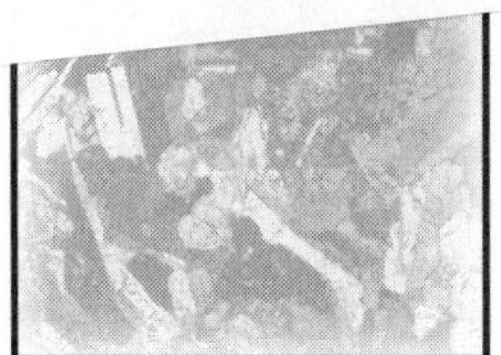

Mastering JavaServer™ Faces

Bill Dudney
Jonathan Lehr
Bill Willis
LeRoy Mattingly

Wiley Publishing, Inc.

Wiley Publishing, Inc.
Vice President and Executive Group Publisher: Richard Swadley
Vice President and Executive Publisher: Robert Ipsen
Vice President and Publisher: Joseph B. Wikert
Executive Editorial Director: Mary Bednarek
Editorial Manager: Kathryn A. Malm
Executive Editor: Robert Elliott
Managing Production Editor: Fred Bernardi
Development Editor: Eileen Bien Calabro, Sharon Nash
Production Editor: Felicia Robinson
Media Development Specialist: Greg Stafford
Text Design & Composition: Wiley Composition Services

Published by Wiley Publishing, Inc., Indianapolis, Indiana
Published simultaneously in Canada

Library of Congress Cataloging-in-Publication Data is available from the publisher.
ISBN: 0-471-46207-1
Printed in the United States of America
10 9 8 7 6 5 4 3 2 1

For Andrew, Isaac, Anna, Sophia, and Isabel—may you dream big dreams and have the courage to pursue them. —BD

To my little Sunshine, who makes me see life in a different light. —BW

For my wife, Kathryn. —JL

Contents

Acknowledgments

First and foremost, I would like to thank Christ, for all He has done in my life to teach me to be more than I was and to inspire me to be more than I am. I would also like to thank my wonderful wife Sarah; without her encouragement and love I'd be lost. And I'd also like to thank my great kids, who keep life interesting. Andrew, Isaac, Anna, and Sophia, you are the definition of joy. Also, I can't begin to express my thanks to Chris Maki who spent many a late hour reviewing the book and making it much better than it was. Thanks again Chris! Finally I'd like to thank Ed Burns for all his feedback late in the cycle under a looming deadline; it's a better book because of his feedback. —BD

Once again, I am indebted to my coauthor, Bill Dudney, for inviting me to participate in the writing of this book, as well as for his valuable input. I am also grateful for the contributions of Eileen Bien Calabro and Chris Maki, which have dramatically improved the content both in terms of readability and (let's hope!) correctness.

Writing several chapters of a technical book such as this in one's spare time is at best a challenging proposition. It might have proven difficult indeed to keep things running smoothly at work were it not for my friend Carl Lindberg's remarkable craftsmanship and extraordinary diligence. He also bore with good cheer my frequent murmuring about my impossible schedule, while acting as my sounding board and contributing a number of useful suggestions. Many thanks, Carl!

Above all, I thank my dear wife Kathryn, who often bore the brunt of this demanding project, tending to things that I no longer had time for and keeping up social obligations that I often had to dodge. Her indispensable patience, love, and support kept me going when the work got overwhelming. I am also grateful to our family and friends for being so sympathetic to our situation, and for their repeated offerings of encouragement. —JL

Thank you to Chris Maki for his valuable input to this book. —BW

About the Authors

Bill Dudney is a Java architect with Object Systems Group. He has been building J2EE applications and software for 6 years and has been doing distributed computing for almost 15 years. Bill has been using EJB since he was at InLine Software and the first public beta was released. Bill has built several J2EE applications as well as tools to help others do the same. He is also a coauthor of *Jakarta Pitfalls* and *J2EE AntiPatterns,* both from Wiley.

Jonathan Lehr is a software developer, architect, mentor and trainer with over 20 years of industry experience, including 12 years of object-oriented programming. He is coauthor of *Jakarta Pitfalls* (Wiley), and has written and taught courses on a variety of programming topics delivered to thousands of developers throughout the United States.

For the past 8 years, he has helped design and implement large-scale e-commerce applications in Java and Objective C for Fortune 500 financial and telecommunications companies. He currently leads a framework development team that provides reusable Struts-based components and infrastructure enhancements for use by development teams at a major financial institution.

Bill Willis has over 10 years of experience in the software industry managing and developing mission-critical systems and innovative, industry-leading products and services. He is an expert in object-oriented methods and Pattern-driven design and development, and has used Java since its introduction. He is currently the director of engineering and technology at ObjectVenture Inc., where he focuses on next-generation, pattern-based tools and technology that help less experienced developers visualize and build well-designed software. He is also the director of PatternsCentral.com, a community portal devoted to "all things Patterns."

LeRoy Mattingly is a senior software engineer with Tecton Software, Inc. He has over 10 year's experience building large scale object–oriented systems. His specialties include project mentoring, use-case–driven development, and applying adaptive process improvements for large software development projects. In addition, he is co-owner and lead software engineer of OSGTools, a subsidiary company of Object Systems Group. At OSGTools, he is the creator and lead software engineer of The Integrator—a specialized tool for authoring and managing the use case process.

Foreword

JavaServer Faces is a holistic solution to several longstanding problems facing software developers and the customers who consume the software. For the end user, JavaServer Faces holds the promise of an easier, more intuitive usage experience for Web-based applications. For software developers, JavaServer Faces provides a standard, object-oriented, easy-to-use application programming interface (API) that takes much of the pain out of bringing a great user experience to the world of Web applications. JavaServer Faces gives users the power, flexibility, and performance that have previously been addressed only in a piecemeal fashion.

JavaServer Faces was developed by a community of Web application experts assembled by the Java Community Process. These experts are the people behind Jakarta Struts, Oracle Application Server, Sun Java Studio, IBM WebSphere Studio, ATG, and many other programs in the Web application development space. Their collective wisdom was brought to bear on the problem of how to take the best patterns from the existing technologies that solve the same problems and combine them into a cohesive whole, as well as filling in the gaps not filled anywhere to date. JavaServer Faces combines the ubiquity of JSP and servlets, the simplicity of JavaBeans, the power of J2EE, and the common-sense chutzpah of frameworks like Jakarta Struts to bring you the best-of-breed way to develop the user interface for a Web application.

I'd like to take this opportunity to thank the members of the Java Community Process Expert Group who contributed directly to the development of JavaServer Faces, also the team of dedicated engineers that brought the first reference implementation to market, and the early adopters in our initial access and beta program who discovered the hard bugs and had the patience to wait for us to get it right the first time.

Now, to the matter of *Mastering JavaServer Faces*. This book is all about getting you up to speed and productive with JavaServer Faces quickly, and providing enough depth to keep you on track once you are. The authors have done a great job of taking the complexity inherent in providing a complete API for Web application user interfaces and pulling out the simple concepts on which this API was built. If you've read any of the author's other books, you know that the author focuses on pitfalls and anti-patterns; this book also emphasizes these things.

Here are just a few of the reasons why I recommend this book: the author keeps the text readable by foreshadowing more interesting content; includes chapters that "put it all together"; provides examples implemented in several different ways, for example, a JavaBeans version and an EJB version; uses the Unified Modeling Language (UML effectively to get the point across instantly; and, most importantly, provides ready-to-use patterns and samples you can immediately work into your application. All of these things combine to make this the book you keep handy at your elbow as you develop JavaServer Faces applications.

Ed Burns, JSF Implementation Lead and Co-Specification Lead

Introduction

JavaServer Faces (JSF) is an exciting new technology that will change the way we build user interfaces for Java 2 Enterprise Edition applications. With the introduction of JSF, we can finally create user interfaces simply with a set of reusable components. And with a component-based framework, Web applications are finally on a more level playing field with client-based User Interface (UI) frameworks such as Swing. Now, Web developers will be able to use and reuse components off the shelf in their applications so we will see tool support and components implemented for JSF.

The Genius of JSF

The genius of JSF is that we only have to learn the UI programming model once, and then apply that knowledge to any JSF-compliant component that we want to use. Now that we finally have a standard component model, programming for the Web is much easier to learn and to do.

What is a component-based, Web-tier UI framework? A component is something that has known attributes and behaviors, i.e., all the components in JSF have at least a base set of attributes and behaviors in common. A component model allows you to reuse components that come from a third party without having to learn a new component model (the model is standard). Typically, components fit into a part/whole hierarchy (see the Composite Pattern discussion in Chapter 2, "Elements of JSF") and can be composed into more complex components.

The component-based model is beneficial to the handling of the user action. A user action, such as a button click, flows through a well-defined process from the button click to the business logic that performs the requested process. JSF provides well-defined points for your code to plug into the flow and be executed.

The component-based model also allows developers to focus on providing great features instead of trying to focus on two or three different models for building Web-based user interfaces. It also allows the promise of reusable off-the-shelf components in the future. In the same way that you can purchase a Swing-based UI component that plots graphs of data, you will be able to buy off-the-shelf JSF components that provide similar functionality.

JSF Makes Things Easy

Another great thing is that JSF offers a standard, ubiquitous technology to learn instead of the fragmented landscape that currently exists in the world of J2EE Web-based UI frameworks. Further, JSF will almost certainly be included in the J2EE specification in the future, ensuring that all the major vendors will have an implementation included out of the box. Eventually, there will be a major body of knowledge and mindshare behind it so that you will have lots of resources to help you implement your applications.

Lets take a quick look at how the JSF component model makes building Web applications easy. The following little sample application will take a customer's first and last name and store it. The UI is very simple: two labels, two text fields, and a button to save the input. The user interface is rendered in Figure Intro.1 below.

Figure Intro.1 Sample customer input form.

The components involved in this user interface are built in a JSP with the following code. The important parts will be discussed below in more detail.

```
<f:view>
  <h:form id="customerForm" >
     <h:panelGrid columns="2">
      <f:facet name="header">
        <h:panelGroup>
          <h:outputText id="header"value="Customer Name"/>
        </h:panelGroup>
      </f:facet>
      <h:panelGroup>
        <h:outputText id="fNameLabel" value="First Name:"/>
        <h:inputText id="fName" value="#{customer.firstName}"/>
      </h:panelGroup>
      <h:panelGroup>
        <h:outputText id="lNameLabel" value="Last Name:"/>
        <h:inputText id="lName" value="#{customer.lastName}"/>
      </h:panelGroup>
      <h:panelGroup>
        <h:commandButton id="cancel" value="Cancel"/>
        <h:commandButton id="save" value="Save"/>
      </h:panelGroup>
    </h:panelGrid>
  </h:form>
</f:view>
```

Listing Intro.1 CustomerInput JSF page.

This code creates a form (which contains the rest of the components) and then creates the subsequent components. This group of components, rooted at the form, is known as a component tree. You will learn all about component trees later in the book, for now think of the tree as a collection of components that know which component is their parent and which components are their children. The cool thing about this page is that the components on it are active. As a request comes in and JSF processes it, the components get to play an active role in how the application acts. For example, the components can post events that are later used to process business logic. So, in our little example here each of these buttons is able to invoke a different piece of logic by posting events.

What Is in the Book

This book is about the JSF UI component model for building Java applications for the Web. The book is practically focused, but has enough information on the programming model to allow you to understand why you are doing what you are doing. This should allow you to have not only a broad understanding of JSF, but also a deep understanding of how the framework works.

How to integrate your UI with the back-end persistent state will also be covered. In a typical J2EE Web application, there are at least three logic tiers, the front-end, or Web, tier; the application tier; and the database tier, where the persistent state of the application is stored. We find this three-tiered approach to building applications in many J2EE applications today. Figure Intro.2 shows how JSF will fit into the three-tier scenario.

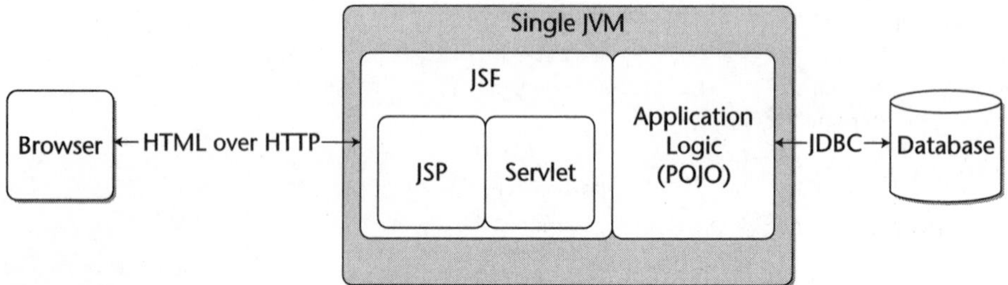

Figure Intro.2 Three-tier JSF configuration.

The Web tier of a J2EE application is based on HTML sent to a browser. The HTML is dynamically generated via JSPs and/or servlets that delegate the application logic to plain old Java objects (POJOs), which interact with the database using JDBC (the application tier) to store and retrieve data for the application. However, in enterprise-scale applications, the application tier will be implemented in EJBs either as sessions or entities, or some combination of both.

With EJBs in the picture, the application is made of four tiers: Web, JSP/Servlet, EJB, and database. JSF fits into the JSP/Servlet tier and provides a component-based approach to building applications. JSF provides a way to build user interfaces and delegate the business processing to the next layer (that is, the EJB layer). We will see a lot more about this in Chapter 1, "JSF Patterns and Architecture." Application logic can take the form of POJOs or EJBs—JSF integrates nicely with either. This book shows you how to build JSF applications that interact with either EJBs or POJOs. Figure Intro.3 shows the four-tier configuration that we would see in a typical JSF application.

The book will also cover the technical details of JSF so that you will be able to do more than simply follow a cookbook; rather, you will be able to invent your own recipes. For example, the validation coverage in Chapter 7, "Navigation, Actions, and Listeners," not only describes how you will ensure that the data you put into the database is valid but also shows the details of how validation works in JSF. Armed with this knowledge, you will be able to confidently build applications that validate their data, and if needed, be able to build your own custom validators.

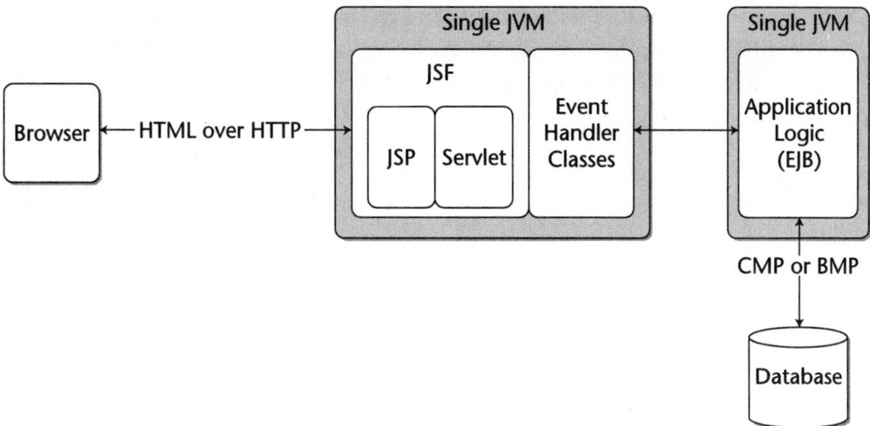

Figure Intro.3 Four-tier JSF configuration.

Layout of the Book

The book is laid out in three parts that cover various aspects of JSF. The first part, "Architecture of JSF," covers the big architectural picture of JSF. The next part, "Elements of JSF," covers the various pieces of the JSF component model. The last part, "Applying JSF," brings the other two parts together, covering issues related to using JSF in applications.

The first part covers the architectural aspects of JSF, from the patterns that are used in the implementation to the life cycle of a typical JSF request/response pair. This part will provide you with a broad understanding of how JSF is put together and functions. This part will provide you with the knowledge you need to understand the more concrete pieces of JSF. The content assumes that you are familiar with Java programming for the Web and that you have at least some exposure to general design patterns. You will also be given a broad overview of the components of JSF. The following chapters are in this part:

Chapter 1: JSF Patterns and Architecture. This chapter covers the architecture of JSF by discussing the patterns used in its implementation. The chapter also compares JSF to its to greatest influences, Struts and Swing.

Chapter 2: Elements of JSF. This chapter provides an introduction to the component mode of JSF by going over briefly the various APIs that make up the component model. This chapter provides a brief summary of the next major section. If you find something here that is interesting, you can jump forward to the chapter that covers that topic in detail.

Chapter 3: JSF Request-Processing Life Cycle. This chapter covers the way that JSF responds to requests and provides the rendered versions of components back to the requestor. Understanding this life cycle is crucial to building JSF applications.

Part 2, "Elements of JSF," covers in detail all the abstractions that make up JSF. The topics covered include components, events, validation, and so on. After reading this section, you will have a broad understand of all of JSF as well as practical knowledge of how to use JSF. Each chapter in this section will focus on a different aspect of the JSF component model and how that aspect fits into building real-world applications. The following chapters are in this section:

Chapter 4: JSF Configuration. This chapter deals with what you have to do to configure your JSF application. Details of the `faces-config.xml` file and what to add to your `Web.xml` file as well as how to get the TagLibs setup will be covered.

Chapter 5: JSP Integration in JSF. This chapter covers the details of how JSF integrates with JSPs through the custom tag feature in JSP implementations. After you read this section, you will have a detailed understanding of how the integration works. We will also cover each of the custom tags required for JSPs to be part of any JSF implementation.

Chapter 6: UI Components. This chapter covers the component API in detail. After reading this chapter, you will know how to use UIComponents to build your user interface. You will be comfortable with the standard components and how they are used in a typical JSF application. You will also understand the various pieces that make up a component and how they are involved in the request-response life cycle.

Chapter 7: Navigation, Actions, and Listeners. This chapter discusses the navigation and event model in JSF. When you are finished with this chapter, you will understand the way that navigation works in a JSF. This chapter also discusses events and how they are used to manage the navigation and invoke state changes in your applications.

Chapter 8: Validation and Conversion. This chapter provides information on ensuring that the data that you store meets the business rules for your application. After reading this chapter, you will understand the validation and conversion model inherent in JSF. You will be able to use the built-in Validators and Converters that come with JSF as well as be able to create your own.

Part 3, "Applying JSF," covers using JSF in the real world to build applications. Specifically covered here are integrating JSF user interfaces with the business tier (be it EJB or POJO), building custom components to render your own user interface components, and converting your existing Struts applications to JSF. The following chapters are included in this part:

Chapter 9: Building JSF Applications. This chapter covers the detail of how to integrate your application with the technology actually used to build enterprise applications. Both EJB integration and POJO through JDBC will be covered. After reading this chapter, you will understand how to build real-world JSF applications that put enterprise data into a browser so that users can manipulate and save that data.

Chapter 10: Custom JSF Components. This chapter shows you how to build your own custom components. After reading this chapter, you will be comfortable with building a component that understands how to render itself as well as integrate itself with a RenderKit. You will also understand how to validate the new component and how events can be queued by the component to invoke custom application logic.

Chapter 11: Converting a Struts Application to JSF. This chapter demonstrates in detail how you can move your application from Struts to JSF. After reading this chapter, you will be comfortable converting your pages and application logic to JSF.

Summary

We are very excited about the promise of JSF and what it means to the average J2EE application developer. With JSF, you will be able to build consistent reusable user interfaces for the Web that interact in well-defined ways with your business process code. It is indeed a good time to be a geek. We hope that you enjoy and get as much out of this book as we did in writing it.

Architecture of JSF

CHAPTER

1

JSF Patterns and Architecture

As with any other framework, gaining an understanding of how JSF is designed is crucial to applying it correctly and transitioning from other similar frameworks. This chapter will discuss the Model-View-Controller (MVC) architectural pattern, which is commonly used in modern user interface frameworks, and how it has been adopted for the Web (and JSF). We'll then take a more detailed look at how the JSF framework implements MVC and other patterns that are commonly used with MVC. This will by no means be an exhaustive or academic patterns study, but it will be enough to highlight the JSF architecture and show you what you can accomplish with it. While doing so, it will be useful to put JSF in perspective with two other frameworks that have heavily influenced it and to which it will undoubtedly be compared against: Swing and Struts.

Overview

Patterns typically exist at a higher level of abstraction than the implementations they describe. Indeed, this is one of the primary benefits of patterns—to describe a general solution to a recurring problem. As such, the purpose of a pattern is not to provide a specific implementation but to provide a reusable design with constraints on its use. At implementation time, the application of a pattern solution will vary according to your specific needs and will be influenced by any number of factors (a good example being the programming language you use). However, it will always adhere to the spirit of the pattern, which is just another way of saying that it will satisfy the constraints that a pattern places on its solution.

It is not uncommon then for a pattern to have any number of different implementations. Here we refer to such an implementation as a *strategy*. Do not confuse the term strategy here with the *Gang of Four* (or GoF) pattern of the same name (Gamma, Helm, Johnson, and Vlissides 1996). We use the term strategy here in the same manner in which you will find in *Core J2EE Patterns* (Alur, Crupi, and Malks 2003). Most documented strategies provide the most common implementations of a particular pattern, thereby aiding in the communication of a pattern solution's lower-level aspects.

In this chapter, we will typically start out with an informal pattern description and then follow with the strategy used for implementing it in each of the three frameworks we are focusing on here. You are encouraged to study these patterns and their various implementation strategies outside of our coverage here to get a fuller understanding of how each framework is designed. Employing such a process should yield a better understanding of how JSF attempts to solve some of the same problems that Swing and Struts were faced with. In the end, you should not be surprised to see how heavily JSF is influenced by both frameworks.

MVC and User Interfaces

MVC was first popularized with Smalltalk (Goldberg & Robson 1983) and is now used in many modern user interface frameworks. One of the primary benefits of MVC is that it provides reusable components for interactive user interfaces. Swing does this admirably for rich Java clients, while Struts does so to a lesser extent on the Web. Even though the introduction of Tiles to Struts provides more reuse, the components are still more page-centric as opposed to Swing's more fine-grained widget-centric approach. Like Struts, JSF is targeted at Java Web applications, but moves closer to Swing with its concentration on reusable user interface widgets (or components).

MVC Pattern

We begin by describing the traditional form of MVC and then discuss how it has been adapted for the Web. Each of the three frameworks is then examined, and their respective implementations of this common pattern are uncovered.

The intent of this pattern is to partition interactive applications into three separate components: Model, View, and Controller. The Model represents core application data and functional logic, the View renders the data and displays it to users of the application, and the Controller handles user interaction or input. All three components communicate via a change-propagation mechanism to stay synchronized.

Motivation

The most volatile part of an interactive software application is the user interface (or the View) because it is what users of the application directly communicate with. In other words, it is the most visible part of most software systems. Besides the everyday changes in requirements, you may also be faced with a requirement like supporting more than one operating system (Windows, Linux, Apple, and so on), each of which may require a different look and feel. A requirement like this can quickly complicate what at first may have been a simple interface.

In highly coupled, monolithic applications, making even the smallest changes can be complicated and error-prone. Changes can propagate throughout the system. Furthermore, user requirements may force you to maintain separate versions of the same application if one user group has sufficiently different presentation requirements than another. This adds an additional dimension of complexity and often results in each version of the same application getting out of synch.

Solution

The MVC Pattern provides a flexible solution to these problems by decoupling the Model, View, and Controller components of an application while providing a uniform interface between them. It is often appropriate if one or more of the following statements are true:

- You wish to provide different representations of the same application data (for example, a table versus a graph).
- You wish to provide different looks and feels (perhaps for different operating systems) for your user interface without affecting the rest of your application.
- User-driven events must immediately update application data or other user interface components, while changes to application data must be reflected immediately in user interface components.
- You wish to reuse one or more user interface components independently of application data.

The structure of the MVC Pattern is provided in Figure 1.1.

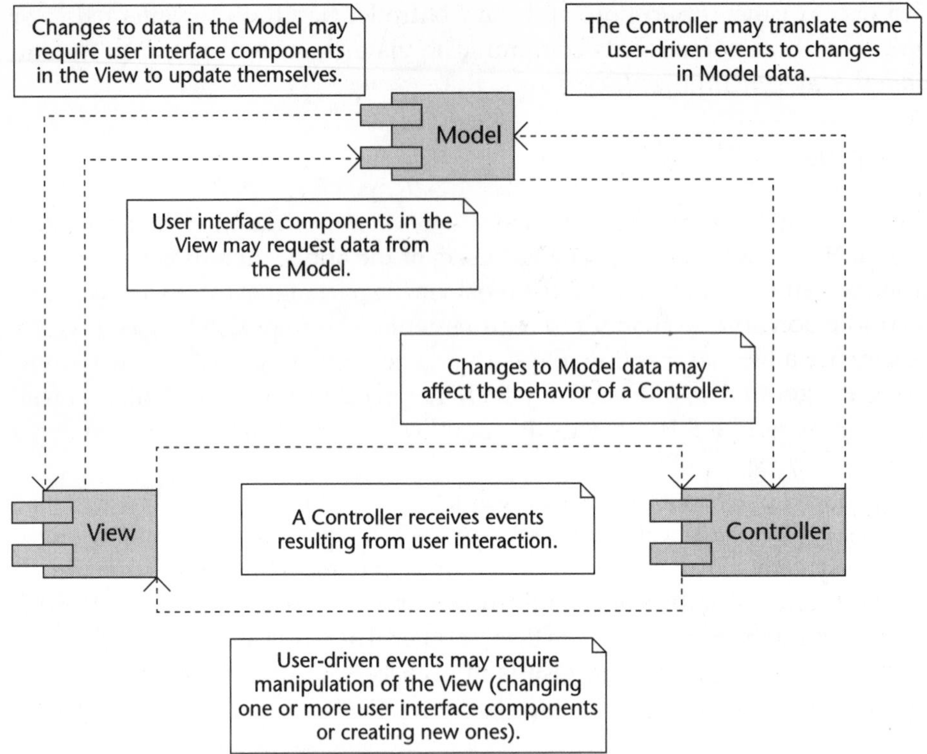
Changes to data in the Model may require user interface components in the View to update themselves.
The Controller may translate some user-driven events to changes in Model data.
Model
User interface components in the View may request data from the Model.
Changes to Model data may affect the behavior of a Controller.
View
A Controller receives events resulting from user interaction.
Controller
User-driven events may require manipulation of the View (changing one or more user interface components or creating new ones).

Figure 1.1 MVC Pattern structure.

As we discussed earlier, there are three main participants in this pattern. We provide here a summary of each participant's responsibilities and explain how they collaborate.

Model. This participant provides a componentized representation of application data (or state) and functional logic. It is essentially the core of the application.

View. This participant provides one or more representations of application data and behavior in a graphical form for user consumption. This is the only participant that a user directly interacts with.

Controller. This participant processes user-driven events, which may result in updates to the Model or direct manipulation of the View.

When a user interacts with user interface components in the View, events are dispatched to one or more Controllers for processing. If the event requires changes to the Model, a Controller may manipulate Model data or invoke application-specific operations. If the event requires changes in other user interface components, a Controller will either manipulate them directly, add new components, or even remove (or hide) existing components.

Views rely on the Model to display and render information to users but they don't change the Model directly. When changes occur in the Model, Views are notified and may then query the Model for additional information. This provides Views with the opportunity to immediately synchronize themselves with changes in the Model.

Views and Controllers are loosely coupled with the Model via this change notification mechanism (see our coverage of the Observer Pattern later in this chapter). Views and Controllers register themselves with the Model, which in turn keeps an internal list of registered observers of changes. When changes to the Model occur, Views and Controllers are notified as necessary.

There are a few well-known consequences to using the MVC Pattern—not all of them good:

- Since the MVC Pattern provides loose coupling between the Model and user interface components, multiple Views of the same data are possible. Multiple Views may exist in the same user session and among multiple users with different presentation requirements.
- Different looks and feels may be provided independent of the underlying application data. This consequence provides user interface portability without requiring changes to the underlying Model.
- The change notification mechanism provides synchronization of dependent Views and Controllers without requiring high coupling. Views and Controllers observe changes to the Model and receive notifications as those changes occur.
- The MVC Pattern encourages reusable user interface components and Controllers that may be interchanged with the same Model.
- The MVC Pattern can result in increased complexity for simple applications that do not benefit from its loose coupling of the Model. However, many applications start out simple and evolve into more complex systems, so this consequence should not be used as an excuse to create highly coupled components.
- Views and Controllers are often closely related, which will limit their reuse. This is not the case in applications that do not require meaningful Controllers (in the case of applications that access read-only data). Some frameworks that implement the MVC Pattern will combine these two components and still achieve effective reuse of the resulting composite component.
- The number of updates received by Views and Controllers can be excessive, so a more fine-grained approach to registration is almost always appropriate. Views and Controllers should be able to register only with those parts of the Model they are interested in.

Model-2 MVC for the Web

Web applications rely on the stateless HyperText Transfer Protocol (HTTP). This alters the way that Web applications implement the MVC Pattern; however, much of the same benefits are still evident. The term *Model 2* refers to an adaptation of the original MVC Pattern to the Web.

A conceptual view of MVC for the Web is provided in Figure 1.2.

Typically a user interacts with a markup page in a Web browser (this could be HyperText Markup Language [HTML]) and ultimately forwards a request for more information back to the server (by pressing a button, for example). A controller servlet is listening for requests with a certain URL that has been designated at design and deployment time. When a request is received, the servlet interacts with the Model and then determines which View (usually a JSP) component to dispatch control to for generating a response. As part of generating a response, the View component may query the Model.

This is actually a relatively simple representation of the Model 2 architecture. Enhancements are commonly made to increase flexibility and scalability for larger applications.

- There is often a single servlet controller for a Web application. This provides a single point of access to handle security concerns, proper user management, and central management of application flow. This type of servlet is often referred to as a *Front Controller* (Alur, Crupi, and Malks 2003).
- A controller servlet often uses helper components and/or XML configurations to define command processing and application flow via forwarding. Helper components may serve as *Command* (Gamma, Helm, Johnson, and Vlissides 1996) objects that interact with the Model and serve to decouple the Controller from the Model. Even the dispatching of requests may be offloaded to a separate helper component, as is the case with the Struts `RequestDispatcher`.
- In larger applications, View components may not interact directly with the Model. The Controller or one of its helper objects typically retrieves a subset of the data, in the form of *Data Transfer Objects* (Alur, Crupi, and Malks 2003), and makes it available to View components by placing them in a session or request scope in the response. The Model in this scenario may then consist of EJBs, object-relational components, or *Data Access Objects* (Alur, Crupi, and Malks 2003).

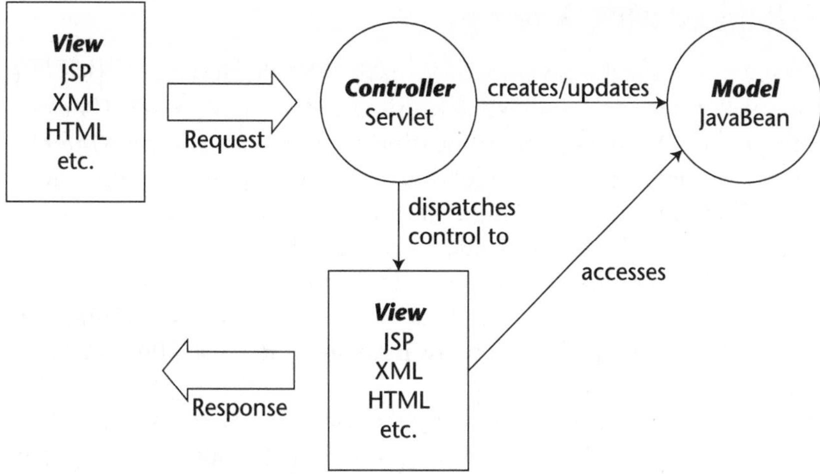

Figure 1.2 Model 2 structure.

There are some differences and limitations with the Model 2 architecture that are worth mentioning. All of them are rooted in the stateless nature of Web browsing.

- There is no mechanism for allowing model changes to propagate immediately to registered Views and Controllers. With Model 2, the Controller servlet or one of its helper objects usually accesses the Model and provides a snapshot of it to the View component that control is dispatched to.
- Views are reconstructed for each response as opposed to simply updating them. This is necessary because Web applications are served up one page or screen at a time via the stateless HTTP protocol.
- A Controller cannot query a View directly upon receiving a request. It must instead inspect the request parameters created by the View and may then need to convert these parameters to a proper type (date, integer, and so on) before interacting with the Model.

Implementing MVC

Now that we've explored the MVC Pattern and the Model-2 variant used for Web-based applications, let's take a look at how each of our frameworks implement the Pattern. What you'll notice is that Swing follows the more traditional form of MVC, Struts uses the Model-2 variant, and JSF is somewhere in between.

Swing Collapsed MVC Strategy

Swing is loosely based on the traditional form of MVC in that it collapses the View and Controller parts into one while keeping the Model separate. The creators of Swing chose this design simplification to deal with complex interactions between the View and Controller that often occur in components. A simplified representation of the Swing collapsed MVC design is provided in Figure 1.3. The combined View-Controller is referred to as a UI delegate. Each Swing component has a delegate object that is responsible for both rendering the View of a component and handling user input events. The UI Manager is an extension of the delegate that globally manages the look and feel of an application's components.

A simple yet concrete example of a Swing component and the MVC Pattern in action is `JTextField`, which is a text component that allows one line of input. A simplified representation of `JTextField` is provided in Figure 1.4. The UI delegate for this component is `BasicTextFieldUI`, while the default model is `PlainDocument` (which itself ultimately implements the `Document` interface).

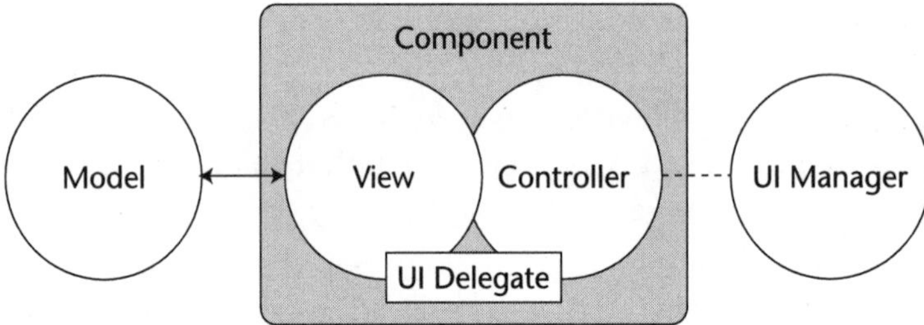

Figure 1.3 Swing's modified MVC.

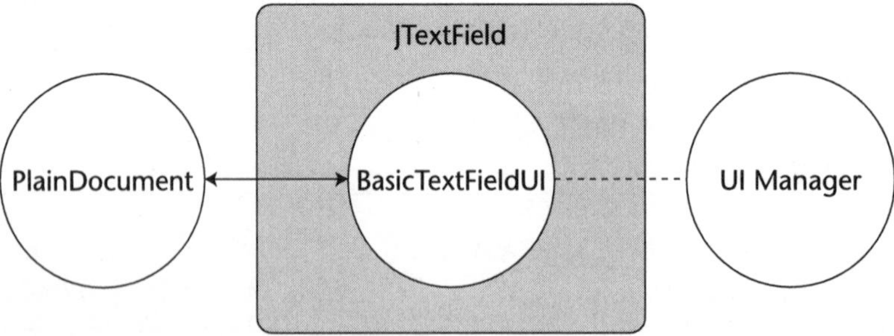

Figure 1.4 JTextField component.

Creating a `JTextField` component is very straightforward. A default model is created for you if you don't specify one, and the UI delegate is internally assigned based on the current look and feel.

```
JTextField textField = new JTextField();
```

You can specify a custom model for the component at creation time by using an alternate constructor. In the case of `JTextField`, it must implement the `Document` interface.

```
JTextField textField = new JTextField(new MyCustomDocument());
```

After creating a component, you have full access to both the model and the UI delegate. To access the model of a `JTextField`, you would use the following methods:

```
Document textDoc = textField.getDocument();
TextField.setDocument(new MyCustomDocument());
```

Other components commonly use `getModel()` and `setModel(...)` instead, but the result is the same. You get access to the model behind the component.

To access the UI delegate of a `JTextField`, you would use the following methods:

```
TextUI textUI = textField.getUI();
TextField.setUI(new MyCustomTextUI());
```

Accessing the UI delegates of other components is very similar. At this point, you could access various properties of the component. Other components, such as `JTable` and `JTree`, aren't this trivial to create, but they still follow the UI delegate design.

We'll look at a less trivial example later in this chapter once we cover how Swing components can be combined to form larger composite components. You may have noticed that we conveniently left out any mention of events here. They will also be covered later in this chapter.

Struts Model-2 MVC Strategy

Struts is designed specifically for Web-based applications, so it naturally employs the popular Model-2 MVC strategy, or architecture. Detailed coverage of Struts is outside the scope of this book, so you are encouraged to visit the Struts Web site and to study one or more of the excellent books on Struts. A simplified overview of the Struts framework is provided in Figure 1.5.

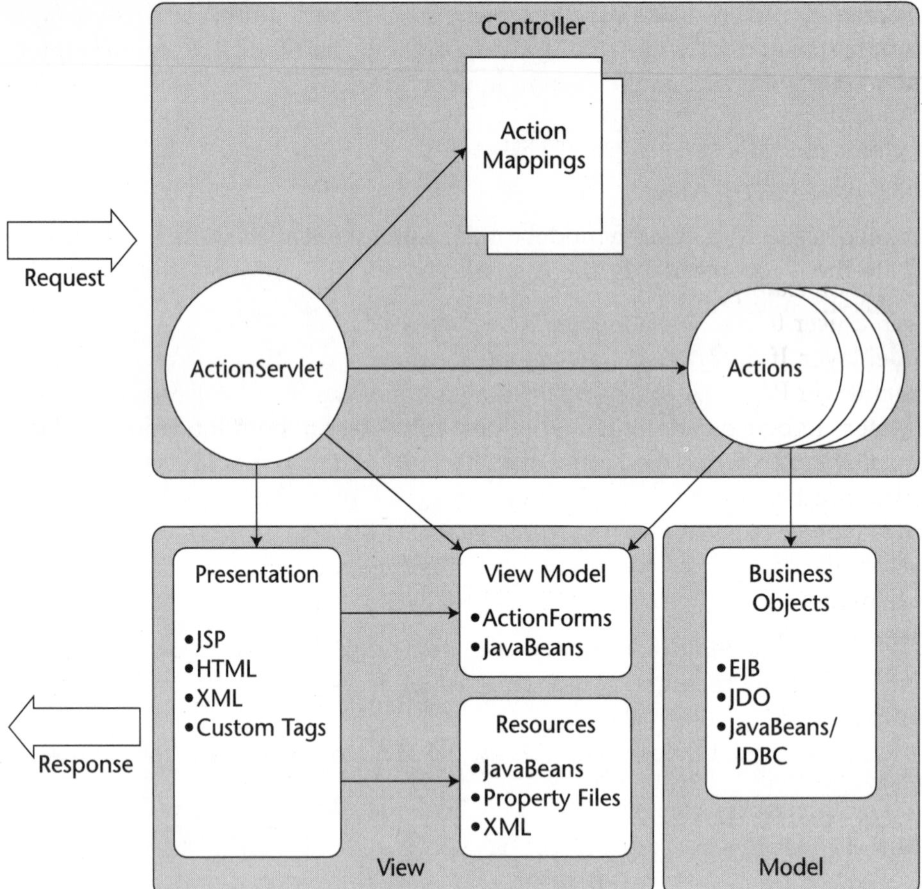

Figure 1.5 Struts Model-2.

The Struts framework has a very well defined notion of the Model, View, and Controller. As we take a closer look at how Struts implements these three pillars of MVC, you will also see how well separated they are (a primary benefit of the MVC Pattern). You may have noticed by now that Struts is really more of an application framework than it is a strict UI component framework, but it still has the primary goal of providing a user interface built from reusable components through which clients may manipulate underlying information (or data).

Controller

The core of the Struts controller is the `ActionServlet`, which is a *Front Controller* servlet (Alur, Crupi, and Malks 2003). The `ActionServlet` serves as a single point of access to a Web application and the brains behind determining how each request is handled. It is responsible for receiving incoming HTTP requests from clients (such as Web browsers) and dispatching them either directly to another Web page or to appropriate handlers that eventually provide a response.

A handler in Struts is an `Action`, which is essentially a *Command* JavaBean (Gamma, Helm, Johnson, and Vlissides 1996) that is responsible for examining information from the request, performing some operation, optionally populating data that will later be used by the presentation components, and then communicating to the `ActionServlet` where control should be forwarded next. A common example of an `Action` would be a `LoginAction` that attempts to log in a user to the system by invoking operations on business objects in the Model layer. If the attempt is successful, control would likely be forwarded to a JavaServer Page (JSP) that may present a home page for the user. Otherwise, control may be forwarded back to the original login JSP with further instructions to the user.

You may be wondering at this point how the `ActionServlet` determines where requests are dispatched. One solution would be to hard-code these decision points in the `ActionServlet` itself, but that would lead to almost immediate maintenance issues. Struts addresses this design problem by providing an external Extensible Markup Language (XML) configuration file (commonly called `struts-config.xml`) that, among other things, defines mappings of request URLs to `Action` classes. Such a mapping is called an `ActionMapping` in Struts. When a Web application is started, the `ActionServlet` reads the configuration files, stores its contents in memory, and later refers to this information when each request comes in from a client. A very simple example of this file is provided in Listing 1.1.

```
<?xml version="1.0"?>
<!DOCTYPE struts-config PUBLIC
  "-//Apache Software Foundation//DTD Struts Configuration 1.1//EN"
  "http://jakarta.apache.org/struts/dtds/struts-config_1_1.dtd" >

<struts-config>
  <form-beans>
    <form-bean name="loginForm" type="login.LoginForm"/>
  </form-beans>
  <action-mappings>
    <action name="loginForm"
            path="/login"
            scope="request"
            type="login.LoginAction">
      <forward name="success" path="/success.jsp"/>
      <forward name="failure" path="/failure.jsp"/>
    </action>
  </action-mappings>
</struts-config>
```

Listing 1.1 Sample Struts configuration file.

This particular configuration file has one mapping defined for a user login. Whenever a request is received that ends with /login, the ActionServlet will forward control to the LoginAction.

You may also be wondering at this point how an Action instructs the ActionServlet where to dispatch control to after it has completed its task. You can hard-code this information in your actions, but that would make them less reusable and maintainable. You'll notice two forward tags in the configuration file named success and failure, respectively. The LoginAction has access to the ActionMapping at run time and can use these logical names instead of actual paths when forwarding control back to the ActionServlet. Changing a path only requires a change to the configuration file and not the actions.

Source code for the simple LoginAction is provided in Listing 1.2 to wrap things up. Among other things, this Action does not contain code for internationalization and logging for brevity.

```
public final class LoginAction extends Action {
    public ActionForward execute(ActionMapping mapping,
                                 ActionForm form,
                                 HttpServletRequest request,
                                 HttpServletResponse response)
        throws Exception {

        User user = null;

        // Extract user information from request
        String userName = (String)
            PropertyUtils.getSimpleProperty(form, "username");
        String password = (String)
            PropertyUtils.getSimpleProperty(form, "password");

        // Access the Login business object.
        UserSecurityService security = new UserSecurityService();

        // Attempt to log in.
        user = service.login(userName, password);

        // If no such user exists, display error page
        if(user == null) {
            return mapping.findForward("failure");
        }

        // Create a new session for this user.
        HttpSession session = request.getSession();
        session.setAttribute(Constants.USER_KEY, user);

        // The user exists and has successfully logged in.
```

Listing 1.2 Sample login Action.

```
            // Display the success page.
            return mapping.findForward("success");
        }
    }
```

Listing 1.2 *(continued)*

You can now see an example of how a business object is accessed and how an `Action` communicates where the `ActionServlet` should forward control to next. There is a clear separation here from the Model layer. Even page flow in the Controller layer is decoupled because logical forwarding names are used instead of hard-coded paths.

Model

The Model, which consists of a domain model represented by an application's business objects, is not explicitly required or enforced by the Struts framework. These business objects are usually represented by either Enterprise JavaBeans (EJBs), Java Data Objects (JDOs or something like Hibernate), or plain JavaBeans that may access databases via JDBC as described by the *Data Access Object* Pattern (Alur, Crupi, and Malks 2003). The place where the Struts controller meets the model is in Struts `Action` objects. As mentioned earlier, an `Action` typically invokes operations on business objects to accomplish its objectives.

NOTE A common mistake made by many less-experienced developers new to Struts is to place business logic inside of their `Action` objects. This pitfall negates the separation between the Struts Controller and the Model and should be avoided. The sample provided in Listing 1.2 gives a good example of how an `Action` should interact with the business layer.

View

The View layer in Struts typically consists of JSPs with custom tags. The Struts framework provides a number of custom tag libraries that are framework-aware. One of these tag libraries is Tiles, which allows you to compose your view with reusable JSP templates. This library will be discussed in the next section.

To continue our login example, the login JSP page is provided in Listing 1.3.

```
<%@ page contentType="text/html;charset=UTF-8" language="java" %>
<%@ taglib uri="/WEB-INF/struts-html.tld" prefix="html" %>
<%@ taglib uri="/WEB-INF/struts-bean.tld" prefix="bean" %>

<html:html>
    <head>
        <title><bean:message key="app.title"/></title>
    </head>

    <body>
        Log on with your username and password.<br/><br/>

        <html:errors/>
        <html:form action="/login">
            Username: <html:text property="username"/><br/>
            Password: <html:password property="password"/><br/>

            <html:submit value="Login"/>
        </html:form>
    </body>
</html:html>
```

Listing 1.3 Sample login JSP.

Up until now, we have conveniently failed to cover how data gets to and from presentation components like JSPs. Struts does this via an `ActionForm`, which is essentially a JavaBean with any number of JavaBean-compliant properties. You can think of it as a View data object. As part of our login example, the `LoginForm` is provided in Listing 1.4.

```
public final class LoginForm extends ActionForm {
    private String password;
    private String username;

    /**
     * Provides the password
     */
    public String getPassword() {
        return (this.password);
    }

    /**
     * Sets the desired password
     */
    public void setPassword(String password) {
        this.password = password;
```

Listing 1.4 Sample login ActionForm.

```
    }

    /**
     * Provides the username
     */
    public String getUsername() {
        return (this.username);
    }

    /**
     * Sets the desired username
     */
    public void setUsername(String username) {
        this.username = username;
    }

    /**
     * Resets all properties to their default values
     */
    public void reset(ActionMapping mapping,
                      HttpServletRequest request) {
        password = null;
        username = null;
    }

    /**
     * Validate the properties that have been set.
     */

    public ActionErrors validate(ActionMapping mapping,
                                 HttpServletRequest request) {

        ActionErrors errors = new ActionErrors();
        if ((username == null) || (username.length() < 1))
            errors.add(
                "username",
                new ActionError("Username Is required.")
            );
        if ((password == null) || (password.length() < 1))
            errors.add(
                "password",
                new ActionError("Password Is required.")
            );

        return errors;
    }
}
```

Listing 1.4 *(continued)*

As shown in Listing 1.3, we are using the Struts HTML tag library to provide the input parameters for a login. When the `ActionServlet` receives a request from this page, it will attempt to load these parameters into a `LoginForm` object. Since we have provided a `validate()` method, it will be invoked by the `ActionServlet`. If errors are reported, the page will be reloaded with any errors displayed. If all goes well, the `ActionServlet` will forward control to the `LoginAction` as directed in Listing 1.1 as part of the action mapping. The `LoginAction` will have access to the `LoginForm` as shown in Listing 1.2 and as specified in the form bean section of Listing 1.1.

NOTE If you look at the Struts framework from an application perspective, an `ActionForm` is not part of the Model layer. It is actually a snapshot that captures a piece of the Model and later used to render a response in the View layer. Therefore, an `ActionForm` is considered part of the View layer in Struts as demonstrated in Figure 1.5.

This covers getting data from a request to an `Action`, but how do we get data from an `Action` to the resulting presentation component that is used as the response? Since each `Action` has access to the `ActionServlet`'s response object, it can place any information it wishes in request or session scope that may later be used by a JSP page. The JSP does not know or care where that data comes from, which provides good separation between the Controller and View layers.

JSF Component-Based Model-2 MVC Strategy

As touched upon earlier, JSF is an attempt to provide more Swing-like components for Web GUIs. When we say Swing-like, we mean that they are composable, event-driven, and can change their appearance to fit common looks and feels. That being said, JSF still makes use of the Model-2 architecture because of its Web-centric focus. A simple overview of the JSF architecture is provided in Figure 1.6.

With Struts, the JSF framework also has a very-well-defined notion of the Model, View, and Controller. The major difference between the two is that the JSF View is composed of a component tree, whereas the Struts View is page-centric (usually JSPs). There are other important differences that we'll examine shortly (most notably with action and event handling).

NOTE The term *Component Tree* in JSF refers to a hierarchy of user interface components that make up a JSP page or other form of presentation. As we will soon discover later in this chapter, component trees in JSF follow the Composite Pattern. We'll begin our coverage of them when discussing this pattern and again in Chapter 2, "Elements of JSF."

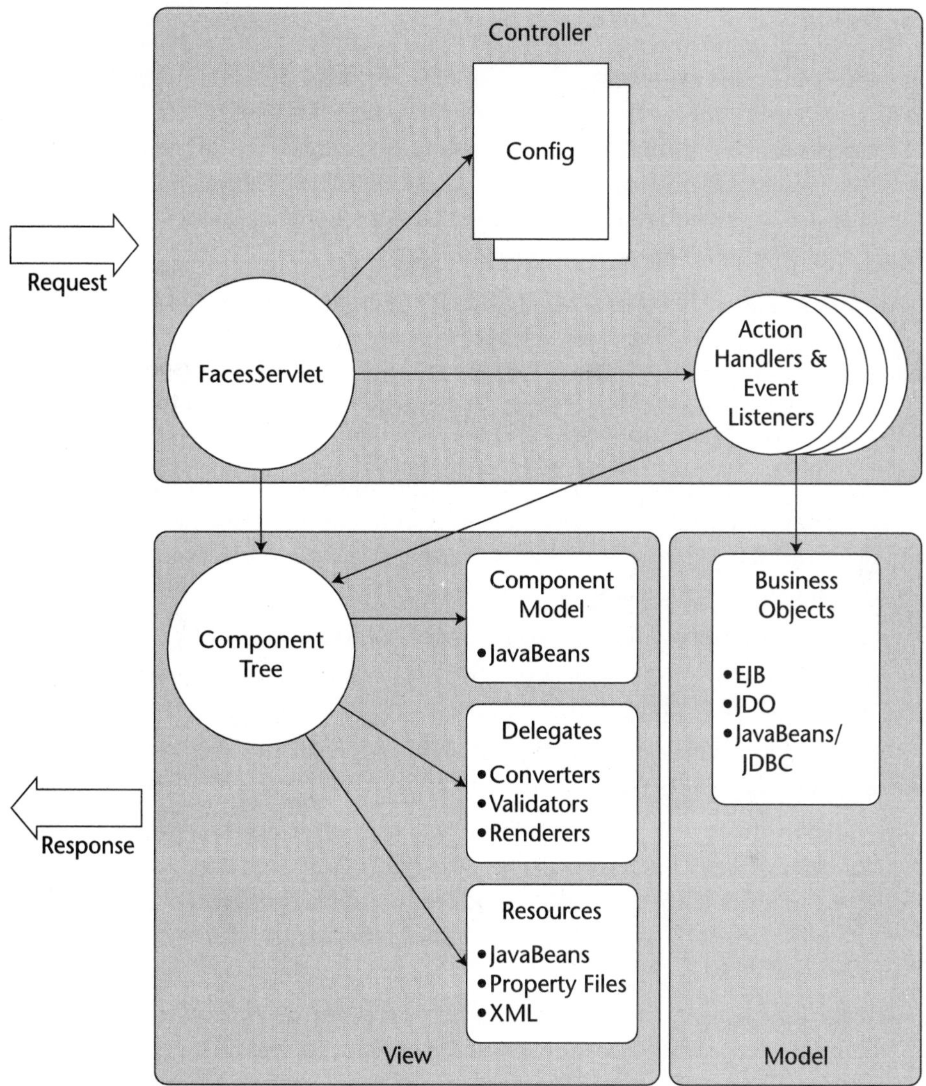

Figure 1.6 JSF Model-2.

You may be wondering if it is possible to combine some aspects of Struts with JSF, particularly when you would like to leverage JSF's event-driven component framework with existing Struts-based applications. The creators of Struts have created an integration library called Struts-Faces that is available on the Struts project Web site that does just that. If you want to convert a Struts application to JSF, we'll take a look at this in detail in Chapter 11, "Converting a Struts Application to JSF."

Controller

The JSF controller consists primarily of a Front Controller servlet called `FacesServlet`, one or more configuration files, and a set of action handlers that are somewhat similar to (but not formally defined like) a Struts `Action`. The `FacesServlet` is responsible for receiving incoming requests from Web clients and then performing a logical set of steps for preparing and dispatching a response. Each step is summarized below.

Restore View. This is essentially the act of creating a component tree for the request page. If this page has been previously displayed in the same user session and the data saved, the `FacesServlet` will build the component tree from this data. Saving component state between requests is an important feature of JSF.

Apply Request Values. Once the component tree has been recovered, it is updated with new information from the request. This includes any user interface component events that need to be broadcast immediately or queued for processing in later steps.

Process Validations. Each user interface component may have internal validation logic or a number of registered Validators that perform correctness checks on its state.

Update Model Values. During this step, each user interface component is asked to update its backing model.

Invoke Application. After updating the user interface component model, the default `ActionListener` will respond to any queued `ActionEvents`, which are normally associated with `UICommand` components (such as a button) that may require interaction with the application's business objects.

Render Response. Based on the result of the request processing we just summarized, either a response will be generated from the current component tree (which may include modifications) or a new component tree. When using JSP pages for the View, each component tree is directly associated with a particular JSP page.

This is really a rudimentary discussion of the request processing performed by the `FacesServlet` and at this point is only intended to give you a flavor for its responsibilities. We will examine each step of this process later in Chapter 3, "JSF Request-Processing Life Cycle."

You'll remember that we just mentioned the similarity between JSF action handlers and Struts `Action` components. Both of them are primarily used to handle application level events, but they differ in how they are represented, configured and invoked. In keeping with our simple login example, the JSF `LoginBean` is provided in Listing 1.5.

```
public final class LoginBean {
    private String password;
    private String userId;
    private Action loginAction;

    /**
     * Provides the password
     */
    public String getPassword() {
        return (this.password);
    }

    /**
     * Sets the desired password
     */
    public void setPassword(String password) {
        this.password = password;
    }

    /**
     * Provides the user ID
     */
    public String getUserId() {
        return (this.userId);
    }

    /**
     * Sets the desired user ID
     */
    public void setUserId(String userId) {
        this.userId = userId;
    }

    /**
     * Attempt to log in the user.
     */
    public String login() {
        // Check for blank input fields.
        if ((userId == null) || (userId.length() < 1))
           return "failure";
        if ((password == null) || (password.length() < 1))
           return "failure";

        User user = null;

        // Access the Login business object.
        UserSecurityService security = new UserSecurityService();

        // Attempt to login.
```

Listing 1.5 JSF LoginForm. *(continued)*

```
        user = service.login(userId, password);

        // If no such user exists, login fails.
        // Otherwise, login succeeds.
        if(user == null)
            return "failure";
        else
            return "success";
    }
}
```

Listing 1.5 *(continued)*

The first thing you'll notice here is that there is no formal notion of an Action component in JSF as there is in Struts. Our action handler here is simply a method in a JavaBean that has no parameters and returns a String. We chose to place this method in our `LoginBean`, which itself is very similar to the Struts `LoginForm`, because the action handler needs access to the login data. In more complex applications, action handlers may be organized differently. A JSF action handler returns a logical result (`success` or `failure` in this case), while a Struts `Action` uses the logical result to actually return what page should be forwarded to next.

As part of the request-processing life cycle, the next component tree (or JSP page in this example) will be determined by the logical result returned by this action handler. As with Struts, JSF allows you to define a configuration file. Among other things, this configuration file provides a mechanism for defining user interface workflow. An example of what the workflow for our example might look like is provided below.

```
<navigation-rule>
    <from-view-id>/login.jsp</from-view-id>
    <navigation-case>
        <from-outcome>success</from-outcome>
        <to-view-id>/home.jsp</to-view-id>
    </navigation-case>
    <navigation-case>
        <from-outcome>failure</from-outcome>
        <to-view-id>/login.jsp</to-view-id>
    </navigation-case>
</navigation-rule>
```

This navigation rule specifies that a failed login should place the user back at the login page, while a successful login should place the user at the home page of the application. For more information on how to configure navigation rules and other elements in a JSF configuration file, see Chapter 4, "JSF Configuration."

We'll talk about how you bind an action to a user interface component shortly when we visit the JSF View. Before we do that, let's take a look at the JSF Model.

Model

When thinking in terms of existing Web frameworks like Struts, it may be a little confusing at first to see a JSF component's data referred to as the Model. This distinction becomes more difficult in JSF because we now have components similar to what we find in Swing. In reality, what is called a Model in JSF is often similar to a Struts `ActionForm` that stores and marshals data between the View and Model layers of a Web application. This is a very important distinction. Whether or not you decide to use business objects directly to back your user interface components, you must resist the temptation to let JSF component data objects influence your real Model (business objects) and vice versa. Failing to do so often results in high coupling between the View and Model layers of the Model-2 architecture.

There are some (even among the authors of this book) who prefer to use business objects to negate the need for a separate set of objects just for the user interface components. In fact, there have been several heated debates in the Struts community alone regarding this preference. As long as you understand the tendency for business object models to be corrupted by such a direct connection (and the separation of Model and View to become blurred), you may certainly do as you wish. Just be aware of the consequences.

That being said, when thinking strictly in terms of UI components, dubbing a component's backing data the Model makes more sense. This is especially true when coming from Swing. So the whole debate over whether or not a component's data is the Model or not is really just based on your point of reference. Just make sure that you are aware of this distinction so you can avoid some of the pitfalls that are associated with it.

With respect to JSF, Figure 1.5 provided a good example of what a user interface component model object looks like. You'll notice that this object is not part of the business object model that is interfaced with in the action handler. You could choose to use the `User` object (if it wasn't an EJB) directly, but we chose not to do that here. Since this object is just your typical JavaBean, there isn't much more to discuss about it in particular. However, we still need to figure out how we bind this object with our user interface components.

The first thing we'll do is declare this JavaBean as a *managed bean* in our JSF configuration file. An example of how you would do this is provided in Listing 1.6.

```
<managed-bean>
    <managed-bean-name>login</managed-bean-name>
    <managed-bean-class>logindemo.LoginBean</managed-bean-class>
    <managed-bean-scope>request</managed-bean-scope>
    <managed-property>
        <property-name>userId</property-name>
        <null-value/>
    </managed-property>
    <managed-property>
        <property-name>password</property-name>
        <null-value/>
    </managed-property>
</managed-bean>
```

Listing 1.6 Declaring a Model object as a managed bean.

When using managed beans, you must ensure that each property you declare exists in the declared class following JavaBean naming conventions. Once declared in this manner, each managed bean and its declared properties can be referenced and bound to user interface components. Your chosen JSF implementation will also handle the task of creating a `LoginBean` instance when one of its properties is invoked by a user interface component. You'll notice that we declaratively initialized each property to `null`. In addition to creating an instance of our `LoginBean`, the JSF implementation will also initialize each property as we have instructed. As you can see, managed beans are very convenient from a management perspective. We'll talk more about them later in Chapter 4, "JSF Configuration," and elsewhere where appropriate. For now, let's take a look at how you create a JSP View in JSF and bind its components to the Model object.

View

As you have probably figured out by now, the View layer in JSF consists primarily of the component tree. One benefit of JSF is that individual components or the whole component tree can be rendered differently to support multiple client user interface types. In most cases, you will be dealing with a markup language such as HTML that is used in a JSP. Depending on the client device type, components could render themselves in the markup language appropriate for that device. We will take a detailed look at JSF component rendering later in Chapter 2, "Elements of JSF," and in Chapter 10, "Custom JSF Components."

Another benefit of JSF is that components bring a more event-driven style to Java Web applications. User interaction with a component (clicking a check box) may result in events being fired that ultimately result in changes to the appearance of that component or others in the component tree. We'll explore events in more detail later in this chapter.

For now, let's take a look at what our login interface might look like in JSF. A JSP example of our JSF login user interface is provided in Listing 1.7.

```
<!doctype html public "-//w3c//dtd html 4.0 transitional//en">
<html>
<head>
    <meta http-equiv="Content-Type"
         content="text/html;
         charset=iso-8859-1">
    <title>Login</title>
    <%@ taglib uri="http://java.sun.com/jsf/core/" prefix="f" %>
    <%@ taglib uri="http://java.sun.com/jsf/html" prefix="h" %>
</head>
<body>
Log in with your User ID and Password.<br/><br/>

<f:view>
<h:form>

    <h:outputLabel for="userId">
        <h:outputText value="User ID"/>
    </h:outputLabel>
    <h:inputText id="userId" value="#{login.userId}"/><br/>

    <h:outputLabel for="password">
        <h:outputText value="Password"/>
    </h:outputLabel>
    <h:inputSecret id="password" value="#{login.password}"/><br/>

    <h:commandButton action="#{login.login}" value="Login"/>

</h:form>
</f:view>

</body>
</html>
```

Listing 1.7 JSF login form using a JSP page.

The first thing we do in our JSP is to declare two of the standard JSF tag libraries. All JSF tags used within a JSP page must be declared within the core `<view>` tag. Inside this tag, we make use of the standard JSF HTML tag library (see Chapter 5, "JSP Integration in JSF," for more information on this and other JSF tag libraries) to construct our login form.

Our User ID and Password properties are both represented here, one via a text input field using the `<inputText>` tag and the other via a text field using the `<inputSecret>` tag that hides what the user enters. Both of these input fields are associated via their `id` attributes with matching labels that provide instructions for users.

You'll notice that each input field has a `value` attribute. This attribute allows you to bind the input fields to properties on an object. In this case, we are binding the input fields to properties on our `LoginBean` JavaBean. Since this class has been declared as a managed bean, an instance of `LoginBean` will be created automatically (if it doesn't already exist), initialized, and placed into Request scope when the JSP page is evaluated. The key to this binding is the first part of the `value` expression. The text `login` must match the name given in the `<managed-bean-name>` tag used when declaring the `LoginBean` as a managed bean in the JSF configuration file (refer back to Listing 1.6 for this). This simple mechanism for binding user interface components to the managed bean allows you to capture user input and validate it with business objects via the `login()` action handler. Furthermore, the simple navigation rules specified earlier will ensure that the user is directed to the next appropriate page only after the login is successful. Our chosen JSF implementation takes care of all the dirty work in between.

You could have made use of Converters, Validators, and even custom Renderers as part of the user interface. In fact, a Converter and Validator component would be useful even in this simple example. These components are very useful for delegating and reusing common user interface tasks. In the interest of simplicity, we decided not to use these special JSF components in our little login example. We'll introduce them in Chapter 2, "Elements of JSF," and then examine them in detail in Chapter 8, "Validation and Conversion." Components for rendering will be covered in Chapter 10, "Custom JSF Components." For now, just be aware that they exist.

Composite Components

In most modern component architectures, components are typically combined to form user interfaces. The primary component is usually a form, frame, or page. Within these root components, other components are arranged hierarchically to achieve the desired interface. This composable nature of components supports the creation of rich user interfaces. The *Composite* (Gamma, Helm, Johnson, and Vlissides 1996) Pattern describes this feature of components and is important in understanding most MVC-based architectures.

You have probably already seen the composable nature of user interface components in each of the three frameworks we have been discussing. What we'll do here is provide a useful summary of the Composite Pattern and then describe how each framework implements the pattern. This exercise will give us important insight into the design of JSF user interface components.

Composite Pattern

We begin by describing the Composite Pattern in general terms as it relates to user interfaces. The intent of this pattern is to form whole-part component hierarchies of arbitrary complexity, while at the same time treating individual components and compositions of components with a uniform interface. Let's first take a look at the motivation behind this pattern.

Motivation

User interfaces are commonly constructed with two basic types of components: container components and primitive components. A container component may have any number of components nested within it, while a primitive component may not. Using these two simple component types, developers can build larger components that then may be composed into even larger, more complex components. Such component hierarchies allow for the creation of those rich user interfaces we spoke of earlier.

When dealing with complex component hierarchies, having to distinguish between container components and primitive components is undesirable. You would routinely be forced to determine the type of component you were dealing with before performing operations common to all components. This adds still more complexity to the equation. The Composite Pattern allows us to treat these component types identically through a common interface.

The Composite Pattern is appropriate if the following statements are true:

- We are representing "part-whole hierarchies" (Gamma, Helm, Johnson, and Vlissides 1996).
- We wish to treat composite components and individual components the same throughout a component hierarchy. This allows uniform treatment of all components, regardless of type.

Now let's take a look at how the Composite Pattern resolves these issues.

Solution

The structure of the Composite Pattern is provided in Figure 1.7.

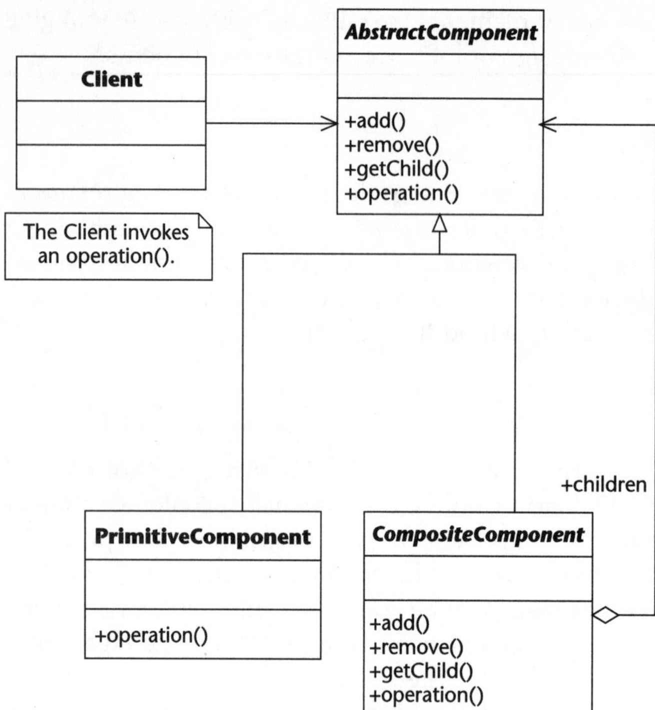

Figure 1.7 Composite Pattern structure.

There are a number of participants in this Pattern. We will first provide a summary of each participant's responsibilities and then explain how they collaborate to provide the uniform interface we are seeking.

AbstractComponent. This participant defines an interface common to all components. It implements this common interface to provide default behavior, a portion of which is used for accessing and managing nested components.

SimpleComponent. This participant represents and defines the behavior of primitive components.

CompositeComponent. This participant represents and defines the behavior of container components. It provides a mechanism for storing and managing nested components by implementing those portions of the `AbstractComponent` interface.

Client. This participant accesses and manipulates component hierarchies through the `AbstractComponent` interface.

When a Client performs an operation on a component, a uniform response is provided regardless of the underlying structure. If the component is a `SimpleComponent`, the operation is performed directly. Otherwise, we have a `CompositeComponent` that asks each nested component to perform the requested operation. The `CompositeComponent` may perform additional operations before responding to the Client. In either case, these interactions are hidden beneath a common interface.

There are a few well known consequences to using the Composite Pattern—not all of them good.

- As stated in the intent, this Pattern provides component hierarchies of arbitrary complexity, while at the same time treating individual components and compositions of components with a uniform interface (Open/Closed Principle).

NOTE The Open/Closed Principle is a software design principle that requires components to be open for extension but closed for modification. Composite components satisfy this principle nicely since they allow you to extend and aggregate existing components without modification.

- Client code is much simpler because it uses a uniform interface to manipulate both composite and primitive components (Liskov Substitution Principle [Liskov 1987]).

NOTE The Liskov Substitution Principle is a software design principle that allows the instance of a component to function as an instance of its super-component. This is accomplished by extending a new component directly or indirectly from `AbstractComponent`**.**

- Adding new component types is very straightforward and requires no change to existing client code.
- Nothing in the composite structure distinguishes one component type from another—they are all treated the same. While this provides a great deal of simplicity and flexibility, it can result in overly generic designs.
- When calling a method such as `add(...)` on a primitive component, an error may result if the component does not support this operation. The Client may then need to account for this possibility, which results in a violation of the Liskov Substitution Principle. In other words, our overly generic interface may require the Client to have knowledge of what that specific component is capable of instead of being able to rely on an appropriate implementation of all the generic interface's methods.

Swing Components and Containers

Swing components form a containment hierarchy that consists of what is called a top-level container and any number of child components. A top-level container may be a frame (`JFrame`), dialog (`JDialog`), or applet (`JApplet`). These top-level containers essentially provide a window within which components can paint themselves.

A simplified view of the Swing Composite structure is provided in Figure 1.8.

All components descend from the `Component` class, which provides basic component properties and services. This includes event handling, painting, and positioning. The `Container` class adds the ability for a component to contain others. This includes managing a list of child components, ordering them, and setting layout managers. The `Container` class in Swing is what provides the uniform Composite interface we discussed in the previous section (referred to as `AbstractComponent`).

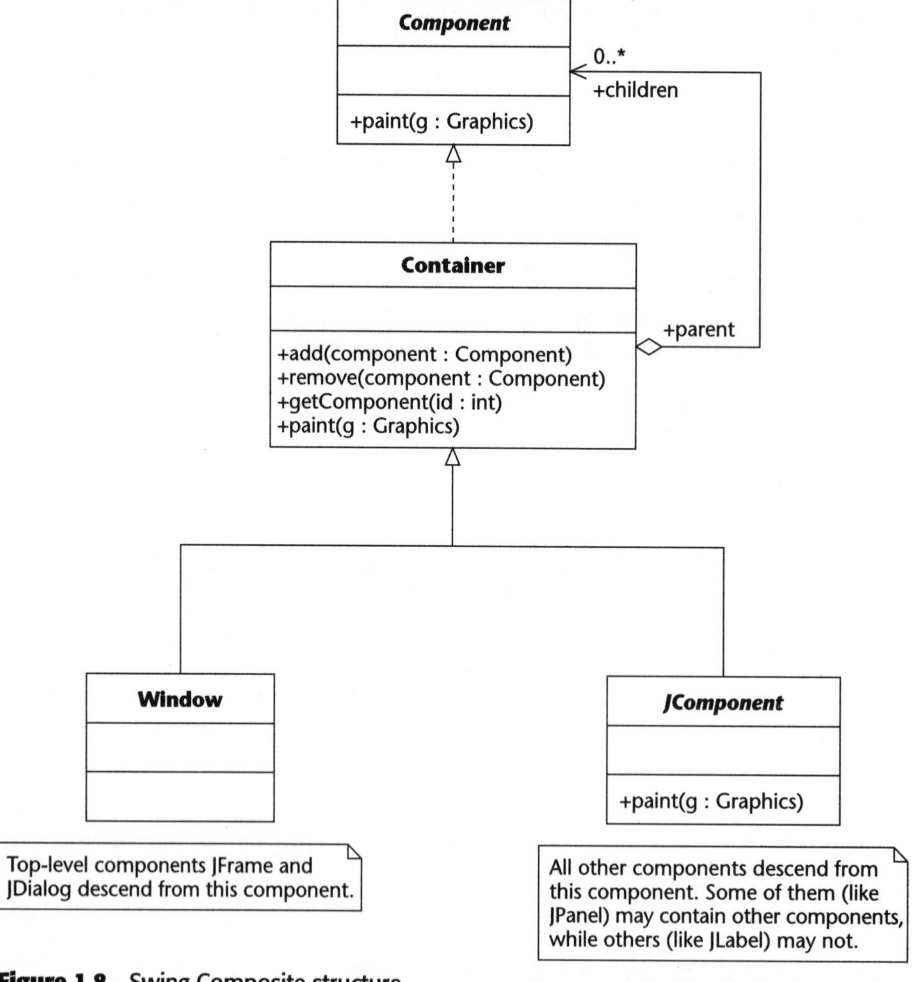

Figure 1.8 Swing Composite structure.

All components that are not top-level containers descend from the JComponent class, which is a direct subclass of Container. JComponent adds access to the application-wide pluggable look and feel, comprehensive keystroke handling, tool tips, accessibility support, custom component properties, and more painting functionality (most notably double buffering and support for borders).

Let's return to our simple login example to see what a Swing composite component structure would look like. The containment hierarchy for our login form is provided in Figure 1.9.

You'll notice that the LoginFrame contains something called a content pane. Each top-level container (in this case a JFrame) has this intermediate container. Instead of adding components to the frame itself, you add them to the frame's content pane. If we consider the content pane part of the frame, then this simple login form is a composite component with a hierarchy of child components four levels deep.

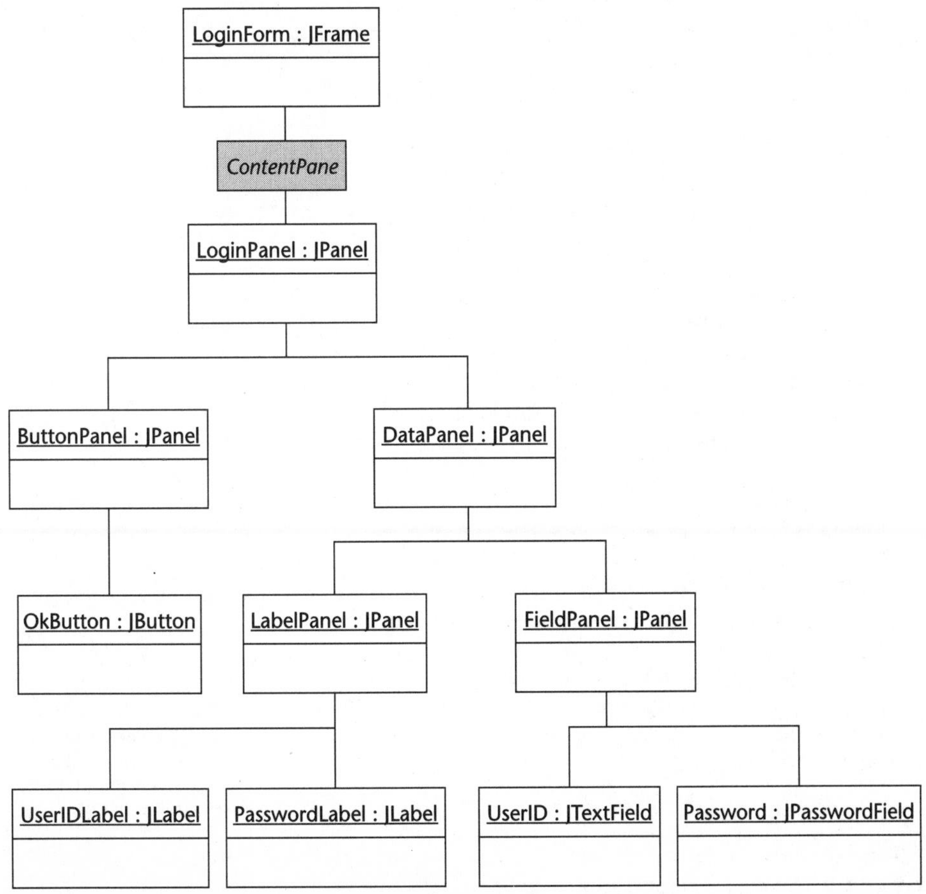

Figure 1.9 Swing login containment hierarchy.

Let's explore this composite a bit more with its source code representation in Listing 1.8. The source code only deals with creating components and laying them out. We have conveniently left out event handling for now because that topic will be covered later in this chapter.

```
class LoginForm extends JFrame {

    LoginForm() {
        super("Login");

        Container contents = getContentPane();;
        contents.add(getLoginPanel(), BorderLayout.CENTER);
        contents.add(getButtonsPanel(), BorderLayout.SOUTH);

        pack();
        setVisible(true);
    }

    JPanel getLoginPanel() {
        JPanel panel = new JPanel(new BorderLayout());

        JPanel labelPanel = new JPanel(new GridLayout(2,0));
        JLabel userIdLabel = new JLabel("User ID:");
        labelPanel.add(userIdLabel);
        JLabel passwordLabel = new JLabel("Password:");
        labelPanel.add(passwordLabel);
        panel.add(labelPanel, BorderLayout.WEST);

        JPanel fieldPanel = new JPanel(new GridLayout(2,0));
        JTextField userIdField = new JTextField();
        fieldPanel.add(userIdField);
        JTextField passwordField = new JTextField();
        fieldPanel.add(passwordField);
        panel.add(fieldPanel, BorderLayout.CENTER);

        return panel;
    }

    JPanel getButtonPanel() {
        JPanel panel = new JPanel(new FlowLayout());

        JButton okButton = new JButton("OK");
        panel.add(okButton);

        return panel;
    }
}
```

Listing 1.8 Swing login form source code.

Our login form basically consists of nested panels, descriptive labels, data fields, and a submit button. The `add(...)` method is used extensively here as the component hierarchy is built. This method allows us to add nested components of any type, so you are seeing one aspect of the Composite interface in action. We could also employ the other methods as well, but there is no need to do so for this example.

With a few minor exceptions, Swing provides a clear example of the Composite Pattern in action. We'll now move onto how Struts implements the same pattern.

Struts and Tiles

Earlier in this chapter we constructed a simple login form as a JSP using some of the Struts form tags. In this section we'll build a more robust login form that would serve as part of a larger Web application. In addition to the Struts form tags; we'll now make use of the Tiles tag library, which provides its own implementation of the Composite Pattern for the Web.

What is Tiles? Here is a definition of Tiles provided in the Struts User Guide:

> *Tiles builds on the "include" feature provided by the JavaServer Page specification to provided a full-featured, robust framework for assembling presentation pages from component parts. Each part, or tile, can be reused as often as needed throughout your application. This reduces the amount of markup that needs to be maintained and makes it easier to change the look and feel of a Web site. (Husted, Burns, and McClanahan 2003)*

A simplified view of the Tiles composite structure is provided in Figure 1.10.

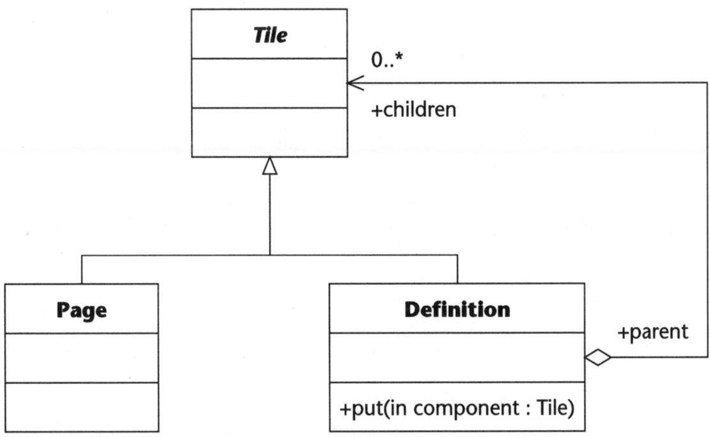

Figure 1.10 Tiles composite structure.

A component in Tiles (called a `Tile` or `Region`) may consist of a `Definition` or a `Page`. A `Definition` is an XML file that defines a reusable parameterized template, whereas a `Page` is usually a JSP. Each `Definition` may accept pages or even other definitions. If you look back at our description of the Composite Pattern, a `Tile` represents the `AbstractComponent`, a `Definition` represents the `CompositeComponent`, and a `Page` represents the `PrimitiveComponent`.

Let's return once again to the simple login example to see what a Tiles composite component structure would look like. The structure of the login form is provided in Figure 1.11.

The Login is a Tiles definition that extends the Base definition. The Base definition defines a standard layout that all pages in the Web application use. This allows us to localize changes to items that will appear on every page (the header and footer in this case). The Base definition expects to be given three pages and a String variable for the title. Each definition is provided below.

```
<!DOCTYPE tiles-definitions PUBLIC
       "-//Apache Software Foundation//DTD Tiles Configuration//EN"
       "http://jakarta.apache.org/struts/dtds/tiles-config.dtd">

<tiles-definitions>
    <definition name=".app.Base" path="/app/common/base.jsp">
      <put name="title"      value ="${title}"/>
      <put name="header"     value="/app/common/header.jsp"/>
      <put name="body"       value="${body}"/>
      <put name="footer"     value="/app/common/footer.jsp"/>
   </definition>
   <definition name=".app.Login" extends=".app.Base">
      <put name="title"      value="Login Form"/>
      <put name="body"       value="/app/login.jsp"/>
   </definition>
   ... other definitions ...
</tiles-definitions>
```

Here is the JSP used for the layout of the Base definition.

```
<%@ taglib uri="/tags/struts-bean" prefix="bean" %>
<%@ taglib uri="/tags/struts-html" prefix="html" %>
<%@ taglib uri="/tags/tiles" prefix="tiles" %>

<html:html>
    <head>
    <html:base/>
    <title><tiles:useAttribute name="title"/></title>
    </head>

    <body>
        <tiles:get name="header"/>
```

```
        <tiles:get name="body"/>
        <tiles:get name="footer"/>
    </body>
</html:html>
```

The JSP used for the login form, which is passed in via the Base definition's body attribute, is provided below.

```
<%@ taglib uri="/WEB-INF/struts-html.tld" prefix="html" %>

Logon with your username and password.<br/><br/>

<html:errors/>
<html:form action="/login">
    Username: <html:text property="username"/><br/>
    Password: <html:password property="password"/><br/>

    <html:submit value="Login"/>
</html:form>
```

Although we examined a simple example of Tiles in action, you could easily imagine the need to create one definition out of not just pages but other definitions as well. This behavior is characteristic of the Composite Pattern. In this case, the parent definition doesn't care whether one of its attributes is providing a page or a template because they both ultimately render markup text.

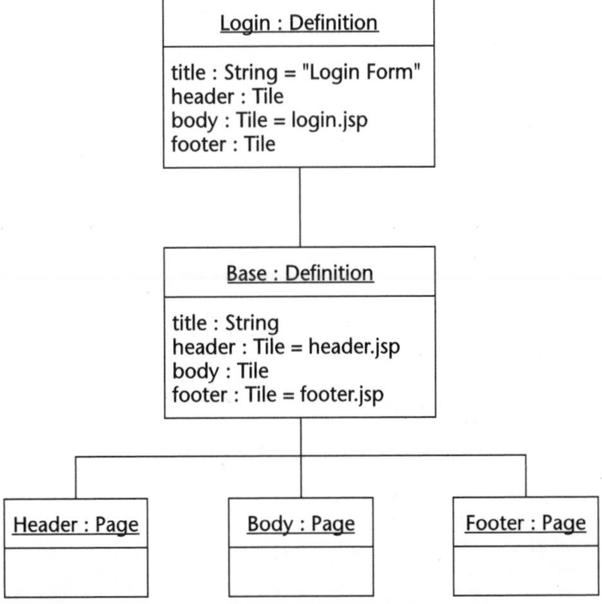

Figure 1.11 Tiles login form composite.

In this section we have just scratched the surface of what is possible with Tiles and Struts. Our purpose here is merely to determine how the Composite Pattern applies to Struts, so any further discussion is outside the scope of this book.

JSF Component Trees

As does Swing, JSF components provide an implementation that is very close to the generic solution presented by the Composite Pattern. Unlike Swing; however, there is no explicit distinction between top-level and regular components. A simplified view of the JSF Composite structure is provided in Figure 1.12.

JSF provides an interface called `UIComponent` that all components implement. The `UIComponentBase` class defines default behavior for the convenience of component developers. JSF supplies a number of basic components, like `UIForm` and `UIInput`, but you may create your own custom components if you wish. When creating custom components, you must either implement the `UIComponent` interface or extend the `UIComponentBase` class.

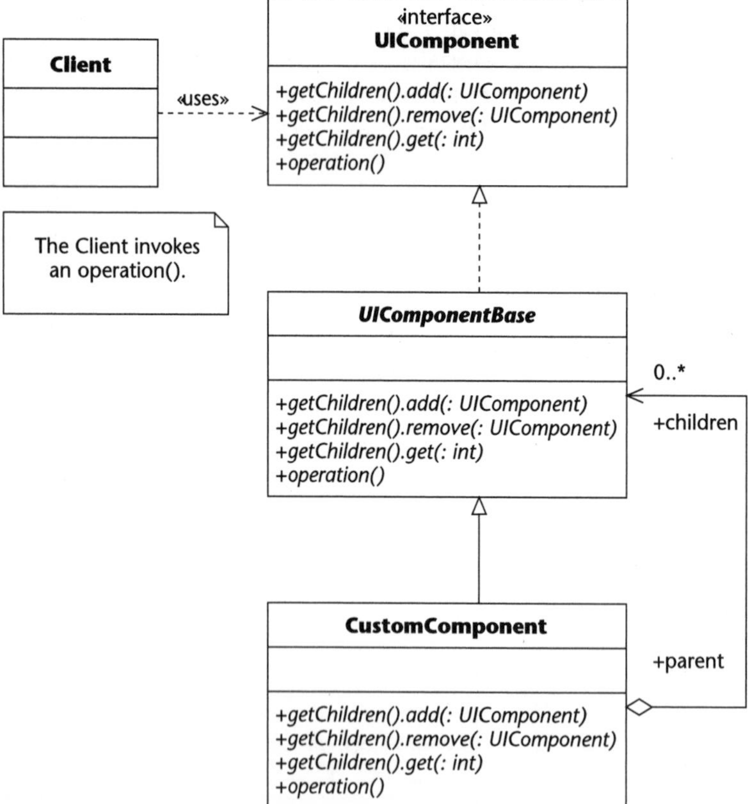

Figure 1.12 JSF Composite structure.

JSF allows you to nest components to form large composite components. Our login example for JSF looks similar to the Swing version we created earlier minus all of the panels. The JSF structure of the login form is provided in Figure 1.13.

For this particular example, the `LoginForm` is composed of a number of other components in a hierarchy that is only one level deep. Each of the components we are using here is provided with JSF by default, but later in this book we'll explore creating custom components for more complicated UIs. We could have deepened the hierarchy by using panels (`UIPanel`) for layout purposes, but the Web interface we will create doesn't require them.

Although we'll use JSPs for our UI in this example, JSF does not force you to use only JSPs when constructing your UI. We'll cover how you may render other markup shortly. For now, refer back to Listing 1.7 for our JSP version of the JSF login interface.

As you can see from the source code, JSF provides a convenient tag library for using the default components it provides. When this page is submitted by a user of the application, the `FacesServlet` we discussed earlier will build the actual component tree from the information presented and gathered by these tags.

You'll notice the use of `login` throughout the JSP. As we discussed earlier, this JavaBean serves as the backing model object for the login form and all of its child components. It is used to gather data entered by the user and to repopulate the page as necessary. Refer back to Listing 1.5 for the `LoginBean` source code. As you can see, any Java object that follows JavaBean naming conventions can be used with your JSF components.

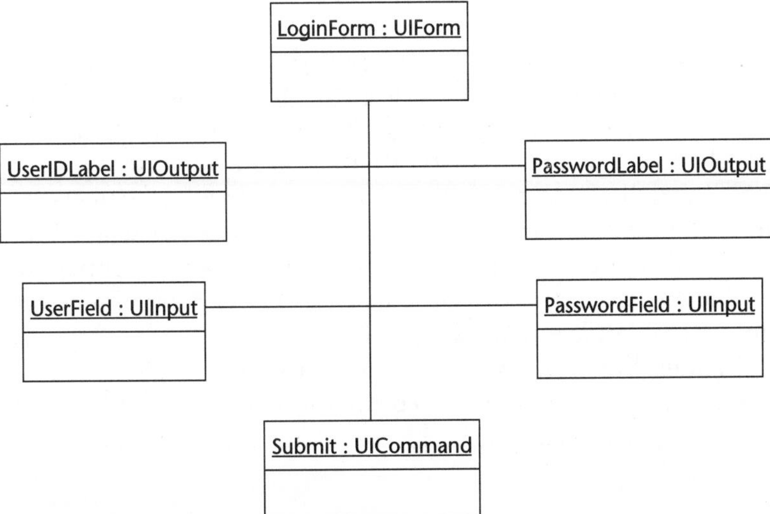

Figure 1.13 JSF login form composite.

Up to this point, you should have a good feel for how JSF implements the Composite Pattern to provide reusable, composable components. In the next section, we'll take this example further to see how JSF uses events to process a form submission.

Component Events

Events are an important aspect of the MVC architecture, so we'll now take a brief look at how each of our frameworks makes use of events in their MVC implementations. Before we get started, though, there is another commonly used pattern that is relevant to this discussion. It is called the *Observer* (Gamma, Helm, Johnson, and Vlissides 1996) Pattern, and it describes a useful mechanism for handling events in MVC-based architectures.

Observer Pattern

As with the Composite Pattern, we will begin by describing the Observer Pattern in general terms as it relates to user interfaces. Each of the three frameworks is then examined and the respective implementation of this common Pattern is uncovered.

The generic intent of this Pattern is to automatically notify dependent objects of a state change in the object they are interested in. For user interfaces, this Pattern provides a flexible and efficient mechanism for the Model, View, and Controller components of the MVC Pattern to communicate with each other.

Motivation

The MVC architecture separates the presentation (View) of its components from the underlying data objects (Model), but presentation components must rely on the data objects along with any changes of state that occur within them to render a consistent view with correct information. We would ideally like to keep this separation so that our components are reusable while at the same time giving the *appearance* that they have intimate knowledge of each other.

We also do not wish to set limits on the number of presentation components (or their types) that are dependent on the same data objects. This allows us to provide multiple user interfaces to the same data.

The Observer Pattern describes how to resolve these seemingly contradictory concerns. This Pattern is based on two primary roles—the *subject* and the *observer*. The subject represents our data objects and may have any number of observers that subscribe to receive notifications of state changes through a generic interface. Upon receiving notification of a change, each observer may query the subject via a generic interface to synchronize its state.

The Observer Pattern is appropriate if the following statements are true:

- You have one set of objects dependent on another, but you wish to maintain and reuse them separately.
- You want a change in one object to affect an unknown number of others of possibly varying types without requiring tight coupling.

Now let's take a look at how the Observer Pattern resolves these issues.

Solution

The structure of the Observer Pattern is provided in Figure 1.14.

There are a number of participants in this pattern. We will first provide a summary of each participant's responsibilities and then explain how they collaborate to meet the stated goals of this pattern.

Subject. The `Subject` provides a generic interface for adding and removing observers as well as notifying registered observers of state changes.

ConcreteSubject. The `ConcreteSubject` implements the `Subject` interface and holds a collection of observers that have registered for notifications. It also provides access to its state.

Observer. The `Observer` provides a generic interface for observing components to receive notification of state changes in the `Subject`.

ConcreteObserver. The `ConcreteObserver` implements the `Observer` interface and holds a copy of the `Subject`'s state. Each time the `Subject` notifies the `ConcreteObserver` of a state change, through its `Observer` interface, the `ConcreteObserver` can query the `Subject` for its new state.

Each component that wishes to observe changes in another registers via the `Subject` interface. The `ConcreteSubject` that implements this interface manages a collection of observing components that have requested to be notified of a state change. When a change occurs, the `ConcreteSubject` iterates through its list of observers and notifies each via the `Observer` interface. Each `ConcreteObserver` that is notified may then query the `ConcreteSubject` to reconcile its state.

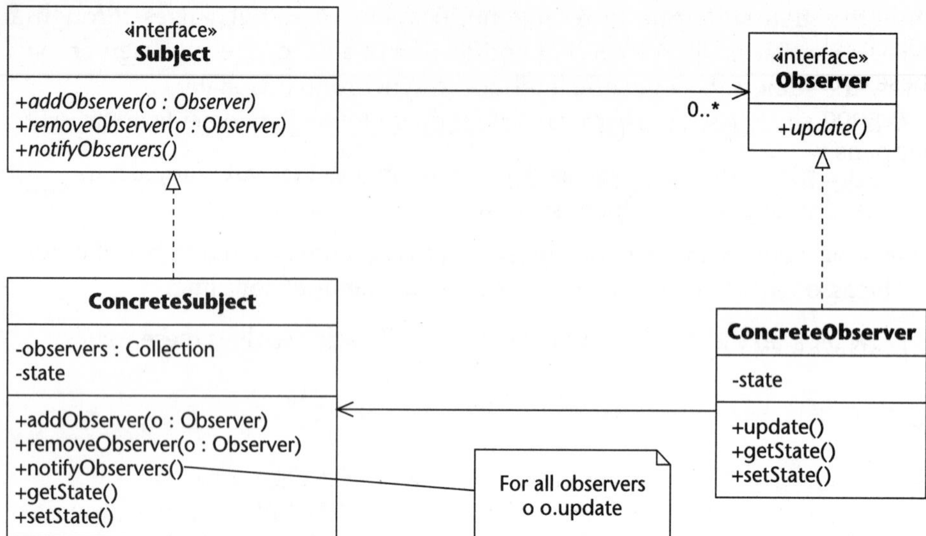

Figure 1.14 Observer Pattern structure.

There are a few well-known consequences to using the Observer Pattern—not all of them good:

- A loose coupling is maintained between a `Subject` and its `Observers`. The `Subject` does not know or care what types of components are observing it, because each of these components implements a simple interface.
- The Observer Pattern supports broadcast notifications. That is to say, the `Subject` doesn't care how many components have registered for change notifications, and it does not make a distinction between types of changes. It simply broadcasts to each registered observer that a change has occurred. It is then up to each observing component to either handle or ignore the notification.
- Receiving only a generic notification can be a disadvantage in that each observer may receive a number of notifications it is not interested in. There is no way to distinguish one notification from another without going back to the `Subject` for more information.

Swing Event Listeners

In the last section, we created a simple login form using Swing components. Although the form demonstrated how Swing components are composable, it didn't do anything interesting. Swing makes heavy use of the Observer

Pattern to allow its components to respond to user-driven events. Any Java object, whether it is a Swing component or not, can register to be notified of these events.

A good example of this behavior is the OK button on the login form. What happens when it is pressed? Nothing at the moment, but we can add a listener (or observer) for this event on the login form itself. Once the listener is registered, it will receive a notification every time the button is pressed. A structural representation of this process is provided in Figure 1.15.

The associated code for this process is provided below.

```
public class LoginForm implements ActionListener {

    public LoginForm() {
        ...
        okButton.addActionListener(this);
        ...
    }

    public void actionPerformed(ActionEvent e) {
        // Implement code here that is similar to that provided in
        // Listing 1.2.
    }
}
```

In this example, the login form is the `Observer` while the OK button is the `Subject`. This solution is very similar to what the Observer Pattern describes with one difference. When a Swing event is dispatched, an event object is included with the notification. The observing component can use this object to get additional information instead of querying the source of the event.

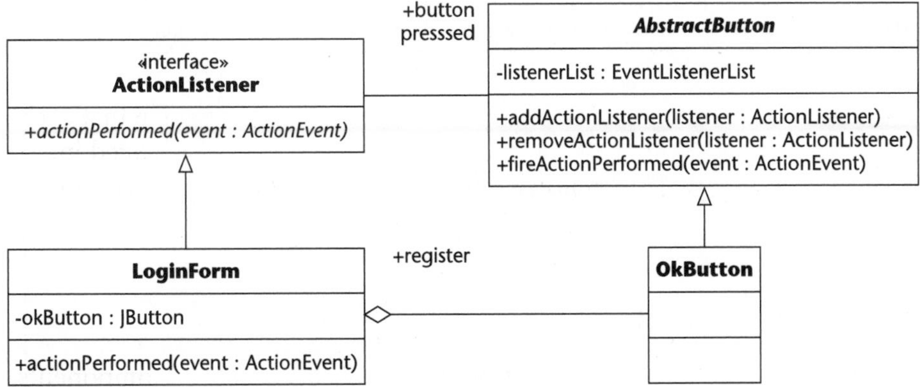

Figure 1.15 Swing login form event notification.

We have only demonstrated one type of Swing listener here. There are actually a number of others that you may use, depending on what the `Subject` component allows. For example, every Swing component may listen for component size changes, focus changes, key presses, mouse clicks, and mouse motion. There are others as well—each of which provides a separate listener interface.

Property Change Listener

One additional type of listener that deserves mention here is the JavaBean property change listener, which is described in the JavaBean specification. This listener is useful for observing bound properties on the backing model object of a Swing component. The structure of this listener is provided in Figure 1.16.

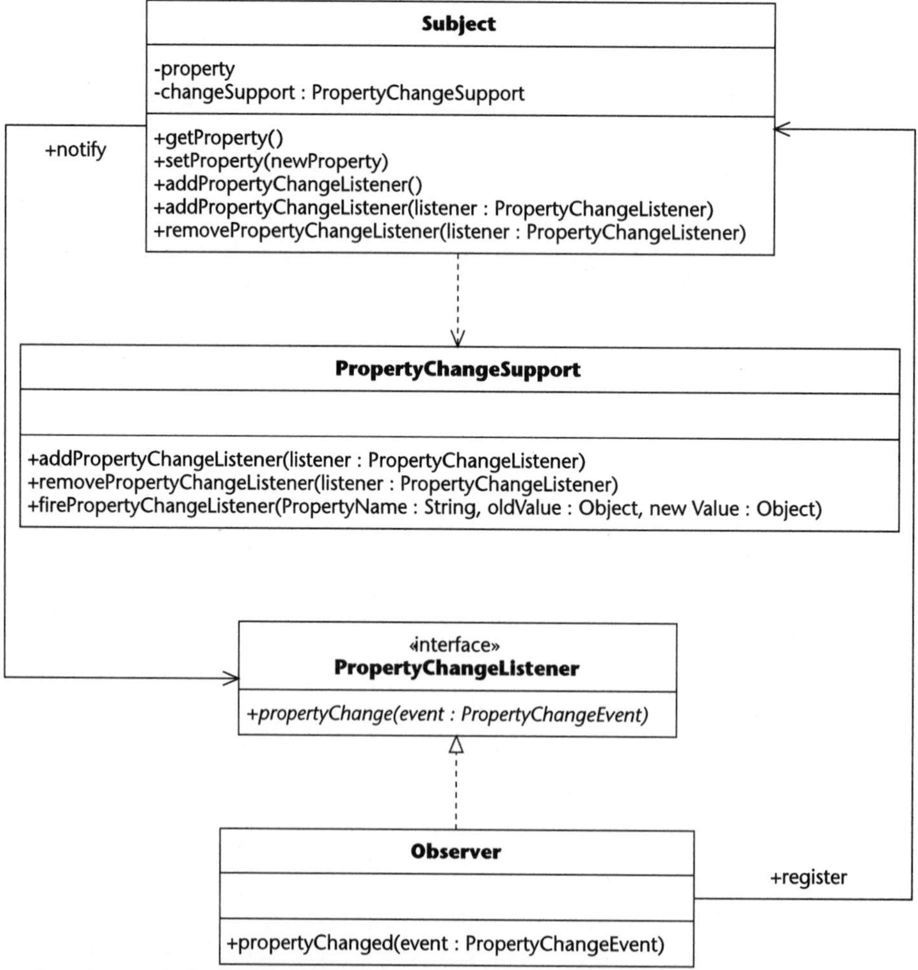

Figure 1.16 Property change listener structure.

The associated code for the `Subject` component is provided below.

```
public class SubjectComponent {
    ...
    String someProperty;
    private PropertyChangeSupport changes =
        new PropertyChangeSupport(this);
    ...

    public void addPropertyChangeListener(PropertyChangeListener l) {
        changes.addPropertyChangeListener(l);
    }

    public void removePropertyChangeListener(PropertyChangeListener l) {
        changes.removePropertyChangeListener(l);
    }

    public void setSomeProperty(String newValue) {
        String oldValue = someProperty;
        someProperty = newValue;
        changes.firePropertyChange("someProperty", oldValue, newValue);
    }
}
```

Although we chose to delegate the handling of property change event broadcasts to the `PropertyChangeSupport` utility class, we could have chosen instead to subclass it. Most Swing model objects already have built-in support for property change notifications, so you simply register with one to receive this type of notification.

```
public class ObserverComponent implements PropertyChangeListener {
    ...
    subject.addPropertyChangeListener(this);
    ...

    public void propertyChange(PropertyChangeEvent e) {
        // Respond to event here
    }
}
```

As you can see, the process for dealing with property change events is very similar to the other types of events Swing offers.

Struts Application Events

Struts has no built-in support for component events. It does, however, have support for what could be called application events. These events are essentially form submissions or links to other Web pages.

If you look back at Figure 1.5, you'll remember that the Struts ActionServlet handles each incoming request and forwards it to the appropriate Action for processing. Take a look at Figure 1.17 for a more event-based representation.

A user submits form data or selects a link on a Struts-based JSP (that is, one using Struts HTML tags). A request is created that, among other things, may contain form data. The ActionServlet serves as an event dispatcher by receiving the request and forwarding it to an appropriate Action. The Action then serves as an event handler by receiving the request, processing it, and letting the ActionServlet know how to respond.

This type of event handling is different from how Swing handles events. Swing allows you to programmatically register multiple listeners on a component, while Struts allows you to declaratively assign one event handler to a component.

JSF Events

JSF provides two kinds of events: *Value Changed* and *Action*. A Value Changed event (javax.faces.event.ValueChangeEvent) is useful for observing changes to a user interface component property (such as expanding a tree node or changing the text in a text field). An Action event (javax.faces.event.ActionEvent) is useful for observing the activation of a user interface component that is a descendent of UICommand (this includes buttons and hyperlinks). Both of these event types ultimately descend from a common ancestor in JSF (javax.faces.event.FacesEvent).

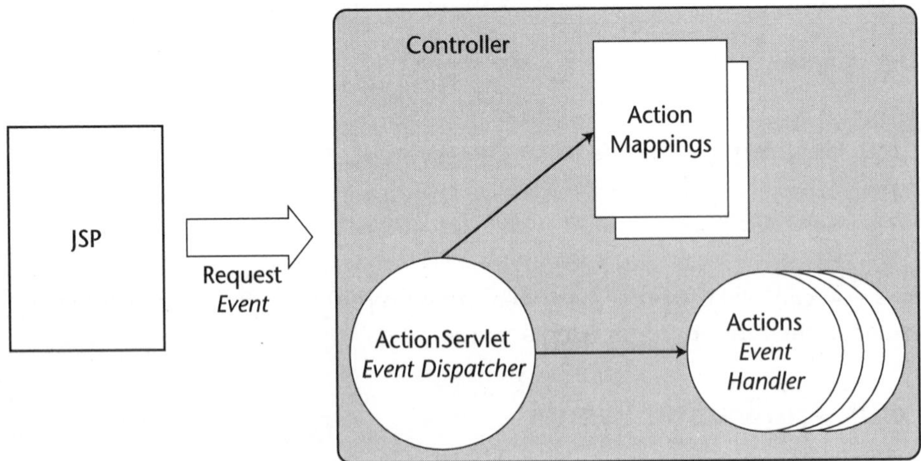

Figure 1.17 Struts application event handling.

Unlike Struts, JSF has a well-defined notion of events. You'll remember our recent discussion about property change events in Swing. JSF events also follow the JavaBean event model with strongly typed event classes and event listener interfaces. JSF's standard set of components emit either Value Changed or Action events, and any other component (user interface or server side) may register for a specific user interface component's events.

There are essentially two steps to capturing events in JSF. The first step is to implement the appropriate listener interface on the component you wish to receive an event. When implementing the `ValueChangeListener` interface, you'll need to add a `processValueChanged(...)` method where you will implement the code that responds to the event. Similarly, when implementing the `ActionListener` interface, you'll need to add a `processAction(...)` method. When an event is dispatched to your listener component, these methods will be called by the JSF implementation.

The second step to capturing an event in JSF is to register your newly created listener. An example of registering a Value Changed event listener on an input text field is provided below.

```
<h:inputText id="userId" value="#{login.userId}">
    <f:valueChangeListener type="logindemo.UserLoginChanged" />
</h:inputText>
```

When a user changes this input field and ultimately submits the changes, the `UserLoginChanged` class will be expected to implement the `ValueChangeListener` interface and an instance will have its `processValueChanged(...)` method called with information about the event.

An example of registering an Action event listener on a command button is provided below.

```
<h:commandButton id="login" commandName="login">
    <f:actionListener type="logindemo.LoginActionListener" />
</h:commandButton>
```

When a user changes this input field and ultimately submits the changes, the `LoginActionListener` class will be expected to implement the `ActionListener` interface and an instance will have its `processAction(...)` method called with information about the event. Another way to process an `ActionEvent` is to register an action handler method directly with this command button. We covered an example of this earlier (see Listing 1.7) when discussing JSF's implementation of the MVC pattern. When you only intend to respond to such an event in one way (such as this case, where you simply attempt to log in a user), you will typically register an action handler method instead of an action event listener. However, if you wish to dynamically change your response to such an event, then registering an action event listener would be more appropriate.

We'll cover JSF events in more detail later in Chapter 2 and in Chapter 7, "Navigation, Actions, and Listeners". The important thing to remember at this point is that JSF events closely resemble that of Swing, while JSF brings the concept of well-defined events and event listeners to the Web. Of course, this is a natural outgrowth of JSF's more component-centric approach to developing user interfaces (as opposed to the Struts page-centric approach).

Summary

Looking at JSF and the other frameworks in terms of Patterns has hopefully been a valuable experience. We covered only a few applicable patterns, so an additional exercise would be to identify other patterns and compare/contrast their use in Swing and Struts versus JSF. Although each of these frameworks is designed to deliver user interface-driven applications, they all provide varying implementations that were influenced by the environments they were designed to operate in. Comparing and contrasting Swing and Struts with JSF helps us understand many of the design decisions made by the authors of JSF.

Before moving on, it is important for you to notice how JSF attempts to bring Swing's event-driven, component-based user interface style to the Web. You'll see this even more clearly as we begin to delve into the specifics of JSF. Without further delay, let's now take a closer look at the essential elements of JSF.

CHAPTER 2

Elements of JSF

Now that we have taken a look at the JSF architecture in relation to other frameworks, it is time to dig into JSF itself. This chapter begins that process by giving an overview of essential JSF elements; in other words, those parts of the framework that are key to understanding how it works. We'll cover JSF UI components, Converters, Validators, Renderers, and much more. In doing so, we'll explore some of the sample applications provided with the *JSF Reference Implementation*. We'll continue with these applications in Chapter 3, "JSF Request-Processing Life Cycle," and Chapter 4, "JSF Configuration," as well while we finish covering the basics of JSF. In future chapters we'll present new sample applications as we cover more advanced topics. The hope here is that you become familiar with the *JSF Reference Implementation* while learning the basics of JSF.

The goal of this chapter is not a complete examination of each element, since that is the purpose of Chapters 5 to 10. Our goal here is simply to get a good feel for how JSF is composed and how those parts work together. At the end of this chapter, you will have a good, albeit basic, understanding of how the most important elements of JSF work.

Overview

JSF is primarily a user interface framework for developing Web-based applications on the Java platform. With the dizzying array of Java Web application frameworks already in existence, you may be wondering why we need another one. Here are a few of the more important motivations:

Standardization. JSF is an attempt to provide a standard user interface framework for the Web where no such standard currently exists. There are many benefits to having a multitude of frameworks to choose from, but such a choice does tend to fragment the Java development community. JSF provides a chance for Java developers to unite behind a standard, component-based user interface framework for the Web. JSF's ultimate inclusion under the J2EE umbrella will further this reality.

Tool Support. Having a standard Web application framework with a well-documented API makes the decision of which framework to support for all Java-based IDEs and other tools much easier. The design of JSF also lends itself well to graphical user interface building tools and will empower tool providers to create more complete and pleasurable development environments for developers at varying levels of experience.

Components. Of all the frameworks out there, very few of them incorporate the concept of reusable user interface components (beyond the concept of a Web page). JSF is just such an attempt, and it is intended to be for Web user interfaces what Swing is for more traditional user interfaces.

Web Development

Although JSF is designed to be independent of specific protocols and markup languages, most Java developers will use it in concert with Java servlets and JSPs to create HTML-based Web applications. These applications can communicate with Java application servers via the now ubiquitous and venerable HTTP. The authors of the JSF specification are aware of this demographic, so one of their primary goals is to resolve a number of issues related to using the stateless HTTP protocol in concert with HTML clients. The specification highlights a number of JSF features related to this goal:

UI Component State. JSF specifically addresses saving user interface component state between requests in a Web client session.

Component Rendering. HTML is just one of many markup languages, and each Web client's support of a particular markup language may vary. JSF provides a rendering mechanism for addressing this variety of target Web clients.

Form Processing. Most Web applications are form-based. JSF provides a number of convenient features for processing multipage and single-page form-based requests.

Form Validation. Along with form processing, validating form data is a critical need. JSF helps automate this process and provide the necessary error reporting.

Event Model. JSF provides a strongly typed component event model for responding to client-generated events with server-side handlers.

Type Conversion. Since Web client requests via HTTP provide form data as strings, a mechanism for converting these strings to and from the application model would be very useful. JSF provides a facility for enabling type conversion.

Error Handling. All applications must deal with application errors and exceptions. JSF provides a mechanism for handling error conditions and reporting them back to the user interface.

Internationalization. Multilanguage support is often a key requirement in Web applications, which are easily accessible from around the world. JSF provides native support of internationalization.

JSF also provides a standard tag library and rendering kits that support JSP development. We'll cover this JSP support in detail in Chapter 5, "JSP Integration in JSF."

UI Components

UI components are the centerpiece of JSF and are used as building blocks to create user interfaces that range from simple to complex. We covered the composable nature (via an implementation of the Composite Pattern) of these components in the previous chapter. Here, we will examine JSF UI components in more detail along with other component types that exist to support them. We'll delve into an even more comprehensive treatment of UI components in Chapter 6, "UI Components."

You are probably familiar with Swing user interface components as well as those from other languages or development environments. As Swing did for rich user interface clients, JSF provides a standard user interface component framework for the Web. This standardization promises more powerful and visual development environments for Web applications and libraries of rich user interface components like calendars, trees, and tables.

JSF also provides a number of other standard component types that play a supporting role to UI components. These include Converters, Validators, Renderers, and others. Like UI components, these components are interchangeable and can be reused throughout the same application and a host of others.

This opens up the possibility of additional libraries of components that cover these common supporting tasks.

So what makes a user interface component? Every user interface component in JSF implements the `javax.faces.component.UIComponent` interface. This comprehensive interface defines methods for navigating the component tree, interacting with backing data models, and managing supporting concerns such as component validation, data conversion, rendering, and a host of others. A convenient base class that implements this interface, `javax.faces.component.UIComponentBase`, is provided for creating new components. It provides default implementations for each method that component developers can then extend to customize the behavior of a component.

When creating new components in JSF, you essentially have three choices: create the component from scratch by directly implementing the `UIComponent` interface when no existing components meet your needs and you expect to override much of what `UIComponentBase` provides; subclass `UIComponentBase` to get default component behavior; or subclass an existing component to customize it for your needs. Subclassing an existing component will most likely be your choice for new individual components because most of the standard JSF components serve as good building blocks (input fields, labels, panels, and so on). Subclassing `UIComponentBase` will likely be your choice for building composite components. If you are creating new components for use with JSPs, you also need to either extend existing tag libraries or create your own so that your new component can be used in a JSP. We'll cover this process in great detail in Chapter 10, "Custom JSF Components."

The standard JSF components (and the standard JSF HTML RenderKit) provide a number of the basic components you'll need when building your Web applications. In most cases, you'll use one of these standard components or those from third-party libraries, so you typically won't need to worry about `UIComponent` or `UIComponentBase`. However, there will be times where you may wish to extend an existing component or have need of one that is not readily accessible. You may also wish to directly manipulate component trees on the server side (outside of JSPs) in a manner similar to that discussed in Chapter 1 with our coverage of the Composite Pattern.

Standard UI Components

Before looking at the UIComponent interface in more depth, let's briefly take a look at what the standard JSF components are. Each component is summarized in Table 2.1. A more detailed description of each component may be found in the *JavaServer Faces Specification*.

Table 2.1 Standard JSF UI Components

COMPONENT	DESCRIPTION
UIColumn	UIColumn represents a column in the parent UIData component. Child components of UIColumn are processed once for each row in the parent UIData component.
UICommand	UICommand represents UI components like buttons, hyperlinks, and menu items that result in application-specific actions or events. These components emit an ActionEvent when triggered that may be processed by a registered ActionListener.
UIData	UIData represents a collection of data wrapped by a DataModel (one of the standard JSF UIComponent model beans) instance. This component is commonly used to render tables, lists, and trees.
UIForm	UIForm represents a user input form and is meant primarily to be a container of other components.
UIGraphic	UIGraphic displays an immutable image or picture.
UIInput	UIInput represents UI components like text input fields, numeric input fields, date input fields, memo fields, and so on. UIInput displays the current value of a field and accepts changes by the user. Each change triggers a ValueChangedEvent that may be processed with a registered ValueChangedListener. It is very common to see registered Validators and Converters attached to this type of component to ensure the validity of data entered by a user.
UIMessage	UIMessage displays error messages for a specified input component.
UIMessages	UIMessages displays error messages not related to a specific component or all error messages.
UIOutput	UIOutput represents UI components like labels, error messages, and any other textual data that is immutable.
UIPanel	UIPanel represents UI components that serve as containers for others without requiring form submissions. UIPanel will typically be used to manage the layout of its child components.
UIParameter	UIParameter represents information that requires no rendering. It is typically used to provide additional information to a parent component. Examples include declaring request parameters for the URL associated with a hyperlink (UICommand component) or input parameters necessary for displaying a registered message.

(continued)

Table 2.1 *(continued)*

COMPONENT	DESCRIPTION
UISelectBoolean	UISelectBoolean represents a Boolean data field and is most often rendered as a check box. This component descends from UIInput, so it emits a ValueChangedEvent when a user checks or unchecks it.
UISelectItem	UISelectItem represents a single item in a selection list. It may be used to insert an item into a UISelectMany or a UISelectOne list.
UISelectItems	UISelectItems is very similar to UISelectItem with the exception that it allows the insertion of multiple items at once.
UISelectMany	UISelectMany represents UI components like combo boxes, list boxes, groups of check boxes, and so on. This component allows the selection of multiple items. Each item is specified by nesting one or more UISelectItem and UISelectItems components. This component descends from UIInput, so it emits a ValueChangedEvent when a user modifies the list of selected items.
UISelectOne	UISelectOne is very similar to UISelectMany with the exception that it only allows the selection of one item.
UIViewRoot	UIViewRoot represents the component tree root and is involved in the state-saving process. This component is not rendered.

A component hierarchy is provided in Figure 2.1. You'll notice how some components build upon and specialize others. This is not uncommon in user interface component libraries, and you can expect to see others extend this component hierarchy with a richer set of UI components.

Each of the sample applications provided with the *JSF Reference Implementation* make use of some or all of these components. You will typically see them used via JSP tags that are defined as part of the default HTML RenderKit that every JSF implementation is required to provide. A summary list of these tags is provided in the "Rendering" section of this chapter.

You may have already noticed an important distinction with respect to JSF UI components. In JSF, function is separated from appearance. In other words, a component like UIInput actually represents a class of user interface components that you are used to dealing with. All of them are functionally similar, but they appear differently. For example, a simple text input field is functionally similar to a password entry field. They are represented by the same component type in JSF, but they have different Renderers (which produce a particular look and feel) associated with them. This is a simple but important concept to understand, especially if you are considering developing your own UI components. Develop components according to function, then create

Renderers to specify different looks and feels as your user interface requires. The concept of delegation (which is actually a simple, yet fundamental, software pattern) is used here to separate function from appearance. You'll see it again when we discuss Validators and Converters shortly.

Identifiers

Identifying components becomes important in complex user interfaces, and JSF addresses this with the concept of a *component identifier*. You set a component's identifier programmatically via its `setComponentId()` method, and you retrieve it via its `getComponentId()` method. However, most developers will set this identifier via a tag attribute in a JSP. Here is an example from the sample login application in Chapter 1.

```
<h:outputLabel for="userId">
    <h:outputText value="User ID"/>
</h:outputLabel>
<h:inputText id="userId" value="#{login.userId}"/>
```

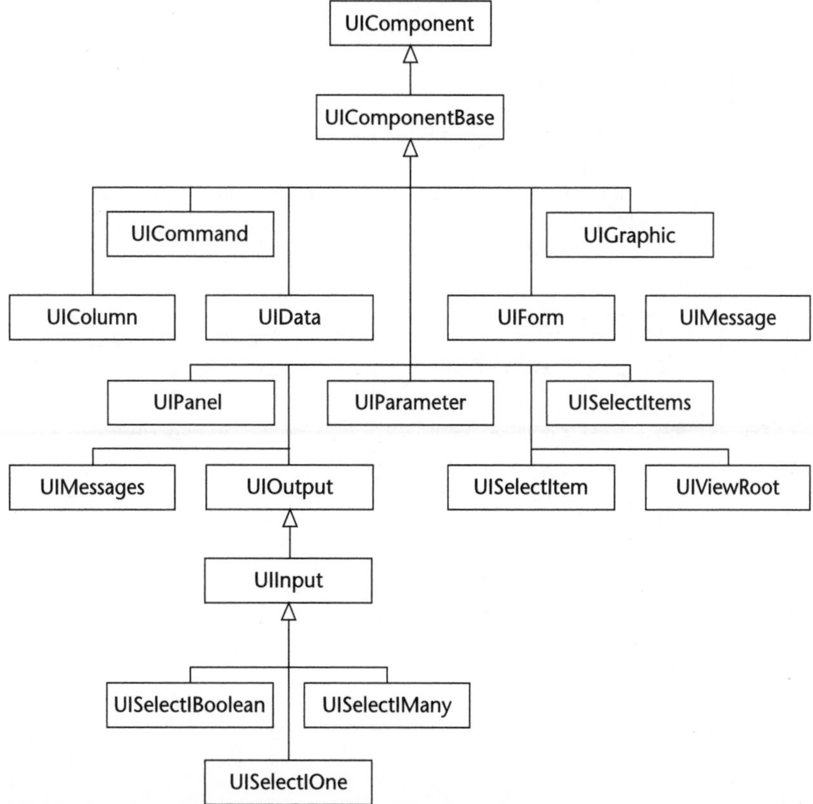

Figure 2.1 Standard JSF UI component hierarchy.

Identifiers are optional, but in this example one is necessary for the label to associate itself with the input field. You should explicitly declare an identifier like this when other UI components or server-side components refer to it. Each identifier is required by the specification to meet the following requirements: should start with a letter; should contain only letters, whole numbers, dashes, and underscores; and should be as short as possible to limit the size of responses generated by JSF.

UI Component Trees

As we discussed in Chapter 1, user interface components in JSF are composable. In other words, you can nest one component within another to form more complex client interfaces. These compositions are referred to as *component trees* in JSF. A simple example of such a tree, the Guess Number sample application provided by the *JSF Reference Implementation*, is provided in Listing 2.1.

```
<html>
    <head> <title>Hello</title> </head>
    <%@ taglib uri="http://java.sun.com/jsf/html" prefix="h" %>
    <%@ taglib uri="http://java.sun.com/jsf/core" prefix="f" %>
    <body bgcolor="white">
    <f:view>
    <h:form id="helloForm" >
        <h2>
            Hi. My name is Duke. I'm thinking of a number from
            <h:outputText value="#{UserNumberBean.minimum}"/> to
            <h:outputText value="#{UserNumberBean.maximum}"/>.
            Can you guess it?
        </h2>

        <h:graphicImage id="waveImg" url="/wave.med.gif" />
        <h:inputText id="userNo" value="#{UserNumberBean.userNumber}"
                    validator="#{UserNumberBean.validate}"/>

        <h:commandButton id="submit" action="success" value="Submit" />
        <p>

        <h:message id="errors1" for="userNo"/>
    </h:form>
    </f:view>
</html>
```

Listing 2.1 JSP component tree.

You'll notice how the root component is a form component, and inside it we have an input component and a command button that submits the contents of the input component. You can of course imagine much more complicated interfaces that involve more input fields, labels, tables, and other components, but this at least provides a simple example of what a component tree looks like.

When the command button is pressed, a request that includes the content of the input field is submitted to the `FacesServlet`. As you'll see in Chapter 3, the servlet goes through a number of steps to process the request and return an appropriate response (in this case, another JSP). During that processing, a Java object version of the component tree is either created (for the initial request) or reconstituted. As a developer, you will work with this version of the component tree in custom Validators, Converters, Renderers, and application components. Fortunately, JSF provides a convenient component API for manipulating these trees programmatically.

Tree Manipulation and Navigation

UI components have access to their parent and children via a number of methods defined by the `UIComponent` interface. These methods should be familiar to you from our discussion of the Composite Pattern in Chapter 1. Let's take another look at the Guess Number sample. A graphical representation of it is provided in Figure 2.2, in which some of those methods are reflected.

Most of these methods are self-explanatory. Invoking `getParent()` on either the input or submit component will return the parent form. You can use `getChildren()` on the form component to retrieve a mutable list of direct children (in this case the input and submit components).

You can change the list of child components in the form by manipulating the `List` returned by `getChildren()`. Invoking `add()` with a new user interface component would add that component either to the end of the list of child components or at a position you specify. Likewise, invoking `remove()` either with a reference to the desired user interface component or its position in the list of children will remove it.

Since these methods are available for every user interface component in JSF, you are provided with a generic interface for navigating and manipulating components in arbitrarily complex tree structures. You just need to remember that the methods in this interface will behave differently based on whether a component actually has children or not.

When dealing with a tree of components, you may wish to search for a particular component. You can do this by invoking the `findComponent()` method on a form, panel, or other container component. The expression argument will typically be the identifier of the component you are looking for. This particular method is convenient for avoiding lengthy traversals of more complex component trees.

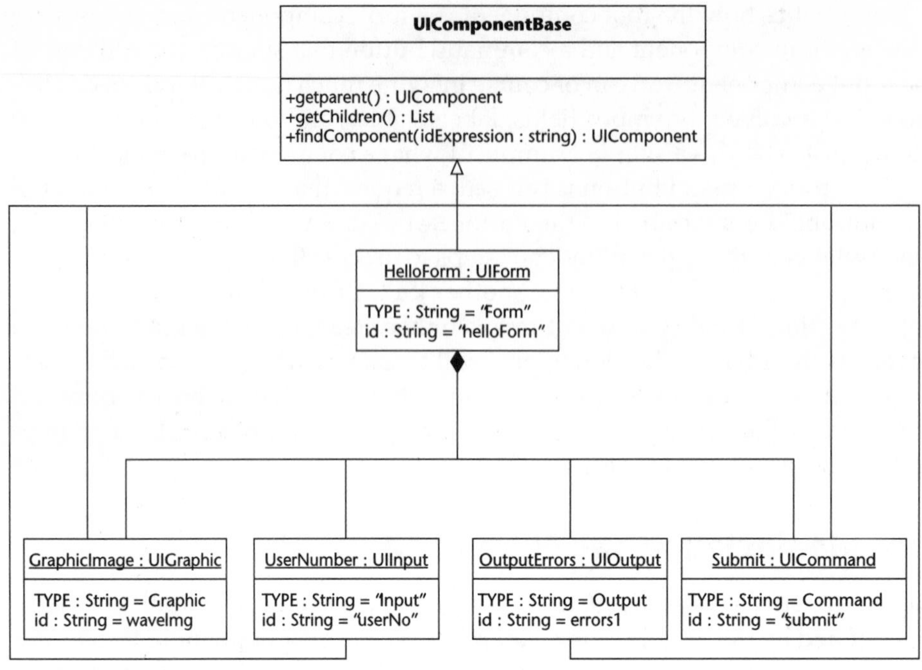

Figure 2.2 Component tree.

Facets

The methods listed above allow you to manipulate and navigate composite components through a generic interface as described by the Composite Pattern. JSF provides an additional facility for defining the roles of subordinate components that may be independent of or orthogonal to the parent-child relationship. These roles are called *facets*.

To understand how facets may be used, let's take a look at the Component sample application provided by the *JSF Reference Implementation*. An excerpt of the `tabbedpanes` JSP is provided in Listing 2.2.

```
<h:form>
<d:stylesheet path="/stylesheet.css"/>
Powered by Faces components:
<d:paneTabbed id="tabcontrol"
        paneClass="tabbed-pane"
        contentClass="tabbed-content"
        selectedClass="tabbed-selected"
        unselectedClass="tabbed-unselected">

    <d:paneTab id="first">
        <f:facet name="label">
            <d:paneTabLabel label="T a b 1" commandName="first" />
        </f:facet>
        ...
    </d:paneTab>

    <d:paneTab id="second">
        <f:facet name="label">
            <d:paneTabLabel image="images/duke.gif"
                            commandName="second"/>
        </f:facet>
        ...
    </d:paneTab>

    <d:paneTab id="third">
        <f:facet name="label">
            <d:paneTabLabel label="T a b 3" commandName="third"/>
        </f:facet>
        ...
    </d:paneTab>
</d:paneTabbed>
</h:form>
```

Listing 2.2 Facets in tabbed pane JSP.

In this example, a facet called `label` is used to identify the label of each tab in the tabbed component. You can already see that the facet is being used here to logically identify a specific component that appears in each tab. To see how the facet is actually used, take a look at an excerpt from the `TabbedRenderer` class in Listing 2.3.

```
public void encodeEnd(FacesContext context, UIComponent component)
    throws IOException {

    ...

    // Render the labels for the tabs.
    String selectedClass =
        (String) component.getAttributes().get("selectedClass");
    String unselectedClass =
        (String) component.getAttributes().get("unselectedClass");

    ...

    kids = component.getChildren().iterator();
    while (kids.hasNext()) {
        UIComponent kid = (UIComponent) kids.next();
        if (!(kid instanceof PaneComponent)) {
            continue;
        }
        PaneComponent pane = (PaneComponent) kid;
        ...
        UIComponent facet = (UIComponent)pane.getFacet("label");
        if (facet != null) {
            if (pane.isRendered() && (selectedClass != null)) {
                facet.getAttributes().put("paneTabLabelClass",
                selectedClass);
            }
            else if (!pane.isRendered() && (unselectedClass != null)) {
                facet.getAttributes().put("paneTabLabelClass",
                unselectedClass);
            }
            facet.encodeBegin(context);
        }
    ...
    }
    ...
}
```

Listing 2.3 Facets in tabbed pane Renderer.

This `Renderer` is used for showing the correct representation of a tabbed pane after the client has performed some action (such as changing the active tab). The `label` facet is used to easily locate the label component of each tab. Once located, the style of the label (or how it appears to the client) is set, based on whether or not the parent tab has been selected by the client. You can see the difference in the selected tab's label compared to those that are not selected in Figure 2.3.

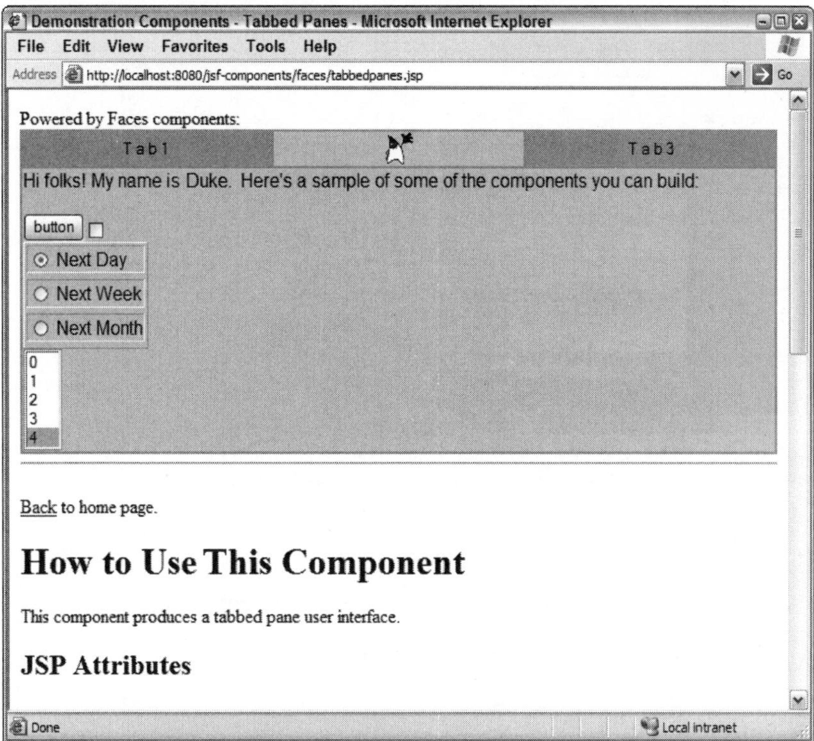

Figure 2.3 Initial tab selection.

If you select a different tab, not only does the content change, but the shading of the tabs themselves also changes. This is shown in Figure 2.4.

We'll talk more about Renderers later, but all you need to know for now is that facets can be used to easily classify and locate a component according to its function in your user interface. Instead of searching through a collection of components to find them, you simply retrieve them via their facet name or role.

It is worth noting that all components have methods for accessing and manipulating facets that have been associated with them. In our example, the `getFacet()` method was invoked along with the name of the facet we were looking for. Another method, `getFacets()`, provides a mutable `Map` of facets that you can use to programmatically add and remove facets. Only one component may be associated with a particular facet name at a time. Adding a facet that already exists has the effect of replacing the associated component.

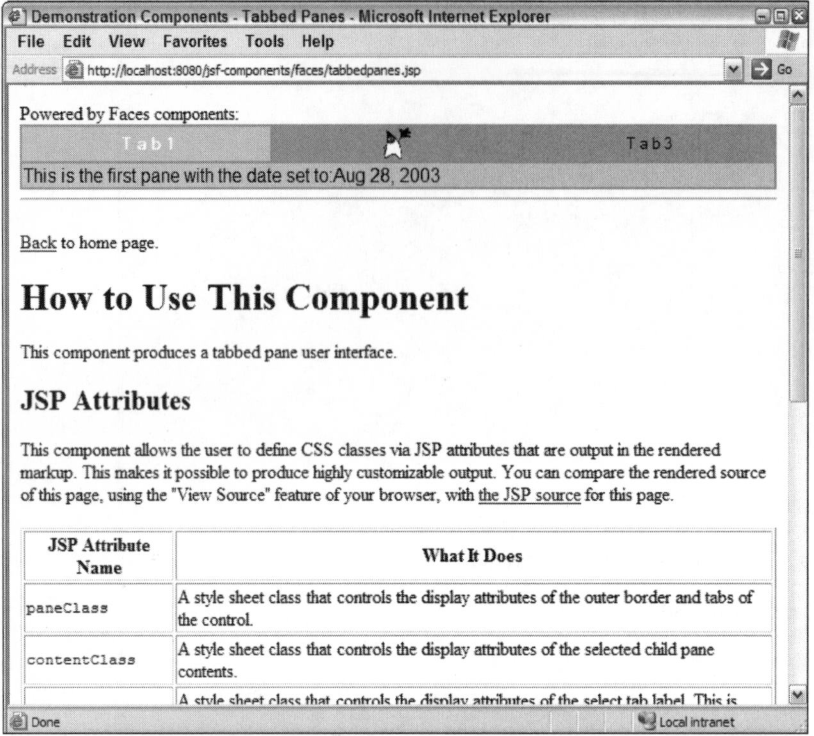

Figure 2.4 Different tab selection.

Generic Attributes

JSF supports the concept of generic attributes, which allow for runtime component metadata that is separate from those properties defined for a component's implementation. Attributes are used frequently for Renderers, Validators, Converters, and events.

Every component has methods for accessing generic attributes. In our previous example, you've already seen the `getAttribute()` and `setAttribute()` methods in action for retrieving and changing the value of a specific attribute by name. The `getAttributeNames()` method may also be used to get a list of all attributes associated with a particular component. You may add attributes to a component at design time (in a JSP) or at run time (in a `Validator`, `Renderer`, and so on) to store pretty much anything.

When defining your own custom components, you may choose to represent properties of a component via the generic attribute mechanism or via standard JavaBean properties (with getters and setters on the component itself). You must weigh the type safety of actual JavaBean properties on the component itself versus the flexible but potentially unsafe use of generic attributes.

If you take another look at the tabbed pane sample we just covered, you'll notice a number of generic attributes set on the tabbed pane itself. The contentClass, selectedClass, and unselectedClass attributes are used by the associated Renderer to properly draw child tabs and their contents via style sheets. The code provided in Listing 2.3 (and the full method provided in the associated sample application) shows how the Renderer uses these attributes together to properly draw each tab in the tabbed pane.

Don't get too caught up in the specifics of this example, because we will cover the concept of component rendering in greater depth later in the book. For now, you should have a good idea of how attributes are used.

Data Models

When working with JSF applications, you will usually deal with two different data models. The first model is associated with user interface components to manage their state. The second model is associated with the server-side application-level model. User interface component models are often populated with snapshots of data from the application model, while changes to component models are propagated back to the application model via application events.

Component Model

A component model object is usually associated with a component via JSF's value-binding facility. If you remember our discussion of managed beans in Chapter 1 while exploring the MVC pattern as applied to JSF, we used a managed bean to hold data from the login form JSP. The LoginBean JavaBean was registered in the associated JSF configuration file as a managed bean and made available to UI components through a unique identifier. To bind a UI component to this bean, we used the value attribute.

```
<h:inputSecret id="password" value="#{login.password}"/>
```

This attribute references the managed bean through its login identifier and then binds to its password property. We'll cover this topic in more detail in Chapter 4, and then again in Chapter 6.

Application Model

Application models represent business data. As such, there are a number of alternatives for representing and persisting such data:

- JavaBeans (where persistence is not required)
- JavaBeans with JDBC

- JavaBeans that use an object-relational (OR) framework
- Enterprise JavaBeans

You will often interface with these application model objects (or business objects) through action handlers and managed beans. Our discussion of the MVC Pattern in Chapter 1 provided a good example of this with the `LoginBean` managed bean and its `login` action handler. You'll see more examples of this in Chapter 7, "Navigation, Actions, and Listeners."

Validation

Performing correctness checks on user-submitted data is an important aspect of all applications that collect information (not just Web applications), even if that information is only temporarily used to perform a calculation of some sort. Being able to catch bad data as it is provided is critical to ensuring the integrity of the information you collect and for your application to perform as expected. It is no surprise, then, that data validation is an integral part of the JSF framework.

In this section, we'll cover `Validator` components in JSF and how they are associated with `UIInput` components. We'll also look at how you register Validators with your applications; before using your first `Validator` component, it will be good to know what standard `Validator` components JSF provides out of the box.

Validators

Validation in JSF comes in two forms: direct validation within a `UIInput` component and delegated validation, which occurs outside of a `UIInput` component. Figure 2.5 provides a graphical summary of this choice. Which method you choose is essentially determined by whether the validation you are performing is specific to a particular `UIInput` component or should be reused among a number of different `UIInput` components. It will not be uncommon for you to use both methods for components that have a nontrivial amount of data behind them, some of which may be unique to that component, while the rest may be common data types seen elsewhere.

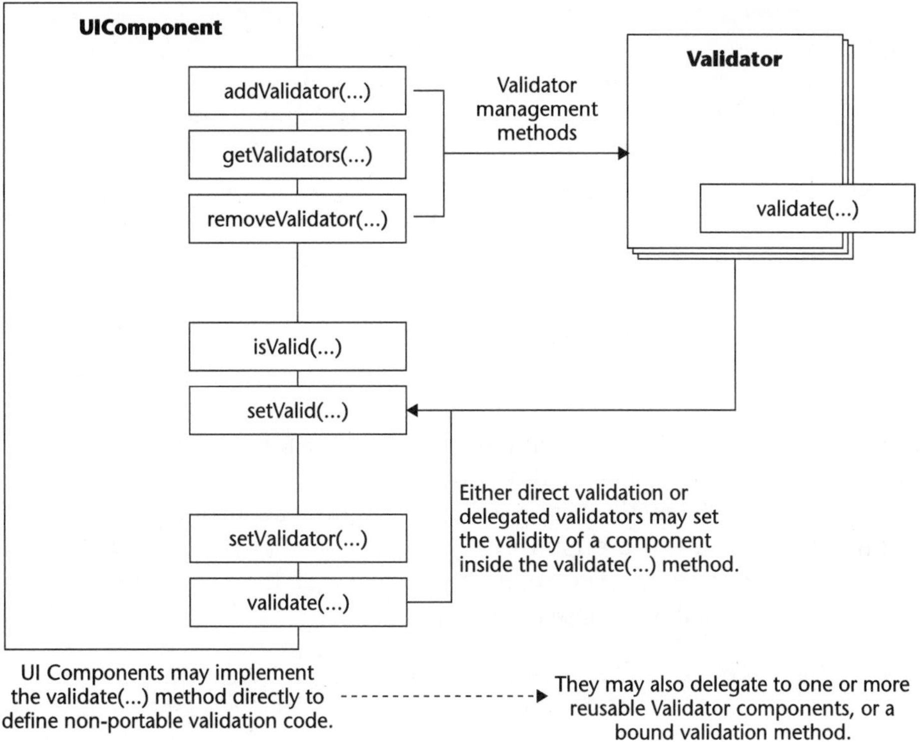

Figure 2.5 Direct validation versus delegated validation.

If your validation is specific to a particular `UIInput` component, then you may implement your validation code within the component by overriding the `validate()` method. At the appropriate point in the request processing life cycle, the JSF framework will invoke this method, thereby executing any code you have provided for correctness checking. This method of validation provides a quick and efficient means of validating your components; the downside is that your validation code is not portable. An additional restriction is that you can only use this method of validation for your own components or you must subclass an existing component to implement the `validate()` method.

Delegated Validation

If your validation should be reused among different user interface component types or if you would like to attach a certain type of validation to an existing component, the JSF framework provides two useful mechanisms: validate method binding and `Validator` components.

The method binding mechanism allows you to delegate component validation to a method on any managed bean or JavaBean in scope. It is similar to direct validation in that you are associating validation logic directly to a UIInput component. The difference, of course, is that you don't have to actually subclass an existing UIInput component to assign the validation logic.

A good example of this mechanism at use appears in the Guess Number sample application we looked at earlier. The input field in the associated JSP page is repeated here:

```
<h:inputText id="userNo" value="#{UserNumberBean.userNumber}"
             validator="#{UserNumberBean.validate}"/>
```

The validator attribute binds the validate method of the UserNumberBean to the userNo UIInput component. When the JSF implementation calls the component's validate method during the request-processing life cycle, it will delegate to the method assigned to the validate attribute on the tag.

A requirement of this mechanism is that you provide three parameters in your validation method. The following excerpt of the UserNumberBean validate method shows these parameters:

```
public void validate(FacesContext context, UIInput component,
                     Object value) throws ValidatorException {
     ...
}
```

You may call the method anything you wish, but make sure that you copy this signature when binding a method for validation.

The other delegated validation mechanism allows you to define reusable Validator components that you can associate with a UIInput component. This mechanism provides a more powerful form of reuse in component form for multiple applications. Each Validator component must implement the javax.faces.validator.Validator interface. This interface contains a method with the same signature as the one we just covered for method-binding validation. You implement your validation code within this method and operate on the generic component instance and value that is passed in.

We previously touched on the possibility of using generic attributes with Validators for the purpose of storing configuration information. For general-purpose Validators, this is certainly a flexible option. You may also define these configuration items via JavaBean properties and/or constructor arguments on the Validator component itself. Either way, you have the flexibility of defining configurable Validators when necessary.

Let's take a look at a simple, but complete, Validator example. The code in Listing 2.4 is an excerpt from the customerInfo JSP page in the Car Demo sample application provided by the *JSF Reference Implementation*.

```
...
<h:form  formName="CustomerForm" >
    ...
    <h:inputText id="ccno" size="16"
                 converter="#{creditCardConverter}" required="true">
        <cs:formatValidator formatPatterns="9999999999999999|
                                            9999 9999 9999 9999|
                                            9999-9999-9999-9999"/>
    </h:inputText>
    ...
</h:form>
```

Listing 2.4 Assigning Validators to a UI component in a JSP.

You'll notice that a `Validator` is being assigned to an input component that is used to collect a credit card number. This `Validator` ensures the string is formatted properly according to the provided input masks. Let's now take a look at the source code in Listing 2.5.

```
public class FormatValidator implements Validator, StateHolder {

    public static final String FORMAT_INVALID_MESSAGE_ID =
        "carstore.Format_Invalid";

    private ArrayList formatPatternsList = null;

    public FormatValidator() {
        super();
    }

    /**
     * <p>Construct a FormatValidator with the specified formatPatterns
     * String.</p>
     *
     * @param formatPatterns <code>|</code> separated String of format
     *                       patterns that this validator must match
     *                       against.
     */
    public FormatValidator(String formatPatterns) {
        super();
        this.formatPatterns = formatPatterns;
        parseFormatPatterns();
    }

    /**
     * <code>|</code> separated String of format patterns that this
     * validator must match against.
```

Listing 2.5 Format Validator. *(continued)*

```
     */
    private String formatPatterns = null;

    /**
     * <p>Return the format patterns that the validator supports.
     */
    public String getFormatPatterns() {
        return (this.formatPatterns);
    }

    /**
     * <p>Set the format patterns that the validator support.</p>
     *
     * @param formatPatterns <code>|</code> separated String of format
     *                       patterns that this validator must match
     *                       against.
     */
    public void setFormatPatterns(String formatPatterns) {
        this.formatPatterns = formatPatterns;
        parseFormatPatterns();
    }

    /**
     * Parses the <code>formatPatterns</code> into validPatterns
     * <code>ArrayList</code>. The delimiter must be "|".
     */
    public void parseFormatPatterns() {
        ...
    }

    public void validate(FacesContext context, UIInput component,
        Object toValidate) {

        boolean valid = false;
        String value = null;
        if ((context == null) || (component == null)) {
            throw new NullPointerException();
        }
        if (!(component instanceof UIOutput)) {
            return;
        }

        if (null == formatPatternsList || null == toValidate) {
            return;
        }

        value = toValidate.toString();
        // Validate the value against the list of valid patterns.
        Iterator patternIt = formatPatternsList.iterator();
```

Listing 2.5 *(continued)*

```
        while (patternIt.hasNext()) {
            valid = isFormatValid(((String) patternIt.next()), value);
            if (valid) {
                break;
            }
        }
        if (!valid) {
            FacesMessage errMsg = MessageFactory.getMessage(
                context,
                FORMAT_INVALID_MESSAGE_ID,
                (new Object[]{formatPatterns})
            );
            throw new ValidatorException(errMsg);
        }
    }

    /**
     * Returns true if the value matches one of the valid patterns.
     */
    protected boolean isFormatValid(String pattern, String value) {
        ...
    }

    ...
}
```

Listing 2.5 *(continued)*

One of the first things you'll notice here is that a constructor parameter is being used to set the acceptable format patterns. This is an alternative to using generic attributes. More importantly, you'll also notice how the `ValidatorException` is used inside the implemented `validate()` method to flag the target component as invalid. When this exception is thrown, the JSF implementation marks the `UIComponent` invalid. If one or more components are marked as invalid, the JSF implementation will stop request processing after the *Process Validations* phase of the life cycle has been completed, and the page will be displayed with the appropriate error messages (like the invalid format error message in this example). In Chapter 3 we'll take a look at what happens in the *Process Validations* phase of the life cycle when components are flagged as invalid.

Validator Registration

When using any of the standard JSF Validators in a JSP, you simply nest the appropriate Validator tag within the `UIInput` component tag. We saw an example of this being done with the `FormatValidator` in Listing 2.4. Although you may assign Validators in JSPs via the standard JSF tag library, they may also be assigned and managed dynamically at run time via the component tree. Every `UIInput` component has a number of methods for adding and removing Validators, as well as getting a list of all active Validators in the order they are assigned (as shown in Figure 2.5).

You may also create and assign your own `Validator` components. When doing so, you must make sure you register each custom `Validator` in your application's associated JSF configuration file (see Chapter 4 for a discussion of how to do this). You may then either create a JSP tag for your JSP or use the standard `<validator>` tag and specify the `Validator` by its type. When using this generic tag, the input field in Listing 2.4 could be rewritten as follows.

```
<h:inputText id="ccno" size="16" converter="#{creditCardConverter}"
             required="true">
    <f:validator type="cardemo.FormatValidator"/>
    <f:attribute name="formatPatterns"
                 value="9999999999999999|
                        9999 9999 9999 9999|
                        9999-9999-9999-9999"/>
</h:inputText>
```

You'll see that the `Validator` is identified by its unique type (which is provided as part of the registration process in the associated JSF configuration file), and its `formatPatterns` attribute is added to and accessible from the text input UI component. The advantage of creating an associated custom JSP tag is that it provides a more user-friendly notation for page authors, especially when the `Validator` requires the use of one or more attributes. For a more complete discussion of `Validator` components, see Chapter 8, "Validation and Conversion."

Standard Validators

The *JSF Specification* requires every JSF implementation to provide some basic but useful Validators. A summary of each standard `Validator` is provided in Table 2.2.

Table 2.2 Standard JSF Validators

VALIDATOR	JSP TAG	DESCRIPTION
DoubleRangeValidator	validateDoubleRange	Validates that an input field provides a String that may be converted to a double and that it is within the supplied maximum and minimum values.

Table 2.2 *(continued)*

VALIDATOR	JSP TAG	DESCRIPTION
LengthValidator	validateLength	Validates that an input field provides a String (or a value that may be converted to a String) and that its length is within the supplied maximum and minimum values.
LongRangeValidator	validateLongRange	Validates that an input field provides a String that may be converted to a long and that it is within the supplied maximum and minimum values.

The associated JSP tags are available via the core JSF tag library, which is declared as follows in your JSP page.

```
<%@ taglib uri="http://java.sun.com/jsf/core" prefix="f" %>
```

You can expect a number of custom `Validator` components for all sorts of correctness checking from third parties. The JSF framework makes this very easy to do. In Chapter 8 we'll cover the process of creating your own custom Validators, which are similar to the format `Validator` we just examined.

Conversion

Web applications capture user data as request parameters over the HTTP protocol. Each of these parameters is in the form of a String, while the backing data for the application on the server side is in the form of Java objects. An example of these two views of the same data is a date. To a Web client, the date may be shown as a String in any number of formats from numbers (03/05/2003) to natural language (March 5, 2003). It may also have some sort of calendar control that allows users to graphically select a date. On the server side, a date is most likely represented with a `java.util.Date` object.

The challenge for you as a developer is to convert this data back and forth between both representations. This can be mind-numbing, error-prone work, but JSF fortunately provides support for reusable data conversion via Converters.

Converters

Just about every user interface component (`UIOutput` and all descendents to be exact) may have an optional `Converter` associated with it. Each `Converter` must implement the `javax.faces.convert.Converter` interface. A custom `Converter` from the Car Demo sample application is provided in Listing 2.6.

```
public class CreditCardConverter implements Converter {

    public static final String CONVERSION_ERROR_MESSAGE_ID =
     "carstore.Conversion_Error";

    /**
     * Parses the CreditCardNumber and strips any blanks or
     * <code>"-"</code> characters from it.
     */
    public Object getAsObject(FacesContext context,
        UIComponent component, String newValue)
        throws ConverterException {

        String convertedValue = null;
        if ( newValue == null ) {
            return newValue;
        }
        // Since this is only a String to String conversion,
        // this conversion does not throw ConverterException.
        convertedValue = newValue.trim();
        if ( ((convertedValue.indexOf("-")) != -1) ||
            ((convertedValue.indexOf(" ")) != -1)) {
            char[] input = convertedValue.toCharArray();
            StringBuffer buffer = new StringBuffer(50);
            for ( int i = 0; i < input.length; ++i ) {
                if ( input[i] == '-' || input[i] == ' '  ) {
                    continue;
                } else {
                    buffer.append(input[i]);
                }
            }
            convertedValue = buffer.toString();
        }
       // System.out.println("Converted value " + convertedValue);
        return convertedValue;
    }

    /**
     * Formats the value by inserting space after every four
     * characters for better readability if they don't already
     * exist. In the process converts any <code>"-"</code>
     * characters into blanks for consistency.
     */
    public String getAsString(FacesContext context,
        UIComponent component, Object value)
```

Listing 2.6 Credit card custom Converter.

```
        throws ConverterException {

        String inputVal = null;
        if ( value == null ) {
            return null;
        }
        // The value must be of the type that can be cast to a String.
        try {
            inputVal = (String)value;
        } catch (ClassCastException ce) {
            FacesMessage errMsg = MessageFactory.getMessage(
                CONVERSION_ERROR_MESSAGE_ID,
                (new Object[] { value, inputVal }));
            throw new ConverterException(errMsg.getSummary());
        }

        // insert spaces after every four characters for better
        // readability if it doesn't already exist.
        char[] input = inputVal.toCharArray();
        StringBuffer buffer = new StringBuffer(50);
        for ( int i = 0; i < input.length; ++i ) {
            if ( (i % 4) == 0 && i != 0) {
                if (input[i] != ' ' || input[i] != '-'){
                    buffer.append(" ");
                  // If there are any "-"'s convert them to blanks.
                } else if (input[i] == '-') {
                    buffer.append(" ");
                }
            }
            buffer.append(input[i]);
        }
        String convertedValue = buffer.toString();
        // System.out.println("Formatted value " + convertedValue);
        return convertedValue;
    }
}
```

Listing 2.6 *(continued)*

This `Converter` implements the `getAsObject()` and `getAsString()` methods as required by the `Converter` interface. Converters are expected to be symmetric in their processing of data. In other words, a `Converter` should typically implement both the `getAsObject` and `getAsString` methods such that a piece of data will be equivalent when it is converted back and forth via these methods.

Converters are not required to be threadsafe because each instance will only be used in the context of the current request-processing thread. In some cases, a `Converter` may require configuration values to operate correctly. You may use JavaBean properties on the Converter or even generic attributes (via the standard <attribute> tag) to capture these values if they are subject to change with use.

Every user interface component has methods for getting and setting a Converter. These methods are getConverter() and setConverter(), respectively, and they may be used to dynamically assign a Converter at any time. Converters are associated via a String-based *converter identifier*, which we will cover in Chapter 4.

Although you may associate a Converter with a user interface component by invoking its setConverter() method, you will typically set a Converter via an associated JSP tag attribute. If you take another look at Listing 2.4, you'll see the custom credit card Converter being assigned to the credit card number input component via the converter attribute. This attribute is provided as part of the standard JSF HTML tag library. Behind the scenes, the <inputText> tag just invokes the setConverter() method for you with the converter identifier provided.

Converter Registration

When using your own custom Converter components, you must first register them with your application in its associated JSF configuration file. This process is covered in Chapter 4 for the credit card Converter we have been using as an example here. As part of the registration process, you provide a unique identifier for the Converter, and this identifier is what you use to associate a Converter with a UIOutput component via its optional converter attribute.

Standard Converters

The *JSF Specification* requires every JSF implementation to provide a basic set of Converters. A summary of each standard Converter is provided in Table 2.3.

These Converters basically give you a few different ways to convert input fields into dates and numbers with various styles and formats. As with standard Validators, you'll need to declare the core JSF tag library in the JSP page you wish to use the Converters. An example usage of one of these standard Converters in use is provided below.

```
<h:inputText id="total" value="#{invoice.total}">
    <h:convertNumber pattern="#,##.00" type="currency"/>
</h:inputText>
```

This input field represents the total amount of an invoice, and the associated Converter will transfer the String entered by users into a Number that represents money.

Table 2.3 Standard JSF Converters

CONVERTER	DESCRIPTION
DateTime	Converts a String or Number to a Date with attributes for controlling the pattern, style, time zone considerations, and type.
Number	Converts a String or Number to a Number with attributes for controlling the number type (currency, percent, integer), pattern, an so on.

As with Validators, you can expect a number of custom Converter components for all sorts of `String` and `Number` conversions (among others) from third parties. The JSF framework makes this very easy to do. In Chapter 8 we'll cover the process of creating your own custom Converters, which are similar to the credit card `Converter` we just examined.

Events and Listeners

Events provide an important mechanism for user interface components to propagate user actions to other components (including server-side components). These components register as listeners to events they are interested in (the pressing of a button or perhaps a change to the value in a text input field). Events were introduced in Chapter 1 in terms of the Observer Pattern, so the concept of events should be very familiar to you. We also discovered that JSF takes an approach to events and event handling that is similar to Swing's. Both of them are based on the *JavaBean Specification* event model. We'll review JSF events here in a bit more detail.

UI Events

Each user interface component may emit any number of events and have any number of listeners registered to have these events broadcast to them. These listeners may be other user interface components or application components. Each supported event must extend the `javax.faces.event.FacesEvent` base class.

The constructor of each event accepts a reference to the user interface component that is responsible for propagating it, while the `getComponent()` method provides access to the originating component. Events may also have useful information (usually involving component state) that they wish to communicate to registered listeners. For this reason, an Event may provide any number of properties and constructors to initialize them. The JavaBean specification recommends that the name of each event class end with the word *Event*.

The JSF specification defines two standard user interface component events. The `javax.faces.event.ActionEvent` is broadcast from the standard `UICommand` component (typically rendered as a push button, a menu item, or a hyperlink) when activated by a user, whereas the `javax.faces.event.ValueChangeEvent` is broadcast from the standard `UIInput` component or subclasses when its value has changed and passed validation.

Listeners

Each event type has a corresponding listener interface that must extend the `javax.faces.event.FacesListener` interface. Application components or other user interface components may implement any number of listener interfaces, as long as they provide the appropriate event handler method for each one. Listener implementations have access to the corresponding event via a parameter that is passed in to the event handler method. The JavaBean specification recommends that each listener interface name be based on the event class it is associated with and end with *Listener*.

The JSF specification defines two standard listener interfaces corresponding to the two standard event types. Listeners of the `ActionEvent` must implement `javax.faces.event.ActionListener` and receive notification via invocation of the `processAction()` method, whereas listeners of the `ValueChangeEvent` must implement `javax.faces.event.ValueChangeListener` and receive notification via invocation of the `processValueChange()` method they are required to implement.

An example of a listener is provided in Listing 2.7 from the Car Demo sample. This particular listener implementation responds to the change of a text input field for a customer first name by placing its new value in session scope.

```
public class FirstNameChanged implements ValueChangeListener {

    public void processValueChange(ValueChangeEvent event)
        throws AbortProcessingException {

        if (null != event.getNewValue()) {
            FacesContext.getCurrentInstance().getExternalContext().
                getSessionMap().put("firstName", event.getNewValue());
        }
    }

    public PhaseId getPhaseId() {
        return PhaseId.ANY_PHASE;
    }
}
```

Listing 2.7 Custom event listener.

Now that we've covered what is required of event listeners, you may be wondering how we register them to receive event notifications. The JavaBean specification requires a component that emits a particular event to define a pair of methods for registering and unregistering listeners. We'll use the standard `ActionListener` as an example of what these methods should look like:

```
public void addActionListener(ActionListener listener);
public void removeActionListener(ActionListener listener);
```

Any component that wishes to register for a certain event must simply call the appropriate `add()` method at any time on the user interface component it wishes to observe. Likewise, if a component no longer wishes to receive event notifications, it must simply call the appropriate `remove()` method on the component it is observing. However, you will typically register listeners in JSPs, as shown for in the `customerInfo` JSP of the Car Demo example in Listing 2.8.

```
<h:outputText value="#{bundle.firstLabel}" />
<h:inputText  id="firstName" value="#{customer.firstName}"
              required="true">
    <f:valueChangeListener type="carstore.FirstNameChanged" />
</h:inputText>
<h:message styleClass="validationMessage" for="firstName"/>
```

Listing 2.8 Custom event listener assigned in JSP.

This registration is done via the standard JSF HTML tag library with the `<valueChangeListener>` tag. The appropriate listener class is associated via the `type` attribute (including the appropriate package structure). Behind the scenes, the `<valueChangeListener>` tag calls the `addValueChangeListener()` method for you on the associated `UIInput` component.

Phase Identifiers

All listener implementations must implement the `getPhaseId()` method from the `FacesEvent` interface to specify at which stage of the request-processing life cycle they wish to receive event notifications. This method returns an instance of `javax.faces.event.PhaseId`, which is an enumerated type that defines each stage at the end of which events may be broadcast to registered listeners. An additional type of `PhaseId.ANY_PHASE` is provided for those listeners who wish to be notified every time a particular event is broadcast. The event listener in Listing 2.7 implements this method.

We'll cover the request-processing life cycle in greater detail in Chapter 3, including the overall process for handling events.

Event Queuing and Broadcasting

During the request-processing life cycle, events may be created in response to user actions, and all of them are queued in the `FacesContext` in the order in which they are received. At the end of each phase where events may be handled, any events in the queue are broadcast to registered listeners that define the appropriate `PhaseId`. As we discussed earlier, this action results in the appropriate event-processing method being invoked on each registered listener.

Rendering

One of the most important aspects of user interfaces is how they look and feel to users. JSF provides a flexible mechanism for rendering responses in Web applications, and it comes in two forms: direct rendering within a user interface component and delegated rendering via RenderKits that occur outside of a user interface component. Figure 2.6 provides a graphical summary of this choice. As with Validators, the method you choose is dependent upon how specific a rendering is to a particular user interface component.

With direct rendering, a user interface component must encode and decode itself by overriding one or more of the rendering methods defined by `UIComponentBase`.

The `decode()` method is invoked on a component after a request is received and is expected to convert request parameters into a user interface component with its current state. This conversion process is aided by a `Converter` if one has been assigned to the component. The set of encode methods, `encodeBegin()`, `encodeChildren()`, and `encodeEnd()`, are invoked when the JSF implementation is preparing a response to a client request. If the component you are rendering has no children, then you only need to implement the `encodeEnd()` method. As with the `decode()` method, a `Converter` may be used if assigned. When performing direct rendering, you must also override the `setRendererType()` method to return `null`.

Direct rendering coupled with the direct validation we discussed earlier allows component authors to build self-contained custom components in single classes. If used correctly, this option can be compact and efficient. On the other hand, it does limit reuse of common rendering and validation among multiple components, which could have a negative impact on maintainability.

Delegated Rendering

Delegating user interface component encoding and decoding to external components allows you to quickly change the look and feel of components and to render appropriate responses to different client types. In essence, the rendering of a user interface component is separated out and becomes pluggable with other possible rendering.

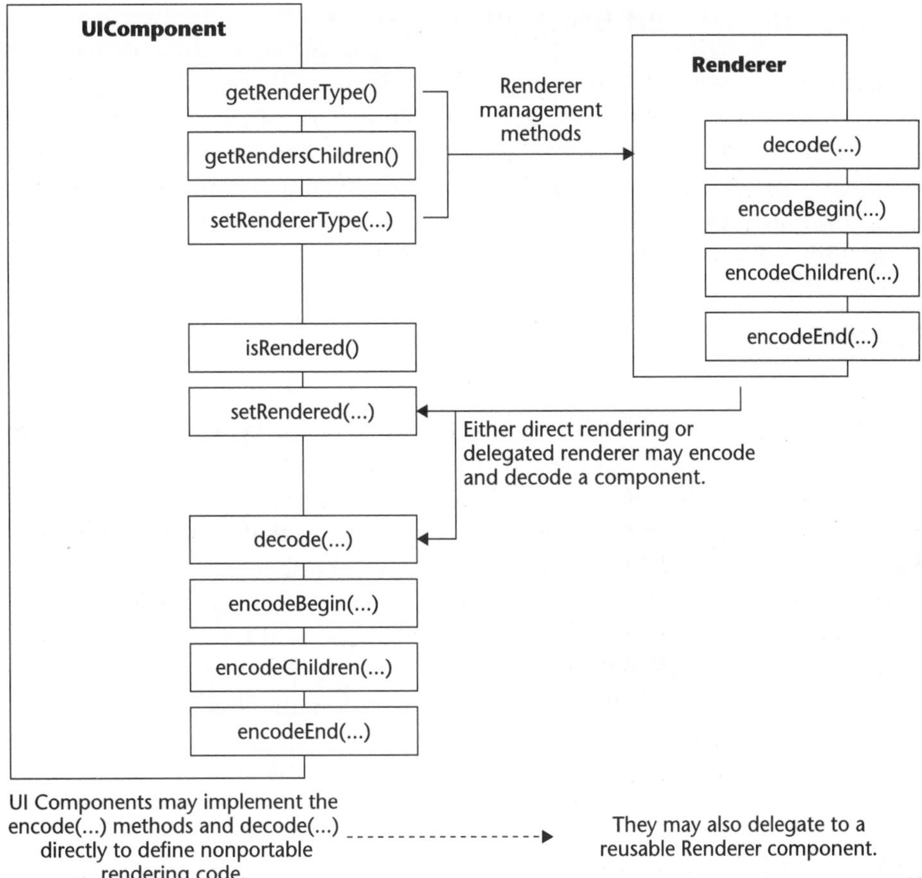

Figure 2.6 Direct rendering versus delegated rendering.

A `Renderer` is a subclass of the abstract class `javax.faces.render.Renderer` and provides the same encode and decode methods that exist on a user interface component for direct rendering. We provided an example of a custom `Renderer` in Listing 2.3. We only showed the `encodeEnd()` method, but if you look at the complete example provided with the *JSF Reference Implementation*, you'll see the other methods as well.

You are probably wondering at this point how to associate a `Renderer` with a UI component. This is done by implementing the `getRendererType()` method and returning the appropriate render type (see the "Registering Renderers" section for more information on render types). At run time, your chosen JSF implementation will call this method when encoding and decoding the UI component to determine which `Renderer`, if any, should be used. This property would return a value of `null` if you choose direct over delegated rendering. When using standard JSF UI components, you don't have to worry about setting a render type, because each of these components already defaults to one in the standard HTML `RenderKit`. You only need to worry about setting a render type when you are creating a new component or customizing the look of an existing one. A good example of handling component rendering for a custom UI component is provided in Chapter 10.

Each Renderer may also recognize certain generic attributes that are used to properly encode and decode an associated user interface component. You'll recall our earlier example in this chapter of a tabbed pane that uses the selected attribute to determine which tab is selected. This tab is then rendered with a different appearance than the others.

Render Kits

A RenderKit is a subclass of the abstract class javax.faces.render .RenderKit;it represents a collection of Renderers that typically specialize in rendering user interface components in an application based on some combination of client device type, markup language, and/or user locale. Render kits are conceptually similar to Swing looks and feels in that they are pluggable and often render user interfaces based on a common theme.

At some point you may wish to customize the Renderers of an existing RenderKit or even create your own RenderKit. You will typically create Renderers for your custom components and register them with existing RenderKits. We'll take a look at that registration process next, and we'll explore custom user interface component rendering in much greater detail in Chapter 10.

Registering Renderers

Before using the tabbed Renderer we have seen more than once so far in this chapter, it must be registered in the associated application's JSF configuration file.

```
<render-kit>
  ...
  <renderer>
    <renderer-type>Tabbed</renderer-type>
    <renderer-class>components.renderkit.TabbedRenderer</renderer-class>
  </renderer>
  ...
</render-kit>
```

The configuration information here registers the Renderer with the default HTML RenderKit (which is the default behavior of not specifying a particular RenderKit). As we discussed earlier in this chapter, your JSF implementation will check each UI component's getRendererType() method to see if it should delegate rendering to a Renderer; otherwise, it will expect the UI component to render itself.

Standard RenderKits

The JSF specification defines a standard `RenderKit` and set of associated Renderers for generating HTML-compatible markup. Each JSF implementation is required to support this `RenderKit`. A summary of the available Renderers is provided in Table 2.4.

Table 2.4 Standard JSF HTML Renderers

RENDERER / TAGS	UICOMPONENTS	DESCRIPTION
Button / <commandButton>	UICommand	Represents your typical command button.
Web Link / <commandHyperlink>	UICommand	Represents a Web link.
Table / <dataTable>	UIData	Represents a table.
Form / <form>	UIForm	Represents a form.
Image / <graphicImage>	UIGraphic	Represents an icon or image.
Hidden / <inputHidden>	UIInput	Represents an invisible field that is useful for a page author.
Secret / <inputSecret>	UIInput	Represents a password input field or one in which the characters are masked.
Input Text / <inputText>	UIInput	Represents plain text in an input field.
TextArea / <inputTextArea>	UIInput	Represents a multiline text input or memo field.
Label / <outputLabel>	UIOutput	Represents a label for an input field.
Output Link / <outputLink>	UIOutput	Displays a localized message.
Output Text / <outputText>	UIOutput	Represents an immutable text field.
Grid / <panelGrid>	UIPanel	Represents a table of UIComponents.
Group / <panelGroup>	UIPanel	Represents a group of related components.
Checkbox / <selectBooleanCheckbox>	UISelectBoolean	Represents a check box.

(continued)

Table 2.4 *(continued)*

RENDERER / TAGS	UICOMPONENTS	DESCRIPTION
Checkbox List / <selectManyCheckbox>	UISeletMany	Represents a list of check boxes.
Listbox / <selectManyListbox> <selectOneListbox>	UISelectMany / UISelectOne	Represents a list of items from which one or more may be selected.
Menu / <selectManyMenu> <selectOneMenu>	UISelectMany / UISelectOne	Represents a menu.
Radio / <selectOneRadio>	UISelectOne	Represents a set of radio buttons from which one choice may be made.

The determination of which `Renderer` you use will be automatically handled based on the tag you use in your JSPs. You have already seen some of these tags in action in our examples, and you'll see more of them throughout the rest of the book. You will no doubt also see more Renderers (and associated tags) from third-party vendors and likely the vendor of your particular JSF implementation.

Summary

Now that we've covered the most important elements of JSF and how many of them work together in JSF applications, it's time to pull everything together with a discussion of the JSF request-processing life cycle. We'll do this in Chapter 3, before rolling up our sleeves and digging into more details.

CHAPTER

3

JSF Request-Processing Life Cycle

In Chapters 1 and 2, we covered the architecture and design behind JSF in contrast to other similar frameworks. We also introduced the elements of JSF along with some simple examples of what they look like in action. Here, we'll discover how these elements fit together in the JSF request-processing life cycle. This life cycle is what each JSF application is required to go through when taking a request and then generating an appropriate response back to the client. We'll deal with how the component tree is constructed and used, how events are processed, how conversions and validations are executed, how the response is generated from rendered components, and much more.

Specifically, we'll cover request-processing scenarios, each step of the request-processing life cycle, and some important elements of the `FacesContext`. This chapter will tie together many of the elements we discussed in the previous chapter and prepare you for more in-depth and advanced topics in the following chapters.

Overview

We first got a glimpse of the JSF request-processing life cycle in Chapter 1, "JSF Patterns and Architecture." The life cycle actually defines the process by which the `FacesServlet`, JSF's version of the Controller in MVC, digests a client request (usually from a Web browser) and returns an appropriate response. A concise view of this life cycle is provided in Figure 3.1.

You may already be familiar with the standard servlet life cycle (which also applies to JSPs) as defined by the *Servlet Specification*. This life cycle defines how servlet containers such as Tomcat process a request that involves servlets. The JSF life cycle builds on this life cycle by adding steps of its own to process JSF UI components. Each step is shown in Figure 3.1 and will be covered in detail later in this chapter.

The steps executed in this life cycle are determined largely by whether or not a request originates from a JSF application and whether or not the response is generated via the *Render Response* phase of the life cycle. We'll discuss four scenarios here: Faces request generates Faces response non-Faces request generates Faces response, Faces request generates non-Faces response, and non-Faces request generates non-Faces response. Once we discuss each scenario, we'll begin our detailed coverage of each phase.

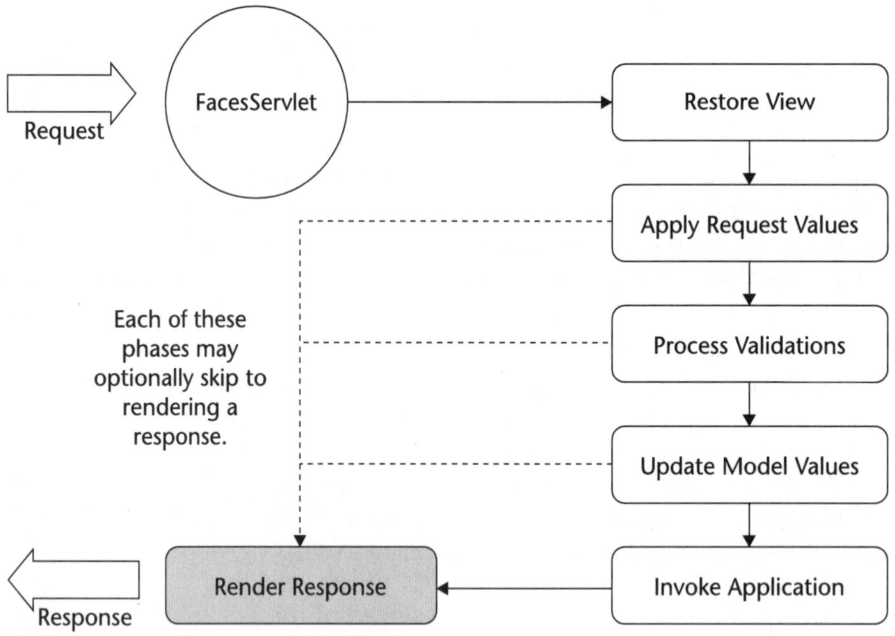

Figure 3.1 JSF request-processing life cycle.

SOME LIFE-CYCLE TERMINOLOGY FROM THE JSF SPECIFICATION

You'll see terms in our discussion of life cycles that may be unfamiliar. Some of these terms are defined below.

Faces Response. **A servlet response that was created by the execution of the Render Response phase of the request-processing life cycle.**

Non-Faces Response. **A servlet response that was not created by the execution of the Render Response phase of the request-processing life cycle. Examples would be a servlet-generated or JSP-rendered response that does not incorporate JSF components, or a response that sets an HTTP status code other than the usual 200 (such as a redirect).**

Faces Request. **A servlet request that was sent from a previously generated Faces Response. Examples would be a hyperlink or form submit from a rendered user interface component, where the request URI was crafted (by the component or Renderer that created it) to identify the component tree to use for processing the request.**

Non-Faces Request. **A servlet request that was sent to an application component (for example, a servlet or JSP page), rather than directed to a Faces component tree.**

Faces Request Generates Faces Response

This is the most common scenario and makes use of most, and often all, steps in the life cycle. Our discussion of the life-cycle phases later in this chapter will be based on this scenario.

Non-Faces Request Generates Faces Response

The most common case of this scenario is when a user clicks on a hyperlink from one JSP that contains no JSF UI components that forwards to another page that actually contains JSF UI components. Linking from one set of pages or application to another is very common on the Web, and it will occur whenever a user enters your JSF application (they have to come from somewhere on the Web to reach your application). An overview of this life cycle is provided in Figure 3.2.

In a nutshell, the `FacesServlet` will a create a component tree from the JSP the hyperlink is forwarding to by going through the *Restore View* phase of the standard life cycle and will then skip to the *Render Response* phase by asking the tree to render itself. Additional requests submitted from this response (a user clicks on a JSF URL, button, and so forth), except for the next scenario we will discuss, will then likely include other phases of the life cycle to process changes to the UI components.

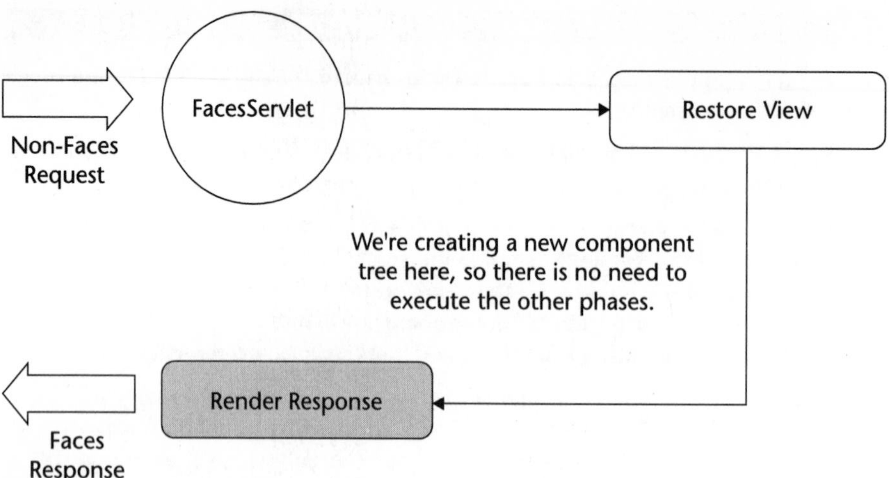

Figure 3.2 Life cycle for generating a Faces response from a non-Faces request.

Faces Request Generates Non-Faces Response

There will be occasions where allowing the response to be generated by the *Render Response* phase of the standard life cycle is not desirable. The most common scenario is when you wish to simply redirect the request to a different Web application. Another scenario would involve generating a response that does not make use of JSF UI components. This would include responding with a binary stream (graphics or sound) or perhaps an XML file that is not intended for human consumption (perhaps only for communicating with an external application). Figure 3.3 provides an overview of this particular life cycle.

Once the non-Faces response is submitted, control is transferred to the other Web application and the JSF client session effectively ends.

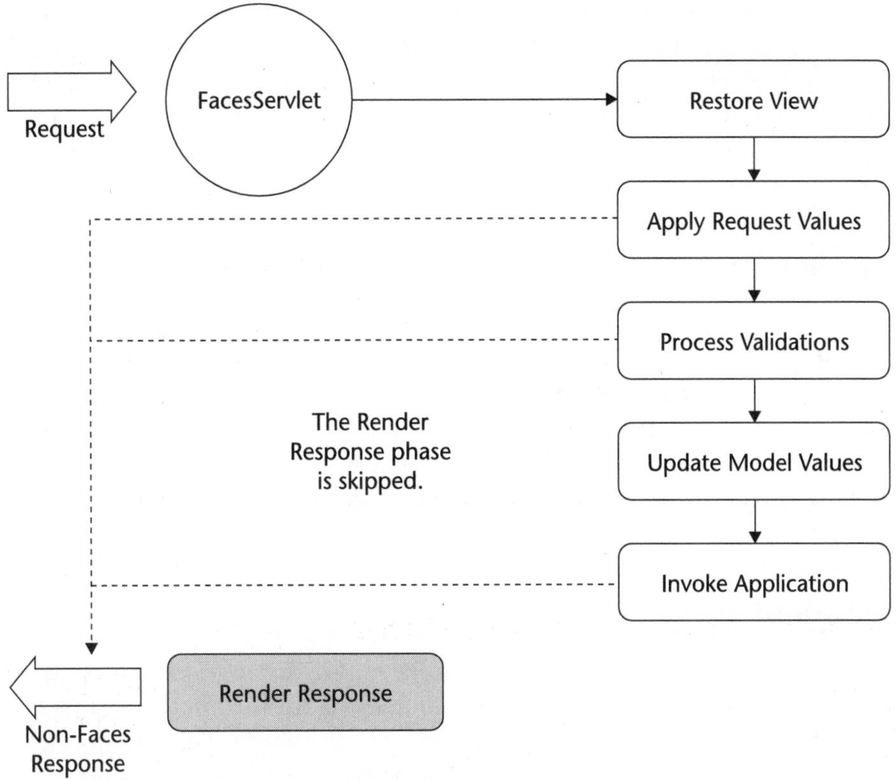

Figure 3.3 Life cycle for generating a non-Faces response from a Faces request.

Non-Faces Request Generates Non-Faces Response

Generating non-Faces responses to non-Faces requests is certainly another possibility, but it has absolutely nothing to do with JSF applications. These requests will be handled and responded to by non-Faces servlets and will not follow the standard JSF request-processing life cycle. Therefore, we don't need to examine this particular life cycle any further.

Faces Context

Before discussing each phase of the life cycle, we need to cover some elements of the `FacesContext`, which plays an important role in the overall life cycle. Each JSF application must store information about the request it is processing. The `FacesContext` holds all contextual information necessary for processing a request and generating a response. More specifically, it manages a queue for messages, the current component tree, application configuration objects, and the life-cycle flow control methods. It also provides generic access to the external context in which the JSF application is running (which in most cases will be the servlet container environment or context). You'll see the `FacesContext` mentioned often in our discussion of the life-cycle phases, so let's examine it before moving on.

Accessing Context

Whether it is the `validate()` method of a `Validator`, the `decode()` method of a `Renderer`, or any number of other extension points in the framework, the `FacesContext` is available where you need it. You can also get the `FacesContext` instance for the current request by calling the static `getCurrentInstance()` method on the `FacesContext` class itself.

Now that we know how to get the current instance of `FacesContext`, let's take a look at what information it manages.

Component Tree

Each JSF implementation is required to store a new or reconstituted component tree in the `FacesContext`. This requirement is fulfilled in the first phase of the request-processing life cycle—the *Restore View* phase. This requirement gives you access to all of the user interface components from the request.

You'll often do much of your work inside an event handler in one of the various supporting components (such as Validators, Converters, and so on). In any case, you have access to the component tree simply by invoking the `getViewRoot()` method on the `FacesContext` at any point in the life cycle.

There are also times where you may wish to replace an entire component tree with another one before the request is generated. This will typically occur within the *Invoke Application* phase, although you may do so in the other phases as well. As we saw in our discussion of the MVC Pattern in Chapter 1, and as you'll see again in Chapter 4, "JSF Configuration," navigating from one tree to another (or one JSP page to another) will typically be defined in your application's JSF configuration file via navigation rules. However, you may do so manually at any time by executing code similar to the following:

```
String treeId = "/login.jsp";
// If you don't already have a handle to the FacesContext...
context = FacesContext.getCurrentInstance();
context.getApplication().getViewHandler().createView(context, treeId);
```

You manually change the current component tree by first getting the current instance of the FacesContext if you don't already have it and then passing it in with the identifier of a component tree (in this case the name and location of a JSP) to the createView method of the current ViewHandler instance. Creating the new view results in its UIViewRoot component (the root of the component tree) being set as the current component tree in the FacesContext. However, before doing this, you should make sure that you have any information you need from the previous tree, because it may no longer be available. Although you can certainly create a component tree programmatically from scratch, you will almost always let the JSF implementation construct the tree from a JSP that uses JSF user interface components. You will see more on the JSP-JSF integration in Chapter 5, "JSP Integration in JSF."

We'll revisit component trees later in this chapter in the discussion of some of the life-cycle phases. For now, just remember three things: the FacesContext stores a reference to the component tree that will be rendered for the request; you have access to the component tree throughout the request-processing life cycle via the FacesContext; and you can modify or replace the current component tree in its entirety throughout the life cycle.

External Context

You will sometimes wish to interact with the external environment in which your JSF implementation runs. This environment is usually a servlet context (for Web applications), but it may also be a Portlet or other container. The FacesContext provides generic access to the external environment via the getExternalContext() method. It returns an ExternalContext object that provides access to the external environment via a standard interface.

You've already seen an example of how this object is used in the previous chapter when we looked at event handling. The FirstNameChanged listener in the Car Demo sample application invokes one of the ExternalContext methods to place the customer's first name in session scope of the Web application. The call is repeated here.

```
FacesContext.getCurrentInstance().getExternalContext().
    getSessionMap().put("firstName", event.getNewValue());
```

There are a variety of other methods that give you access to objects in the external context. These objects include request and response objects as well as cookies. We'll take another look at this example later in this chapter. The thing to remember here is that the FacesContext gives you convenient access to these objects when you need them.

Flow Control

The FacesContext contains methods that allow you to alter the sequential execution of life-cycle phases. You would normally access these methods in event listeners, Validators, and user interface components for the purpose of skipping to the *Render Response* phase or to stop the life cycle for the current request.

When invoked, the renderResponse() method skips to the *Render Response* phase of the life cycle once the current phase is completed and events are processed. For example, an event handler for a tree control may wish to expand a node, when it is selected, to show its children. In this case, you would want to render a response immediately to show the change in the tree's state. After taking care of the tree expansion in the event handler, you would call the renderResponse() method so that all other life-cycle phases are skipped and the current page is redisplayed with the altered tree structure.

When invoked, the responseComplete() method terminates the life cycle for the current request after the current phase is completed. You'll typically use this method inside event handlers and user interface components to send a redirect or to manually handle a response. If you remember the discussion earlier in this chapter, the response object is available via the External Context object in the FacesContext.

If both the renderResponse() and responseComplete() methods have been invoked, the responseComplete() method is honored. The getRenderResponse() and getResponseComplete() methods, which return Boolean values, allow you to check whether or not the other two have been called.

Localization

If you wish to programmatically determine what locale is set for the client in the current request, the FacesContext gives you easy access to it. The default locale (taken ultimately from the HTTP request header in Web applications) is set by the JSF implementation when the FacesContext for the current request is created. You may simply invoke the getViewRoot().getLocale() method at any point in the request-processing life cycle to retrieve the currently set locale. You may also change the locale at any point in the life cycle by invoking the getViewRoot().setLocale() method.

JSF makes use of Java's built-in localization support. Of particular interest are the Locale and ResourceBundle classes in the java.util package. When you invoke either the getLocale() or setLocale() method on the UIViewRoot reference in the FacesContext, you are working with objects of type Locale. In applications that support multiple languages, just about every static piece of information you display to users (such as the label of an input field) is associated with a key value and stored externally in property files. You use resource bundles to retrieve information based on key values.

The standard JSF HTML `RenderKit` tag library provides some useful tags for accessing internationalized information. A simple example is provided in Listing 3.1.

```
<%@ taglib uri="http://java.sun.com/jsf/html" prefix="h" %>
<%@ taglib uri="http://java.sun.com/jsf/core" prefix="f" %>

<html>
<head>
    <title>Welcome to CarStore</title>
    <link rel="stylesheet" type="text/css"
          href='<%= request.getContextPath() + "/stylesheet.css" %>'>
</head>
<body bgcolor="white">

<f:loadBundle baseName="carstore.bundles.Resources" var="bundle"/>
<f:view>
    <h:form>
        <h:graphicImage  url="/images/cardemo.jpg" />

        <h:panelGrid id="thanksPanel" columns="1"
                     footerClass="subtitle" headerClass="subtitlebig"
                     styleClass="medium"
                     columnClasses="subtitle,medium">
            <f:facet name="header">
                <h:outputMessage  value="#{bundle.thanksLabel}">
                    <f:parameter value="#{sessionScope.firstName}"/>
                </h:outputMessage>
            </f:facet>
        </h:panelGrid>
    </h:form>
    <jsp:include page="bottomMatter.jsp"/>
</f:view>

</body>
</html>
```

Listing 3.1 Localization in JSPs.

This excerpt is the `finish` JSP in its entirety from the Car Demo sample application provided by the *JSF Reference Implementation*. As shown in the next code sample, the `<loadBundle>` tag loads the desired resource bundle by identifying a property file.

```
<f:loadBundle baseName="carstore.bundles.Resources" var="bundle"/>
```

In this case, it identifies the `Resources.properties` file. You must be sure to provide the fully qualified name of the file, which in this case resides in the `carstore.bundles` package. A short excerpt of this file is provided here.

```
thanksLabel=Thanks, {0}, for using CarStore! Your car will ship soon.
```

You'll notice that the information on the right is associated with a key on the left. Specifying the `thanksLabel` key will return the text on the right. If you look at our example JSP again, this is exactly what the `<outputMessage>` tag does. This tag is responsible for displaying a message, and in this particular case, it does so by getting text from the loaded resource bundle. This particular example also makes use of a parameter, which represents the first name of the customer. Here is the relevant snippet of code from our example.

```
<h:outputMessage  value="#{bundle.thanksLabel}">
    <f:parameter value="#{sessionScope.firstName}"/>
</h:outputMessage>
```

For additional languages, you'll notice that the Car Demo application has other properties files with the same base name of `Resources` with locale abbreviations appended. A corresponding excerpt of one of these files is provided below.

```
thanksLabel=Gracias, {0}, para usar CarStore! Tu carro enviado pronto.
```

You'll notice that the `thanksLabel` key (as well as others) is repeated with information in Spanish. Each time you set up a resource bundle, the JSF implementation will pick up the correct file based on the user's locale in the `FacesContext`. For English speakers, the default file will be used; for Spanish speakers, the JSF implementation will use the same base name of `Resources` with the characters `es` appended to it. If a specific locale is not supported, the default (in this case, `Resources.properties`) will be used. You can add as many translations as you wish without having to recompile code (just remember to put them all in the same package), and that is one of the beauties of supporting localization.

If you are still a little fuzzy about the ins and outs of localization, don't worry. We'll touch on it later throughout Chapters 5 to 11. For now, just remember that JSF supports internationalization, and that you have access to the current locale via the `FacesContext`.

Message Queue

During the request-processing life cycle, errors may occur for any number of reasons (such as a component failing validation). The `FacesContext` stores a queue of messages that may be associated either with a `UIComponent` or with the component tree itself (an entire JSP page). You can use the `getMessages()` method on the `FacesContext` to retrieve a collection of all messages or by `UIComponent`.

You will usually add messages to the queue when validating and converting user interface components. An example of a `Validator` queuing a message is provided in Listing 3.2.

```
public void validate(FacesContext context, UIInput component,
    Object toValidate) {

    boolean valid = false;
    String value = null;
    if ((context == null) || (component == null)) {
        throw new NullPointerException();
    }
    if (!(component instanceof UIOutput)) {
        return;
    }

    if (null == formatPatternsList || null == toValidate) {
        return;
    }

    value = toValidate.toString();
    // Validate the value against the list of valid patterns.
    Iterator patternIt = formatPatternsList.iterator();
    while (patternIt.hasNext()) {
        valid = isFormatValid(((String) patternIt.next()), value);
        if (valid) {
            break;
        }
    }
    if (!valid) {
        FacesMessage errMsg = MessageFactory.getMessage(
            context,
            FORMAT_INVALID_MESSAGE_ID,
            (new Object[]{formatPatterns})
        );
        throw new ValidatorException(errMsg);
    }
}
```

Listing 3.2 A Validator queues an error message.

You probably remember this example from our discussion of Validators in the previous chapter. The excerpt in Listing 3.2 comes from the `FormatValidator` class in the *JSF Reference Implementation* Car Demo example. A good portion of the `validate()` method source code is busy determining whether or not the credit card number entered by a customer is valid. The following source code is executed when the number is invalid.

```
FacesMessage errMsg = MessageFactory().getMessage(
     context,
     FORMAT_INVALID_MESSAGE_ID,
     (new Object[] {formatPatterns})
);
throw new ValidatorException(errMsg);
```

The basic process for assigning the resulting error message is taken care of when you create a `FacesMessage` object and use it to initialize the `ValidatorException`. The JSF implementation later adds the error message to the message queue after capturing the exception. Don't worry about how this particular error message is created, because Chapter 8, "Validation and Conversion," covers internationalization of messages. In this particular example, the validation code is executed in the *Process Validations* phase of the request-processing life cycle. At the end of this phase, the JSF implementation will skip to the *Render Response* phase if any messages are in the queue (as in this case).

When rendering a response, you have access to queued messages so that you can display useful information to the client along with instructions for correcting any problems. An example of how this is done inside a JSP is provided in Listing 3.3.

```
<h:outputText value="#{bundle.ccNumberLabel}" />
<h:inputText id="ccno" size="16" converter="#{creditCardConverter}"
             required="true">
    <cs:formatValidator formatPatterns="9999999999999999|
                                        9999 9999 9999 9999|
                                        9999-9999-9999-9999"/>
</h:inputText>
<h:message styleClass="validationMessage" for="ccno"/>
```

Listing 3.3 Displaying an error message.

The excerpt in Listing 3.3 comes from the `customerInfo` JSP in the Car Demo sample. The source code specifies an input field where customers enter a credit card number. The `FormatValidator` we just explored is attached to this field. You'll also notice a `<message>` tag that appears after the input field. It's repeated in the following.

```
<h:message styleClass="validationMessage" for="ccno"/>
```

What this tag does is display all queued messages associated with the input field component; so if an invalid credit card number is entered, this tag will display the resulting error message right after the input field. It is associated via the input field's identifier.

For now, don't concentrate too much on how these tags work, because this example is only intended to show how the message queue in the FacesContext is used. We'll explore the <message> tag in more detail later in Chapter 8.

Event Queues

Event handling is an important part of the request-processing life cycle, so before moving onto a discussion of each phase in the life cycle, let's examine the event queue and how it is handled with the help of an example.

As we discussed in Chapters 1 and 2, there are two basic types of events in JSF: value change events (ValueChangeEvent) and action events (ActionEvent). You'll remember that value change events are typically emitted from a UIInput component to notify others of a change in its value, while action events are typically emitted from a UICommand component to notify others of a button click (perhaps for a form submission) or link selection. All events, whether they are fired as the result of a user action or during the request-processing life cycle in response to a user action, are queued in either their respective UIComponent or the UIViewRoot for the current request.

In most cases, you will not need to manually add events to the queue during the request-processing life cycle. This is because most JSF user interface components fire one or more FacesEvents by default. You must simply register listeners to the events you are interested in. We touched on the process for registering listeners in the last chapter, but we'll cover events in much greater detail in Chapter 7, "Navigation, Actions, and Listeners."

You cannot access the event queue directly, but you can add an event of type FacesEvent to the queue by invoking the queueEvent() method on a particular UIComponent or the UIViewRoot. Events may be added up to and including the *Invoke Application* phase of the request-processing life cycle and will be processed at the end of each phase from the *Apply Request Values* phase to the *Invoke Application* phase. We'll discuss this in a bit more detail shortly.

For now, let's look at a typical example of how an event is treated. Let's start by looking at some commands in a JSP, an excerpt of which is provided below.

```
<h:outputText value="#{bundle.firstLabel}" />
    <h:inputText id="firstName" value="#{customer.firstName}"
                required="true">
        <f:valueChangeListener type="carstore.FirstNameChanged" />
    </h:inputText>
<h:message styleClass="validationMessage" for="firstName"/>
```

This excerpt comes from the `customerInfo` JSP in the Car Demo sample application. What is displayed here is a text input field where the customer provides a first name. The `FirstNameChanged` class is registered as a listener to changes in the text input field's value. We covered this particular example in the previous chapter when discussing events. If the customer changes his or her first name on the input form, the registered listener will be notified. As part of the request-processing life cycle, the JSF implementation will queue this event during the *Apply Request Values* phase of the life cycle. At the end of the phase, the event will be dispatched to the `FirstNameChanged` class because it was registered as a listener.

You'll remember from our earlier introduction to events that each listener is required to implement the appropriate listener interface for the type of event it is designed to observe. Let's take another quick look at the `FirstNameChanged` class in Listing 3.4.

```
public class FirstNameChanged implements ValueChangeListener {

    public void processValueChange(ValueChangeEvent event)
        throws AbortProcessingException {

        if (null != event.getNewValue()) {
            FacesContext.getCurrentInstance().getExternalContext().
                getSessionMap().put("firstName", event.getNewValue());
        }
    }

    public PhaseId getPhaseId() {
        return PhaseId.ANY_PHASE;
    }
}
```

Listing 3.4 Handling the name change request.

The first thing you'll notice is that the `ValueChangeListener` interface is implemented. As such, it is required to implement the `getPhaseId()` and `processValueChange()` methods. Before allowing the listener to process the name change event, the JSF implementation will call the `getPhaseId()` method. This method specifies that it will process that event during any appropriate phase of the request-processing life cycle.

Once the JSF implementation reaches the end of the *Apply Request Values* phase, it will invoke the `processValueChange()` method on the listener. What our listener then does is get the new first name and place it in session scope to be used by JSP pages that may find it inconvenient to use the corresponding `CustomerBean` property.

Let's take a look at what would happen if the getPhaseId() method returned a different value.

```
public PhaseId getPhaseId() {
    return PhaseId.PROCESS_VALIDATIONS;
}
```

In this case, the FirstNameChanged handler would not be notified until after the *Process Validations* phase was completed. The phase ID allows you to control when your handler is notified of events.

Now that we've looked at how events are handled, let's take a closer look at what goes on behind the scenes when processing events in the queue throughout the request-processing life cycle.

During several of the life-cycle phases, previously queued events must be broadcast to registered listeners. The JSF implementation initiates the process after each respective phase has been completed. For each queued event, it first checks the getPhaseId() method to determine whether or not the event should be processed during the current phase (similar to the listener shown in the previous example). It then calls the getComponent() method to get a reference to the owning UIComponent. The broadcast() method on the component is then invoked with a reference to the event.

The broadcast() method, in turn, notifies each registered listener that can accept the event (by checking the getPhaseId() method) in the current phase. It then returns a boolean value that communicates to the JSF implementation whether or not the event has been completely handled (all registered listeners have been notified). If the event has been completely handled, the event is removed from the queue.

It is possible for event handlers of the listeners to queue other events. Every JSF implementation is required to support the dynamic addition of new events throughout the life cycle. Each event will be processed at the end of the current or next phase that handles events in the order they were received unless the phase ID restricts when the event may be broadcast.

We'll cover events in more detail in Chapter 7. For now, just remember that events are queued in the component tree and that the JSF implementation manages this queue while notifying registered listeners. You should also remember that this queue is available to you throughout the life cycle for adding events programmatically as necessary.

Standard JSF Request-Processing Life Cycle

Now that we have covered some important pieces of FacesContext and how the event queue is managed, let's finally take a look at each phase of the request-processing life cycle. We'll cover each step in order based on Figure 3.1.

Restore View

After receiving a client request, the JSF implementation will attempt to restore the component tree. This is done in the *Restore View* phase of the life cycle, which is shown graphically in Figure 3.4.

The JSF implementation first checks an init parameter in the external context to determine whether state was previously saved in the request or on the server (usually in session scope). If tree state exists and the corresponding identifier matches the request URI, the component tree will be restored from its previously saved state.

If the identifier does not exist or does not match the request URI, a new component tree is constructed from the extra path info on the request URI and set in the `FacesContext`. The final step in this phase is to set the locale. This is either retrieved from the saved state or set to the default locale from the external context request object.

At the end of this phase, a reference to the component tree is passed to the `FacesContext` via the `setViewRoot()` method, and it will reflect either the saved state from the previous request (if any) or the default state. If the request contains no `POST` data or query parameters, the `renderResponse()` method is called on the `FacesContext` so that all other phases of the life cycle are skipped and the tree is rendered in the *Render Response* phase.

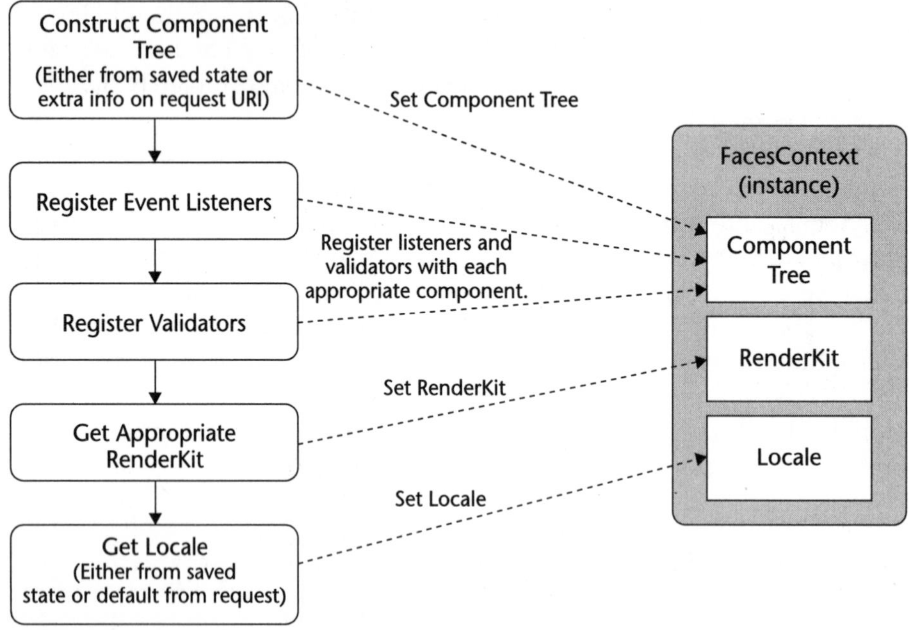

Figure 3.4 The Restore View phase.

TREE IDENTIFIERS AND REQUEST URI'S

Each component tree is required to have a unique identifier. In Web applications with JSPs, this identifier typically corresponds to the *extra path info* portion of the request URI. For example, when using the standard servlet mapping of `javax.faces.Webapp.FacesServlet` to `/faces/*`, the extra path info is that portion of the URI after `/faces`. So if the request URI is `/faces/login.jsp`, then the tree identifier will be `/login.jsp`.

Apply Request Values

The purpose of this phase is to allow each component in the component tree the opportunity to update itself with new information from the request. This phase is shown graphically in Figure 3.5.

If you remember the `FirstNameChanged` listener example from earlier in this chapter, this update would allow the first name text component to set its value from the old value to the new one. The JSF implementation accomplishes this by calling the `processDecodes()` method on the `UIViewRoot` component in the component tree. This action results in the `processDecodes()` method of each child component in the component tree to be called recursively.

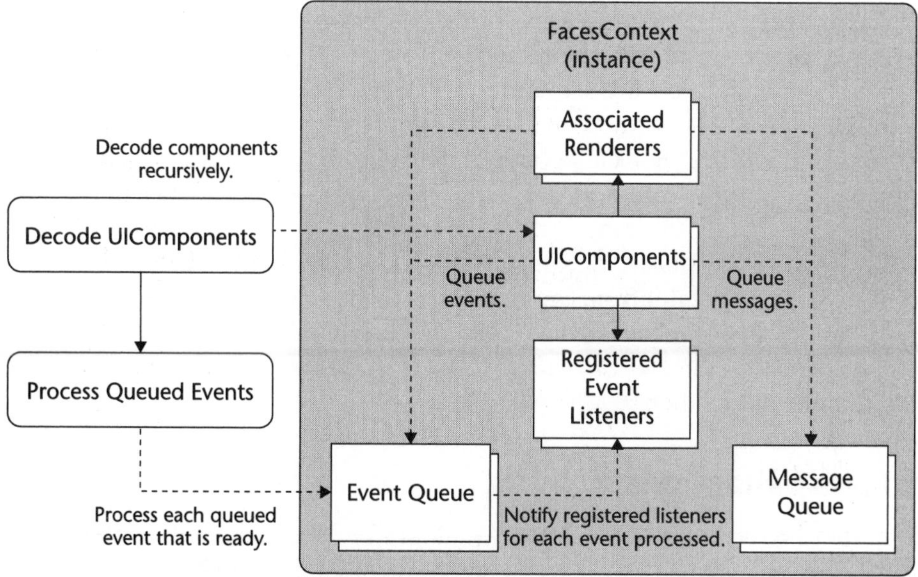

Figure 3.5 The Apply Request Values phase.

Within the `processDecodes()` method, a component first calls the `processDecodes()` method of all child facets and components. The `decode()` method of the component is then called. If a `Converter` has been associated with the UI component, it will be invoked here to convert the `String` value entered by the user into its proper object form in the component's backing model object. Remember from our earlier discussion on component rendering that decoding may be delegated to an associated `Renderer` at this point. If the conversion process of one or more components fails, messages may be queued in the `FacesContext` via the `addMessage()` method we covered earlier. For each conversion that fails, the `setValid()` method on the user interface component will be called with a value of `false`. This ultimately will result in the JSF implementation skipping to the *Render Response* phase to notify the user of input errors.

During the process of updating component values, events may be queued for processing either by UI components or associated `Renderers`. In the case of the first name changed example in the Car Demo sample application, a `ValueChangeEvent` would be placed in the event queue. After each component value has been updated via the conversion process, the JSF implementation will process this and other queued events in the order that they were queued before moving to the next phase.

If any of the event handlers or `decode()` methods on the UI components (or their associated `Renderers`) calls the `responseComplete()` method on the `FacesContext`, the processing of the current request will be terminated once this phase has been completed. Likewise, if any event handlers or `decode()` methods on the UI components (or their `Renderers`) calls the `renderResponse()` method on the `FacesContext`, the JSF implementation will skip to the *Render Response* phase of the life cycle once this phase has been completed. The most common cause of this action is the occurrence of a conversion error that requires input from the user.

At the end of this phase, all components will be updated with any new values (or changes in state) from the request. It is also possible that events have been queued and some (or all) have been processed. At this point, the life cycle will proceed to the *Process Validations* phase, skip to the *Render Response* phase, or terminate all together.

Process Validations

Similarly to `Renderers`, each UI component may associate with one or more `Validator` components and/or directly implement its `validate()` method. We introduced the topic of `Validators` in the previous chapter, as well as both methods of performing validation. The purpose of this phase is to give each UI component the opportunity to validate its state. Each step in this phase is shown graphically in relation to the others in Figure 3.6.

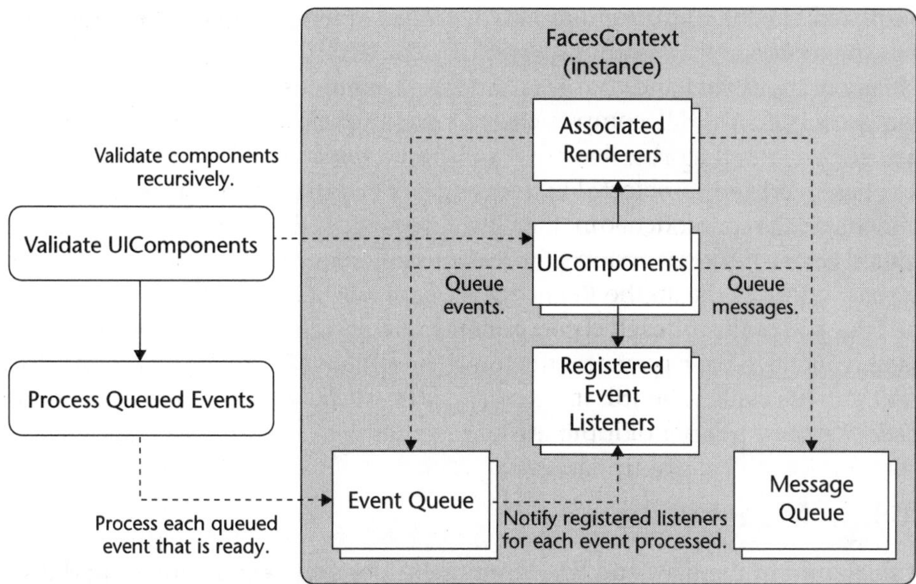

Figure 3.6 The Process Validations phase.

If you remember our credit card example in Listing 3.3, the credit card number input component has a `Validator` associated with it. This update would allow the Validator to execute their validation code to verify the correctness of the supplied credit card number. The JSF implementation accomplishes this by calling the `processValidators()` method on the `UIViewRoot` component in the component tree. This action results in the `processValidators()` method of each child `UIInput` component in the component tree being called recursively.

Within the `processValidators()` method, a component first calls the `processValidators()` method of all child facets and components. The `validate()` method of the component is then called on each associated `Validator` and finally on the component itself. We introduced `Validators` in the previous chapter, including associating separate `Validator` components as well as implementing the `validate()` method on the UI component itself, so you may want to refresh your memory if the concept of Validators is a bit fuzzy. We'll also cover them in much greater detail in Chapter 8.

If the validation process of one or more user interface components fails, messages may be queued in the `FacesContext` via the `addMessage()` method we covered earlier. For each validation that fails (usually via a thrown `ValidatorException`), the `setValid()` method on the component will be called with a value of `false`. This ultimately will result in the JSF implementation skipping to the *Render Response* phase to notify the user of input errors.

During the validation process, events may be queued for processing either by user interface components or associated Validators. After all validations are completed, the JSF implementation will process queued events before moving to the next phase.

If any of the event handlers or `validate()` methods on the components (or their associated Validators) calls the `responseComplete()` method on the `FacesContext`, the processing of the current request will be terminated once this phase has been completed. Likewise, if any event handlers or `validate()` methods on the components (or their Validators) calls the `renderResponse()` method on the `FacesContext`, the JSF implementation will skip to the *Render Response* phase of the life cycle once this phase has been completed.

At the end of this phase, all components will be validated. It is also possible that events have been queued and some (or all) have been processed. At this point, the life cycle will proceed to the *Update Model Values* phase, skip to the *Render Response* phase, or terminate all together.

Update Model Values

At this point in the life cycle, the component tree has been restored, updated with new data from the request, and successfully validated. The purpose of this phase is to update each user interface component's data model in preparation for processing any application level events. Each step in this phase is shown graphically in relation to the others in Figure 3.7.

The JSF implementation updates the model by calling the `processUpdates()` method on the `UIViewRoot` component in the component tree. This action results in the `processUpdates()` method of each child `UIInput` component in the component tree to be called recursively.

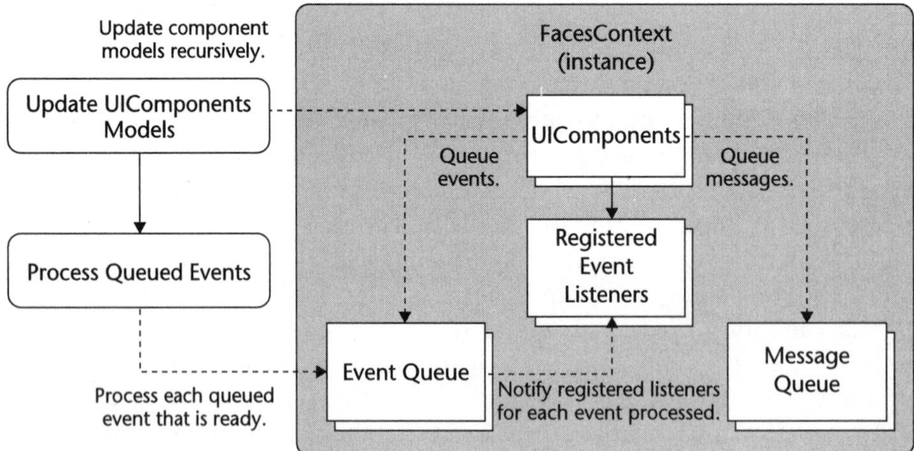

Figure 3.7 The Update Model Values phase.

Within the `processUpdates()` method, a component first calls the `processUpdates()` method of all child facets and UI components. The `updateModel()` method of the UI component is then called. If the updating process of one or more UI components fails, messages may be queued in the `FacesContext` via the `addMessage()` method we covered earlier. For each update that fails, the `setValid()` method on the associated component will be called with a value of `false`. This ultimately will result in the `FacesServlet` skipping to the *Render Response* phase to notify the user of input errors.

During the updating process, events may be queued for processing by the user interface components. After all updates are completed, the JSF implementation will process queued events before moving to the next phase.

If any component in the component tree calls the `responseComplete()` method on the `FacesContext` within its `updateModel()` method, the processing of the current request will be terminated once this phase has been completed. Likewise, If any component in the component tree calls the `renderResponse()` method on the `FacesContext` within its `updateModel()` method, the JSF implementation will skip to the *Render Response* phase of the life cycle once this phase has been completed.

At the end of this phase, all components models will be properly updated. It is also possible that events have been queued and some (or all) have been processed. At this point, the life cycle will proceed to the *Invoke Application* phase, skip to the *Render Response* phase, or terminate all together.

Invoke Application

The purpose of this phase is to process any `ActionEvents` that have been previously queued (typically by `UICommand` components). The JSF implementation initiates this process by invoking the `processApplication()` method on the `UIViewRoot` component.

Render Response

The purpose of this phase is to render the current state of the component tree and prepare a response to the current request. Each step in this phase is shown graphically in relation to the others in Figure 3.8.

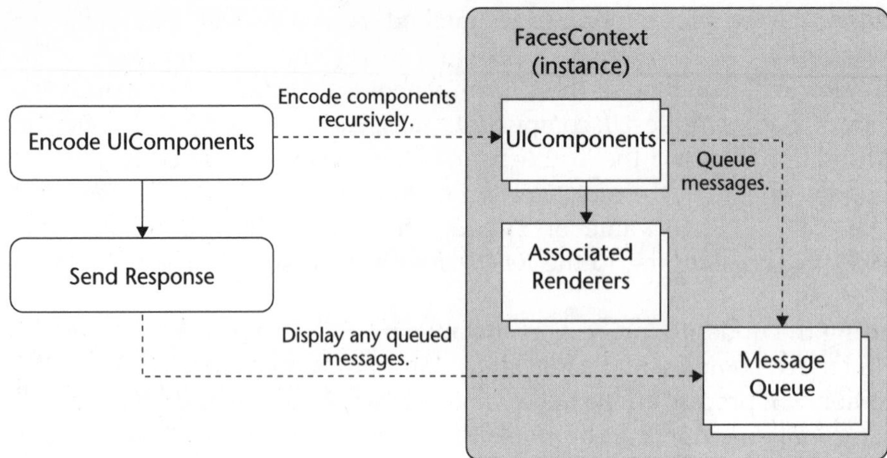

Figure 3.8 The Render Response phase.

On a basic level, the response is generated from encoding performed directly by the components in the component tree and by their associated Renderers. The JSF specification also allows for other methods of generating responses, all of which involve interleaving UI component encoding with other content. Interleaving is something that mostly JSF implementers will be interested in, but you should be aware of it before using your chosen JSF implementation.

View Handlers

The generation of response content is handled by a `ViewHandler` in JSF. A `ViewHandler` is a class that implements the `javax.faces.lifecycle.ViewHandler` interface. All JSF implementations are required to provide a default `ViewHandler` that is used unless it is overridden, so most developers don't need to worry about dealing with this interface.

However, this interface can be implemented and the resulting implementation registered to alter the way content is generated for responses. That makes it an important extension mechanism for those developers that wish to generate something other than, say, JSPs.

Regardless of what method of response generation is used, every JSF implementation is required to follow certain requirements. Most of these have to do with what order component rendering occurs, while some place restrictions on how additional components may be added and the relationship between parent and child components in controlling encoding. See the *JSF Specification* for more details.

Encoding

Putting the interleaving of content aside for clarity, the JSF implementation will call the `encodeBegin()` method of a component or its associated `Renderer` to generate its content for the response. If the component returns a value of `true` for the `rendersChildren()` method, the JSF implementation will then call the `encodeChildren()` and `encodeEnd()` methods in order.

Once the response has been completely rendered, the JSF implementation must save the state of the current component tree for later use by the *Restore View* phase in future requests. This state must be saved in the request itself or on the server (usually in the session scope for Web applications). Once the state is saved, the request-processing life cycle is completed, and we start all over again with the next request!

Summary

This draws to a close our introduction to JSF. At this point, you should have a solid understanding of how JSF is designed, what its major elements are, and how it processes client requests to produce responses. Don't worry if some of the things we have covered are still a bit fuzzy. You should actually have a number of detail-oriented questions at this point, and the following chapters will help you answer them.

Elements of JSF

CHAPTER

4

JSF Configuration

The JSF framework requires two separate types of configuration files to function properly inside a Web application container (such as Tomcat). In Chapters 1, "JSF Patterns and Architecture," and 2, "Elements of JSF," we took a look at a variety of JSF components and how they function within the JSF request-processing life cycle. Here we will examine how you configure, package, and deploy these components as a Web application. Part of this discussion will be a review of what is required for a standard Java Web application.

Overview

Before moving on to more detailed coverage of JSF, we need to set up our JSF environment and examine how JSF applications are configured. We will actually cover each element of JSF configuration files with pointers to other chapters later in this book that provide more detail. The goal here is to get you set up to run JSF applications, to play with one of the *JSF Reference Implementation* sample applications, and to introduce you to how JSF applications can be configured.

Getting Started

The best way to get started is to download and install the *JSF Reference Implementation*. You'll find a link to the latest distribution and installation instructions at the following Web site:

```
http://java.sun.com/j2ee/javaserverfaces/index.jsp
```

The download includes libraries for the reference implementation itself, Javadocs for the API, and some sample applications to get started with.

You have the choice of using your own servlet container or a version of the free servlet reference implementation, Tomcat. You'll find a link to the latest distributions of Tomcat, installation instructions, documentation, and even source code at the following Web site:

```
http://jakarta.apache.org/tomcat/index.html
```

Once you have Tomcat or any other servlet container set up, you'll find a WAR for each *JSF Reference Implementation* application ready to deploy in the `[JSFInstallDir]/samples` directory. Most containers, including Tomcat, have simple procedures for deploying and running packaged applications as well as convenient management consoles.

Introduction to Sample Application

We'll use the Car Demo sample application *from the JSF Reference Implementation* throughout this chapter to demonstrate how a JSF application is properly configured, packaged, and deployed. We'll introduce some alternative scenarios along the way but Car Demo will be our starting point.

The first page of the Car Demo sample is the preferred locale map. Once you select a suitable locale, which directs the application to display text in a language you are comfortable with, you are presented with a list of cars to choose from. This list of cars is shown with English descriptions in Figure 4.1. Each car has a picture, description, and a button for more information. Once you choose a car, you'll see an input form that helps you equip your chosen car and then buy it.

After choosing to buy a car, you are presented with a summary screen to double-check your options and prices. After verifying the specifics of your purchase, you are asked for some personal information, which includes how you wish to pay for the car. The last page you see is a thank you for purchasing a car. A page flow diagram is provided in Figure 4.2.

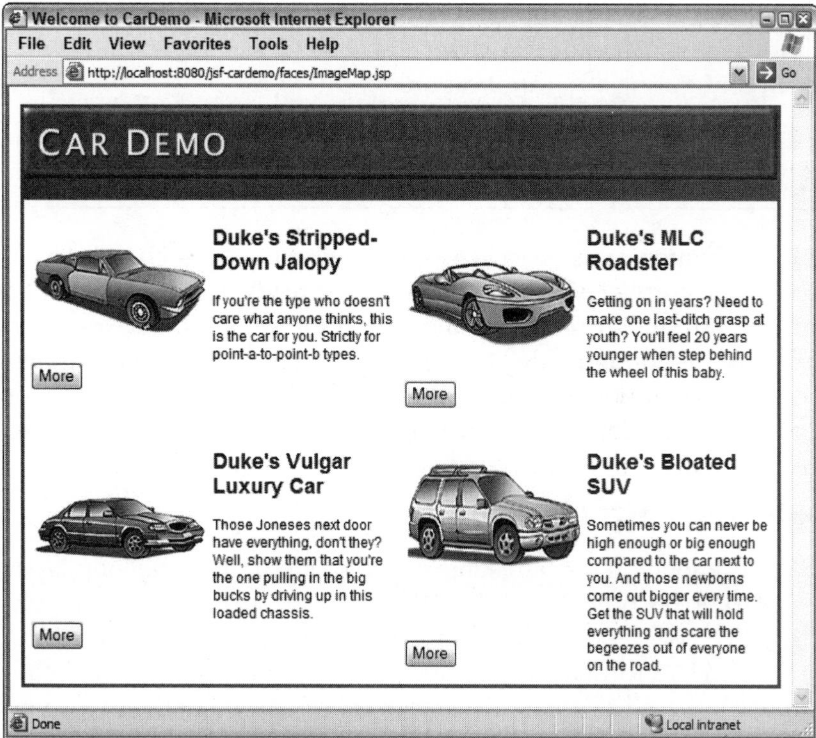

Figure 4.1 Car Demo sample application.

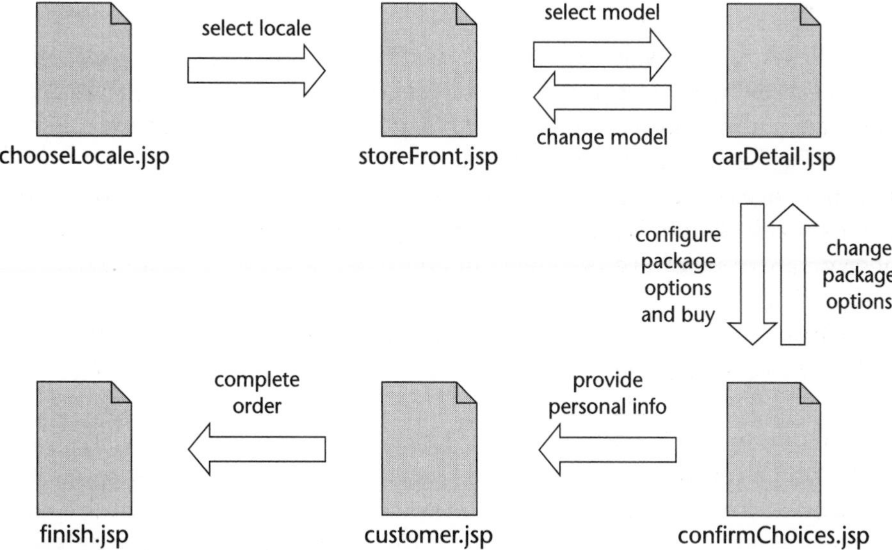

Figure 4.2 Car Demo page flow.

This is admittedly a simple application, and you are probably thinking of ways to improve upon it already. However, it will serve well for learning what is necessary in configuring a JSF application.

A Word about Web Applications

A typical JSF application at its heart is a Web application. As such, it is based in part on the Java servlet specification. We've already touched upon the `FacesServlet` as the controller for a JSF application, and in the next section we'll discuss how you configure the `FacesServlet` for your JSF applications. But before we do that, it would be a good idea to review what is required for deploying any Java Web application.

Web Application Structure

Every Web application will contain some combination of the following types of resources: Markup documents (JSP, HTML, XML, and so on), servlets, graphics files (GIF, JPEG, PNG, and so on), multimedia files (Flash, WAV, and so on), classes, libraries (in JAR format), applets, style sheets, scripts (JavaScript being the most popular), as well as others. The servlet specification defines how you package these files and deploy them to your servlet container of choice. You'll find the latest version of the servlet specification using the following URL:

```
http://java.sun.com/products/servlet/index.jsp
```

In addition to the usual structuring of directories to organize application files, the servlet specification defines some special directories for certain types of files. Each of these directories, along with how they relate to each other, is shown in Figure 4.3. The root of a Web application may contain any number of directories to organize your application files, but certain types of resources must be contained in these special directories for your Web application to work properly in a standard Java servlet container.

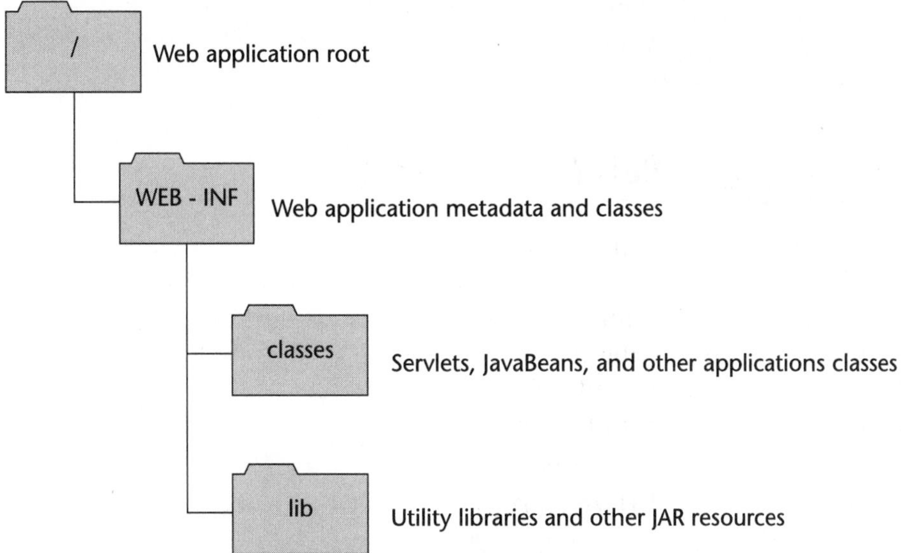

Figure 4.3 Web application directory structure.

The `WEB-INF` directory contains meta-information about a Web application. As required by the servlet specification, its contents are private and not accessible to Web clients. However, classes and servlets within your Web application DO have access to the contents of this directory and any nested subdirectories. The deployment descriptor for a Web application must be placed here, and you will typically find other configuration files and resources located here as well. We'll cover the deployment descriptor shortly.

The `WEB-INF/classes` directory must contain all classes and servlets in your application that are not otherwise packaged in Java Archive (JAR) files. If these classes are scoped within Java packages, then the directory structure beneath the `classes` directory must represent the package structure.

As an example, let us suppose you had a class named `Customer.java` located in the `com.acme` package. The resulting directory structure is provided in Figure 4.4.

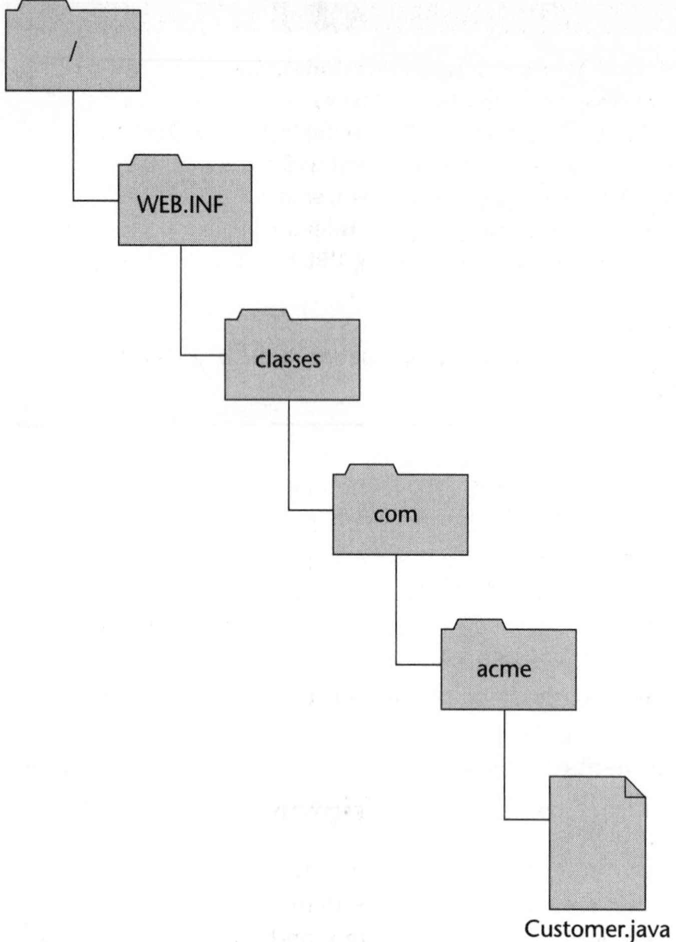

Figure 4.4 Package structure within a Web application.

The WEB-INF/lib directory must contain all JAR resources, which would include utility libraries and reusable sets of classes that you use among multiple applications. The class loader (or loaders) in your servlet container will pick up these JAR files and those class files contained in the classes directory when loading your Web application at startup time. The servlet specification requires that resources in the WEB-INF/classes directory be loaded before those in the WEB-INF/lib directory.

Other than the above-stated requirements, you are free to place your other resources wherever you wish. Just remember that you will want to place any files that you don't wish to be accessible by Web clients within the WEB-INF directory.

WEB APPLICATION ROOT

When deploying a Web application as a set of directories, the servlet container will provide a method for mapping the root context for your application (usually via a simple XML configuration file). When deploying a Web application in WAR format, the servlet container will usually use the name of the WAR as the root context by default. For the Car Demo sample, deploying the `jsf-cardemo.war` file that is provided by the reference implementation to Tomcat on a local machine results in the following URL mapping to the Car Demo application:

```
http://localhost:8080/jsf-cardemo/
```

In this case, `jsf-cardemo` is automatically set as the root context for the Car Demo application.

You may certainly deploy your Web application as a set of directories and files under an application root directory. However, the servlet specification provides a more convenient mechanism for packaging and deploying your applications. It is referred to as a Web Archive (or WAR), which basically follows the structure we just covered packaged in JAR format. The resulting file must have a `.war` extension. Servlet containers can accept WAR files and are capable of unpacking them with their directory structure intact before loading them.

Web Application Deployment Descriptor

Other than the structuring of certain resources in your Web application, a servlet container will use a special XML-based file to properly configure your application and its resources before loading it and making it available to Web clients. As required by the servlet specification, this file must be called `web.xml` and be located in the `WEB-INF` directory of your Web application.

The structure of all Web application deployment descriptors must follow a certain format. Since the descriptor is XML-based, this format is defined in a Document Type Definition (DTD) file and is available online at the following address:

```
http://java.sun.com/dtd/web-app_2_3.dtd
```

The servlet specification defines each element of the descriptor and gives you detailed guidelines for properly constructing it. Each descriptor must have the following declaration at the top of the file to be recognized appropriately by servlet containers:

```
<!DOCTYPE web-app PUBLIC
 "-//Sun Microsystems, Inc.//DTD Web Application 2.3//EN"
 "http://java.sun.com/dtd/web-app_2_3.dtd">
```

This declaration specifies that the file is a standard Java Web application descriptor and that it follows the structure defined in the referenced DTD. Make sure this is the first element in your web.xml files.

Configuring a Web Application for JSF

Now that we've covered what a standard Web application requires, let's take a look at what is required to create a JSF Web application. Listing 4.1 shows the contents of the web.xml file for the Car Demo sample application.

```
<!DOCTYPE web-app PUBLIC
    "-//Sun Microsystems, Inc.//DTD Web Application 2.3//EN"
    "http://java.sun.com/dtd/web-app_2_3.dtd">

<web-app>
    <display-name>Car Store</display-name>
    <description>Buy a car.</description>
    <context-param>
        <param-name>javax.faces.STATE_SAVING_METHOD</param-name>
        <param-value>client</param-value>
    </context-param>

    <!-- Faces Servlet -->
    <servlet>
        <servlet-name>Faces Servlet</servlet-name>
        <servlet-class>javax.faces.webapp.FacesServlet</servlet-class>
        <load-on-startup> 1 </load-on-startup>
    </servlet>


    <!-- Faces Servlet Mapping -->
    <servlet-mapping>
        <servlet-name>Faces Servlet</servlet-name>
        <url-pattern>*.jsf</url-pattern>
    </servlet-mapping>
</web-app>
```

Listing 4.1 Car Demo web.xml file.

The first thing you see is the document type declaration we discussed previously. This tells the servlet container that this file is a standard Web application descriptor. Both the <description> and <display-name> tags provide descriptive information about the application and are not explicitly required. The other tags need a bit more explanation.

FacesServlet Mapping

As we discussed in Chapter 1 in our discussion of the MVC Pattern, the FacesServlet is the controller for your JSF applications. The servlet container you deploy your application to needs to know about the FacesServlet as well as the request URLs it should handle. You declare the FacesServlet by using the <servlet> tag in the Web application descriptor.

```
<!-- Faces Servlet -->
<servlet>
    <servlet-name>Faces Servlet</servlet-name>
    <servlet-class>javax.faces.webapp.FacesServlet</servlet-class>
    <load-on-startup> 1 </load-on-startup>
</servlet>
```

The <load-on-startup> tag specifies whether or not the container loads the servlet when the application is started. A value of 0 or any positive integer directs the container to load the servlet when the application is started, while a negative integer or no value at all directs the container to load the servlet whenever it chooses. The smaller the positive integer value, the higher the priority of starting the servlet before others. What the above XML basically states is that the container should load the standard JSF FacesServlet when the Car Demo application is started.

Now that the FacesServlet has been declared, you map possible request URLs for your application to the FacesServlet by using the <servlet-mapping> tag.

```
<!-- Faces Servlet Mapping -->
<servlet-mapping>
    <servlet-name>Faces Servlet</servlet-name>
    <url-pattern>*.jsf</url-pattern>
</servlet-mapping>
```

The <servlet-name> tag matches the name just assigned to the FacesServlet while the <url-pattern> tag directs the container to send all Web client requests that end with *.jsf, where the asterisk denotes any filename text, to the servlet. This form of mapping is known as extension mapping. The *JSF Specification* recommends the use of faces as the extension, but this is not required (as shown here with the alternate jsf extension). The FacesServlet translates the name to a corresponding JSP. For example, the following URLs

```
http://localhost:8080/index.jsf
http://localhost:8080/index.faces
```

would translate to

```
http://localhost:8080/index.jsp
```

The other form of mapping is known as prefix mapping. The mapping section of the configuration file could be rewritten as follows:

```
<!-- Faces Servlet Mapping -->
<servlet-mapping>
    <servlet-name>Faces Servlet</servlet-name>
    <url-pattern>/faces/*</url-pattern>
</servlet-mapping>
```

In this case, the `<url-pattern>` tag directs the container to send all Web client requests that end with `/faces/*`, where the asterisk denotes any additional path or file information, to the servlet. As an example, the following request URLs would be sent to the `FacesServlet` as configured:

```
http://localhost:8080/jsf-cardemo/faces/
http://localhost:8080/jsf-cardemo/faces/index.jsp
```

We'll talk about the `STATE_SAVING_METHOD` context parameter in the next section.

JSF Application Configuration Files

In addition to the `web.xml` file, you will have at least one JSF configuration file. All JSF implementations are required to search for these files in the following order:

- Look for a resource named `/META-INF/faces-config.xml` in every JAR resource that is located in the `/WEB-INF/lib` directory of the Web application. If such a resource exists, the configuration file is loaded at application startup. A good example of this method is the Components sample application that is packaged with the *JSF Reference Implementation* (look for the `demo-components.jar`).
- Next, look for a context initialization parameter named `javax.faces.application.CONFIG_FILES` in the `web.xml` file for one or more JSF configurations that should be loaded. The value of this parameter is a comma delimited list of context relative resource paths (each starting with `/`). This particular method is useful when you wish to split up a large JSF application into manageable pieces.

- If the initialization parameter does not exist, look for a resource named `faces-config.xml` in the `/WEB-INF/` directory of the Web application. This is the simplest and most common method for configuring a JSF Web application. In this case, your `faces-config.xml` file is located alongside your `web.xml` file.

The Car Demo application uses the third method, and we'll examine the JSF configuration file it uses in the next section. However, if you would like to make use of the second method for declaring multiple configuration files, you would declare the `javax.faces.application.CONFIG_FILES` property as a servlet context initialization parameter in the `web.xml` file.

```
<context-param>
    <param-name>javax.faces.application.CONFIG_FILES</param-name>
    <param-value>
        /WEB-INF/faces-config1.xml,
        /WEB-INF/faces-config2.xml,
        ...
    </param-value>
</context-param>
```

The names of these files can be whatever you wish and they may be located wherever you wish within the application. However, you will almost always want to place them under the `WEB-INF` directory to keep them private from Web clients. If you are familiar with Struts, then this method of declaring multiple configuration files will look familiar.

Another commonly used context parameter is the one we saw in the previous section for controlling how component tree state is saved between client requests.

```
<context-param>
    <param-name>javax.faces.STATE_SAVING_METHOD</param-name>
    <param-value>client</param-value>
</context-param>
```

The `STATE_SAVING_METHOD` context parameter directs the JSF implementation to save state either on the `client` or on the `server`. Refer to the documentation of your particular JSF implementation for the pros and cons of each.

Necessary Classes and Resources

In addition to your own classes (which may be in JAR format), a number of other resources are required for your JSF application to properly function. These resources are listed in Table 4.1.

Table 4.1 Required JSF Resources

RESOURCE NAME	DESCRIPTION
jsf-api.jar	This JAR contains the standard JSF API classes and interfaces that all JSF implementations must satisfy.
jsf-ri.jar	This JAR represents the reference implementation's implementation of the JSF API. If you are using another JSF implementation (which may be named differently), then substitute that JAR for this one.
jstl.jar standard.jar	These JAR files contain the Java Standard Tag Library files and resources upon which the standard HTML JSF tag library is based upon in the reference implementation. It is likely that other JSF implementations will use these same libraries, but you should check to make sure.
commons-beanutils.jar commons-digester.jar commons-collections.jar commons-logging.jar	The *JSF Reference Implementation* uses these Apache Jakarta utilities but other implementations may not. You should consult your implementation's documentation to be sure.

In addition to these resources, other JSF implementations may require additional resources. You should always check your implementation's documentation before deploying your application for the first time to make sure that you have all of the required files packaged with your application.

SHARED CLASS FACILITY

Most servlet containers have a shared classes facility that allows you to make a resource like the `jsf-api.jar` file available in the classpath of every Web application that the container manages. This saves you the trouble of packaging up the same files with multiple Web applications. For example, Tomcat allows you to do this by simply dropping `jsf-api.jar` file in its `shared/lib` directory.

Each of the reference implementation samples does not make use of this feature. Instead, they package up each of the required resources in the WAR file. This makes deploying the sample applications very easy, because they each contain all of the files they need with no external dependencies. However, in practice you will usually want to make use of the shared classes facility to lower the footprint of each application and to avoid duplicating resources. Incidentally, one reason not to use this feature is if one or more applications have a dependency on an older version of a resource.

It is likely that future versions of the J2EE specification will require support for JSF. If this happens, most containers will ship with resources like `jsf-api.jar` and the associated implementation. As always, check to see what resources your container already provides or automatically shares across applications before you package and deploy your first application.

Now that we know what is required to configure a Web application for JSF, it is time to look at how we configure the JSF application itself. At the heart of this process is the JSF configuration file.

Configuring a JSF Application

As we discussed in the "JSF Application Configuration Files" section earlier in this chapter, each JSF application will have one or more configuration files for registering and initializing JSF-specific resources. In most cases, these settings will be provided in a file named `faces-config.xml` in the `WEB-INF` directory of a Web application.

Configuration File Format

The `faces-config.xml` file for the Car Demo sample application is provided in Listing 4.2. We'll discuss each part of this configuration file in the following sections, which will be organized in roughly the same manner as they appear in the associated DTD file that defines the structure of every JSF configuration file.

```
<!DOCTYPE faces-config PUBLIC
    "-//Sun Microsystems, Inc.//DTD JavaServer Faces Config 1.0//EN"
    "http://java.sun.com/dtd/web-facesconfig_1_0.dtd">

<faces-config>
  <application>
    <message-bundle>carstore.bundles.Messages</message-bundle>
    <locale-config>
      <default-locale>en</default-locale>
      <supported-locale>de</supported-locale>
      <supported-locale>fr</supported-locale>
      <supported-locale>es</supported-locale>
    </locale-config>
  </application>

  <validator>
    <description>
        Registers the concrete Validator implementation,
        carstore. FormatValidator with the validator
        identifier, FormatValidator.
    </description>
    <validator-id>FormatValidator</validator-id>
    <validator-class>carstore.FormatValidator</validator-class>
    <attribute>
```

Listing 4.2 JSF configuration for Car Demo. *(continued)*

```
      <description>
        List of format patterns separated by '|'. The validator
        compares these patterns against the data entered in a
        component that has this validator registered on it.
      </description>
      <attribute-name>formatPatterns</attribute-name>
      <attribute-class>java.lang.String</attribute-class>
    </attribute>
  </validator>

  <!-- converter -->
  <converter>
    <description>
        Registers the concrete Converter implementation,
        carstore.CreditCardConverter using the ID,
        creditcard.
    </description>
    <converter-id>creditcard</converter-id>
    <converter-class>carstore.CreditCardConverter</converter-class>
  </converter>

  <!-- Initialize Image Map Hotspot Data -->
  <managed-bean>
    <description>
      Causes the default VariableResolver implementation to instantiate
      the managed bean, NA of the class, components.model.ImageArea in
      application scope if the bean does not already exist in any scope
      and initialize the shape, alt, and coords properties with the
      values specified by the managed-property elements.
    </description>
    <managed-bean-name> NA </managed-bean-name>
    <managed-bean-class>components.model.ImageArea</managed-bean-class>
    <managed-bean-scope> application </managed-bean-scope>
    <managed-property>
      <description>
        Initializes the shape property of the managed bean, NA with
        the value, poly.
      </description>
      <property-name>shape</property-name>
      <value>poly</value>
    </managed-property>
    <managed-property>
      <description>
        Initializes the alt property of the managed bean, NA with
        the value, NAmerica.
      </description>
      <property-name>alt</property-name>
      <value>NAmerica</value>
```

Listing 4.2 *(continued)*

```
    </managed-property>
    <managed-property>
      <description>
        Initializes the coords property of the managed bean, NA with
        the value specified by the value element.
      </description>
      <property-name>coords</property-name>
      <value>
        53,109,1,110,2,167,19,168,52,149,67,164,67,165,68,167,70,168,72,
        170,74,172,75,174,77,175,79,177,81,179,80,179,77,179,81,179,81,
        178,80,178,82,211,28,238,15,233,15,242,31,252,36,247,36,246,32,
        239,89,209,92,216,93,216,100,216,103,218,113,217,116,224,124,
        221,128,230,163,234,185,189,178,177,162,188,143,173,79,173,73,
        163,79,157,64,142,54,139,53,109
      </value>
    </managed-property>
  </managed-bean>

  ...

  <!-- Business Logic Beans -->

  <managed-bean>
    <description>
      Causes the default VariableResolver implementation to instantiate
      the managed bean, CustomerBean of the class, carstore.CustomerBean
      in session scope if the bean does not already exist in any scope.
    </description>
    <managed-bean-name> customer </managed-bean-name>
    <managed-bean-class> carstore.CustomerBean </managed-bean-class>
    <managed-bean-scope> session </managed-bean-scope>
  </managed-bean>

  <managed-bean>
    <description>
      The main backing file mean
    </description>
    <managed-bean-name> carstore </managed-bean-name>
    <managed-bean-class> carstore.CarStore </managed-bean-class>
    <managed-bean-scope> session </managed-bean-scope>
  </managed-bean>

  <navigation-rule>
    <from-view-id>/chooseLocale.jsp</from-view-id>
    <navigation-case>
      <description>
        Any action on chooseLocale should cause navigation to
        storeFront.jsp
```

Listing 4.2 *(continued)*

```
      </description>
      <to-view-id>/storeFront.jsp</to-view-id>
    </navigation-case>
  </navigation-rule>

  <navigation-rule>
    <from-view-id>/storeFront.jsp</from-view-id>
    <navigation-case>
      <description>
        Any action that returns "carDetail" on storeFront.jsp should
        cause navigation to carDetail.jsp
      </description>
      <from-outcome>carDetail</from-outcome>
      <to-view-id>/carDetail.jsp</to-view-id>
    </navigation-case>
  </navigation-rule>

  <navigation-rule>
    <from-view-id>/carDetail.jsp</from-view-id>
    <navigation-case>
      <description>
        Any action that returns "confirmChoices" on carDetail.jsp should
        cause navigation to confirmChoices.jsp
      </description>
      <from-outcome>confirmChoices</from-outcome>
      <to-view-id>/confirmChoices.jsp</to-view-id>
    </navigation-case>
  </navigation-rule>

  <navigation-rule>
    <from-view-id>/confirmChoices.jsp</from-view-id>
    <navigation-case>
      <description>
        Any action that returns "carDetail" on confirmChoices.jsp should
        cause navigation to carDetail.jsp
      </description>
      <from-outcome>carDetail</from-outcome>
      <to-view-id>/carDetail.jsp</to-view-id>
    </navigation-case>
  </navigation-rule>

  <navigation-rule>
    <from-view-id>/confirmChoices.jsp</from-view-id>
    <navigation-case>
      <description>
        Any action that returns "customerInfo" on confirmChoices.jsp
        should cause navigation to customerInfo.jsp
```

Listing 4.2 *(continued)*

```
      </description>
      <from-outcome>customerInfo</from-outcome>
      <to-view-id>/customerInfo.jsp</to-view-id>
    </navigation-case>
  </navigation-rule>

  <navigation-rule>
    <from-view-id>/customerInfo.jsp</from-view-id>
    <navigation-case>
      <description>
        Any action that returns "finish" on customerInfo.jsp should
        cause navigation to finish.jsp
      </description>
      <from-outcome>finish</from-outcome>
      <to-view-id>/finish.jsp</to-view-id>
    </navigation-case>
  </navigation-rule>
</faces-config>
```

Listing 4.2 *(continued)*

The first thing you'll notice, as with the `web.xml` file, is a document type declaration at the top of the file. The JSF specification defines the structure of a JSF configuration file via a publicly available DTD:

```
http://java.sun.com/dtd/web-facesconfig_1_0.dtd
```

Each JSF configuration file must adhere closely to this DTD or the associated application will likely fail to start.

As part of the Car Demo sample, a JAR file named `demo-components.jar` is packaged in the `/WEB-INF/lib/` directory of the WAR. This JAR is actually the result of another sample application called Demo Components that demonstrates the use of custom GUI components and Renderers. The associated `faces-config.xml` file is provided in Listing 4.3. We'll refer to this file later when we discuss declaring UI components and Renderers.

```
<!DOCTYPE faces-config PUBLIC
  "-//Sun Microsystems, Inc.//DTD JavaServer Faces Config 1.0//EN"
  "http://java.sun.com/dtd/web-facesconfig_1_0.dtd">

<faces-config>

  <!-- Custom Components -->
```

Listing 4.3 JSF Configuration for custom UI components and Renderers. *(continued)*

```
<component>
  <component-type>DemoArea</component-type>
  <component-class>
    components.components.AreaComponent
  </component-class>
  <property>
    <description>
      Alternate text if we synthesize an ImageArea bean.
    </description>
    <property-name>alt</property-name>
    <property-class>java.lang.String</property-class>
  </property>
  <property>
    <description>
      Hotspot coordinates if we synthesize an ImageArea bean.
    </description>
    <property-name>coords</property-name>
    <property-class>java.lang.String</property-class>
  </property>
  <property>
    <description>
      Shape (default, rect, circle, poly) if we synthesize an
      ImageArea bean.
    </description>
    <property-name>shape</property-name>
    <property-class>java.lang.String</property-class>
  </property>
</component>

<component>
  <component-type>Graph</component-type>
  <component-class>
    components.components.GraphComponent
  </component-class>
</component>

<component>
  <component-type>DemoMap</component-type>
  <component-class>
    components.components.MapComponent
  </component-class>
  <property>
    <description>
      Alternate text for the currently selected child AreaComponent.
    </description>
    <property-name>current</property-name>
    <property-class>java.lang.String</property-class>
  </property>
```

Listing 4.3 *(continued)*

```
</component>

<component>
  <component-type>Pane</component-type>
  <component-class>
    components.components.PaneComponent
  </component-class>
</component>

<component>
  <component-type>Scroller</component-type>
  <component-class>
    components.components.ScrollerComponent
  </component-class>
</component>

  <!-- Custom Renderers -->
<render-kit>
  <renderer>
    <description>
      Renderer for a components.components.AreaComponent component.
    </description>
    <renderer-type>DemoArea</renderer-type>
    <renderer-class>components.renderkit.AreaRenderer</renderer-class>
    <attribute>
      <description>
        Context-relative path to an image to be displayed when the
        mouse is not hovering over this hotspot.
      </description>
      <attribute-name>onmouseout</attribute-name>
      <attribute-class>java.lang.String</attribute-class>
    </attribute>
    <attribute>
      <description>
        Context-relative path to an image to be displayed when the
        mouse is hovering over this hotspot.
      </description>
      <attribute-name>onmouseover</attribute-name>
      <attribute-class>java.lang.String</attribute-class>
    </attribute>
    <attribute>
      <description>
        CSS style class to use when rendering this component.
      </description>
      <attribute-name>styleClass</attribute-name>
      <attribute-class>java.lang.String</attribute-class>
    </attribute>
    <supported-component-class>
```

Listing 4.3 *(continued)*

```
        <component-class>
          components.components.AreaComponent
        </component-class>
      </supported-component-class>
    </renderer>

    <renderer>
      <description>
        Renderer for a components.components.MapComponent component.
      </description>
      <renderer-type>DemoMap</renderer-type>
      <renderer-class>components.renderkit.MapRenderer</renderer-class>
      <attribute>
        <description>
          CSS style class to use when rendering this component.
        </description>
        <attribute-name>styleClass</attribute-name>
        <attribute-class>java.lang.String</attribute-class>
      </attribute>
      <supported-component-class>
        <component-class>
          components.components.MapComponent
        </component-class>
      </supported-component-class>
    </renderer>

    <renderer>
      <renderer-type>MenuBar</renderer-type>
      <renderer-class>
        components.renderkit.MenuBarRenderer
      </renderer-class>
    </renderer>

    <renderer>
      <renderer-type>MenuTree</renderer-type>
      <renderer-class>
        components.renderkit.MenuTreeRenderer
      </renderer-class>
    </renderer>

    <renderer>
      <description>
        Renderer for a UIData component that can serve as the basis for
        different markup creation for the components that are children
        of the child UIColumn components.
      </description>
```

Listing 4.3 *(continued)*

```
      <renderer-type>Repeater</renderer-type>
      <renderer-class>
        components.renderkit.RepeaterRenderer
      </renderer-class>
    </renderer>

    <renderer>
      <renderer-type>Stylesheet</renderer-type>
      <renderer-class>
        components.renderkit.StylesheetRenderer
      </renderer-class>
    </renderer>

    <renderer>
      <renderer-type>TabLabel</renderer-type>
      <renderer-class>
        components.renderkit.TabLabelRenderer
      </renderer-class>
    </renderer>

    <renderer>
      <renderer-type>Tab</renderer-type>
      <renderer-class>
        components.renderkit.TabRenderer
      </renderer-class>
    </renderer>

    <renderer>
      <renderer-type>Tabbed</renderer-type>
      <renderer-class>
        components.renderkit.TabbedRenderer
      </renderer-class>
    </renderer>
  </render-kit>
</faces-config>
```

Listing 4.3 *(continued)*

The <faces-config> Element

This element is the root of every faces configuration file and contains all configuration settings for a JSF application other than those defined in the Web application descriptor. A summary of each possible child element is provided in Table 4.2.

Table 4.2 <faces-config> Child Elements

CHILD ELEMENT	MULTIPLICITY	DESCRIPTION
application	zero to many	You may optionally replace the default action listener, navigation handler, property resolver, and variable resolver for your application.
factory	zero to many	Provides factory implementations of things like faces context, life cycle, render kit, and application resources.
component	zero to many	Custom UI components (other than standard JSF components).
converter	zero to many	Converters for encoding and decoding UI component values.
managed-bean	zero to many	Objects that are automatically created, initialized, and placed into proper scope when invoked by a UI component.
navigation-rule	zero to many	Navigation rules that are used in the decision flow of your application.
referenced-bean	zero to many	Bean references that are expected to be in scope where used in your user interface code.
render-kit	zero to many	RenderKits for rendering UI components in your application.
lifecycle	zero to many	Provides modifications to the default life cycle.
validator	zero to many	Validators for ensuring the correctness of data entered by users in application UI components.

We'll cover each of these elements, along with their child elements, in the following sections.

The <application> Element

This element allows you to replace the default action handler, navigation handler, and resolvers for properties and variables. Replacing the defaults provided with your JSF implementation is unnecessary for most applications but may be done if one or more of them are inadequate. A summary of each possible child element is provided in Table 4.3.

Table 4.3 <application> Child Elements

CHILD ELEMENT	MULTIPLICITY	DESCRIPTION
action-listener	zero to many	The fully qualified class name of the concrete ActionListener implementation class that processes action events emitted from UI components.
message-bundle	zero to many	Base name (and optionally package when appropriate) of a resource bundle that contains message resources for the application (see the JavaDocs for java.util.ResourceBundle for more information).
navigation-handler	zero to many	The fully qualified class name of the concrete NavigationHandler implementation class that determines next steps in application flow.
view-handler	zero to many	The fully qualified class name of the concrete ViewHandler implementation class that is called by the *Restore View* and *Render Response* phases of the request processing life cycle.
property-resolver	zero to many	The fully qualified class name of the concrete PropertyResolver implementation class that resolves all property references in your application.
variable-resolver	zero to many	The fully qualified class name of the concrete VariableResolver implementation class that resolves all variable references in your application.
local-config	zero to many	Provides supported locales supported by the application (including an optional default).

The Car Demo application, like typical JSF applications, does not replace these default resources provided by the JSF implementation.

The <factory> Element

This element allows you to declaratively provide factory implementations of things like the faces context, life cycle, render kits, and application resources. A summary of each possible child element is provided in Table 4.4.

Table 4.4 <factory> Child Elements

CHILD ELEMENT	MULTIPLICITY	DESCRIPTION
application-factory	zero to many	The fully qualified class name of the ApplicationFactory implementation class (its instances provide a host of basic resources and behavior needed by JSF applications) that should replace the default provided by your JSF implementation.
faces-context-factory	zero to many	The fully qualified class name of the FacesContextFactory implementation class (which provides FacesContext instances) that should replace the default provided by your JSF implementation.
lifecycle-factory	zero to many	The fully qualified class name of the LifecycleFactory implementation class (the Lifecycle instances it provides manage the entire JSF request-processing life cycle) that should replace the default provided by your JSF implementation.
render-kit-factory	zero to many	The fully qualified class name of the RenderKitFactory implementation class (provides access to available render kits) that should replace the default provided by your JSF implementation.

This element allows you to add custom extensions to your JSF implementation. Most JSF developers won't use this mechanism, but it is very useful when adjustments to a particular JSF implementation are necessary.

The <message-bundle> and <local-config> Elements

The `<message-bundle>` element represents a bundle of localized messages, while the `<local-config>` element defines all supported locales (including an optional default). You can use these elements to support internationalization in your application. Listing 4.2 provides a good example of these elements in action.

```
<application>
  <message-bundle>carstore.bundles.Messages</message-bundle>
  <locale-config>
    <default-locale>en</default-locale>
```

```
      <supported-locale>de</supported-locale>
      <supported-locale>fr</supported-locale>
      <supported-locale>es</supported-locale>
    </locale-config>
  </application>
```

The `<message-bundle>` tag defines the base name of a resource file, including the package when appropriate. The `<default-local>` tag specifies English as the default locale, so the following resource file will be the default.

```
carstore.bundles.Messages_en.properties
```

Each other supported locale is specified via a `<supported-locale>` tag.

The <attribute> Element

This element provides a method for declaratively defining generic attributes for UI components, Converters, Renderers, and Validators. Each attribute is available to the programming logic of the parent component as well as other components (including event handlers) that manipulate it. A summary of each possible child element is provided in Table 4.5.

Table 4.5 <attribute> Child Elements

CHILD ELEMENT	MULTIPLICITY	DESCRIPTION
description	zero to many	A textual description of the generic attribute.
display-name	zero to many	A short, descriptive name of the generic attribute for representing the generic attribute in JSF tools.
icon	zero to many	Small and large icons for representing the generic attribute that are intended for JSF tools.
attribute-name	exactly one	The name under which the generic attribute is stored in its parent (UI components, Converters, and so on) and its value is keyed on.
attribute-class	exactly one	Defines the Java type for the generic attribute (java.lang.String, and so forth).
suggested-value	zero or one	Provides a value for the attribute that is used for tools when populating palettes.
attribute-extension	zero to many	Provides a place for content specific to a particular JSF implementation.

You'll notice that the FormatValidator in Listing 4.2 provides a formatPatterns attribute for specifying format patterns that a particular value (from a UIInput component) will be validated against.

```
<attribute>
  <description> List of format patterns separated by '|'.  The
    validator compares these patterns against the data entered
    in a component that has this validator registered on it.
  </description>
  <attribute-name>formatPatterns</attribute-name>
  <attribute-class>java.lang.String</attribute-class>
</attribute>
```

To see this attribute in action, check out the customerInfo.jsp page in Car Demo and its use of the FormatValidator.

```
<h:outputText value="#{bundle.zipLabel}" />
<h:inputText id="zip" value="#{customer.zip}" size="10"
             required="true">
    <cs:formatValidator formatPatterns="99999|99999-9999|### ###"/>
</h:inputText>
<h:message styleClass="validationMessage" for="zip"/>
```

You can see here how the formatPatterns attribute is set inside the JSP. To see how the attribute is accessed and used, take a look at the FormatValidator and FormatValidatorTag classes.

The <property> Element

This element provides a method for declaratively defining standard JavaBean properties for UI components, Converters, and Validators. You will typically use this element to make properties available for tool manipulation. A summary of each possible child element is provided in Table 4.6.

Table 4.6 <property> Child Elements

CHILD ELEMENT	MULTIPLICITY	DESCRIPTION
description	zero to many	A textual description of the property.
display-name	zero to many	A short, descriptive name of the property for display in JSF tools.
Icon	zero to many	Small and large icons for representing the property in JSF tools.
property-name	exactly one	The name of the property (following standard JavaBean naming conventions).

Table 4.6 *(continued)*

CHILD ELEMENT	MULTIPLICITY	DESCRIPTION
property-class	exactly one	Defines the Java type for the property (java.lang.String, for example).
suggested-value	zero or one	Provides a value for the property that is used for tools when populating palettes.
property-extension	zero to many	Provides a place for content specific to a particular JSF implementation.

The <component> Element

This element allows you to declare a new UI component for your application or replace an existing one, while registering it under a unique identifier. Along with each component, you will also declare the component's available attributes and properties. Each UI component you use in your application, other than the standard components provided with JSF, will be declared using this element. A summary of each possible child element is provided in Table 4.7.

Table 4.7 <component> Child Elements

CHILD ELEMENT	MULTIPLICITY	DESCRIPTION
description	zero to many	A textual description of the UI component.
display-name	zero to many	A short, descriptive name of the UI component for display in JSF tools.
icon	zero to many	Small and large icons for representing the UI component in JSF tools.
component-type	exactly one	Represents the name under which the UI component will be registered; this name must be unique within your application.
component-class	exactly one	Defines the fully qualified type of the UI component, which must be an implementation of UI component.
attribute	zero to many	Defines a generic attribute for the UI component.
property	zero to many	Defines a generic JavaBean property on the UI component.
component-extension	zero or more	Provides a place for content specific to a particular JSF implementation.

There are a number of custom UI components defined in Listing 4.3, one of which is repeated here.

```
<component>
  <component-type>DemoArea</component-type>
  <component-class>components.components.AreaComponent</component-class>
  <property>
    <description>
      Alternate text if we synthesize an ImageArea bean.
    </description>
    <property-name>alt</property-name>
    <property-class>java.lang.String</property-class>
  </property>
  <property>
    <description>
      Hotspot coordinates if we synthesize an ImageArea bean
    </description>
    <property-name>coords</property-name>
    <property-class>java.lang.String</property-class>
  </property>
  <property>
    <description>
      Shape (default, rect, circle, poly) if we synthesize an ImageArea
      bean
    </description>
    <property-name>shape</property-name>
    <property-class>java.lang.String</property-class>
  </property>
</component>
```

The type for this component is specified as `DemoArea` and is associated with the `AreaComponent` class. In JSP-based Web applications, you will normally create a custom tag to go with each UI component. In this example, the `AreaTag` class is provided along with an entry in the associated `components.tld` file. All of these files are provided in the `demo-components.jar` file that is contained within the `/WEB-INF/lib/` directory of the Car Demo application.

```
<tag>
  <name>area</name>
  <tag-class>components.taglib.AreaTag</tag-class>
  <body-content>empty</body-content>
  <description>
    Description of a single hotspot in a client-side image map. This
    tag MUST be nested inside a &lt;map&gt; tag.  To specify the
    hotspot characteristics, you must specify EITHER a value OR the
    alt, coords, and shape attributes.
  </description>

  ...
```

```
  <attribute>
    <name>id</name>
    <required>false</required>
    <rtexprvalue>false</rtexprvalue>
    <description>
      Component id of this component.
    </description>
  </attribute>

  <attribute>
    <name>onmouseout</name>
    <required>false</required>
    <rtexprvalue>false</rtexprvalue>
    <description>
      Context-relative path to the image to be displayed for this
      hotspot when the mouse is not hovering over it
    </description>
  </attribute>

  <attribute>
    <name>onmouseover</name>
    <required>false</required>
    <rtexprvalue>false</rtexprvalue>
    <description>
      Context-relative path to the image to be displayed for this
      hotspot when the mouse is hovering over it
    </description>
  </attribute>

  <attribute>
    <name>targetImage</name>
    <required>true</required>
    <rtexprvalue>false</rtexprvalue>
    <description>
      Specifies the ID if the image component.
    </description>
  </attribute>

  ...

  <attribute>
    <name>value</name>
    <required>false</required>
    <rtexprvalue>false</rtexprvalue>
    <description>
      Value reference expression pointing at an ImageArea bean
      describing the characteristics of this hotspot.  If not
      present, an ImageArea bean will be synthesized from the
      values of the alt, coords, and shape attributes.
    </description>
  </attribute>
</tag>
```

To see an example of how this component is used in a JSP, check out the chooseLocale.jsp page in the Car Demo application. The following code shows the tag library being declared and the DemoArea component being used.

```
<%@ taglib uri="http://java.sun.com/jsf/demo/components" prefix="d" %>
...
<d:area id="NAmerica" value="#{NA}"
        onmouseover="/images/world_namer.jpg"
        onmouseout="/images/world.jpg"
        targetImage="mapImage" />
```

See Chapter 6, "UI Components," for more information about creating and configuring custom UI components.

The <converter> Element

This element allows you to declare each of the custom Converters that are used in your application. As with UI components, you will also declare the Converter's available attributes and properties. A summary of each possible child element is provided in Table 4.8.

Table 4.8 <converter> Child Elements

CHILD ELEMENT	MULTIPLICITY	DESCRIPTION
description	zero to many	A textual description of the Converter.
display-name	zero to many	A short, descriptive name of the Converter for display in JSF tools.
icon	zero to many	Small and large icons for representing the Converter in JSF tools.
converter-id	exactly one	Represents the identifier under which the Converter will be registered; this identifier must be unique within your application.
converter-class	exactly one	Defines the fully qualified type of the Converter, which must be an implementation of Converter.
attribute	zero to many	Defines a generic attribute for the Converter.
property	zero to many	Defines a generic JavaBean property on the Converter.

The CreditCardConverter in Listing 4.2 is registered in the Car Demo application with an identifier of creditcard.

```
<converter>
  <description>
    Registers the concrete Converter implementation,
    carstore.CreditCardConverter using the ID, creditcard.
  </description>
  <converter-id>creditcard</converter-id>
  <converter-class>carstore.CreditCardConverter</converter-class>
</converter>
```

This makes the Converter available to the customerInfo.jsp JSP page, which uses it to convert the credit card number provided by the user of the application.

```
<h:outputText value="#{bundle.ccNumberLabel}" />
  <h:inputText id="ccno" size="16" converter="#{creditCardConverter}"
               required="true">
  ...
  </h:inputText>
<h:message styleClass="validationMessage" for="ccno"/>
```

See Chapter 8, "Validation and Conversion," for more information about creating and configuring Converter components.

The <managed-bean> Element

This element declares UI component model objects represented by JavaBeans and can be used to dynamically instantiate and initialize them when first invoked by UI components. A summary of each possible child element is provided in Table 4.9.

Table 4.9 <managed-bean> Child Elements

CHILD ELEMENT	MULTIPLICITY	DESCRIPTION
description	zero to many	A textual description of the managed bean.
display-name	zero to many	A short, descriptive name of the managed bean for display in JSF tools.
icon	zero to many	Small and large icons for representing the managed bean in JSF tools.

(continued)

Table 4.9 *(continued)*

CHILD ELEMENT	MULTIPLICITY	DESCRIPTION
managed-bean-name	exactly one	Represents the attribute name under which the bean may be located and stored (if the scope is something other than "none"); this name must be unique within your application.
managed-bean-class	exactly one	Defines the fully qualified type of the class that represents the managed bean and that will be used to create instances when invoked.
managed-bean-scope	exactly one	Specifies the scope of the managed bean, which may be either "request," "session," "application," or "none." A value of "none" results in the managed bean's not being persisted between requests.
managed-property	zero to many	Defines an individual property of the managed bean.

You will most likely use this element to configure and initialize UI component model objects. Listing 4.2 provides an example of this element in use for the Car Demo application.

```
<managed-bean>
  <description>
    Causes the default VariableResolver implementation to instantiate
    the managed bean, CustomerBean of the class, carstore.CustomerBean
    in session scope if the bean does not already exist in any scope.
  </description>
  <managed-bean-name> customer </managed-bean-name>
  <managed-bean-class> carstore.CustomerBean </managed-bean-class>
  <managed-bean-scope> session </managed-bean-scope>
</managed-bean>
```

Here, we are defining the `Customer` object that will support the input form presented in the `Customer.jsp` page. An identifier (or name) is provided along with the backing JavaBean class that the JSF implementation must create an object from when necessary. We have also specified that the `Customer` object be placed in session scope when created.

Table 4.10 <managed-property> Child Elements

CHILD ELEMENT	MULTIPLICITY	DESCRIPTION
description	zero to many	A textual description of the managed property.
display-name	zero to many	A short, descriptive name of the managed property for display in JSF tools.
icon	zero to many	Small and large icons for representing the managed property in JSF tools.
property-name	exactly one	Represents the corresponding JavaBean property on the parent managed bean.
property-class	zero or one (optional)	Defines the fully qualified type of the class that represents the managed property; this class should be specified if the configuration file will be used to generate the managed bean and its properties.
map-entries, null-value, value, list-entries	exactly one	A managed property may be initialized as a Map (map-entries), a List or array (list-entries), a value of null (null-value), or a literal value (value).

The <managed-property> Element

This element represents a property of a managed bean and allows you to declaratively define initialization parameters that will be set when the parent managed bean is automatically initialized by the JSF implementation you are using. A summary of each possible child element is provided in Table 4.10.

You will typically want to declare each property on a managed bean that you wish to initialize before use. The North American image map from the `chooseLocale.jsp` JSP page provides a good example of this.

```
<managed-bean>
  <description>
    Causes the default VariableResolver implementation to instantiate
    the managed bean, NA of the class, components.model.ImageArea in
    application scope if the bean does not already exist in any scope
    and initialize the shape, alt, and coords properties with the
    values specified by the managed-property elements
  </description>
```

```
    <managed-bean-name> NA </managed-bean-name>
    <managed-bean-class> components.model.ImageArea </managed-bean-class>
    <managed-bean-scope> application </managed-bean-scope>
    <managed-property>
      <description>
        Initializes the shape property of the managed bean, NA with the
        value, poly
      </description>
      <property-name>shape</property-name>
      <value>poly</value>
    </managed-property>
    <managed-property>
      <description>
        Initializes the alt property of the managed bean, NA with the
        value, NAmerica.
      </description>
      <property-name>alt</property-name>
      <value>NAmerica</value>
    </managed-property>
      <managed-property>
      <description>
        Initializes the coords property of the managed bean, NA with the
        value specified by the value element
      </description>
      <property-name>coords</property-name>
      <value>
        53,109,1,110,2,167,19,168,52,149,67,164,67,165,68,167,70,168,
        72,170,74,172,75,174,77,175,79,177,81,179,80,179,77,179,81,179,
        81,178,80,178,82,211,28,238,15,233,15,242,31,252,36,247,36,246,
        32,239,89,209,92,216,93,216,100,216,103,218,113,217,116,224,
        124,221,128,230,163,234,185,189,178,177,162,188,143,173,79,173,
        73,163,79,157,64,142,54,139,53,109
      </value>
    </managed-property>
  </managed-bean>
```

The name of each property follows JavaBean naming conventions and is expected to match properties on the associated JavaBean class that is provided in the `<managed-bean>` element. You'll notice that all of the properties in this example are initialized to a String value (via the `<value>` element).

You don't need to declare every property on a managed bean for it to be accessible at runtime. You only need to declare each property that should be initialized before use or that may be used by tools.

The <map-entries> Element

For a managed property of type `java.util.Map`, this element allows you to initialize it with a set of key value pairs. A summary of each possible child element is provided in Table 4.11.

Table 4.11 <map-entries> Child Elements

CHILD ELEMENT	MULTIPLICITY	DESCRIPTION
key-class	zero or one (optional)	Defines the fully qualified class name to which each "key" element in a set of "map-entry" elements will be converted to; if omitted, java.lang.String is assumed.
value-class	zero or one (optional)	Defines the fully qualified class name to which each "value" element will be converted to, prior to adding it to the "values" list for a managed property that is a Collection or Array; if omitted, java.lang.String is assumed.
map-entry	zero or more	A key-value pair that will be used to initialize a managed property of type java.util.Map.

In addition to initializing a property to a single value or object, you may also initialize a property to a map of values. For example, we could choose to represent options and their prices for the SUV in a map.

```
<managed-bean>
  ...
  <managed-property>
    ...
    <map-entries>
      <value-class>java.math.BigDecimal</key-class>
      <map-entry>
        <key>Sun Roof</key>
        <value>1000.00</value>
      </map-entry>
      <map-entry>
        <key>Cruise Control</key>
        <value>500.00</value>
      </map-entry>
      <map-entry>
        <key>Keyless Entry</key>
        <value>1000.00</value>
      </map-entry>
      ...
    </map-entries>
  </managed-property>
</map-entries>
```

We didn't define a value class, so it will default to a type of String. We specified the class for all values so that they will automatically be converted to a type of `java.math.BigDecimal`. You must be sure that your values (and

Table 4.12 <map-entry> Child Elements

CHILD ELEMENT	MULTIPLICITY	DESCRIPTION
key	exactly one	Provides the String representation of the key.
null-value or value	exactly one	Provides the value associated with the key as a value of null (null-value) or a literal value.

keys if a key class is specified) can be converted to the specified class. See the *JavaServer Pages 2.0 Specification* for more information on conversion rules.

The <map-entry> Element

This element represents a single key-value pair that will be used to initialize its parent managed property of type `java.util.Map`. We looked at an example of this in the previous section. A summary of each possible child element is provided in Table 4.12.

The <list-entries> Element

This element represents a number of elements that will be used to initialize a managed property that is either a List or an array. A summary of each possible child element is provided in Table 4.13.

Similarly to the `<map-entries>` element, you may use the `<values>` element to define a compound property made up of a List or an array. For example, we could choose to represent all of the state codes in a collection.

Table 4.13 <list-entries> Child Elements

CHILD ELEMENT	MULTIPLICITY	DESCRIPTION
value-class	zero or one (optional)	For a managed property of type List, you may optionally specify a fully qualified type that each element will be converted to before being added to the List. This is very useful for Lists that require all elements to have the same type.
null-value or value	zero or more	This provides the value, which may be either null (null-value) or a literal value.

```
<managed-bean>
  ...
  <managed-property>
    ...
    <list-entries>
      <value-class>java.lang.String</value-class>
      <value>AL</value>
      <value>AK</value>
      <value>AZ</value>
      ...
    </list-entries>
  </managed-property>
</managed-bean>
```

The <navigation-rule> Element

This element defines one decision point in the flow of your application's user interface. The navigation rule elements you define will be used by the default `NavigationHandler` of your JSF implementation (or the one you optionally replace it with using the application element) to determine next steps in your workflow. A summary of each possible child element is provided in Table 4.14.

Table 4.14 <navigation-rule> Child Elements

CHILD ELEMENT	MULTIPLICITY	DESCRIPTION
description	zero to many	A textual description of the navigation rule.
display-name	zero to many	A short, descriptive name of the navigation rule for display in JSF tools.
icon	zero to many	Small and large icons for representing the navigation rule in JSF tools.
from-view-id	zero or one (optional)	Defines the component tree identifier for which the navigation rule applies; if no identifier is supplied, then the navigation rule will apply to all component trees.
navigation-case	zero to many	Defines one possible outcome for the navigation rule.

The <navigation-rule> element is used to define either an outcome that applies to all pages in the application or one that applies specifically when coming from a particular page. The code in Listing 4.2 provides the application flow for Car Demo, a piece of which is repeated here.

```
<navigation-rule>
  <from-view-id>/chooseLocale.jsp</from-view-id>
  <navigation-case>
    <description>
      Any action on chooseLocale should cause navigation to
      storeFront.jsp.
    </description>
    <to-view-id>/storeFront.jsp</to-view-id>
  </navigation-case>
</navigation-rule>

<navigation-rule>
  <from-view-id>/storeFront.jsp</from-view-id>
  <navigation-case>
    <description>
      Any action that returns "carDetail" on storeFront.jsp should
      cause navigation to carDetail.jsp.
    </description>
    <from-outcome>carDetail</from-outcome>
    <to-view-id>/carDetail.jsp</to-view-id>
  </navigation-case>
</navigation-rule>

<navigation-rule>
  <from-view-id>/carDetail.jsp</from-view-id>
  <navigation-case>
    <description>
      Any action that returns "confirmChoices" on carDetail.jsp should
      cause navigation to confirmChoices.jsp.
    </description>
    <from-outcome>confirmChoices</from-outcome>
    <to-view-id>/confirmChoices.jsp</to-view-id>
  </navigation-case>
</navigation-rule>

<navigation-rule>
  <from-view-id>/confirmChoices.jsp</from-view-id>
  <navigation-case>
    <description>
      Any action that returns "carDetail" on confirmChoices.jsp should
      cause navigation to carDetail.jsp.
    </description>
```

```
    <from-outcome>carDetail</from-outcome>
    <to-view-id>/carDetail.jsp</to-view-id>
  </navigation-case>
</navigation-rule>

<navigation-rule>
  <from-view-id>/confirmChoices.jsp</from-view-id>
  <navigation-case>
    <description>
      Any action that returns "customerInfo" on confirmChoices.jsp
      should cause navigation to customerInfo.jsp.
    </description>
    <from-outcome>customerInfo</from-outcome>
    <to-view-id>/customerInfo.jsp</to-view-id>
  </navigation-case>
</navigation-rule>

<navigation-rule>
  <from-view-id>/customerInfo.jsp</from-view-id>
  <navigation-case>
    <description>
      Any action that returns "finish" on customerInfo.jsp should
      cause navigation to finish.jsp.
    </description>
    <from-outcome>finish</from-outcome>
    <to-view-id>/finish.jsp</to-view-id>
  </navigation-case>
</navigation-rule>
```

Here, we have several rules. The first one specifies, via the `<from-tree-id>` tag, that the Web client must currently be viewing the `chooseLocale.jsp` page for the nested `<navigation-case>` elements to be evaluated. The other rules are specified in a similar manner. If you do not specify which page (or component tree) must currently be viewed, it will be evaluated for all pages when an action is performed by the Web client.

It is possible for each rule to have several cases that must be evaluated. For example, it is not uncommon to see a `failure` and `success` case in the same rule.

The <navigation-case> Element

This element provides one possible outcome for a navigation rule and specifies what component tree should be displayed next, based on that outcome. A summary of each possible child element is provided in Table 4.15.

Table 4.15 <navigation-case> Child Elements

CHILD ELEMENT	MULTIPLICITY	DESCRIPTION
description	zero to many	A textual description of the navigation case.
display-name	zero to many	A short, descriptive name of the navigation case for display in JSF tools.
icon	zero to many	Small and large icons for representing the navigation case in JSF tools.
from-action	zero or one (optional)	A value reference expression that must be executed for this case to apply; this is usually a button click or some other UI component action that the user initiates.
from-outcome	zero or one (optional)	Defines a logical outcome such as "success" or "failure" that is returned from an action.
to-view-id	exactly one	Defines the next component tree that should be displayed if this case is matched and executed.
redirect	zero or one (optional)	Indicates that navigation to the specified to-view-id should be accomplished by performing an HTTP redirect rather than through the usual JSF ViewHandler mechanism.

You'll see that each `<navigation-case>` element in our example specifies an outcome via the `<from-outcome>` element. In this case, the `UICommand` component that is executed by the Web client provides an explicit outcome via its `action` attribute (if used in a JSP). Let's take a look at the code for the `customerInfo.jsp` page's finish button.

```
<h:commandButton value="#{bundle.finishButton}" action="finish" />
```

The `action` attribute explicitly declares an outcome of `finish` when the finish button is pressed. The `NavigationHandler` will then make the next page `thanks.jsp` based on the success case in our `customerInfo.jsp` rule.

The outcome does not have to be explicitly declared like this. Let's take a look at another `UICommand` in the `carDetail.jsp` page.

```
<h:commandButton action="#{carstore.buyCurrentCar}"
                 value="#{bundle.buy}" />
```

In this case, the `NavigationHandler` will call the `buyCurrentCar()` method of the `CarStore` bean. The action handler is expected to return a String result (such as `success` or `failure`). The nice thing about this approach is that the result can be dynamically determined by the action handler at run time (usually based on current form data). Once the appropriate result is returned by the action handler, the navigation rules are consulted as before to determine the next page. In this case the logical result `confirmChoices` is returned, which results in the `confirmChoices.jsp` page being displayed.

The <referenced-bean> Element

This element provides a reference to a Java object outside of your particular application that is expected to exist at run time in scope. It is not used by the JSF implementation at run time but is intended instead for tools to help you design your user interfaces. A summary of each possible child element is provided in Table 4.16.

An example of this element is a data source that a tool would use to help you set up an input form page for collecting data.

Table 4.16 <referenced-bean> Child Elements

CHILD ELEMENT	MULTIPLICITY	DESCRIPTION
Description	zero to many	A textual description of the referenced bean.
Display-name	zero to many	A short, descriptive name of the referenced bean for display in JSF tools.
Icon	zero to many	Small and large icons for representing the referenced bean in JSF tools.
referenced-bean-name	exactly one	Represents the attribute name under which the referenced bean is expected to be located in one of the scopes.
referenced-bean-class	exactly one	Represents the fully qualified class name of the Java class or interface implemented by the corresponding referenced bean.

```
<referenced-bean>
  <description>
    A JDBC data source that supplies our Customer information will be
    initialized and made available in some scope for the Car Demo
    application when it is actually run. This information is only used
    by tools.
  </description>
  <referenced-bean-name>customerDataSource</referenced-bean-name>
  <referenced-bean-class>javax.sql.DataSource</referenced-bean-class>
</referenced-bean>
```

The <render-kit> Element

This element allows you to declare a `RenderKit` other than the default provided by your JSF implementation, while registering it under a unique identifier. If you do not supply an identifier, each nested `Renderer` that you declare will be added to the default `RenderKit`. A summary of each possible child element is provided in Table 4.17.

Each JSF implementation is required to provide a default HTML `RenderKit`. If you have created your own custom UI components or wish to provide support for a presentation technology other than HTML in JSPs, then you will need to register a `RenderKit` and associated Renderers with your application. The Car Demo application does the former by including and using a JAR file containing a number of custom UI components. The configuration information for these components is provided in Listing 4.3 and summarized here.

Table 4.17 <render-kit> Child Elements

CHILD ELEMENT	MULTIPLICITY	DESCRIPTION
description	zero to many	A textual description of the RenderKit.
display-name	zero to many	A short, descriptive name of the RenderKit for display in JSF tools.
icon	zero to many	Small and large icons for representing the RenderKit in JSF tools.
render-kit-id	zero or one (optional)	Represents a unique identifier for the RenderKit.
render-kit-class	zero or one (optional)	Represents the fully qualified class name of a concrete RenderKit implementation class.
Renderer	zero to many	A Renderer supplied by the RenderKit.

```
<render-kit>
  ...
  <renderer>
    <renderer-type>MenuBar</renderer-type>
    <renderer-class>
      components.renderkit.MenuBarRenderer
    </renderer-class>
  </renderer>
  ...
</render-kit>
```

Since no RenderKit identifier is provided, the JSF implementation will register the associated Renderers with the default HTML RenderKit. This is the desired result. If you wish to provide the associated Renderers in a separate RenderKit, then you would include <render-kit-class> and <render-kit-id> elements that specify the RenderKit implementation class and a unique identifier for it.

The <renderer> Element

This element registers a Renderer with its parent RenderKit. Each Renderer must be associated with a RenderKit. A summary of each possible child element is provided in Table 4.18.

Table 4.18 <renderer> Child Elements

CHILD ELEMENT	MULTIPLICITY	DESCRIPTION
description	zero to many	A textual description of the Renderer.
display-name	zero to many	A short, descriptive name of the Renderer for display in JSF tools.
icon	zero to many	Small and large icons for representing the Renderer in JSF tools.
renderer-type	exactly one	Represents a unique identifier for the Renderer.
renderer-class	exactly one	Represents the fully qualified class name of a concrete Renderer implementation class.
attribute	zero to many	Defines a generic attribute for the Renderer.
supported-component-type	zero to many	Registers support for rendering a UI component by its type identifier.

(continued)

Table 4.18 *(continued)*

CHILD ELEMENT	MULTIPLICITY	DESCRIPTION
supported-component-class	zero to many	Registers support for rendering a UI component by its implementation class name.
renderer-extension	zero or many	Provides a place for content spe-cific to a particular JSF implemen-tation.

The example used for the `<render-kit>` element shows the `MenuBar Renderer`. It is given a unique render type and the associated `Renderer` implementation class. If you look at the associated `MenuBarTag` implementation, you'll see that it references its respective `Renderer` by the type assigned to it in the configuration file.

See Chapter 2 and Chapter 10, "Custom JSF Components," for more detailed information about creating and configuring RenderKits and their associated Renderers.

The <validator> Element

This element allows you to declare each of the custom Validators that are used in your application. As with UI components and Converters, you will also declare the Validator's available attributes and properties. A summary of each possible child element is provided in Table 4.19.

Table 4.19 <validator> Child Elements

CHILD ELEMENT	MULTIPLICITY	DESCRIPTION
description	zero to many	A textual description of the Validator.
display-name	zero to many	A short, descriptive name of the Validator for display in JSF tools.
icon	zero to many	Small and large icons for representing the Validator in JSF tools.
Validator-id	exactly one	Represents the identifier under which the Validator will be registered; this identifier must be unique within your application.
Validator-class	exactly one	Defines the fully qualified type of the Validator, which must be an implementation of Validator.

Table 4.19 *(continued)*

CHILD ELEMENT	MULTIPLICITY	DESCRIPTION
Attribute	zero to many	Defines a generic attribute for the Validator.
Property	zero to many	Defines a generic JavaBean property on the Validator.

The FormatValidator in Listing 4.2 is registered in the Car Demo application with an identifier of FormatValidator.

```
<validator>
  <description>
      Registers the concrete Validator implementation,
      carstore. FormatValidator with the validator
      identifier, FormatValidator.
  </description>
  <validator-id>FormatValidator</validator-id>
  <validator-class>carstore.FormatValidator</validator-class>
  <attribute>
    <description>
      List of format patterns separated by '|'.  The validator
      compares these patterns against the data entered in a
      component that has this validator registered on it.
    </description>
    <attribute-name>formatPatterns</attribute-name>
    <attribute-class>java.lang.String</attribute-class>
  </attribute>
</validator>
```

This makes the Validator available to the customerInfo.jsp page, which uses it to ensure the proper format of credit card numbers and zip codes.

```
<h:outputText value="#{bundle.zipLabel}" />
  <h:inputText id="zip" value="#{customer.zip}" size="10"
             required="true">
    <cs:formatValidator formatPatterns="99999|99999-9999|### ###"/>
  </h:inputText>
  <h:message styleClass="validationMessage" for="zip"/>
```

The Validator is assigned in the above example by using the <format Validator> custom tag associated with the FormatValidator. See Chapter 8 for more information about creating and configuring Validator components.

Tool Support for JSF Configurations

Tools will play a large part in the creation of JSF applications. Whether they help you design your GUI screens/pages (perhaps via drag-and-drop interfaces), create and manage custom components, configure your applications, or provide a host of other useful functions, these tools will make developing JSF applications much easier. The creators of the JSF specification recognize this and have made an effort to accommodate tool support wherever possible. The JSF configuration file provides a number of tags that give display names, descriptions, icons, and properties to JSF components and associated elements in direct support of tools.

You can expect a range of tools in support of JSF from all of the major Java IDE companies as well as some innovative supporting technologies from others. Some of these same companies will also provide their own JSF implementations for you to use, and their associated tools may be customized for these specific implementations.

Our purpose in this chapter is to provide an understanding of how a JSF application is properly configured. There is already at least one tool available to help you deal with JSF configuration files, and it is available for free at the following Web address:

```
http://www.jamesholmes.com/JavaServerFaces/console/
```

The Faces Console fully supports the creation and modification of JSF configuration files and plugs into many widely used Java IDEs. Those of you familiar with the popular Struts Console tool will feel right at home with this one. The Car Demo configuration file is shown with Faces Console in Figure 4.5.

There will likely be more visual, drag-and-drop-style tools in the near future as well as tools that also help you package and deploy your applications, but Faces Console is a free and easy way to deal with the complexities of JSF configuration files.

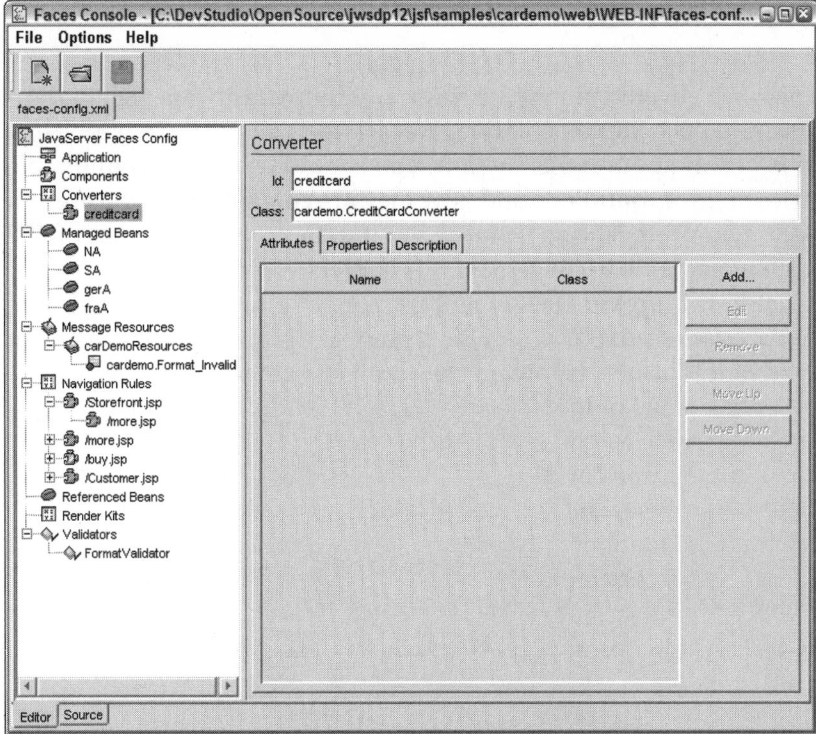

Figure 4.5 Car Demo sample application in Faces Console.

Building the Sample JSF Application

Most JSF applications you create will be built and deployed using Ant. It is available separately from the *JSF Reference Implementation* at the following Web address:

```
http://ant.apache.org/
```

The Ant script for the Car Demo sample application is provided with the *JSF Reference Implementation*. It defines a number of targets, one of which actually packages up the application in a WAR that is ready to deploy. You can actually use this script and its associated properties file as a starting point for your own JSF Web applications.

Summary

In this chapter, we covered setting up your environment to run JSF applications with the reference implementation. We also took a brief look at each element in the JSF configuration file. By now, you should be getting comfortable with the basics of JSF applications and how they are configured. If you are still unclear about some things, don't worry. We'll explore each element of JSF again in much more detail in the remaining chapters.

Now we get to roll up our sleeves and examine the nitty-gritty process of creating JSF applications. We'll work with a number of fun examples and even cover some advanced concepts toward the end! Let's get started . . . .

CHAPTER

5

JSP Integration in JSF

While JSPs are not the only way to build user interfaces with JSF, they will probably be the most common way for quite some time. So if you are going to build JSF applications, it is important that you understand the integration between JSF and JSP. It is also very important that you know how to build applications with JSPs. If you are unfamiliar with JSP development, I suggest you pick up a good book on the subject (the references section has a couple of recommendations).

JSF is integrated with JSPs through TagLibs. JSF provides a rich set of tags that link the server-side component model of JSF to the client-side model (typically HTML, but others like WML, XML, and JavaScript/HTML can easily be imagined and implemented). With the integration tags, you can build a large and interesting component tree that is rendered into the client model and decoded from subsequent requests.

Overview

One of the major goals of the JSF specification team was to make sure that JSF was a natural fit with the current knowledge base of JSP developers. In this chapter, we will see just how well they succeeded in that goal.

The average JSP programmer will be able to pick up JSF very quickly because of the easy integration that has been built with the JSP tags that we will be going over in this chapter. About the only thing that the average JSP programmer will have to unlearn is putting Java code into his or her pages, because that is, thankfully, no longer needed with JSF application development.

Quick JSF/JSP Integration Example

Let's get started with a quick example of how the JSF integration works with JSPs. JSF provides tag libraries that give you complete control over the component tree of your application. There are two libraries. The first is called the core library and has tags for configuring the components, managing the event listeners, validating user input, and other functions. The second tag library has tags for attaching HTML Renderers to the components. There is one tag for each combination of Renderer and component. For example, the UIInput tag can be rendered as a simple text field or secret field (the content is not displayed, like a password). For a text field, the tag is named `inputText`, for a secret field the name is `inputSecret`. When you use `inputSecret` you are specifying that you want to use the UIInput component with a Renderer that creates fields that are not visible (i.e., an input field in HTML with type password). The tag attached to `inputSecret` (you can see the class responsible for this in the .tld file for the library) is then responsible for all the JSF API calls that are needed to make sure that happens. The tree structure of the component tree is conveyed by the structure of the document; if you place a component tag within the tag of another component a parent-child relationship is set up between the two components. Listing 5.1 below shows a typical JSF user interface built with a JSP.

```
<%@ taglib uri="http://java.sun.com/jsf/html" prefix="h" %>
<%@ taglib uri="http://java.sun.com/jsf/core" prefix="f" %>
<html>
  <head>
    <meta HTTP-EQUIV="Content-Type"
                                   CONTENT="text/html;CHARSET=iso-8859-1">
    <title>Small JSF Example</title>
  </head>
  <body>
    <f:view>
      <h:form id="simpleForm">
        <h:outputText id="favoriteLabel"
                      value="Enter Your Favorite Value:"/>
        <h:inputText id="favoriteValue" value="#{simple.longValue}">
            <f:validateLongrange maximum="20" minimum="0"/>
        </h:inputText>
```

Listing 5.1 Example of JSF – JSP integration.

```
        <p/>
        <h:commandButton id="submit" value="#{simple.label}"

action="#{simple.simpleActionMethod}"/>
      </h:form>
    </f:view>
  </body>
</html>
```

Listing 5.1 *(continued)*

In this page, you can see several of the concepts of the integration illustrated. First, you see one of the core tags, `view`. You will see more about this tag later in the chapter. You can also see several components being configured with the `form`, `outputText`, `inputText`, and `commandButton` tags. Not only do these tags build the components, but they also set up the tree based on their relative positioning within the page. Since the `outputText`, `inputText`, and `commandButton` tags are within the `form` tag, they are added to the form's list of children.

In order to use the JSF tags, you must import the two TagLibs. This is done with the two import statements repeated here from Listing 5.1 for clarity.

```
<%@ taglib prefix="h" uri="http://java.sun.com/jsf/html" %>
<%@ taglib prefix="f" uri="http://java.sun.com/jsf/core" %>
```

These statements declare the TagLibs needed to integrate with JSF. The core library is declared with *f* as the prefix, and the HTML library is declared with *h* as its prefix. It is not required that you use these two prefixes, but it is recommended. You will always have to use the core library (`view` is required for all JSF pages). The HTML library provides the link between the standard HTML RenderKit and the JSP runtime. The prefix used for these tags is not mandatory, but it is recommended in the specification that we all stick with *h* and *f* for the HTML and core libraries, respectively. This will make it more likely that we will be able to read each other's code.

The next block of code to look at in this JSP is just a standard HTML title declaration. The code is repeated here from Listing 5.1 for clarity.

```
<html>
  <head>
    <meta HTTP-EQUIV="Content-Type"
          CONTENT="text/html;CHARSET=iso-8859-1">
    <title>Small JSF Example</title>
  </head>
  <body>
```

Keep in mind that even though we are integrating this JSP with JSF, it is still just a standard JSP. The only JSF-specific code in this JSP is the JSF tags, and they do nothing more than take advantage of the TagLib extension mechanism built into JSPs. Therefore, almost anything that you might do in a non-JSF JSP will work as expected. The reason we say almost is that there are a few small caveats to the way other tags interact with JSF. First, you must put identifiers on any components that are inside tags that conditionally render their children (like the JSTLs c:if tag). Second, you must not put JSF tags inside non-JSF tags that iterate over their content (like the JSTL c:forEach tag). Third, programmatically added UIComponents must be nested inside components that render their children. Finally, putting JSP template text and/or other tags inside a UIComponent tag that renders its children is not acceptable either.

The next line of code from Listing 5.1 is `view`. This tag provides a place for the JSF implementation to save the state of the component tree before returning the response to the user. This is why you are required to put all JSF related tags within the `view` tag. The `view` tag does not usually contribute to the response unless you have configured your JSF application to store the state in the response. If you have, the `view` tag will usually write the state (that is, the component tree) into the response as a hidden form field. However, the particular way the state is stored is implementation-dependent.

The next section of JSP code from Listing 5.1 is a group of components that provide the visible part of the user interface being built. The code is repeated here for quick reference.

```
<h:form id="simpleForm">
  <h:outputText id="favoriteLabel"
                value="Enter Your Favorite Value:"/>
  <h:inputText id="favoriteValue" value="#{simple.longValue}">
    <f:validateLongrange maximum="20" minimum="0"/>
  </h:inputText>
  <p/>
  <h:commandButton id="submit" value="#{simple.label}"
                   action="#{simple.simpleActionMethod}"/>
</h:form>
```

The first tag, `form`, creates an HTML form. The next tag, `outputText`, is simply a means to output any kind of text into the HTML that is sent back to the browser. The `inputText` element is rendered as an HTML input element typed as text, which is a typical text file that can be used by the user to input strings. Finally, `commandButton` creates another HTML input element with the *submit* type. This page is rendered in a browser in Figure 5.1.

This example builds a component tree that contains one form with three UIComponents as children. Figure 5.2 illustrates the object graph created by this JSP.

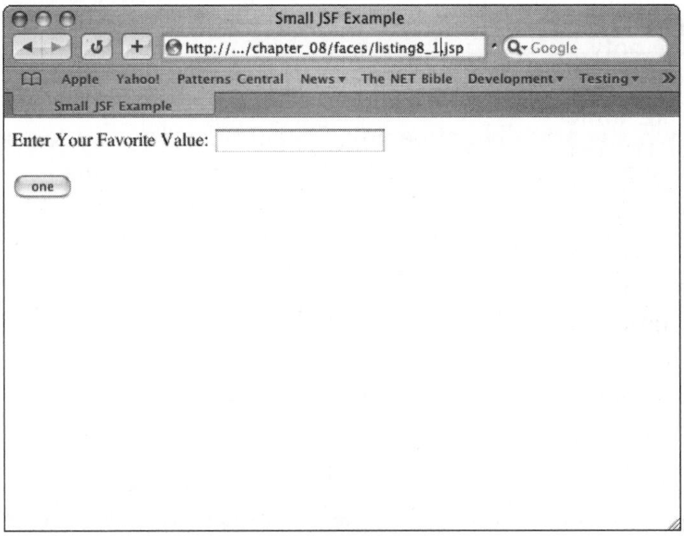

Figure 5.1 Example page rendered.

Recall that this graph is achieved because of the nesting of the tags in the JSP page. The input, output, and button tags are nested inside the form tag so the components that these three tags represent become children of the form component. With the core tag library, you can also add event and change listeners to any component as well as add Validators. We will go into detail on this topic later in this chapter.Keep in mind that this JSP is converted into a servlet by the Web container and the generated servlet simply invokes the JSF API. For example, during the first request for this page, during the *Render Response* phase, the tags in this page will create four UIComponents, a UIForm with the ID *simpleForm*, a UIOutput with ID *favoriteLabel*, a UIInput with the ID *favoriteValue*, and finally a UICommand with the ID *submit*. Each of these components is then stored (by the doEndTag method on the `view` tag) for use in subsequent requests for this page. During the *Restore View* phase, it is these components that will be reconstituted into the tree and will then be carried through the rest of the phases. We will see more about the *Render Response* phase in the next section.

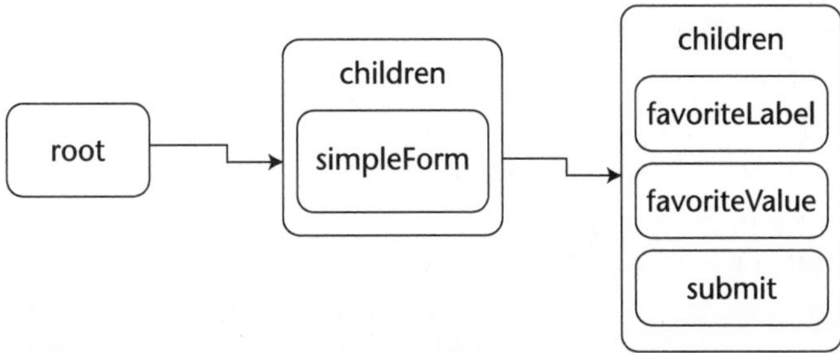

Figure 5.2 Example UIComponent tree.

JSP Integration and the Render Response Phase

Now that we have seen an example of how the JSF/JSP integration works, let's get into the detail of what is actually happening. Specifically, we want to go into more depth about what happens with the JSP integration during the *Render Response* phase (where the HTML is generated) of the request life cycle. There are two types of requests to consider: new JSF requests and a subsequent request that continues a JSF session. Of course, non-JSF requests could also happen, but this type of request does not involve JSF, so there is no need to cover it here.

New JSF Requests

Any request without preexisting state resident on the server can be considered a new request. This preexisting state is called the component tree (we cover the component tree in Chapter 6, "UI Components"), and it is identified by the view ID, which is derived from the request URI. When a request is received, JSF first looks to see if there is an existing tree; if one is not found, a new one is created. The tree is initialized with the default RenderKit and an implementation-dependent root component that will become the parent of any components on the page.

Before we go into any more detail, let's consider a simple example of an application. This application will perform temperature conversion from degrees Fahrenheit to degrees Celsius. We focus on the JSP integration points. The application will perform the conversion when the user submits the form. Figure 5.3 shows the example rendered in a Web browser.

> **THE ROOT UICOMPONENT**
>
> **The root component is used as an easy-to-find (or well-known) entry point into the tree. You can always get at the root (and thus the rest of the components) in the tree by asking the context for it with the `getRoot` method. You can set up the parent-child relationship between the components with the placement of your tags. Children are added to the root component in your JSP by adding JSF tags as direct children of the `view` tag.**

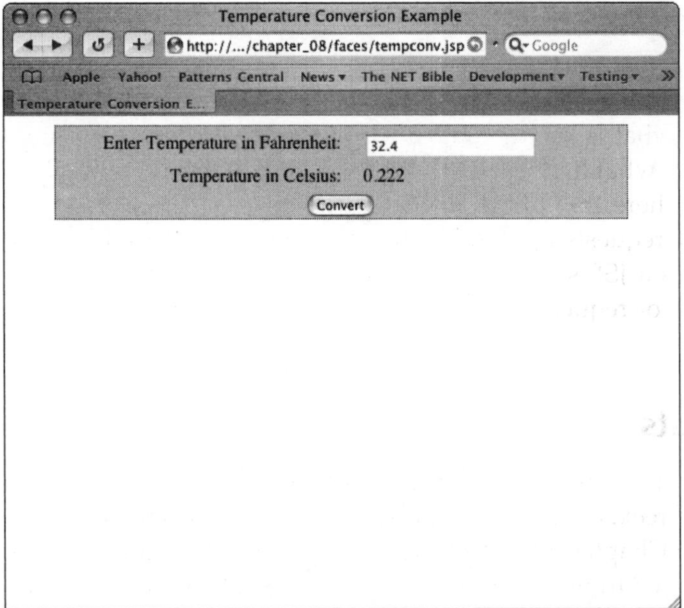

Figure 5.3 Temperature Conversion Sample Page.

This is a very simple form to allow the user to type in the degrees Fahrenheit, submit the form, and get back the conversion into degrees Celsius. Listing 5.2 shows the JSP code for the example.

```
<%@ taglib uri="http://java.sun.com/jsf/html" prefix="h" %>
<%@ taglib uri="http://java.sun.com/jsf/core" prefix="f" %>
<html>
  <head>
    <meta HTTP-EQUIV="Content-Type"
         CONTENT="text/html;CHARSET=iso-8859-1">
    <title>Temperature Conversion Example</title>
    <style type="text/css">
      .red {color:red;}
      .black {color:black;}
      div.row {
        clear: both;
        padding-top: 5px;
        text-align: center;
      }
      .label {
        float: left;
        width: 250px;
        text-align: right;
      }
      .formElement {
```

Listing 5.2 Temperature conversion JSP. *(continued)*

```
        float: right;
        width: 230px;
        text-align: left;
      }
      .form {
        width: 500px;
        background-color: #ccc;
        border: 1px dotted #333;
        padding: 0px;
        margin: 0px auto
      }
    </style>
  </head>
  <body>
    <f:view>
      <h:form>
        <div class="row">
          <h:outputText id="fahrenheitLabel" styleClass="label"
                        value="Enter Temperature in Fahrenheit:"/>
          <span class="formElement">
            <h:inputText id="temperature"
                         value="#{tc.fahrenheitTemp}">
              <f:validateDoublerange minimum="-100.0" maximum="100.0"/>
              <f:valuechangeListener
                      type="tempconv.page.TCChangedListener"/>
            </h:inputText>
          </span>
        </div>
        <div class="row">
          <h:outputText id="celsiusLabel" styleClass="label"
                        value="Temperature in Celsius:"/>
          <span class="formElement">
          <h:outputText id="celsiusValue"
                        value="#{tc.celsiusTemp}">
            <f:convertNumber maxFractionDigits="3" type="number"/>
          </h:outputText>
          </span>
        </div>
        <div class="row">
          <h:commandButton value="Convert"
                           action="#{tc.convert}">
          </h:commandButton>
        </div>
      </h:form>
    </f:view>
  </body>
</html>
```

Listing 5.2 *(continued)*

At the top of Listing 5.2, you can see the import of the JSF TagLibs. As discussed earlier, JSF pages must import at least the core JSF tag libraries (so that the page will have access to `f:view`). The standard HTML tag library is also imported, and it contains the bulk of the JSP integration tags. Next is some simple template text that is handled in the typical manner by the Web container. Following that is the `f:view` tag. The rest of the tags on this page create the components that make up the page.

Now that you have had an overview of the example, let's look at how the tags interact during the *Render Response* phase of the first request for this page. Since this is just a JSP page, all the normal JSP activities happen; the JSP is turned into a servlet, and template text is copied directly from the JSP into a servlet that just writes the strings directly into the output stream. Tags are invoked as normal. The JSF tags are interesting only because they are invoking the JSF APIs (application programming interfaces); otherwise, they are just normal tags.

When the UIComponentTag receives the `doStartTag` method, any attributes of the tag are used to set attribute values on the component. For example, in the temperature conversion example shown in Listing 5.2, consider the `h:inputText` tag with the ID `temperature`. Here is the code again for reference:

```
<h:inputText id="temperature"
             value="#{tc.fahrenheitTemp}">
  <f:validateDoublerange minimum="-100.0" maximum="100.0"/>
  <f:valuechangeListener
                type="tempconv.page.TCChangedListener"/>
</h:inputText>
```

This tag sets the `id` (the component identifier), the `styleClass` and the `value` of the underlying UIInput component. What the tag does is to call `setAttribute(String name, Object value)` for each attribute specified in the JSP for the tag. In other words, you can set any of the attributes for `h:inputNumber` and that attribute will be translated into a call to `setAttribute(String name, Object value)` on the UIInput component by the tag. Some of the attributes are used by the component and some are used by the Renderer.

An important thing to keep in mind with respect to the tags setting values on the components is that the tag will not replace a value that has previously been set on the component. You can think of this as being like the default argument when getting a system property. If the property was specified, then it is returned; otherwise, the default that was provided will be returned (see the javadoc for System.getProperty(String, String) for more info). The values specified in a tag are used only if there is no other value set on the component. For example, since we are currently considering a new request there will be no values set on the component, so all the attributes specified in the tag will be set on the component. The next time this page is invoked, though, all the values will be set, so the tag will not reset any of the values. Consider also that in event processing or other application-specific logic, you might change some attribute of a component. The tag will not replace the value that you set when the *Render Response* phase is invoked. You will see more about this in the next section on processing of subsequent requests.

The next section of code from Listing 5.2 is the addition of an event listener for the UIInput component. The code is repeated here for quick reference.

```
<h:inputText id="temperature"
             value="#{tc.fahrenheitTemp}">
  <f:validateDoublerange minimum="-100.0" maximum="100.0"/>
  <f:valuechangeListener
                type="tempconv.page.TCChangedListener"/>
</h:inputText>
```

The addition happens as a result of the `f:valuechangeListener` tag. This event listener is fired if the value in the field changes on subsequent requests. The *Render Response* phase does not post any events, so this component will have to wait until the next request to post events. Since it's a new request there is no user input to consider anyway.

Finally, we will look at the specification of the UICommand from Listing 5.2. The code is repeated here for clarity.

```
<div class="row">
  <h:commandButton value="Convert"
                   action="#{tc.convert}">
  </h:commandButton>
</div>
```

This code is setting up the UICommand to invoke the `convert()` method when the button is clicked. For more detail on the UICommand and its action method reference, see Chapter 6.

Finally, the closing `view` tag is reached. The usual JSP container action happens, which is to call the `doEnd` tag method. This in turn causes the encoding process to navigate through the entire component tree. Typically, the components delegate to their Renderers to do the actual HTML generation but that step is implementation-dependent. After the components have rendered themselves, the JSP engine (Web container) takes over again and returns the response to the browser. Figure 5.4 is a conceptual sequence diagram showing the high-level steps to the *Render Response* phase and how they are accomplished via the JSP integration.

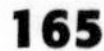

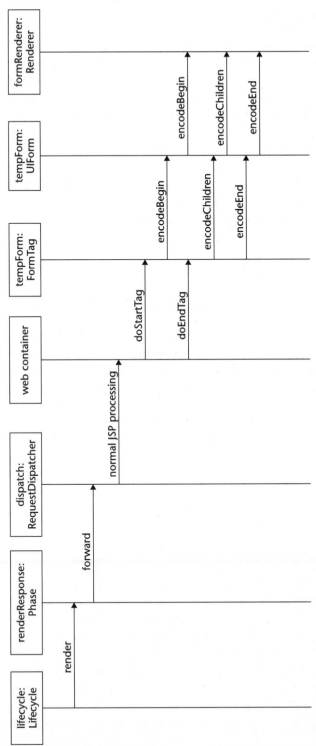

Figure 5.4 Sequence diagram for Render Response phase.

Subsequent JSF Requests

After the initial request is processed for the page, the tree is built and is ready to be reconstituted with further requests. When the second request arrives, the full life cycle is invoked since the components are active and in memory (the objects get into memory as a result of the Restore View phase). The JSP integration is again invoked when the life cycle proceeds to the *Render Response* phase.

The important difference to keep in mind here is that the tags will find existing components instead of creating new ones. Also, the tags will not replace any previously set value on the components they represent. For example, let's return to the temperature input component (Listing 5.2) that we discussed in the previous section. Here again is the code for quick reference.

```
<h:inputText id="temperature"
              value="#{tc.fahrenheitTemp}">
  <f:validateDoublerange minimum="-100.0" maximum="100.0"/>
  <f:valuechangeListener
                 type="tempconv.page.TCChangedListener"/>
</h:inputText>
```

With the ID `temperature` the tag finds the component it represents. Whereas during the first request the tag created the component and set the values for `componentId`, `styleClass` and `value` according to the values specified in the JSP, on subsequent requests the tag will not set the values if they are already set. The conditional setting of values gives you flexibility in the way that your application interacts with the components. For example, let's slightly modify the code above to specify a CSS (Cascading Style Sheet) class for the component. The result is:

```
<h:inputText id="temperature" styleClass="black"
              value="#{tc.fahrenheitTemp}">
```

In this code snippet, the `styleClass` specifies the CSS class to use for the input element that will eventually be generated into the resulting output stream. Let's assume that if the user puts a temperature in that is less than zero, the text should be red, but if the number is greater than zero, then the text should be black. In order to do that the ValueChange event listener can look at the number and set the styleClass to red if the value is less than zero. When this tag is processed during the *Render Response* phase, the tag will not change the `styleClass` attribute on the UIInput component, since it is already set. The processing of tag attributes is a lot like the typical processing of default values: If the component does not have a value, then set the value from the tag; otherwise, leave the value unchanged. It is important to keep this attribute processing in mind as you write your application code. If any of your code sets the value of an attribute, it must also change it back and not rely on the JSP processing to do that. The code for the event listener that changes the value is shown in Listing 5.3.

```
public class TCChangedListener implements ValueChangeListener {

  public TCChangedListener() {
    super();
  }

  public void processValueChange(ValueChangeEvent event)
    throws AbortProcessingException {
    UIComponent comp = event.getComponent();
    Object value = event.getNewValue();
    if (null != value) {
      float curVal = ((Number) value).floatValue();
      Map values = comp.getAttributes();
      if (curVal < 0) {
        values.put("styleClass", "red");
      } else {
        values.put("styleClass", "black");
      }
    }
}
```

Listing 5.3 Value-change event listener.

Notice that this event handler manages setting the value to red and black and does not rely on the JSP; make sure to keep that in mind as you are building your application code. Alternately, you could set the value to null, which would allow the JSP tag to reset the value back to black.

JSF – JSP Integration Example

Now that the overview of the integration is done, let's go through a slightly more sophisticated example with more than one page. In this case, we have a user registration example that will allow a user to type in his or her first and last names, requested username, and password. If the username is not already taken and the password meets the validation (that is, it's eight characters, has at least one uppercase character, and has one nonalphabetic character), the user is welcomed to the new system. Listing 5.4 shows the code for the user to register at the site.

```
<!doctype html public "-//w3c//DTD HTML 4.0 Strict//en">
<%@ taglib uri="http://java.sun.com/jsf/html" prefix="h" %>
<%@ taglib uri="http://java.sun.com/jsf/core" prefix="f" %>
<html>
  <head>
    <meta HTTP-EQUIV="Content-Type"
      CONTENT="text/html;CHARSET=iso-8859-1">
    <title>Register</title>
    <style type="text/css">
      .centered {align:center}
      .grayCentered {align:center;background-color:gray}
      .wideCentered {align:center;width:100%}
    </style>
  </head>
  <body>
    <f:view>
      <h:form>
        <h:panelGrid columns="2"
                     rowClasses="centered"
                     footerClass="centered" border="1">
          <h:outputText value="First Name:"/>
          <h:inputText value="#{regPage.user.firstName}">
            <f:validateLength maximum="20" minimum="0"/>
          </h:inputText>
          <h:outputText value="Last Name:"/>
          <h:inputText value="#{regPage.user.lastName}">
            <f:validateLength maximum="20" minimum="0"/>
          </h:inputText>
          <h:outputText value="User name:"/>
          <h:inputText value="#{regPage.user.userName}">
            <f:validateLength maximum="20" minimum="0"/>
          </h:inputText>
          <h:outputText value="Password:"/>
          <h:inputSecret value="#{regPage.user.password}">
            <f:validator validatorId="passwordValidator"/>
          </h:inputSecret>
          <f:facet name="footer">
          <h:panelGrid id="buttonGrid" columns="2"
                     columnClasses="centered" width="100%">
            <h:commandButton value="Cancel"
                         action="#{regPage.cancel}"/>
            <h:commandButton value="Save"
                         action="#{regPage.save}"/>
          </h:panelGrid>
          </f:facet>
        </h:panelGrid>
      </h:form>
```

Listing 5.4 Registration JSP.

```
    </f:view>
  </body>
</html>
```

Listing 5.4 *(continued)*

Figure 5.5 relates the output from the JSP rendered in a browser.

The bean for this page is set up in the `faces-config.xml` file as usual as a managed bean. The example starts with importing the two JSF TagLibs. As stated earlier, it is recommended by the specification that you use *h* for the HTML taglib and *f* for the core TagLib.

The next section of code in Listing 5.4 is some JSF tags. As in other examples, the first tag is `view`. Remember that this tag must always surround all JSF tags on your page in order for the *Restore View* phase to work properly on subsequent requests. The `view` tag is also responsible for setting up the root of the component tree.

The first component is the UIForm created by the h:form tag. The form Renderer automatically generates the action that is posted for this form so that you don't have to generate it yourself. The action is simply the context root plus the additional URI component from the url-pattern that you deployed in the FacesServlet under in your web.xml file, plus the tree identifier. Next is the list of components that make up the visible aspects of the user interface.

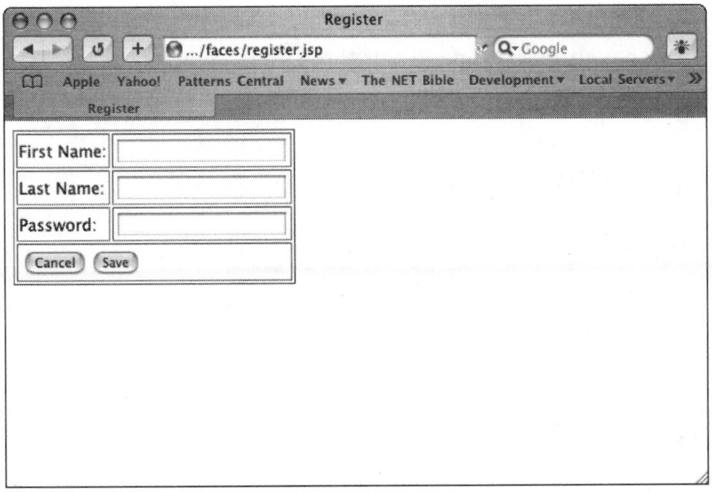

Figure 5.5 Registration page.

The `UIPanel` is used to manage the layout of the rest of the components. The children of the panel are arranged in a grid two columns wide and as many rows as needed to make room for all the child components. In other words, since the `columns` attribute is set for this panel, two components at a time will be placed into a row, then a new row will be created for the next two, until there are no more child components. The grid Renderer creates an HTML `<table>` element for the `UIPanel` component. The panel renders its children so that it can manage the layout by rendering the components inside the rows and cells of the table. Here is the code for the opening of the `panelGrid` tag from Listing 5.4 for quick reference.

```
<h:panelGrid id="registrationPanel" columns="2"
              rowClasses="centered"
              footerClass="centered" border="1">
```

The `rowClasses` attribute specifies the CSS classes to apply to each row. The Renderer will apply the value specified in this attribute to every row in the table. If you'd like to alternate colors or some other aspect of the row, you can comma-delimit the different CSS classes in this attribute. For example, if you wanted every other row to have a gray background, you could specify the value of `rowClasses` like this:

```
<h:panelGrid id="registrationPanel" columns="2"
            rowClasses="centered, grayCentered"
            footerClass="grayCentered" border="1">
```

The table will be rendered with every other row having its class set to `grayCentered`. Figure 5.6 shows the page rendered with every other row in gray.

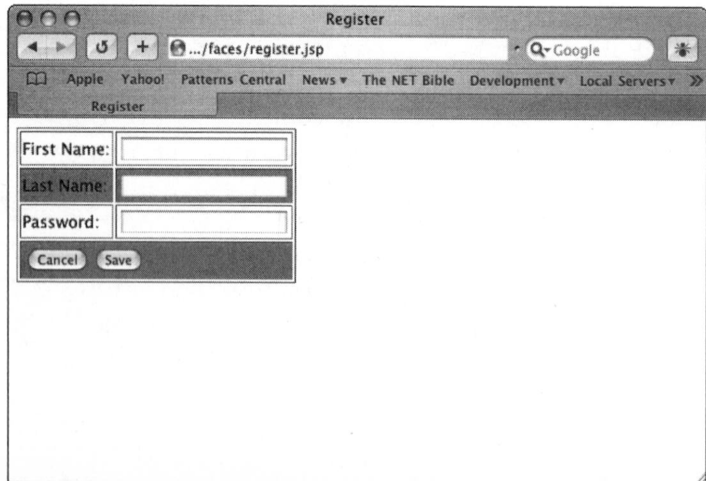

Figure 5.6 Row class example.

The next block of code from Listing 5.4 creates the UIOutput and UIInput components that allow the users to enter their information for registration. There are four UIOutput components that make up the labels and four UIInput components that make up the text fields. Let's look in detail at the password entry label and text field component pair to get a better understanding of how these tags work. Here is the code for the components:

```
<h:outputText value="Password:"/>
<h:inputSecret value="#{regPage.user.password}">
  <f:validator validatorId="passwordValidator"/>
</h:inputSecret>
```

You will see more about it in the discussion of the next component. First, we'd like to look at the `outputText` tag. As expected, this tag creates a `UIOutput` component and sets its render type to `text`. The value is set to Password:, which is written directly to the output when this component is rendered. The next component is a `UIInput` with its render type set to secret.

The `UIInput` component has its `value` set to `user.password`. It is important that you understand the `value` attribute and how it works to use the JSF/JSP integration effectively. The model reference can be thought of as a path through your objects. In this case, the root of the path is `user`, which is specified in the `faces-config.xml` file. Essentially, the object becomes visible as a local variable on this page when it is used; the managed bean mechanism will create the object if it is not already present. The mechanism works a lot like the `jsp:useBean` tag. If the bean is already present in the scope specified, then the tag will do nothing; otherwise, it will create the bean. The next part of the path is `password`. This is a property of the `user` object, and it is assumed that there is an accessor pair for that property that follows the JavaBean naming convention (that is, there is a `get/setPassword` method pair on the `user` bean). The JSF runtime will get the value used to display this component from the model with the `getPassword` method (since this is a secret `UIInput`, it will not display the characters though) during the *Render Response* phase. If the user changes the value of one of the components and the value passes all the validations, the JSF runtime will set the value on the `user` object using the `setPassword` method during the *Update Model Values* phase.

The next section of this JSP, from Listing 5.4 again, is the footer facet. A facet is a special kind of child component that is rendered separately from the rest of the children. The typical use of a facet is to provide special user interface sections such as the footer for this panel. There is more detail on facets in Chapter 6.

The footer contains another UIPanel that has two submit buttons for this page. The code for the footer is copied here for reference.

```
<f:facet name="footer">
  <h:panelGrid id="buttonGrid" columns="2"
```

```
                    columnClasses="centered" width="100%">
      <h:commandButton value="Cancel"
                             action="#{regPage.cancel}"/>
      <h:commandButton value="Save"
                             action="#{regPage.save}"/>
    </h:panelGrid>
  </f:facet>
```

The two UICommand components in this facet are very similar. The `commandButton` tag sets the Renderer type for the `UICommand` to button, which causes an HTML button to be rendered. Both of the buttons also have an `actionListener` specified. When either button is pressed, the action referred to by the respective `action` attribute will be invoked.

After the button is pressed and the action is invoked the returned "logical outcome" will be compared with the navigational rules specified in the `faces-config.xml` file. When the Save button is pressed, the navigation rules specify that the user be taken to the `welcome.jsp` page. In this simplified example, the welcome page simply displays the newly registered user's name and says Welcome. The code for that page is listed here:

```
<HTML>
  <head>
    <meta HTTP-EQUIV="Content-Type"
          CONTENT="text/html;CHARSET=iso-8859-1">
    <title>Welcome!</title>
    <%@ taglib uri="http://java.sun.com/jsf/html" prefix="h" %>
    <%@ taglib uri="http://java.sun.com/jsf/core" prefix="f" %>
  </head>
  <BODY>
    <f:view>
      <h:outputMessage
            value="Welcome {0} {1}, to the Registration Demo!">
        <f:parameter value="#{regPage.user.firstName}"/>
        <f:parameter value="#{regPage.user.lastName}"/>
      </h:outputMessage>
    </f:view>
  </BODY>
</HTML>
```

The interesting thing to notice here is the use of the `f:parameter` tag. The special tags (numbers between { and }) in the `outputMessage` are replaced by the values specified by the parameter tags. So, the welcome message will have the user's first and last name substituted into it.

Summary

In this chapter, we have looked at the details of how JSF integration works with JSPs. You saw that even though a JSP is using the JSF integration tags, there is nothing special about what is happening; it's just normal JSP processing that takes place to invoke JSF API. We also covered a sample page in detail so that you could see the integration in action. In the next chapter, you will see more detail on UIComponent.

CHAPTER

6

UI Components

The notion of UI components is one of the main axes around which the JavaServer Faces framework pivots. The specification defines a User Interface Component Model, in which classes that extend the `UIComponent` class—generically referred to as components—are the centerpiece. But there is much more to the Component Model than just this class hierarchy.

The `UIComponent` class sits at the nexus of a broad and diverse set of collaborating classes. These come in several varieties. There are the taglib classes—subclasses of `UIComponentTag`—that provide a mechanism whereby JSP developers can gain access to the power of components. There are the helpers—Converter, Renderer, Validator—to which components often delegate some of their functionality. Then, there are listeners and the events that drive them, plugging components firmly into the bedrock of the framework's (and each application's) dynamic behavior. And finally there are the model objects with which components perform an intricate dance, as they coordinate their state with the state of the user interface.

Beyond that, components form a buffer between a server-based Web application and its clients, mediating between them to handle differences in data representation (formatted strings for the client, Java types for the application's model), providing a focal point for basic services such as type conversion, formatting, validation, and error messaging, while buffering input values for presentation back to the user in the event of a conversion or validation error.

In this chapter, we'll explore these many aspects of components and gain an understanding of their framework collaborations, rooting our knowledge in concrete examples of usage. We'll walk step by step through the User Interface Component Model, examining each of its salient features in turn.

We'll begin by taking a guided tour through a JSP containing some basic Faces tags, exploring how JavaServer Faces implements their behavior behind the scenes—including how the framework builds a tree of components to represent the page's elements. Next, we'll examine the role of components in binding values from model objects to the user interface using concrete examples to further our understanding.

As we work our way through the chapter, we'll progressively build an example application, gradually incorporating more complex components, including panel, facets, and select lists. We'll learn how to configure type conversion, validation, and error messaging in the sample application as well, at the same time examining the underlying implementation of each feature.

We'll also learn how to use actions and listeners to provide dynamic behavior. Toward the end of the chapter, you'll see an example of a listener that manipulates the view dynamically, modifying the user interface in response to user actions.

Overview

Learning about JavaServer Faces components requires covering a broad range of topics. First, of course, there is the `UIComponentBase` class itself, an abstract subclass of the `UIComponent` class, which we will gradually unfold throughout the chapter. At the beginning and again at the end of each request/response cycle, the JSF framework either builds or retrieves an object graph—referred to as the *view*—of `UIComponents` and their dependents. Collectively, these objects represent the state of a Web page and the rendering logic required to generate it.

The view can be configured in JSP or built dynamically in Java code, though many applications will likely do some of both—defining most of the user interface in JSP, but at times manipulating it by adding, removing, or modifying components programmatically.

Components play a central role in binding values from the user interface directly to model objects, providing with the aid of helpers, all the necessary parsing, type coercion, formatting, and validation behavior. Developers can use JSP or Java code to configure a Converter (a Converter converts the string values found in the browser to the values expected by the components such as Integers etc.) as well as one or more Validators (a Validator ensures that a value meets some defined criteria, such as a certain length, before allowing it to be passed on to the component) on any given component. This configuration capability provides a handy set of extension points, allowing developers to provide custom versions of these helper classes whenever and wherever necessary—even allowing developers to change them dynamically.

JavaServer Faces implements a sophisticated event model that closely mirrors the JavaBean event model, as well as a navigation scheme that incorporates the Command Pattern. Components are deeply involved here as well, queuing and receiving events. Developers can register one or more listeners on a component via JSP or Java, allowing the listeners to respond to events associated with the component.

Components also collaborate with configurable Renderers to generate their own UI representation. Because components have direct access to model objects, they participate both in formatting model values into their appropriate UI string representations, and in rendering the HTML elements used to present the values.

Throughout the chapter, we will describe the various tags defined by the JSF specification, presenting examples of their usage to drive home the concepts and terminology. We'll describe how tags are used to pair components with specific Renderers, allowing several components to share a single rendering behavior, while also allowing a single component to have several different rendering behaviors.

Using Components

Because the UI Component Model is fairly complex and its workings are central to nearly everything the framework does, we will focus in this section on what is going on behind the scenes as we look at examples that illustrate its usage. We'll begin by analyzing how the framework would process a simple JSP, using the JSP responsible for rendering the Modify Invoice page depicted in Figure 6.1 as a starting point.

Let's assume that the form fields in the Modify Invoice page are bound to a simple invoice bean (Listing 6.1), which represents model values for an invoice in a billing system.

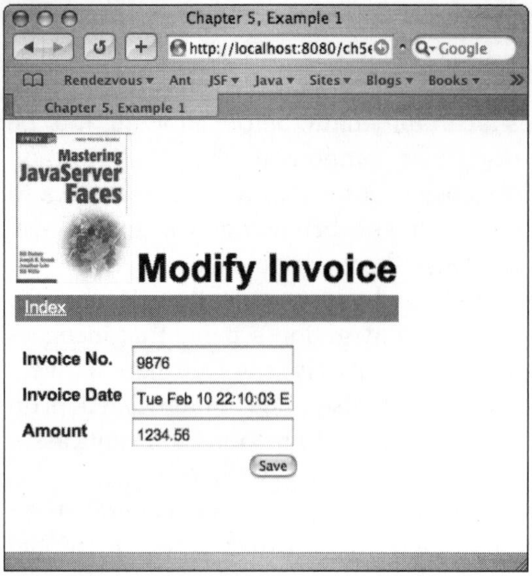

Figure 6.1 The Modify Invoice page.

```
package com.wiley.masteringjsf.ch6ex1;

import java.io.Serializable;
import java.math.BigDecimal;
import java.util.Date;

/**
 * A bean that models a simple invoice
 */
public class InvoiceBean implements Serializable
{
    // Initialize with arbitrary values
    private Integer invoiceNumber = new Integer(9876);
    private Date invoiceDate = new Date();
    private BigDecimal amount = new BigDecimal("1234.56");

    public InvoiceBean() { }

    public String save() {
        // Code to perform save and setup for next page would go here.
        // For now just return null to rerender the current page.
        return null;
    }

    /*--------  Accessor methods --------*/
```

Listing 6.1 A simple invoice bean.

```
    public Integer getInvoiceNumber() {
        return invoiceNumber;
    }
    public void setInvoiceNumber(Integer number) {
        this.invoiceNumber = number;
    }

    public Date getInvoiceDate() {
        return invoiceDate;
    }
    public void setInvoiceDate(Date invoiceDate) {
        this.invoiceDate = invoiceDate;
    }

    public BigDecimal getAmount() {
        return amount;
    }
    public void setAmount(BigDecimal amount) {
        this.amount = amount;
    }
}
```

Listing 6.1 *(continued)*

Apart from the `save()` method, `InvoiceBean` is a simple bean that can be used as a data container for invoice values. The extra method is needed in order to enable the Save button in the sample page.

ACTIONS AND NAVIGATION

You may have noticed that the `InvoiceBean` class in Listing 6.1 contains a simple action method, `save()`, that takes no arguments and returns a string. Although a good portion of Chapter 7, "Navigation, Actions, and Listenters," is devoted to actions, we provide a brief introduction here because it should prove helpful to our understanding of components.

Actions represent responses to UI controls such as buttons and hyperlinks. Action methods are invoked reflectively, and must conform to a simple convention: they must take no arguments, return `String`, and have public visibility.

Action methods are bound to `UICommand` components via the `action` attribute of the `command_button` and `command_link` tags. Because no arguments are passed to action methods, they must rely on other properties of the bean to provide whatever context they need to carry out their tasks. For example, an action method triggered by clicking a Save button might be responsible for transfering the bean's values to a persistence service in the business tier.

The values of the InvoiceBean in Listing 6.1 are bound to components configured by Faces tags in ModifyInvoice.jsp (see Listing 6.2). In the next few pages, we'll walk through the main elements of the JSP, in the process getting a quick overview of components and their associated tags.

```
<html>
<head>
   <meta http-equiv="Content-Type"
         content="text/html; charset=iso-8859-1">
   <link rel="stylesheet" href="/ch6ex1/styles.css" type="text/css">
   <title>Chapter 6, Example 1</title>
   <%@ taglib uri="http://java.sun.com/jsf/html" prefix="h" %>
   <%@ taglib uri="http://java.sun.com/jsf/core" prefix="f" %>
</head>
<body>

<%-- Faces view root --%>
<f:view>
   <%-- Page Heading --%>
   <table>
    <tr valign="bottom">
        <td class="TableCellGraphic">
            <h:graphicImage id="bookImage"
                                 url="/Book.jpg"/>
        </td>
        <td>
            <h:outputText id="pageHeading"
                               styleClass="PageHeading"
                               value="Modify Invoice"/>
        </td>
    </tr>
    <tr>
        <td class="Banner" colspan="2">
            <h:outputLink id="indexLink"
                               styleClass="ReverseLink"
                               value="index.jsp">
                <f:verbatim escape="true">Index</f:verbatim>
            </h:outputLink>
        </td>
    </tr>
    </table>
    <p>
    <h:messages/>
    <p>
    <%-- Invoice form --%>
    <h:form id="invoiceForm" action="#{invoiceBean.save}">
        <table>
        <tr>
```

Listing 6.2 ModifyInvoice.jsp.

```
            <td>
                <h:outputText id="invoiceNumberLabel"
                              styleClass="FieldLabel"
                              value="Invoice No."/>
            </td>
            <td>
                <h:inputText id="invoiceNumber"
                             styleClass="TextInput"
                             value="#{invoiceBean.invoiceNumber}"/>
            </td>
        </tr>
        <tr>
            <td>
                <h:outputText id="dateLabel"
                              styleClass="FieldLabel"
                              value="Invoice Date"/>
            </td>
            <td>
                <h:inputText id="date"
                             styleClass="TextInput"
                             value="#{invoiceBean.invoiceDate}"/>
            </td>
        </tr>
        <tr>
            <td>
                <h:outputText id="amountLabel"
                              styleClass="FieldLabel"
                              value="Amount"/>
            </td>
            <td>
                <h:inputText id="amount"
                             styleClass="TextInput"
                             value="#{invoiceBean.amount}"/>
            </td>
        </tr>
        <tr>
            <td colspan="2" align="right">
                <h:commandButton
                          styleClass="Button"
                        value="Save"
                        action="#{invoiceBean.save}"/>
            </td>
        </tr>
        </table>
    </h:form>
</f:view>

</body>
</html>
```

Listing 6.2 *(continued)*

The first thing you will notice right at the top of `ModifyInvoice.jsp` is the pair of scriptlet statements that import the Faces taglibs. Note that the prefixes, which are recommended by the Faces specification, are *h:* for the Faces HTML taglib, and *f:* for the Faces Core taglib.

```
<%@ taglib uri="http://java.sun.com/jsf/html" prefix="h" %>
<%@ taglib uri="http://java.sun.com/jsf/core" prefix="f" %>
```

If you take a quick scan of the JSP code, you'll notice that most of the tags are preceded by 'h:', the exception being the `f:view` tag that encloses the Faces portion of the JSP. This denotes the root of the *view*, which is represented at run time by an instance of `UIViewRoot`. `UIViewRoot` is a subclass of `UIComponentBase` that implements methods for broadcasting events to the other components in the tree.

The next thing you'll likely notice is an `id` attribute that uniquely identifies each of the Faces HTML components. You can use the value of this attribute to locate a given component on the server at run time. JSF allows you to modify and even add or remove components dynamically. You can also easily address the elements with JavaScript. This a powerful and quite useful feature.

Before the beginning of the HTML table, you'll see a Faces `form` tag, which is responsible for rendering a corresponding HTML `form` tag. Just above that is a `graphicImage` tag, which is used to render an HTML `img` tag, and an `outputLink` tag, which renders an anchor.

There are several `outputText` tags that—in the current example—do nothing more than render the hard-coded strings specified by their `value` attributes. Obviously, the strings could have been directly in the JSP without the use of Faces tags, but given that the framework allows dynamic manipulation of components on the server, there can be advantages to the approach used here. In addition, the `outputText` tag provides a `styleClass` attribute, which allows us to assign a CSS class to be used to style the string. As a result, the string will be rendered inside an HTML `span` tag bound to the specified CSS class.

The `input_text` tags in `ModifyInvoice.jsp` are used to render HTML text input elements. The tags' `value` attributes bind each input field to a corresponding `InvoiceBean` property. The framework supplies default conversion facilities that allow the field values to be coerced to Numbers, Dates, and other common Java types as necessary.

Finally, near the end of the sample code there is a `command_button` that is used to render an HTML submit button. Listing 6.3 displays the HTML that results when JavaServer Faces renders `ModifyInvoice.jsp`. Note how the framework automatically combines the form ID with the field ID to generate unique identifiers for the `name` attributes of the HTML input tags, for example `name="invoice:invoiceNumber"` for the Invoice Number field:

```
<html>
<head>
   <meta http-equiv="Content-Type"
         content="text/html; charset=iso-8859-1">
   <link rel="stylesheet" href="/ch6ex1/styles.css" type="text/css">
   <title>Chapter 6 Example 1</title>
</head>
<body>
   <table>
    <tr valign="bottom">
        <td class="TableCellGraphic">
            <img id="bookImage" src="/ch6ex1/Book.jpg" alt="" />
        </td>
        <td>
            <span class="PageHeading">Modify Invoice</span>
        </td>
    </tr>
    <tr>
        <td class="Banner" colspan="2">
            <a href="index.jsp" class="ReverseLink">Index</a>
        </td>
    </tr>
    </table>
    <p>
    <p>
    <form id="invoiceForm" method="post"
          action="/ch6ex1/faces/ModifyInvoice.jsp">
        <table>
        <tr>
            <td>
                <span class="FieldLabel">Invoice No.</span>
            </td>
            <td>
                <input type="text"
                       name="invoiceForm:invoiceNumber"
                       value="9876"
                       class="TextInput" />
            </td>
        </tr>
        <tr>
            <td>
                <span class="FieldLabel">Invoice Date</span>
            </td>
            <td>
                <input type="text"
                       name="invoiceForm:date"
                       value="Sun Feb 01 13:14:28 EST 2004"
                       class="TextInput" />
                </h:inputText>
```

Listing 6.3 HTML generated from ModifyInvoice.jsp. *(continued)*

```
            </td>
        </tr>
        <tr>
            <td>
                <span class="FieldLabel">Amount</span>
            </td>
            <td>
                <input type="text"
                       name="invoiceForm:amount"
                       value="1234.56"
                       class="TextInput" />
            </td>
        </tr>
        <tr>
            <td colspan="2" align="right">
                <input type="submit"
                       name="invoiceForm:saveButton"
                       value="Save"
                       title="Save changes"
                       class="Button" />
            </td>
        </tr>
        </table>
        <input type="hidden"
               name="invoiceForm"
               value="invoiceForm" />
    </form>

</body>
</html>
```

Listing 6.3 *(continued)*

The View

When a request is submitted to the server to navigate to the Modify Invoice page for the first time, the Faces implementation builds a tree of `UIComponent` instances to represent all of the Faces tags that it finds in `ModifyInvoice.jsp`. (Note that it will only find Faces tags that are nested inside a `view` tag.)

When the Faces implementation renders the response, the view is then referenced to determine how to render the components. When a user submits the form contained in the Modify Invoice page back to the server, the view is used again, playing an integral role in every step of the framework's request-processing functionality.

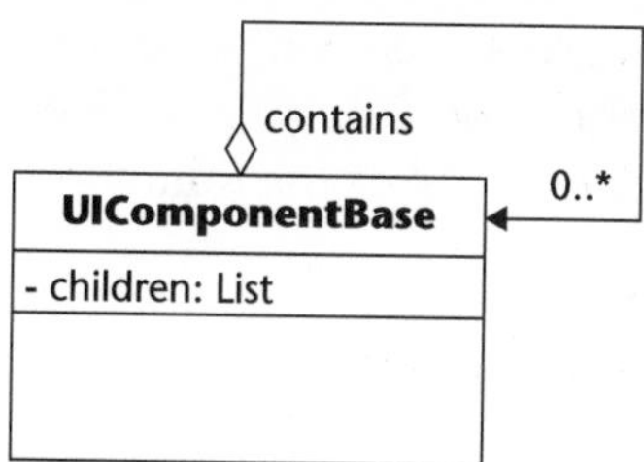

Figure 6.2 The UIComponentBase class.

The `UIComponentBase` class defines a `children` property of type List to allow instances to be assembled into a tree (see Figure 6.2). Let's take a look at the view that the framework would generate to represent the Faces tags in `ModifyInvoice.jsp`. Figure 6.3 provides a conceptual diagram.

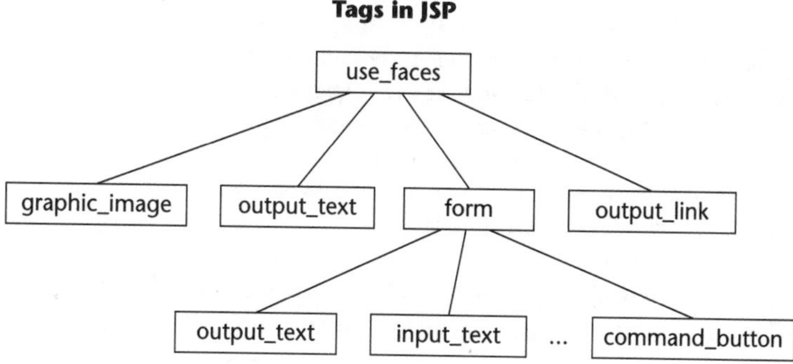

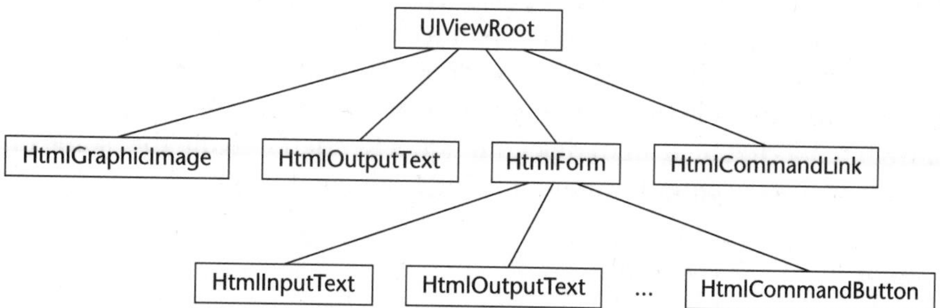

Figure 6.3 The Component tree for the Modify Invoice page.

During the *Render Response* phase, the framework gives each component in the tree an opportunity to render itself, and appends the resulting HTML string to the response. The abstract UIComponent class declares the following set of encoding methods for this purpose:

```
public abstract void encodeBegin(FacesContext facescontext)
    throws IOException;
public abstract void encodeChildren(FacesContext facescontext
    throws IOException;
public abstract void encodeEnd(FacesContext facescontext)
    throws IOException;
```

Components may delegate some or all of their rendering behavior to a Renderer instance. JSF encourages this approach, but doesn't enforce it. To provide this flexibility, the Renderer abstract base class provides default implementations of a set of encoding methods that are parallel to those of UIComponent.

```
public void encodeBegin(FacesContext facescontext,
    UIComponent uicomponent) throws IOException {... }
public void encodeChildren(FacesContext facescontext,
    UIComponent uicomponent) throws IOException { ... }
public void encodeEnd(FacesContext facescontext,
    UIComponent uicomponent) throws IOException { ... }
Public Boolean getRenderersChildren()
```

Renderers are simple helper classes whose purpose is to allow common rendering functionality to be abstracted out of components. This allows for reuse, in that different components can share the same Renderer. More importantly, making Renderers pluggable allows a single component to have multiple visual representations. As you can see from Figure 6.3, the UICommand component can be rendered either as a hyperlink or as a button.

In general, Faces tags are designed to pair a component with a specific Renderer. However, there are a handful of components that either require no rendering at all—for example the view tag we encountered earlier—or that do all of their own rendering instead of delegating to a Renderer. (Note that some of these details may vary among different JSF implementations.)

Subviews

JSF pages are only allowed to contain a single view tag. However, the Faces tag library provides a subview tag that can be used to nest content from a separate JSP inside a view tag. This provides a convenient way for your pages to share common snippets of JSF markup.

For example, the Modify Invoice page's header is rendered by the following table (as seen in Listing 6.2):

```
<%-- Page Heading --%>
<table>
 <tr valign="bottom">
     <td class="TableCellGraphic">
         <h:graphicImage id="bookImage"
                         url="/Book.jpg"/>
     </td>
     <td>
         <h:outputText id="pageHeading"
                       styleClass="PageHeading"
                       value="Modify Invoice"/>
     </td>
 </tr>
 <tr>
     <td class="Banner" colspan="2">
         <h:outputLink id="indexLink"
                       styleClass="ReverseLink"
                       value="index.jsp">
             <f:verbatim escape="true">Index</f:verbatim>
         </h:outputLink>
     </td>
 </tr>
</table>
```

We might want share this code amongst a set of pages. We can start by creating a new JSP file (in our example, `Header.jsp`) containing the code we want to reuse:

```
<html>
<head>
   <link rel="stylesheet" href="/ch6ex2/styles.css" type="text/css">
   <%@ taglib uri="http://java.sun.com/jsf/html" prefix="h" %>
   <%@ taglib uri="http://java.sun.com/jsf/core" prefix="f" %>
</head>
<body>

   <table>
    <tr valign="bottom">
        <td class="TableCellGraphic">
            <h:graphicImage id="bookImage"
                            url="/Book.jpg"/>
        </td>
        <td>
            <h:outputText id="pageHeading"
                          styleClass="PageHeading"
                          value="Modify Invoice"/>
        </td>
    </tr>
    <tr>
        <td class="Banner" colspan="2">
```

```
            <h:outputLink id="indexLink"
                          styleClass="ReverseLink"
                          value="index.jsp">
                <f:verbatim escape="true">Index</f:verbatim>
            </h:outputLink>
        </td>
    </tr>
    </table>

</body>
</html>
```

We can then replace the table in ModifyInvoice.jsp with a subview tag. Inside the subview tag we'll use a jsp:include tag to reference the content of Header.jsp:

```
...
<f:subview id="header" flush="true"/>
    <jsp:include page="Header.jsp" />
</f:subview>
...
```

This will cause the HTML rendered by Header.jsp to be included in place when the Modify Invoice page is rendered. The subview tag will cause any Faces components specified in Header.jsp to be added to the view defined by the enclosing view tag. Note that in addition to the subview tag you must also wrap any HTML markup with f:verbatim so that it is rendered properly.

One problem with the previous example is that we have hard-coded "Modify Invoice" as the page name. To make Header.jsp truly reusable, we would need to pass the page name as a parameter:

```
...
<f:subview id="header"/>
    <jsp:include page="Header.jsp" flush="true">
        <jsp:param name="pageName" value="Modify Invoice"/>
    </jsp:include>
</f:subview>
...
```

The value of the pageName parameter could then be referenced inside Header.jsp as follows:

```
...
<h:outputText id="pageHeading"
              styleClass="PageHeading"
              value="#{param.pageName}"/>
...
```

Here is the code for the `Header.jsp`:

```
<html>
<head>
   <link rel="stylesheet" href="/ch6ex2/styles.css" type="text/css">
   <%@ taglib uri="http://java.sun.com/jsf/html" prefix="h" %>
   <%@ taglib uri="http://java.sun.com/jsf/core" prefix="f" %>
</head>
<body>
  <f:subview>
    <h:panelGrid id="headerPanel"
                 columns="2"
                 columnClasses="TableCellGraphic, PageHeading"
                 footerClass="Banner">
        <h:graphicImage id="bookImage"
                        url="/Book.jpg"/>
        <h:outputText id="pageHeading"
                      value="#{param.pageName}"/>
        <f:facet name="footer">
            <h:outputLink id="indexLink"
                          styleClass="ReverseLink"
                          value="index.jsp">
                <f:verbatim escape="true">Index</f:verbatim>
            </h:outputLink>
        </f:facet>
    </h:panelGrid>
  </f:subview>
</body>
</html>
```

The `panelGrid` and `facet` tags used in the previous example will be explored in detail later in this chapter.

Value Binding

One of the responsibilities of the `UIComponent` class is to provide a UI representation of the model property to which it is bound. `UIComponent` defines a `value` property to buffer this value for both the inbound and outbound portions of the request/response cycle. This field also temporarily stores the result of any conversion applied to the submitted value during the *Apply Request Values* phase. Ultimately, the content of the component's `value` field is transferred to the corresponding bean property during the *Update Model Values* phase.

JSF provides a value binding mechanism to make it easy to access bean properties from within Faces tags. The entry point to this mechanism is the value attribute used by the inputText and ouput_text tags we saw in Listing 6.2:

```
<h:input_text id="amount"
              value="#{invoiceBean.amount}">
```

Expressions that begin with a '#{' and are terminated with a trailing '}' are evaluated by the framework's value binding mechanism. This mechanism provides a bidirectional facility for mapping values between UIComponents and the model bean properties to which they are bound. In fact, the whole JSP 2.0 Expression Language (EL) is honored, so you can do things like #{myBean.value < 16}.

In the previous example, the expression #{invoiceBean.amount} would be resolved at run time by evaluating each dot-separated substring (minus the opening '#{' and the trailing '}') in turn from right to left. (We'll refer to the substrings as *keys*, and the entire string as a *keypath*.) The first key is always assumed to be an object in one of the scopes accessible to the JSP—session, request, or application. Successive keys are assumed to reference properties of the object represented by the preceding key.

In the previous example, the value binding mechanism would resolve the keypath invoiceBean.amount by using reflection to access the amount property of invoiceBean. If a property matching the key 'amount' could not be found on invoiceBean, the associated component's value would be set to null.

The value binding mechanism can be applied to nested, indexed, and mapped properties. Let's look at a couple of examples. First, we'll add a new value object to our model. AccountBean contains values that span multiple invoices—for example, the company name—as well as a list of invoices that belong to the account it represents. To make things more interesting, we'll create a reciprocal relationship between AccountBean and InvoiceBean, as depicted in Figure 6.4.

Listing 6.4 contains the code for the AccountBean class.

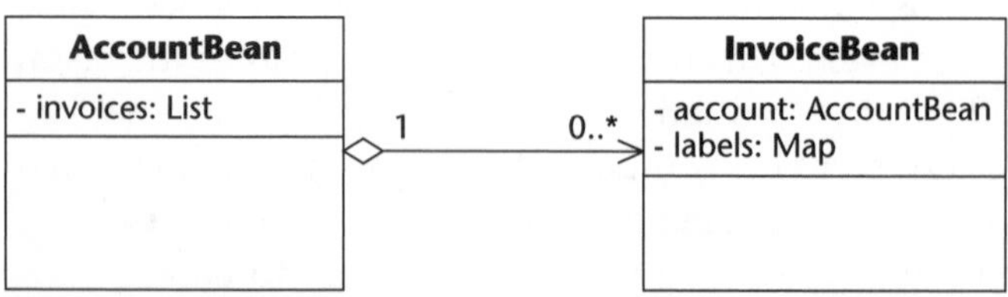

Figure 6.4 AccountBean/InvoiceBean relationship.

```
package com.wiley.masteringjsf.ch6ex2;

import java.io.Serializable;
import java.util.ArrayList;
import java.util.List;

/**
 * Aggregates a list of invoices
 */
public class AccountBean implements Serializable
{
    private String companyName;
    private List invoices = new ArrayList();

    public AccountBean() {
        // Construct with predefined values for now . . .
        setCompanyName("Some Company, Inc.");
        createFakeInvoices();
    }

    private void createFakeInvoices() {
        addInvoice(new InvoiceBean("1001", "1325.58"));
        addInvoice(new InvoiceBean("1002", "675.95"));
    }

    public void addInvoice(InvoiceBean invoice) {
        invoice.setAccount(this);
        invoices.add(invoice);
    }
    public void removeInvoice(InvoiceBean invoice) {
        invoice.setAccount(null);
        invoices.remove(invoice);
    }

    /*--------  Accessor methods --------*/

    public String getCompanyName() {
        return companyName;
    }
    public void setCompanyName(String companyName) {
        this.companyName = companyName;
    }

    public List getInvoices() {
        return invoices;
    }
    public void setInvoices(List invoices) {
```

Listing 6.4 AccountBean.java. *(continued)*

```
        this.invoices = invoices;
    }
}
```

Listing 6.4 *(continued)*

We'll need to make some subtle changes to the `InvoiceBean` class as well. In particular, we'll add an `account` property, as well as an extra convenience constructor, as shown in Listing 6.6.

We'll also add a JavaBean to represent the Modify Invoice page. This will give us a place to put page-related state, as well as behavior (in the form of action methods). For example, we can move the `save()` method from the earlier version of `InvoiceBean` (Listing 6.1) to our new class, `ModifyInvoicePage`, depicted in Listing 6.5.

```
package com.wiley.masteringjsf.ch6ex2;

import java.io.Serializable;
import java.util.HashMap;
import java.util.Map;

public class ModifyInvoicePage implements Serializable
{
    /** The value object managed by this page */
    private InvoiceBean invoice;
    /** Field labels for the user interface. */
    private static Map labels = new HashMap();

    static {
        labels.put("invoiceNumber", "Invoice No.");
        labels.put("invoiceDate", "Invoice Date");
        labels.put("amount", "Amount");
    }

    public ModifyInvoicePage() {
        // Construct with predefined values for now . . .
        InvoiceBean anInvoice = (InvoiceBean)
            new AccountBean().getInvoices().get(0);
        setInvoice(anInvoice);
    }

    public String save() {
        // Code to perform save and setup for next page would go here.
        // For now, just returns null to rerender the current page.
        return null;
```

Listing 6.5 ModifyInvoicePage.java.

```
    }

    /*--------  Accessor methods --------*/

    public Map getLabels() { return labels; }

    public InvoiceBean getInvoice() {
        return invoice;
    }
    public void setInvoice(InvoiceBean invoice) {
        this.invoice = invoice;
    }
}
```

Listing 6.5 *(continued)*

Listing 6.6 is a new version of `InvoiceBean` that implements the relationship with `AccountBean`. The SaveAction no longer appears here because it is now in the ModifyInvoicePage.

```
package com.wiley.masteringjsf.ch6ex2;

import java.io.Serializable;
import java.math.BigDecimal;
import java.util.Date;

/**
 * A bean that models a simple invoice
 */
public class InvoiceBean implements Serializable
{
    private Integer invoiceNumber;
    private Date invoiceDate;
    private BigDecimal amount;
    private AccountBean account;

    public InvoiceBean() { }

    public InvoiceBean(String number, String amount) {
        setInvoiceNumber(new Integer(number));
        setAmount(new BigDecimal(amount));
        setInvoiceDate(new Date());
    }

    /*--------  Accessor methods --------*/
```

Listing 6.6 InvoiceBean.java with reciprocal relationship to AccountBean. *(continued)*

```
    public Integer getInvoiceNumber() {
        return invoiceNumber;
    }
    public void setInvoiceNumber(Integer number) {
        this.invoiceNumber = number;
    }

    public Date getInvoiceDate() {
        return invoiceDate;
    }
    public void setInvoiceDate(Date invoiceDate) {
        this.invoiceDate = invoiceDate;
    }

    public BigDecimal getAmount() {
        return amount;
    }
    public void setAmount(BigDecimal amount) {
        this.amount = amount;
    }

    public AccountBean getAccount() {
        return account;
    }
    public void setAccount(AccountBean account) {
        this.account = account;
    }
}
```

Listing 6.6 *(continued)*

We now need to update the bindings in `ModifyInvoice.jsp` to reflect the new layout of our objects. For example, the code to present the Invoice Number field would now look like this:

```
<h:inputText id="invoiceNumber"
             converter="#{Integer}"
             value="#{modifyInvoicePage.invoice.invoiceNumber}">
</h:inputText>
```

The value binding expression associated with the `value` attribute now contains a longer keypath. The first element of the new keypath is `'modify InvoicePage'`, which is the key under which the `ModifyInvoicePage` instance is stored in the session (either by adding a `jsp:useBean` tag to the page, or by configuring it with the JSF managed bean facility). The next element, `'invoice'`, references the invoice property of the `ModifyInvoice Page` instance. The final portion of the keypath references the `invoice Number` property of the `InvoiceBean`.

Suppose that we now wanted to add a field to display the company name on our Modify Invoice page. We could simply provide an `outputText` tag with the appropriate `value` binding to access the nested property in `AccountBean`, as in the following:

```
<h:outputText
    id="companyName"
    value="#{modifyInvoicePage.invoice.account.companyName}"/>
```

We could also go the other way to access an `InvoiceBean` in the `AccountBean's invoices` list. For example, if an instance of `AccountBean` were stored in the session under the key *accountBean*, we could change the `value` binding in the amount field from its current setting,

```
value="#{modifyInvoicePage.invoice.amount}"/>
```

to something like this,

```
value="#{accountBean.invoices[0].amount}"/>
```

assuming, of course, that the invoice we were interested in was stored at array index 0. There wouldn't be any advantage to doing this in our simple Modify Invoice page as currently written, but the technique might be useful if we were coding a page that presented a list of invoices. The keypath before this paragraph contains a nested property, `invoices`, which as we know is of type List. The array index notation causes the value binding mechanism to access the element at the specified index (in this case, '0'). After retrieving the `InvoiceBean` at that location, the framework evaluates the final portion of the keypath by calling `getAmount()` on the `InvoiceBean`.

We can access the values in the ModifyInvoicePage's `labels` Map using the same syntax:

```
<h:outputText id="invoiceNumberLabel"
              value="#{modifyInvoicePage.labels.invoiceNumber}"/>
```

or with a JavaScript-like syntax:

```
<h:outputText
      id="invoiceNumberLabel"
      value="#{modifyInvoicePage.labels['invoiceNumber']}"/>
```

The square brackets in the previous expression indicate that we are accessing an element of the Map stored in the `labels` property. The quoted string inside the brackets is the key to use to access the value that we're interested in. The two syntaxes are equivalent.

Listing 6.7 contains the complete text of an updated version of `ModifyInvoice.jsp`.

```
<html>
<head>
   <meta http-equiv="Content-Type"
         content="text/html; charset=iso-8859-1">
   <link rel="stylesheet" href="/ch6ex2/styles.css" type="text/css">
   <title>Chapter 6,  Example 2</title>
   <%@ taglib uri="http://java.sun.com/jsf/html" prefix="h" %>
   <%@ taglib uri="http://java.sun.com/jsf/core" prefix="f" %>
</head>
<body>

<%-- Faces view root --%>
<f:view>
    <%-- Page heading --%>
    <f:subview id="header"/>
        <jsp:include page="Header.jsp" flush="true">
            <jsp:param name="pageName" value="Modify Invoice"/>
        </jsp:include>
    </f:subview>
    <p>
    <h:messages/>
    <p>
    <%-- Invoice form --%>
    <h:form id="invoiceForm" action="#{modifyInvoicePage.save}">
        <table>
        <tr>
            <td>
                <h:outputText
                    id="invoiceNumberLabel"
                    styleClass="FieldLabel"
                    value="#{modifyInvoicePage.labels.invoiceNumber}"/>
            </td>
            <td>
                <h:inputText
                   id="invoiceNumber"
                   styleClass="TextInput"
                   converter="#{Integer}"
                   value="#{modifyInvoicePage.invoice.invoiceNumber}"/>
            </td>
        </tr>
        <tr>
            <td>
                <h:outputText
```

Listing 6.7 ModifyInvoice.jsp with nested keypaths.

```
                id="dateLabel"
                styleClass="FieldLabel"
                value="#{modifyInvoicePage.labels.invoiceDate}"/>
        </td>
        <td>
            <h:inputText
                id="date"
                styleClass="TextInput"
                converter="#{Date}"
                value="#{modifyInvoicePage.invoice.invoiceDate}"/>
        </td>
    </tr>
    <tr>
        <td>
            <h:outputText
                id="amountLabel"
                styleClass="FieldLabel"
                value="#{modifyInvoicePage.labels.amount}"/>
        </td>
        <td>
            <h:inputText
                id="amount"
                styleClass="TextInput"
                converter="#{BigDecimal}"
                value="#{modifyInvoicePage.invoice.amount}"/>
        </td>
    </tr>
    <tr>
        <td colspan="2" align="right">
            <h:command_button
                    id="saveButton"
                    title="Save changes"
                    styleClass="Button"
                    value="Save"
                    action="#{modifyInvoicePage.save}"/>
        </td>
    </tr>
    </table>
  </h:form>
</f:view>

</body>
</html>
```

Listing 6.7 *(continued)*

Converting between Model Properties and UI Strings

Note that the `amount` property in the `InvoiceBean` in Listing 6.6 is typed as a `BigDecimal`. That presents a couple of challenges for the presentation layer. One issue is that the `BigDecimal` will need to be converted to an appropriate string representation so that it can be appended to the response. The other is that a `BigDecimal` value could be presented in a variety of different formats depending on context, for example as a percentage, a currency value, and so on.

The JSF architecture permits components to provide the necessary conversion and formatting functionality themselves, or to delegate the behavior to another object that implements the Converter interface. Implementations are expected to provide at a minimum a default set of Converter classes that supply the functionality required by the standard Faces tags.

In the case of the `amount` field, the `inputText` tag in the example JSP includes a `converter` setting to configure the associated `UIInput` component to use a `BigDecimal`Converter to convert between model properties and their formatted string representations. (Conceptually at least—it is left to the JSF implementation to define precisely where and how this is done. In theory, the conversion functionality could be implemented in the tag's Renderer, or even in the component itself, though that approach would be less flexible.)

We can take advantage of this flexibility to solve a problem with the current implementation of the Modify Invoice page. In Listing 6.7, we used an `inputText` tag to render the invoice amount:

```
<h:inputText
    id="amount"
    styleClass="TextInput"
    converter="BigDecimal"
    value="#{modifyInvoicePage.invoice.amount}"/>
```

However, as of this writing, the `BigDecimal`Converter's formatting behavior is to simply call `toString()`, and its conversion behavior is similarly inflexible. As a consequence, values are formatted without thousands separators, which would tend to make larger values difficult for users to read. But worse than that, if a user were to enter a number with a thousands separator (for example, 9,995.00) and submit it back to the server, a `ConverterException` would be thrown. This behavior is likely to vary between JSF implementations and will likely be fixed in a subsequent release of the *Reference Implemention.*

To solve this problem, we can use a nested tag to specify the Converter type. Not only does this let us pick a specific converter (including potentially a custom one of our own devising), but it also allows us to set attributes on the selected converter to customize its behavior, as in the following example:

```
<h:inputText
    id="amount"
    styleClass="TextInput"
    value="#{modifyInvoicePage.invoice.amount}">
    <f:convertNumber type="currency"/>
</h:inputText>
```

The previous `convertNumber` tag binds the tag's `UIInput` component to an instance of NumberConverter, setting the value of its `type` attribute to `'currency'`.

Like the Amount field, the Invoice Date field in `ModifyInvoice.jsp` has formatting problems. In Listing 6.7, the `inputText` tag uses a `converter` binding to select the DateTimeConverter. Although this works when rendering the page, the default date format that is applied results in UI values being rendered in the form 'Sat Feb 07 15:59:24 EST 2004'. Interestingly, the DateTimeConverter is unable to parse the string that it renders (because of an underlying bug in the `java.text.DateFormat` class), so submitting the form without changing any of the rendered values results in a `Converter Exception`.

POTENTIAL NUMBER FORMATTING ISSUES

Note that the previous snippet includes a `convertNumber` tag to set the number type of the `NumberConverter` to `'currency'`. The `Number Converter` class uses java.text.NumberFormat to provide its formatting functionality. The `NumberFormat` class in turn uses `java.util.Locale` to determine how to format and parse predefined numeric types (such as `'currency'` and `'percent'`). If you don't override the default locale, the default locale's number patterns will require a leading dollar sign ($) for currency values (in the United States). Percent values will truncate decimal digits (so 12.5% would be rendered as 12%, for example), and will require a trailing percent sign (%) during parsing.

Failing to enter a leading dollar sign or trailing percent sign will cause a `NumberFormatException` to be thrown, resulting in a conversion error on the field in question. Needless to say this can be a bit annoying if you aren't expecting it, and fiddling with locale format pattern settings is probably not the most flexible solution. One of the examples in Chapter 8, "Validation and Conversion," shows how to write a custom Converter as a more straightforward way to address problems such as these.

As with the Amount field, we can use a nested tag to specify the Converter. Unlike the previous example though, we are going to specify the same Converter class as the one that the `converter` attribute uses. The difference is that we can now supply the additional settings that we need to exercise finer control over the date format. Here's what we had originally:

```
<h:inputText
    id="date"
    styleClass="TextInput"
    converter="Date"
    value="#{modifyInvoicePage.invoice.invoiceDate}"/>
```

Modifying this to include a nested `convertDateTime` tag will allow us to set the `type` attribute to `'date'` (as opposed to `'time'`, or `'both'` (the default), and set the `dateStyle` to `'short'` (to render the date as '2/7/04' instead of 'Feb 7, 2004'). If quotation marks aren't part of code, delete them. They are

```
<h:inputText
    id="date"
    styleClass="TextInput"
    value="#{modifyInvoicePage.invoice.invoiceDate}">
    <f:convertDateTime type="date"
                       dateStyle="short"/>
</h:inputText>
```

Here the binding `converter="Number"` associates the `UIInput` component with an instance of NumberConverter. (A word of caution: The value of the `converter` attribute is assumed to be the name of the Converter class minus the "Converter" suffix. Some JSF implementations may use a case-sensitive comparison, so, for example, the string `'number'` wouldn't match, though `'Number'` would.)

You can use the `pattern` attribute of the `convertDateTime` tag instead of specifying `type` and `dateStyle` to further customize the formatting behavior. The following example yields a result similar to the previous one, except that the year is formatted with four digits (as in '2/7/2004'):

```
    <f:convertDateTime pattern="M/d/yyyy">
```

The JSF architecture allows you to add your own custom Converters, either by extending existing Converter classes or by creating new ones of your own that implement the Converter interface. Please see Chapter 8, for details on implementing custom Converters.

Processing Submitted Form Values

Let's continue with the Modify Invoice example, but this time let's consider what happens when a user modifies the form and then submits it. As you may recall from the section on life-cycle phases in Chapter 3, "JSF Request-Processing Life Cycle," JSF first retrieves the view, creating it if necessary. It then updates the components in the tree with the submitted form values from the request (the *Apply Request Values* phase). This step is initiated when the framework invokes the `processDecodes()` method on the view's root object. The message is propagated recursively, ultimately causing another method, `decode()`, to be called on all the components in the tree. It is up to each component to coerce the string value it is handed in the request into the appropriate Java type, based on the data type of the bean property specified by the component's `value` attribute. The component delegates the actual conversion to its Converter, if one is registered.

You may recall that a component may be implemented to register a Converter in any of the following ways:

- It may register a default Converter on itself.
- A developer may register a Converter declaratively in the JSP, using a tag's Converter attribute.
- A developer may register a Converter programmatically at run time by invoking the component's `setConverter()` method.

If conversion fails the component does the following:

- Stores the invalid string as its `value`, so that it can be presented back to the user when the page is rerendered
- Throws a `ConverterException`
- Sets its `valid` property to false

Otherwise, it stores the converted value in its value field. It is from here that the converted value is accessed during the *Process Validations* and *Update Model Values* phases. If validation succeeds, the value is transferred to the bean property to which it is bound as part of the latter phase.

This process continues until all the components in the tree for which request values were submitted have been updated. Note that request values that map to bean properties typed as `String` may not require conversion, though a custom Converter could define a specific string format and throw a `ConverterException` if the submitted value didn't match it.

DISPLAYING ERROR MESSAGES

Error messages generated during this phase (and the later *Process Validations* phase) can be presented to the user by adding a `messages` **tag, or one or more** `message` **tags to the JSP. The** `messages` **tag renders the entire list of errors aggregated for the components in the page, while the** `message` **tag renders only the message for a given field. The following snippet is all it takes to include the entire list of errors in the page:**

```
<f:messages/>
```

Optionally, you can use the `message` **tag to display the error message (if any) for a given component, as in the following example:**

```
<h:inputText id="invoiceNumber"
             value="#{modifyInvoicePage.invoice.invoiceNumber}">
</h:inputText>

<h:message for="invoiceNumber"/>
```

Notice that the value of the `for` **attribute matches that of the** `id` **attribute of the** `inputText` **tag. The** `message` **tag uses this value to determine which error message to display. The strings must match exactly in order for this to work.**

Validators

After applying request values to the view, the JSF framework passes control to the *Process Validations* phase to execute the `validate()` methods of any registered Validators (instances of classes that implement the Validator interface). Except in the case where the `immediate` attribute is set to `true`, in this case the validation happens right away in the *Apply Request Values* phase. Validator registration is similar to Converter registration, with the difference that you can register more than one Validator on a given component. As is the case with Converters, Validators can be registered on a component in the following ways:

- The component implementation may register default validations on itself.
- A developer can register zero or more Validators on a component declaratively in JSP.
- Validators can be added to a component programatically by calling the component's `addValidator()` method. Validators also can be removed programatically by calling `removeValidator()`, or you can specify a validate method to be called by setting the `validator` attribute on the component. The `validator` attribute must be set to a MethodBinding expression with the following format `void <methodName>(FacesContext, UIInput)`.

In addition, UIComponents may implement validation logic directly in their validate() methods. For example, UIInput has a required property that can be configured directly by input tags, as in the following example:

```
<h:inputText
    id="invoiceNumber"
    styleClass="TextInput"
    converter="#{Integer}"
    required="true"
    value="#{modifyInvoicePage.invoice.invoiceNumber}"/>
```

If the required property is set to true and the submitted value is blank, the UIInput component sets its valid flag to false and adds an error message to the FacesContext. Otherwise, if the submitted value is non-null, the component delegates to any registered Validators for additional validations.

JavaServer Faces defines a default set of Validators (classes that implement the javax.faces.validator.Validator interface) that can be extended by implementers as well as by application developers. The default set includes two range Validators (LongRangeValidator and DoubleRangeValidator) and a string length Validator (LengthValidator).

To register Validators in JSP, simply nest one or more Validator tags inside a Faces input tag. For instance, the following example uses a nested validate_longrange tag to validate the fact that the submitted value for invoiceNumber is at least 1,000:

```
<h:inputText
    id="invoiceNumber"
    styleClass="TextInput"
    converter="#{Integer}"
    value="#{modifyInvoicePage.invoice.invoiceNumber}">
  <f:validate_longrange minimum="1000"/>
</h:inputText>
```

Chapter 8, "Validation and Conversion," provides further details on configuring and using the JSF default Validators and writing custom Validator classes.

Configuring Event Listeners

Some JSF components can register listeners for specific types of events. UIInput defines methods for adding and removing objects that implement the ValueChangeListener interface. UICommand provides additional methods to register objects that implement the ActionListener interface. All this behavior is due to the UIInput (or any UIComponent for that matter) that implements the EditableValueHolder and ActionSource interfaces.

Each interface defines a method to invoke: `processValueChange()` for `ValueChangeListener`, and `processAction()` for `ActionListener`. Chapter 7 contains further information, as well as detailed examples of both listener types. However, here's a brief example that illustrates how to configure an `ActionListener` on a `UICommand` component.

Suppose that we wanted the Modify Invoice page in Listing 6.7 to contain an optional portion of the user interface that the user could hide or display by clicking a button. One way to accomplish this would be to add one or more table rows (we'll just add one in our example) that would initially render empty cells. Most browsers will simply ignore a row containing empty cells, which gives us an easy way to hide the elements. Listing 6.8 shows the modified portion of the JSP:

```
...
<f:view>
    ...
    <h:form id="invoiceForm" action="#{modifyInvoicePage.save}">
       <table>
        ...
        <tr>
            <td>
                <h:outputText
                    id="discountLabel"
                    styleClass="FieldLabel"
                    rendered="false"
                    value="#{modifyInvoicePage.labels.discount}"/>
            </td>
            <td>
                <h:inputText
                    id="discount"
                    styleClass="TextInput"
                    rendered="false"
                    value="#{modifyInvoicePage.invoice.discount}">
                    <f:convertNumber type="percent"/>
                </h:inputText>
            </td>
            <td><h:message for="discount"/></td>
        </tr>
        <tr>
            <td colspan="2" align="right">
                <h:command_button
                        id="saveButton"
                        title="Save changes"
                        styleClass="Button"
                        value="Save"
                        action="#{modifyInvoicePage.save}"/>
                <h:command_button
```

Listing 6.8 ModifyInvoice.jsp with Show Detail button and new table row.

```
                            id="showDetailButton"
                            title="Show less/more details"
                            styleClass="Button"
                            value="Show Detail">
                            <f:action_listener
                                type="com.wiley.[...].ShowDetailListener"/>
                        </h:command_button>
                    </td>
                </tr>
                </table>
            </h:form>
        </f:view>

        </body>
        </html>
```

Listing 6.8 *(continued)*

Note that the two new Faces tags are quite similar to the other tags inside the table, with the addition of a `rendered` attribute that is initialized to `'false'`. This setting short-circuits the underlying `UIComponent's` `encodeXxx()` methods, causing their rendering logic to be skipped. As a result, the new table cells will be empty the first time the page is rendered. We can later change these settings in the components dynamically so that their content will be rendered, and the new table row will appear in the browser. Although the JSP settings are used to initialize the components when the view is first created, they are never checked again, and thus won't interfere with these dynamic changes.

We have also added a Show Detail button inside our form. The new button has a nested `action_listener` tag, binding it to the `ActionListener` class containing the particular implementation of `processAction()` that we want the framework to invoke when the button is clicked. Note that we don't need to specify an action setting for the surrounding `command_button` tag, because none is needed—the `ActionListener` will provide all the necessary behavior.

Figure 6.5 shows how the new version of the Modify Invoice page will appear the first time it is rendered:

The other change we made to `ModifyInvoice.jsp` in Listing 6.8 was to add a Show Detail button. When the user clicks this button, we want the hidden row to show up and display the label and value for the Discount field. We also want the button's label to change from Show Detail to Hide Detail (see Figure 6.6). Each successive time the user clicks the button, these values should be toggled, causing the Discount field to appear and disappear, and the button's title to alternate between Hide Detail and Show Detail.

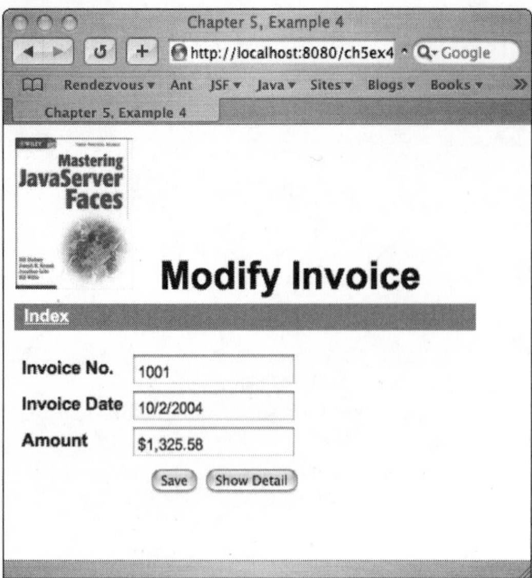

Figure 6.5 Modify Invoice Page with Show Detail button. Discount field is temporarily hidden from view.

Listing 6.9 contains the code for an implementation of `ActionListener` that will toggle the Discount fields and the button title whenever the framework invokes its `processAction()` method.

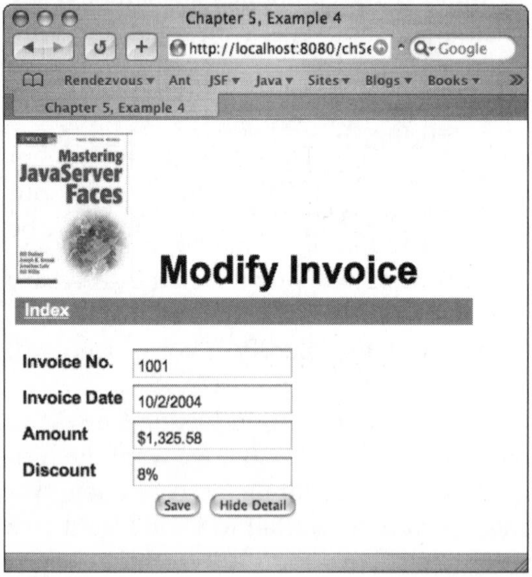

Figure 6.6 Modify Invoice Page after clicking the Show Detail button.

```
package com.wiley.masteringjsf.ch6ex4;

import javax.faces.component.UICommand;
import javax.faces.event.ActionEvent;
import javax.faces.event.ActionListener;

public class ShowDetailListener implements ActionListener {
    public final static String SHOW_DETAIL = "Show Detail";
    public final static String HIDE_DETAIL = "Hide Detail";

    public void processAction(ActionEvent event) {
        UICommand button = (UICommand) event.getComponent();
        boolean shouldRender = button.getValue().equals(SHOW_DETAIL);
        button.setValue(shouldRender ? HIDE_DETAIL : SHOW_DETAIL);
        button.findComponent("discountLabel").setRendered(shouldRender);
        button.findComponent("discount").setRendered(shouldRender);
    }
}
```

Listing 6.9 InvoiceActionListener.java.

The ShowDetailListener in Listing 6.9 uses the `findComponent()` method to locate the UIOutput components for the discount and discount label, and then toggles their `rendered` properties based on the current value of the button. When the button's value is `'Show Detail'`, `rendered` is set to `true`; otherwise, it is set to false, effectively hiding the components. The button's label is also toggled as necessary.

JSF provides another mechanism for registering listeners that has some advantages over the approach we've covered so far. This alternate approach allows you to use the value binding mechanism to specify the location of a method that implements the required functionality. The `UIInput` component has a `valueChangeListener` property that can be bound from any input tag, and `UICommand` provides an `actionListener` property that can be bound from any command tag.

We could use this approach to reimplement the previous example. First, we can simply move all the code from the `ShowDetailListener` to the `ModifyInvoicePage` class and rename the `processAction()` method whatever we please. The only proviso is that the listener method must return `void` and take an argument of type `ActionEvent`, as shown in the example following:

```
public class ModifyInvoicePage implements Serializable
{
    public final static String SHOW_DETAIL = "Show Detail";
    public final static String HIDE_DETAIL = "Hide Detail";
    ...
    public void showDetail(ActionEvent event) {
```

```
            UICommand button = (UICommand) event.getComponent();
            boolean shouldRender = button.getValue().equals(SHOW_DETAIL);
            button.setValue(shouldRender ? HIDE_DETAIL : SHOW_DETAIL);
            button.findComponent("discountLabel").setRendered(shouldRender);
            button.findComponent("discount").setRendered(shouldRender);
        }
        ....
    }
```

It is now a simple matter to change the JSP code in `ModifyInvoice.jsp` to use the `actionListener` binding. We simply remove the nested `action_listener` tag, and replace it with an `actionListener` attribute on the `command_button` tag. That will allow us to rewrite this:

```
<h:command_button
    id="showDetailButton"
    title="Show less/more details"
    styleClass="Button"
    value="Show Detail">
    <f:action_listener
        type="com.wiley.masteringjsf.ch6ex4.ShowDetailListener"/>
</h:command_button>
```

as follows:

```
<h:command_button
    id="showDetailButton"
    title="Show less/more details"
    styleClass="Button"
    value="Show Detail"
    actionListener="#{modifyInvoicePage.showDetail}"/>
```

Working with Tables

JSF supplies two different component hierarchies for managing tables. UIData and its subclasses are designed to work with a list of repeating elements, while UIPanel and its subclasses manage heterogeneous items—the kind of table that is most often used simply to control the positioning of HTML elements on the page. JSF implementations provide a set of tags to represent these components and their constituent parts in the markup. For example the `dataTable` tag is used to represent a UIData, and it typically is used with one or more nested `column` tags; `panelGrid` is used to represent a UIPanel, and the `facet` and `panelGroup` tags can be used with either.

Using Facets

Facets can be registered on a component via JSP markup (using the `facet` tag) or programmatically by calling `addFacet()`. Facets are used to define relationships that are orthogonal to the typical parent-child associations embodied in the view.

Facets are essentially identifiers for nested components that require special handling. For example, the UIData component aggregates a list of UIColumns, each of which represents a single column in the table. In JSP, this is done by nesting one or more `column` tags inside a `dataTable` tag. The `column` tag, in turn, contains a nested tag representing the HTML element to be rendered in the column, as in the following example:

```
<h:dataTable id="table"
             value="#{viewAccountsPage.accounts}"
             var="account">
    <h:column>
        <h:outputText value="#{account.companyName}"/>
    </h:column>
</h:dataTable>
```

Here we have defined a UIData that gets its value from accessing the collection stored in `myBean.accounts`. The `var` attribute defines a request scope variable that will contain the current item from the collection when the collection is iterated through. The nested `column` tag defines a single column for the table, and it in turn contains an `outputText` tag that will be bound to the current account object's `companyName` attribute during rendering. The result will be a simple HTML table of company names similar to the following:

```
<table rows="0">
  <tr><td></td></tr>
  <tbody>
    <tr><td>Foo, Inc.</td></tr>
    <tr><td>Bar Corp.</td></tr>
    <tr><td>Quux Co.</td></tr>
  </tbody>
  <tr><td></td></tr>
</table>
```

Now, suppose we want to add a heading to the column. The UIData will need some way to distinguish itself because it has to be rendered differently from a regular table cell value—that is, as a single table header cell, before the body rows. We can use a Facet to identify the heading value as follows:

```
<h:dataTable id="table"
             value="#{viewAccountsPage.accounts}"
             var="account">
```

```
    <h:column>
        <f:facet name="header">
            <h:outputText value="Phone No."/>
        </f:facet>
        <h:outputText value="#{account.companyName}"/>
    </h:column>
</h:dataTable>
```

The UIData's Renderer looks for a Facet stored under the key `'header'` and renders its value at the top of the column. Keep in mind that the facet must have only one child; if a more complex header is required, nest the other components in a `h:panelGroup` tag. Here is the resultant HTML:

```
<table rows="0">
  <tr><td>Phone No.</td></tr>
  <tbody>
    <tr><td>Foo, Inc.</td></tr>
    <tr><td>Bar Corp.</td></tr>
    <tr><td>Quux Co.</td></tr>
  </tbody>
  <tr><td></td></tr>
</table>
```

A dataTable Example

Let's take a look at a more complete example that will serve to illustrate some additional features of the `dataTable` tag. The example will result in a page like the one in Figure 6.7.

The example makes use of a simple page bean, `ViewInvoicesPage`, as shown in Listing 6.10; it also includes the `InvoiceBean` in Listing 6.6, as well as the `AccountBean` in Listing 6.4, with the addition of the following new method:

```
    public double getTotal() {
        double total = 0.0;
        Iterator invoiceIter = invoices.iterator();
        while (invoiceIter.hasNext()) {
            InvoiceBean invoice = (InvoiceBean) invoiceIter.next();
            Double amount = invoice.getAmount();
            if (amount != null)
                total += amount.doubleValue();
        }
        return total;
    }
```

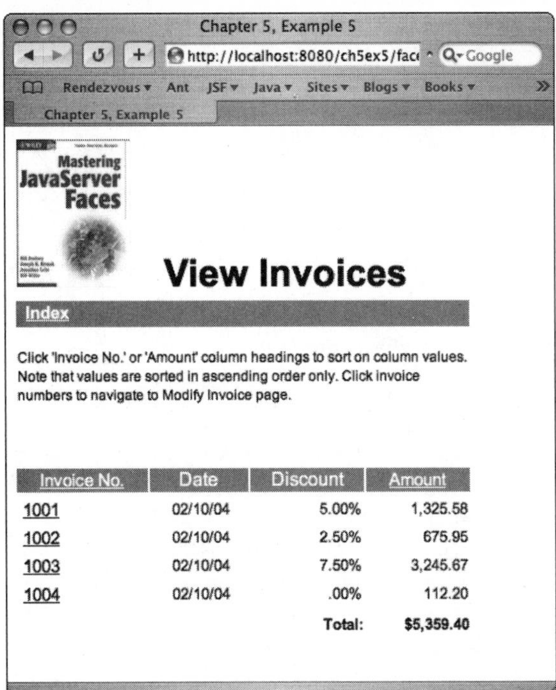

Figure 6.7 View Invoices page.

Listing 6.10 provides the code of the `ViewInvoicesPage` class.

```
package com.wiley.masteringjsf.ch6ex5;

import java.io.Serializable;
import java.util.*;

import javax.faces.component.UIData;
import javax.faces.component.UIViewRoot;
import javax.faces.context.FacesContext;
import javax.faces.el.ValueBinding;

import com.sun.faces.util.Util;

/**
 * Presents a list of invoices and provides methods for sorting the list
 * and for viewing individual invoices
 */
public class ViewInvoicesPage implements Serializable
{
    /** The list of invoices to display */
```

Listing 6.10 ViewInvoicesPage.java. *(continued)*

```
private List invoices = new ArrayList();

public ViewInvoicesPage() {
    setInvoices(new AccountBean().getInvoices());
}

protected void sortWithComparator(Comparator comparator) {
    Collections.sort(invoices, comparator);
}

/** Sort the invoice list on the amount property. */
public String sortByAmount() {
    sortWithComparator(new InvoiceBean.InvoiceAmountComparator());
    return null;
}
/** Sort the invoice list on the invoiceNumber property. */
public String sortByInvoiceNumber() {
    sortWithComparator(new InvoiceBean.InvoiceNumberComparator());
    return null;
}

/**
 * Sets up the detail page by getting the bean backing the current
 * row in the UIData table and passing it to the detail page.
 * An alternative implementation would be to stuff the invoice
 * bean into the request under a well-known key and let the
 * detail page find it.
 * @return the navigation outcome.
 */
public String modifyInvoice() {
    FacesContext facesContext = FacesContext.getCurrentInstance();

    UIViewRoot root = facesContext.getViewRoot();
    UIData table = (UIData)
        root.findComponent("invoiceForm").findComponent("table");
    InvoiceBean invoice = (InvoiceBean) table.getRowData();

    ValueBinding binding =
        Util.getValueBinding("#{modifyInvoicePage}");
    ModifyInvoicePage detailPage = (ModifyInvoicePage)
        binding.getValue(facesContext);

    detailPage.setInvoice(invoice);

    return "modifyInvoice";
}

/**
```

Listing 6.10 *(continued)*

```
     * Totals the invoice amounts of the currently displayed
     * invoices
     * @return The total amount.
     */
    public double getTotal() {
        double total = 0.0;
        Iterator invoiceIter = invoices.iterator();
        while (invoiceIter.hasNext()) {
            InvoiceBean invoice = (InvoiceBean) invoiceIter.next();
            Double amount = invoice.getAmount();
            if (amount != null)
                total += amount.doubleValue();
        }
        return total;
    }

    public List getInvoices() { return invoices; }
    public void setInvoices(List invoices) {
        this.invoices = invoices;
    }
}
```

Listing 6.10 *(continued)*

The JSP for the View Invoices page is presented in Listing 6.11. It uses a `dataTable` tag to present a list of invoices in an HTML table. The tag's `value` attribute, which in the example is set to `#{viewInvoicesPage.invoices}`, points to the collection of model objects that the tag will iterate over. The tag's `var` attribute defines a request-scope variable that will refer to an invoice from the `invoices` collection during a given iteration.

The `dataTable` tag surrounds several `column` tags, each containing tags to render the values of the column's cells. The tags for header and footer elements are nested inside `facet` tags, to distinguish them from ordinary column values.

```
<html>
<head>
   <meta http-equiv="Content-Type"
         content="text/html; charset=iso-8859-1">
   <link rel="stylesheet" href="/ch6ex5/styles.css" type="text/css">
   <title>Chapter 6, Example 5</title>
   <%@ taglib uri="http://java.sun.com/jsf/html" prefix="h" %>
   <%@ taglib uri="http://java.sun.com/jsf/core" prefix="f" %>
</head>
```

Listing 6.11 ViewInvoices.jsp. *(continued)*

```
<body>

<f:view>
    <f:subview id="header"/>
        <jsp:include page="Header.jsp" flush="true">
            <jsp:param name="pageName" value="View Invoices"/>
        </jsp:include>
    </f:subview>
    <p><p>
    <table class="MediumTable"><tr><td class="InstructionText">
    Click 'Invoice No.' or 'Amount' column headings to sort on
    column values. Note that values are sorted in ascending order only.
    Click invoice numbers to navigate to Modify Invoice page.
    </td></tr></table>
    <h:form id="invoiceForm">
    <h:dataTable id="table"
                value="#{viewInvoicesPage.invoices}"
                var="invoice"
                styleClass="MediumTable"
                headerClass="Header"
                footerClass="ListTotal"
                columnClasses="ListLeft, ListCenter,
                               ListRight, ListRight">
        <h:column>
            <f:facet name="header">
                <h:commandLink
                    id="heading1"
                    styleClass="SortLink"
                    title="Sort column values"
                    value="Invoice No."
                    action="#{viewInvoicesPage.sortByInvoiceNumber}">
                    <f:verbatim escape="true">Invoice No.</f:verbatim>
                </h:commandLink>
            </f:facet>
            <h:commandLink
                id="viewInvoice"
                styleClass="Link"
                title="View invoice details"
                value="#{invoice.invoiceNumber}"
                action="#{viewInvoicesPage.modifyInvoice}">
                <h:outputText id="invoiceNumber"
                              value="#{invoice.invoiceNumber}"/>
            </h:commandLink>
        </h:column>
        <h:column>
            <f:facet name="header">
                <h:outputText value="Date"/>
```

Listing 6.11 *(continued)*

```
            </f:facet>
            <h:outputText id="invoiceDate"
                          value="#{invoice.invoiceDate}">
                <f:convertDateTime pattern="MM/dd/yy"/>
            </h:outputText>
        </h:column>
        <h:column>
            <f:facet name="header">
                <h:outputText value="Discount"/>
            </f:facet>
            <h:outputText id="discount"
                          value="#{invoice.discount}">
                <f:convertNumber pattern="##.00%"/>
            </h:outputText>
            <f:facet name="footer">
                <h:outputText value="Total:"/>
            </f:facet>
        </h:column>
        <h:column>
            <f:facet name="header">
              <h:panelGroup>
                <h:commandLink
                    id="heading4"
                    styleClass="SortLink"
                    title="Sort column values"
                    value="Amount"
                    action="#{viewInvoicesPage.sortByAmount}">
                    <f:verbatim escape="true">Amount</f:verbatim>
                </h:commandLink>
              </h:panelGroup>
            </f:facet>
            <h:outputText id="amount"
                          value="#{invoice.amount}">
                <f:convertNumber pattern="#,###.00"/>
            </h:outputText>
            <f:facet name="footer">
                <h:outputText value="#{viewInvoicesPage.total}">
                    <f:convertNumber type="currency"/>
                </h:outputText>
            </f:facet>
        </h:column>
    </h:dataTable>
    </h:form>
  <p>
</f:view>
</body>
</html>
```

Listing 6.11 *(continued)*

Note that the various classes referred to in the dataTable tag in Listing 6.11 (panelClass, headerClass, etc.) are CSS classes defined in the file styles.css, which is imported in the head section at the top of the page. The styleClass attribute determines the style class for the HTML table, while headerClass sets the style for the header row, footerClass does so for the footer row, and columnClasses takes a comma-separated list of CSS class names, one for each of the columns. These settings are all optional.

Using a panelGrid

The dataTable tag is great for presenting tables with repeating rows, but many times HTML tables are used simply to position things neatly on the page. The rows in this type of table contain arbitrary elements. The panelGrid tag is useful for rendering these kinds of tables. A panelGrid is similar to a dataTable, except that it doesn't use column tags to define columns in the table; instead it provides a columns attribute that allows you to specify the number of columns you want. It then calculates which nested elements are in which column dynamically.

Let's look at a simple example. We can use a panelGrid to clean up the JSP for the ModifyInvoice page from Listing 6.8. Listing 6.12 contains the rewritten version:

```
<html>
<head>
   <meta http-equiv="Content-Type"
         content="text/html; charset=iso-8859-1">
   <title>Chaper 6, Example 5</title>
   <link rel="stylesheet" href="/ch6ex5/styles.css" type="text/css">
   <%@ taglib uri="http://java.sun.com/jsf/html" prefix="h" %>
   <%@ taglib uri="http://java.sun.com/jsf/core" prefix="f" %>
</head>
<body>
<f:view>
    <f:subview id="header"/>
         <jsp:include page="Header.jsp" flush="true">
              <jsp:param name="pageName" value="Modify Invoice"/>
              <jsp:param name="linkUrl" value="ViewInvoices.jsp"/>
              <jsp:param name="linkText" value="Back to List"/>
         </jsp:include>
    </f:subview>
    <p>
    <h:messages styleClass="ErrorMessage"/>
    <h:form id="invoiceForm" action="#{modifyInvoicePage.save}">
         <h:panelGrid id="invoicePanel"
                      columns="2"
```

Listing 6.12 Replacing the HTML table in ModifyInvoice.jsp with a panelGrid.

```
                    columnClasses="FieldLabel,TextInput"
                    footerClass="TableCellRight">
            <h:outputText
                id="invoiceNumberLabel"
                value="#{modifyInvoicePage.labels.invoiceNumber}"/>
            <h:inputText
                id="invoiceNumber"
                styleClass="TextInput"
                converter="#{Integer}"
                required="true"
                value="#{modifyInvoicePage.invoice.invoiceNumber}">
                <f:validate_longrange minimum="1000"/>
            </h:inputText>
            <h:outputText
                id="invoiceDateLabel"
                value="#{modifyInvoicePage.labels.invoiceDate}"/>
            <h:inputText
                id="invoiceDate"
                styleClass="TextInput"
                required="true"
                value="#{modifyInvoicePage.invoice.invoiceDate}">
                <f:convertDateTime pattern="M/d/yyyy"/>
            </h:inputText>
            <h:outputText
                id="amountLabel"
                value="#{modifyInvoicePage.labels.amount}"/>
            <h:inputText
                id="amount"
                styleClass="TextInput"
                required="true"
                value="#{modifyInvoicePage.invoice.amount}">
                <f:convertNumber pattern="$#,###.00"/>
            </h:inputText>
            <h:outputText
                id="discountLabel"
                rendered="false"
                value="#{modifyInvoicePage.labels.discount}"/>
            <h:inputText
                id="discount"
                styleClass="TextInput"
                rendered="false"
                value="#{modifyInvoicePage.invoice.discount}">
                <f:convertNumber type="percent"/>
            </h:inputText>
            <f:facet name="footer">
                <h:panelGroup>
                    <h:command_button
                        id="saveButton"
                        title="Save changes"
```

Listing 6.12 *(continued)*

```
                    styleClass="Button"
                    value="Save"
                    action="#{modifyInvoicePage.save}">
                </h:command_button>
                <h:command_button
                   id="showDetailButton"
                   title="Show less/more details"
                   styleClass="Button"
                   value="Show Detail"
                  actionListener="#{modifyInvoicePage.showDetail}"/>
            </h:panelGroup>
        </f:facet>
    </h:panelGrid>
  </h:form>
</f:view>
</body>
</html>
```

Listing 6.12 *(continued)*

Working with Select Lists

JavaServer Faces has a group of related components for managing HTML select lists, as well as a support class, `SelectItem`, for representing select list items in your JavaBeans. There are several things you will need to do to set up a select list.

- Add a property to hold the current selected value
- Add a property to hold the list of `SelectItems`
- Populate the list of `SelectItems`
- Add tags to the JSP to reference the new values and render them in the desired format

For example, the following is the code we would need to add to the `InvoiceBean` class in Listing 6.6 to support a drop-down menu:

```
...
    /* List of payment term options from which users can choose */
    private List paymentTerms = new ArrayList();

    /* Currently selected payment term */
    private String paymentTerm = "";

    ...
```

```
    public InvoiceBean() {
        ...
        paymentTerms.add(new SelectItem("0", "On Receipt", ""));
        paymentTerms.add(new SelectItem("30", "Net 30 Days", ""));
        paymentTerms.add(new SelectItem("60", "Net 60 days", ""));
    }

    public List getPaymentTerms() { return paymentTerms; }
    public void setPaymentTerms(List paymentTerms) {
        this.paymentTerms = paymentTerms;
    }

    public String getPaymentTerm() { return paymentTerm; }
    public void setPaymentTerm(String paymentTerm) {
        this.paymentTerm = paymentTerm;
    }
...
```

Now we can add tags to `ModifyInvoice.jsp` (see Listing 6.12) to render a drop-down menu based on the list of `SelectItems` stored in the `paymentTerms` property:

```
<h:selectOneMenu  id="terms"
                  value="#{modifyInvoicePage.invoice.paymentTerm}">
   <f:selectitems  value="#{modifyInvoicePage.invoice.paymentTerms}"/>
</h:selectOneMenu>
```

The `selectOneMenu` tag will render a drop-down list that is bound to the bean property referenced by the tag's `value` attribute (in this case the `InvoiceBean`'s `paymentTerm` field). The options list in the resulting HTML `select` element will be generated from the list of `SelectItems` contained in the `paymentTerms` field identifed by the nested `selectItems` tag.

Similarly, we could follow the same set of steps used in the previous example to add a set of radio buttons. First, here's the new code we need to add to the `InvoiceBean` class:

```
...
    /* List of possible order status codes  */
    private List statusCodes = new ArrayList();

    /* Current order status */
    private String statusCode = "";

    ...

    public InvoiceBean() {
        ...
        statusCodes.add(new SelectItem("1", "Open", ""));
        statusCodes.add(new SelectItem("2", "Past Due", ""));
```

```
        statusCodes.add(new SelectItem("3", "Paid", ""));
    }

    public List getStatusCodes() { return statusCodes; }
    public void setStatusCodes(List statusCodes) {
        this.statusCodes = statusCodes;
    }

    public String getStatusCode() { return statusCode; }
    public void setStatusCode(String statusCode) {
        this.statusCode = statusCode;
    }
...
```

Now we can add the JSP tags:

```
<h:selectOneRadio  id="status"
                   value="#{modifyInvoicePage.invoice.statusCode}">
    <f:selectItems  value="#{modifyInvoicePage.invoice.statusCodes}"/>
</h:selectOneRadio>
```

As you can see, the only real difference between the drop-down list and the radio button list is the tag name, since both the `selectOneRadio` and the `selectOneMenu` tags are backed by subclasses of `UISelectOne`.

Check boxes are a bit different. They are backed by the `UISelectBoolean` component, which binds its value to a single property of type boolean, rather than to a list of `SelectItems`. To add check boxes to a page, we simply add `boolean` properties to the bean class, one per check box, and then add a tag for each check box in our JSP. Here's the additional Java code we would need to add to the `InvoiceBean` to support a pair of check boxes:

```
...
boolean newCustomer;
boolean expedited;

...

public boolean isNewCustomer() { return newCustomer; }
public void setNewCustomer(boolean newCustomer) {
    this.newCustomer = newCustomer;
}

public boolean isExpedited() { return expedited; }
public void setExpedited(boolean expedited) {
    this.expedited = expedited;
}
...
```

We could then add the following to our JSP:

```
...
     <h:selectBooleanCheckbox
                    id="expedited"
                    value="#{modifyInvoicePage.invoice.expedited}">
     </h:selectBooleanCheckbox>
     ...
     <h:selectBooleanCheckbox
                    id="newCustomer"
                    value="#{modifyInvoicePage.invoice.newCustomer}">
     </h:selectBooleanCheckbox>
...
```

Figure 6.8 shows how the Modify Invoice page would look with the added fields:

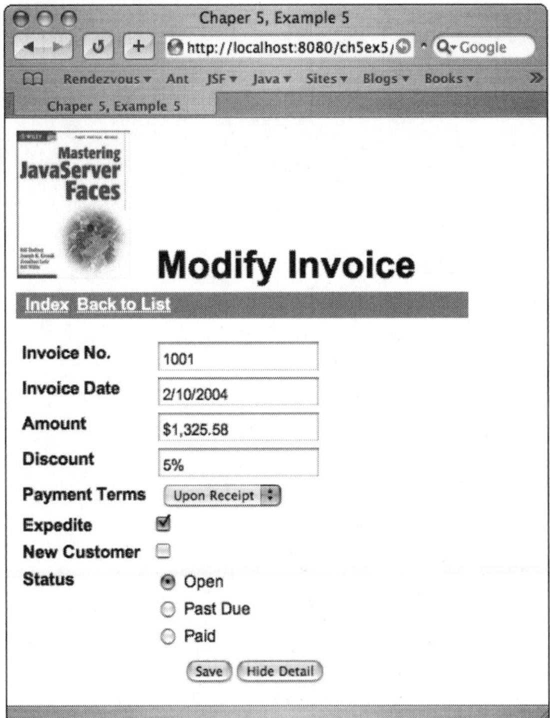

Figure 6.8 Modify Invoice page with a drop-down menu, radio buttons, and check boxes.

Summary

As we have seen, components play a central role in JavaServer Faces. They collaborate with tags and Renderers to generate the presentation, work with Converters to convert values between Java types and their UI representations, assist in validation along with any registered Validators, provide a registry for listeners, and implement the mechanisms needed to assemble and manage the view.

CHAPTER

7

Navigation, Actions, and Listeners

In the previous chapter, "UI Components," we learned about JSF's rendering and value binding facilities. From an MVC perspective, our focus was primarily on understanding how to implement the view portion of a JSF-based Web application. Now let's turn our attention to the controller tier.

JavaServer Faces provides facilities for binding UI controls to arbitrary methods on backing beans that can be used to define how an application responds to user-initiated events. These action methods then collaborate with a built-in navigation management system that allows developers to specify navigation rules declaratively in XML.

Under the covers, JSF uses an Event/Listener model, familiar to many UI developers, which allows developers to access and manipulate component state at any stage of the request/response cycle. It also provides convenient extension points for customizing the framework's behavior.

In combination, these facilities provide a straightforward foundation for building the controller layer of an MVC Model 2 Web application.

Overview

In this chapter, we will explore the framework's navigation mechanism. We'll do so by progressively developing an example application composed of several related pages—modeled on a typical, real-world business application scenario. We'll learn how to code action methods that provide the required application logic, as well as how to configure navigation rules in the application configuration file (by default, `faces-config.xml`) to manage the application's page flows.

We'll also learn about how and when to implement `ActionListeners` and `ValueChangeListeners` to handle some of the subtler issues that can arise when using JSF to develop nontrivial Web applications.

Actions and Navigation

Implementations of JSF must provide an implementation of the `ActionListener` interface to serve as a default listener at the application level. When the framework generates the component tree for a given page (during *Restore View* or *Render Response*), any components of type UICommand are registered with this listener.

A component that implements the `ActionSource` interface (for example, UICommand) will queue an `ActionEvent` when the framework invokes its `processDecodes()` method. At the end of the *Invoke Application* phase (or the *Apply Request Values* phase if the component's `immediate` property is set to `true`), the default `ActionListener` is responsible for dispatching these events by evaluating the component's method binding expression to locate an action method that it can then invoke. Action methods must take no arguments and return a string.

The default `ActionListener` passes the string returned from the action method to the framework's default `NavigationHandler`. The `NavigationHandler` in turn looks for a matching navigation rule in the application configuration file. If a matching value is found, the `NavigationHandler` calls `setViewRoot()` on the `FacesContext` with the name of the new view. If no match is found, the current view (and its tree of components) remains unchanged. At the end of the *Invoke Application* phase (*Apply Request Values* if `immediate` was set to `true`), the framework passes control to the *Render Response* phase, at which point the current view in the `FacesContext` is rendered.

You can customize the framework's behavior if desired by substituting your own implementations for the default `ActionListener`, the default `NavigationHandler`, or both if you wish, by calling `setApplicationListener()` or `setNavigationHandler()` on the application instance as necessary.

JSF provides several features that allow you to manage navigation between your application's pages. The simplest of these is to use an `outputLink` tag to render an HTML anchor tag that references a JSP page, as in the following example:

```
<f:view>
    ...
    <h:outputLink id="searchLink"
                  styleClass="Link"
                   value="Search.jsp">
        <f:verbatim >Search by Account Number</f:verbatim>
    </h:outputLink>
    ...
</f:view>
```

JSF implementations would typically render this in HTML as follows:

```
<a href="Search.jsp" class="Link">Search by Account Number</a>
```

While this works for simple navigation, it doesn't provide for the dynamic behavior that many of the pages in typical Web applications require. For example, suppose that we were creating a simple search page similar to the one in Figure 7.1.

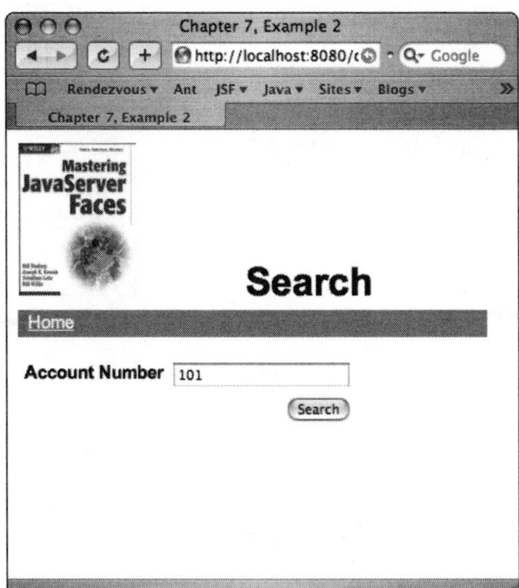

Figure 7.1 A simple search page.

The Search page picture in Figure 7.1 provides a single input field into which a user may enter an account number, and a button to submit the enclosing form. When the form is submitted, there are actually two separate bits of dynamic behavior that the application should carry out. One is the actual search, which in the example code we'll be looking at shortly is delegated to a business tier service. The other is deciding which page to navigate to based on the outcome of the search. That is, if a matching account is found, we want to navigate to a page that displays the results. Otherwise, we want to rerender the Search page with an error message indicating that no matching account was found.

To make implementing these types of scenarios as easy as possible, the `UICommand` component provides an `action` attribute that can be bound to an arbitrary method on a backing bean via a *method binding expression* (a special type of value binding expression), as follows:

```
<f:view>
    ...
    <h:form id="searchForm">
        ...
        <h:command_button id="searchButton"
                          value="Search"
                          action="#{searchPage.search}"/>
        ...
    </h:form>
    ...
</f:view>
```

In this example, the button's action is bound to the `search()` method of a bean located in either the request or the session under the key `searchPage` The previous example would result in the following HTML:

```
...
<form id="searchForm" method="post" action="/ch7ex1/faces/Search.jsp">
    ...
    <input type="submit"
           name="searchForm:searchButton"
           value="Search"
           title="Search by account number"/>
    <input type="hidden" name="searchForm" value="searchForm" />
    ...
</form>
...
```

Note that the `UICommand` component's Renderer adds a hidden form attribute to identify which form has been submitted, in case there are multiple forms on the page. The Renderer also prefixes the button's client ID with the form name (`searchForm:searchButton`) to ensure that the resulting string it is unique within the page.

If we wanted to use a hyperlink instead of a button to submit the form, we could simply replace the commandButton tag in the previous example with a commandLink tag as in the following code:

```
<h:commandLink id="link"
               action="#{searchPage.search}">
    <f:verbatim>Search</f:verbatim>
</h:commandLink>
```

In this case, the component's Renderer would add a bit of JavaScript to the resulting HTML to enable the hyperlink to submit the form:

```
<form id="form" method="post" action="/ch7ex1/faces/Search.jsp">
    ...
    <a href="#"
         onmousedown="document.forms[0][form:link'].value=form:link';
                     document.forms[0].submit()">
       Search
    </a>
    <input type="hidden" name="form:link"/>
    <input type="hidden" name="form" value="form" />
    ...
</form>
```

Note that the Renderer also adds another hidden form field, this time to identify the control that submitted the form, since the HTML anchor tag doesn't provide an id attribute.

Implementing Application Actions

Methods that are bound to a UICommand's action attribute via a method reference expression are referred to as *application actions*. JSF uses reflection at run time to locate and execute application actions, provided that they observe the following API convention: they must be public methods that take no parameters and return String. For example, here's the signature that would be required for the search() method:

```
public String search()
```

When a button or hyperlink backed by a UICommand component is clicked, JSF will look for a method whose signature conforms to this guideline and attempt to invoke it dynamically. To create a working example of a search() method, we would need to code a JavaBean exposing an application action method whose name corresponds to the final portion of the method binding expression. For example, let's take a look at the search() method in the SearchPage class in Listing 7.1.

```
package com.wiley.masteringjsf.ch7ex1;

...

/**
 * Page bean used to find the invoices for a given account
 */
public class SearchPage implements Serializable
{
...

    public SearchPage() { }

    /**
     * Searches for an AccountBean instance corresponding to the value
     * of the <code>accountNumber</code> attribute. If no match is
     * found, adds an error message to the FacesContext and returns
     * <code>null</code>. Otherwise, returns "viewInvoices" after
     * locating the ViewInvoicesPage and passing it the AccountBean's
     * list of invoices.
     */
    public String search() {
        AccountBean account = null;

        try {
            account = delegate.findAccount(accountNumber);
        }
        catch (BusinessDelegate.NotFoundException e) {
            FacesContext context = FacesContext.getCurrentInstance();
            context.addMessage(null, MessageFactory.
                getMessage("noMatch", new Object[] { accountNumber }));
            return null;
        }

        // Do some setup for the next page . . .

        ...

        return "viewInvoices";
    }

...

}
```

Listing 7.1 SearchPage.java.

Note that the `search()` method in Listing 7.1 returns either `null`, or the string `'viewInvoices'`. In general, the value returned by an application action method is referred to as its *outcome*. The outcome is mapped to a *navigation rule* specified in the application configuration file. To get our application action working, we must configure a navigation rule to define a mapping for the `viewInvoices`outcome.

Specifying Navigation Rules

Listing 7.2 is a simple navigation rule that binds the `viewInvoice` outcome to the file `ViewInvoices.jsp`, which we will use to display the search results:

```
...
  <navigation-rule>
    <from-view-id>/Search.jsp</from-view-id>
    <navigation-case>
      <from-outcome>viewInvoices</from-outcome>
      <to-view-id>/ViewInvoices.jsp</to-view-id>
    </navigation-case>
  </navigation-rule>
...
```

Listing 7.2 A simple navigation rule.

The `from-tree-id` element tells the framework that this rule applies only to navigations that result from the evaluation of a method binding expression referenced by an `ActionSource` component in the `Searchpage.jsp` component tree. In this example, that would be the reference to `searchPage.search` in the `commandLink` tag in `SearchPage.jsp`:

```
<h:commandButton id="searchButton"
                 title="Search by account number"
                 styleClass="Button"
                 value="Search"
                 action="#{searchPage.search}"/>
```

The navigation-case element in Listing 7.2 pairs a `from-outcome` element with a `to-tree-id` element. A single navigation rule may contain many navigation cases. The `from-outcome` defines one of the possible outcomes (return values) of an application action. If the action returns a string that matches a `from-outcome`, the framework will navigate to the page defined by the associated `to-tree-id` element, in this case `ViewInvoices.jsp`.

Note that we can optionally code the outcome string directly in the JSP instead of providing a method binding expression, as shown in the following code:

```
<h:commandLink id="homeLink"
               styleClass="Link"
               action="homePage">
    <f:verbatim>Home </f:verbatim>
</h:commandLink>
```

Here, the `action` attribute has been configured with a literal outcome string for which we can now add a navigation case. In this case, because the Home link is likely to be available as an outcome from most, if not all of our application's pages, we can create a global definition as shown in Listing 7.3.

```
...
  <navigation-rule>
      <navigation-case>
        <from-outcome>home</from-outcome>
          <to-tree-id>/Home.jsp</to-tree-id>
      </navigation-case>
  </navigation-rule>
...
```

Listing 7.3 A global navigation rule for the Home page.

This navigation rule simply omits the `from-tree-id` element, allowing the rule to be accessed from any JSP. These are just a few examples of the configuration options available for navigation rules. For further details, please see Chapter 4, "JSF Configuration."

Working with Forms

Listing 7.4 contains a complete source listing for the JSP that renders the Search page we described earlier (Listing 7.1).

```
<html>
<head>
   <meta http-equiv="Content-Type"
         content="text/html; charset=iso-8859-1">
   <link rel="stylesheet" href="/ch7ex1/styles.css" type="text/css">
   <title>Chapter 7, Example 1</title>
   <%@ taglib uri="http://java.sun.com/jsf/html" prefix="h" %>
   <%@ taglib uri="http://java.sun.com/jsf/core" prefix="f" %>
</head>
```

Listing 7.4 Search.jsp.

```
<body>
<f:view>
    <f:subview id="header">
        <jsp:include page="Header.jsp" flush="true">
            <jsp:param name="pageName" value="Search"/>
        </jsp:include>
    </f:subview>
    <p>
    <h:messages styleClass="ErrorMessage"/>
    <h:form id="searchForm">
        <h:panelGrid columnClasses="FieldLabel,TextInput"
                     footerClass="TableCellRight"
                     columns="2">
            <h:outputText value="Account Number"/>
            <h:inputText id="accountNumber"

value="#{searchPage.accountNumber}"/>
            <f:facet name="footer">
                <h:commandButton id="searchButton"
                                 title="Search by account number"
                                 styleClass="Button"
                                 value="Search"
                                 action="#{searchPage.search}"/>
            </f:facet>

        </h:panelGrid>
    </h:form>

</f:view>
</body>
</html>
```

Listing 7.4 *(continued)*

When rendered by the JSF reference implementation, the code in Listing 7.4 results in (approximately) the HTML shown in Listing 7.5.

```
<html>
<html>
<head>
   <meta http-equiv="Content-Type"
         content="text/html; charset=iso-8859-1">
   <link rel="stylesheet" href="/ch7ex1/styles.css" type="text/css">
   <title>Chapter 7, Example 1</title>
</head>
```

Listing 7.5 HTML generated by Search.jsp. *(continued)*

```
<body>

...  <!-- HTML generated by heading subview omitted --!>

<form id="searchForm" method="post"
      action="/ch7ex3/faces/Search.jsp"
      enctype="application/x-www-form-urlencoded">

    <table>
        <tfoot>
            <tr>
                <td class="TableCellRight" colspan="2">
                    <input id="searchForm:searchButton"
                           type="submit"
                           name="searchForm:searchButton"
                           value="Search"
                           title="Search by account number"
                           class="Button"/>
                </td>
            </tr>
        </tfoot>
        <tbody>
            <tr>
                <td class="FieldLabel">Account Number</td>
                <td class="TextInput">
                    <input type="text"
                           name="searchForm:accountNumber"
                           value="101"/>
                </td>
            </tr>
        </tbody>
    </table>

    <input type="hidden" name="searchForm" value="searchForm" />
</form>

</body>
</html>
```

Listing 7.5 *(continued)*

When the search button in Listing 7.5 is activated (by a user clicking it), JSF will respond by invoking the default `ActionListener's processAction()` method, passing it an `ActionEvent` instance that includes a reference to the ActionSource (in this case a `UICommand`) associated with the button. The `ActionListener` will then call the component's `getAction()` method to obtain its method binding (an instance of `MethodBinding`), and then it calls the binding's `invoke()` method, which uses reflection to invoke the actual method referenced by the binding. In this case that will be the `SearchPage` class's `search()` method, as shown in Listing 7.6, which delegates the actual search to the `findAccount()` method of a helper class named `BusinessDelegate`.

```
package com.wiley.masteringjsf.ch7ex1;

import java.io.InvalidObjectException;
import java.io.Serializable;

import javax.faces.context.FacesContext;
import javax.faces.el.ValueBinding;

import com.sun.faces.util.MessageFactory;
import com.sun.faces.util.Util;

/**
 * Page bean used to find the invoices for a given account
 */
public class SearchPage implements Serializable
{
    private Integer accountNumber;
    private transient BusinessDelegate delegate =
        BusinessDelegate.getDelegate();

    public SearchPage() { }

    /**
     * Searches for an AccountBean instance corresponding to the value
     * of the <code>accountNumber</code> attribute. If no match is
     * found, adds an error message to the FacesContext and returns
     * <code>null</code>. Otherwise, returns "viewInvoices" after
     * locating the ViewInvoicesPage and passing it the AccountBean's
     * list of invoices.
     */
    public String search() {
        AccountBean account = null;

        try {
            account = delegate.findAccount(accountNumber);
        }
        catch (BusinessDelegate.NotFoundException e) {
            FacesContext context = FacesContext.getCurrentInstance();
            context.addMessage(null, MessageFactory.
                getMessage("noMatch", new Object[] { accountNumber }));
            return null;
        }
```

Listing 7.6 Complete code for SearchPage.java. *(continued)*

```
        // Note: you could place the account values in the request
        // and let ViewInvoicesPage instances retrieve them as necessary
        // instead of setting them directly the way we do here.
        ValueBinding binding =
            Util.getValueBinding("#{viewInvoicesPage}");
        ViewInvoicesPage viewInvoicesPage = (ViewInvoicesPage)
            binding.getValue(FacesContext.getCurrentInstance());
        viewInvoicesPage.setInvoices(account.getInvoices());
        viewInvoicesPage.setAccountNumber(account.getAccountNumber());
        viewInvoicesPage.setCompanyName(account.getCompanyName());

        return "viewInvoices";
    }

    /**
     * Reconstitues the BusinessDelegate instance when deserialized
     */
    protected Object readResolve() throws InvalidObjectException {
        delegate = BusinessDelegate.getDelegate();
        return this;
    }

    public Integer getAccountNumber() { return accountNumber; }
    public void setAccountNumber(Integer accountNumber) {
        this.accountNumber = accountNumber;
    }
}
```

Listing 7.6 *(continued)*

Note that the actual implementation of the BusinessDelegate is unimportant to our example—the BusinessDelegate is simply a placeholder here for whatever functionality would be required to access the application's persistence services.

The BusinessDelegate's findAccount() method throws a specific exception type if there is no match for the provided account number. If that happens, the search() method catches the exception and adds an appropriate error message to the FacesContext, returning null to cause the current page to be rerendered. Otherwise, it prepares the next page for rendering and returns viewInvoices.

Once the search() method exits, control returns to the default ActionListener's processAction() method. The ActionListener then invokes the handleNavigation() method on the application's default NavigationHandler, passing it the application action's outcome value. The

NavigationHandler would then search for a navigation rule in the application configuration file that matches the provided outcome (in this case viewInvoices). Here's an example of a matching navigation rule:

```
<navigation-rule>
  <from-view-id>/Search.jsp</from-view-id>
  <navigation-case>
    <from-outcome>viewInvoices</from-outcome>
    <to-view-id>/ViewInvoices.jsp</to-view-id>
  </navigation-case>
</navigation-rule>
```

The NavigationHandler then sets the view ID stored in the FacesContext to that of the view selected by the navigation case, which in the example is the path /ViewInvoices.jsp identifying the page we'll use to display the search results. Note though that if the NavigationHandler doesn't find a match for the outcome value in any of the application's navigation rules—for example if our search() method returns null—the view ID is left unchanged. In either case, the framework then passes control to the *Render Response* phase, at which point the component tree referenced by the view ID will be rendered. If the view ID hasn't changed, the current component tree (representing the page that was just submitted) is rerendered.

In our example, we add an error message to the FacesContext and return null if no match was found. This results in the Search page being regenerated with the new error message. Otherwise, we return 'viewInvoices', which changes the view ID, causing the View Invoices page (ViewInvoices.jsp in Listing 7.7, backed by ViewInvoicesPage.java in Listing 7.9) to be rendered.

However, before the new page can be rendered, we must arrange for the ViewInvoicesPage bean to receive the search results that are to be displayed. The search() method uses a ValueBinding to locate the object in the available scopes. It then invokes one of the bean's mutators to pass it the search results. An alternative approach would be to place the results in the request or the session under a well-defined, globally unique key.

Complex Forms

The View Invoices page presents two different scenarios where you might prefer to use a hyperlink rather than a button to submit a form. As you will see, JSF supports this transparently. The file ViewInvoices.jsp shown in Listing 7.7 contains a dataTable that renders an HTML table consisting of a header, a footer, and an arbitrary number of body rows (depending on the size of the list returned by a given search).

```
<html>
<head>
   <meta http-equiv="Content-Type"
         content="text/html; charset=iso-8859-1">
   <link rel="stylesheet" href="/ch7ex1/styles.css" type="text/css">
   <title>Chapter 7, Example 1</title>
   <%@ taglib uri="http://java.sun.com/jsf/html" prefix="h" %>
   <%@ taglib uri="http://java.sun.com/jsf/core" prefix="f" %>
</head>
<body>

<f:view>
    <f:subview id="header"/>
        <jsp:include page="Header.jsp" flush="true">
            <jsp:param name="pageName" value="View Invoices"/>
            <jsp:param name="linkUrl" value="Search.jsp"/>
            <jsp:param name="linkText" value="Search Again"/>
        </jsp:include>
    </f:subview>
    <p>

    <h:form id="invoiceForm">

    <h:outputText id="companyName"
                  styleClass="Heading"
                  value="#{viewInvoicesPage.companyName}"/>

    <h:dataTable id="table"
                  value="#{viewInvoicesPage.invoices}"
                  var="invoice"
                  styleClass="MediumTable"
                  headerClass="Header"
                  footerClass="ListTotal"
                  columnClasses="ListCenter, ListLeft, ListCenter,
                                 ListRight, ListRight">
        <h:column>
            <f:facet name="header">
                <h:outputText value="Select"/>
            </f:facet>
            <h:selectBooleanCheckbox value="#{invoice.selected}"/>
             <f:facet name="footer">
                <h:commandButton
                    id="deleteButton"
                    title="Delete selected invoices"
                    value="Delete"
                    action="#{viewInvoicesPage.delete}">
                </h:commandButton>
            </f:facet>
        </h:column>
```

Listing 7.7 ViewInvoices.jsp.

```
<h:column>
    <f:facet name="header">
        <h:commandLink
            id="invoiceNumber"
            styleClass="SortLink"
            title="Sort column values"
            action="#{viewInvoicesPage.sortInvoiceNumber}">
            <f:verbatim>Invoice No.</f:verbatim>
        </h:commandLink>
    </f:facet>
    <h:commandLink
        id="modifyInvoice"
        styleClass="Link"
        title="Modify this invoice"
        value="#{invoice.invoiceNumber}"
        action="#{viewInvoicesPage.modifyInvoice}">
        <h:outputText id="invoiceNumber"
                      value="#{invoice.invoiceNumber}"/>
    </h:commandLink>
</h:column>
<h:column>
    <f:facet name="header">
        <h:commandLink
            id="invoiceDate"
            styleClass="SortLink"
            title="Sort column values"
            action="#{viewInvoicesPage.sortInvoiceDate}">
            <f:verbatim>Date</f:verbatim>
        </h:commandLink>
    </f:facet>
    <h:outputText id="invoiceDate"
                  value="#{invoice.invoiceDate}">
        <f:convertDateTime pattern="MM/dd/yy"/>
    </h:outputText>
</h:column>
<h:column>
    <f:facet name="header">
        <h:commandLink
            id="discountId"
            styleClass="SortLink"
            title="Sort column values"
            action="#{viewInvoicesPage.sortDiscount}">
            <f:verbatim>Discount</f:verbatim>
        </h:commandLink>
    </f:facet>
    <h:outputText id="discount"
                  value="#{invoice.discount}">
        <f:convertNumber pattern="##.00%"/>
    </h:outputText>
```

Listing 7.7 *(continued)*

```
<f:facet name="footer">
                <h:outputText value="Total:"/>
            </f:facet>
        </h:column>
        <h:column>
            <f:facet name="header">
              <h:panelGroup>
                <h:commandLink
                    id="amountId"
                    styleClass="SortLink"
                    title="Sort column values"
                    action="#{viewInvoicesPage.sortAmount}">
                    <f:verbatim>Amount</f:verbatim>
                </h:commandLink>
              </h:panelGroup>
            </f:facet>
            <h:outputText id="amount"
                           value="#{invoice.amount}">
                <f:convertNumber pattern="#,###.00"/>
            </h:outputText>
            <f:facet name="footer">
                <h:outputText value="#{viewInvoicesPage.total}">
                    <f:convertNumber type="currency"/>
                </h:outputText>
            </f:facet>
        </h:column>
    </h:dataTable>
    </h:form>
  <p>
</f:view>
</body>
</html>
```

Listing 7.7 *(continued)*

The dataTable tag's value attribute takes a value reference expression that you can bind to a bean property containing the Collection to be iterated, as shown here:

```
<h:dataTable id="table"
             value="#{viewInvoicesPage.invoices}"
             var="invoice"
             styleClass="MediumTable"
             headerClass="Header"
             footerClass="ListTotal"
             columnClasses="ListCenter, ListLeft, ListCenter,
                            ListRight, ListRight">
```

The `dataTable` tag's `var` attribute defines a key that can be used to access the current bean during a given iteration of the Collection. Nested tags can then use the key in value reference expressions to access individual properties of the current bean. Let's take a closer look at a single column. Here's the code for the Invoice Date column:

```
<h:column>
    <f:facet name="header">
        <h:commandLink
            id="invoiceDateId"
            styleClass="SortLink"
            title="Sort column values"
            action="#{viewInvoicesPage.sortInvoiceDate}">
            <f:verbatim>Date</f:verbatim>
        </h:commandLink>
    </f:facet>
    <h:outputText id="invoiceDate"
                  value="#{invoice.invoiceDate}">
        <f:convertDateTime pattern="MM/dd/yy"/>
    </h:outputText>
</h:column>
```

Nested inside the column is an `outputText` tag that renders the invoice date, and a header facet containing a `commandLink` bound to the `sort InvoiceDate()` method on the `ViewInvoicesPage` bean. Here's what the `sortInvoiceDate()` method looks like:

```
/** Sort the invoice list on the invoiceDate property. */
public String sortInvoiceDate() {
    Collections.sort(invoices,
        new InvoiceBean.InvoiceDateComparator());
    return null;
}
```

Because we need the hyperlink to submit the form, the `commandLink's` Renderer automatically inserts the necessary JavaScript. For example, the HTML for the Invoice No. anchor tag would look something like this:

```
<a id="form:tbl:invNum"
   href="#"
   title="Sort column values"
   onclick="document.forms['form']['form:tbl:num'].value='form:tbl:num';
            document.forms['form'].submit(); return false;"
   class="SortLink">
        Invoice No.
</a>
```

Actually to get this to fit neatly on the page, we had to shorten the `id` values: `invoiceForm` was shortened to `form`, `table` to `tbl`, and `invoiceNumber` to `num`. This brings up an interesting point. Since the values of the `id` attributes of `UIComponents` are rendered in the resulting HTML tags, it's probably a good idea to keep the names short, though longer names can aid readability. You might try using longer names at first when you are experimenting with the framework, to make the HTML as readable as possible. That's often helpful for getting an initial understanding of what's going on.

Also, note that JSF will autogenerate unique identifiers wherever you don't supply your own. Since these are provided mainly to aid in client-side scripting, (though they can come in quite handy on the server side as well) these autogenerated IDs may not be to your taste, but then to each his own.

Anyway, the idea behind the column header hyperlinks we have been looking at here is simply to allow a user to sort on the values of any given column by clicking on the column's heading, as shown in Figures 7.2 and 7.3.

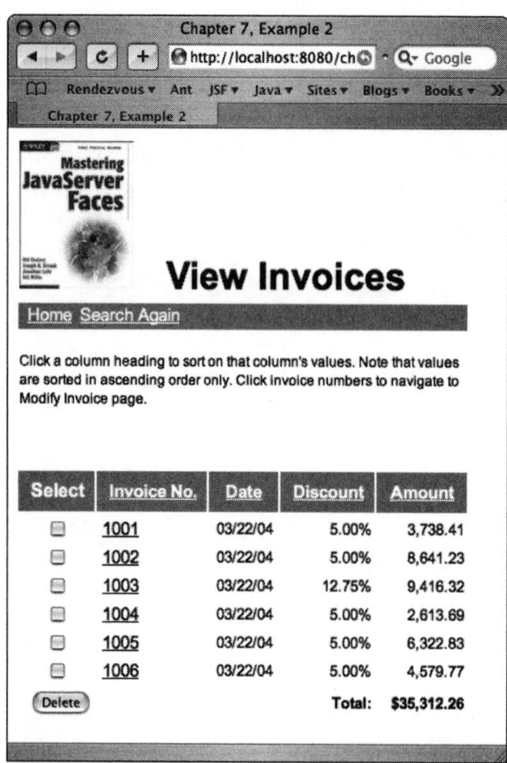

Figure 7.2 The View Invoices page displaying a list of invoices.

For example, clicking the Amount column heading on the page shown in Figure 7.2 would switch the table from being sorted by invoice number to being sorted by amount. The result would be the changed ordering shown in Figure 7.3. Of course this example is a bit simplistic, in that it only provides for sorting in ascending order; a bit more JSP code would be required to keep track of the sort direction for each column.

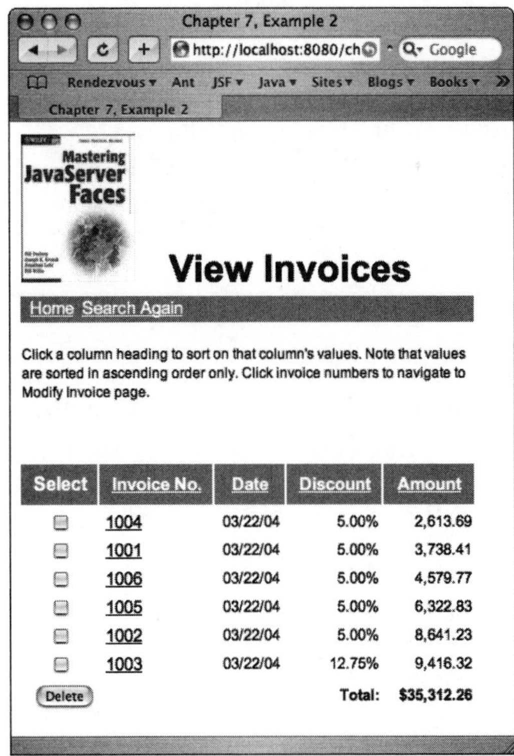

Figure 7.3 The View Invoices page after clicking the Amount hyperlink.

> **HOW NAVIGATION WORKS BEHIND THE SCENES**
>
> **When it builds the component tree for a given page, the framework automatically registers all the `UICommand` components with the application's default `ActionListener`. If the user activates one of these components (by clicking it in the user interface) the component adds an event to the event queue. During the *Invoke Application* phase, the framework handles the event by invoking the listener's `processAction()` method.**
>
> **The `ActionListener's processAction()` method has two possible means of determining the action's outcome. If the component's `action` attribute is set with a simple string value, the literal value is used as the outcome. If the attribute's value is in the form of a method reference expression, the listener uses the value as a method binding and attempts to invoke the referenced method reflectively. The outcome then is the invoked method's return value.**
>
> **This value is then passed to the `NavigationHandler`, which uses it to select the next component tree to render.**

One other interesting point about this JSP is that the Invoice No. column values are also rendered as hyperlinks. Here's the JSP that renders the column:

```
<h:column>
    <f:facet name="header">
        <h:commandLink
            id="invoiceNumber"
            styleClass="SortLink"
            title="Sort column values"
            action="#{viewInvoicesPage.sortInvoiceNumber}">
            <f:verbatim>Invoice No.</f:verbatim>
        </h:commandLink>
    </f:facet>
    <h:commandLink
        id="modifyInvoice"
        styleClass="Link"
        title="Modify this invoice"
        value="#{invoice.invoiceNumber}"
        action="#{viewInvoicesPage.modifyInvoice}">
        <h:outputText id="invoiceNumber"
                      value="#{invoice.invoiceNumber}"/>
    </h:commandLink>
</h:column>
```

The `commandLink` tag that renders the invoice number is bound via a method reference expression to the `modifyInvoice()` application action in the `ViewInvoicesPage` bean. Because the tag is inside a `dataTable`, the Renderer automatically adds a row index to the generated form submission JavaScript, which looks something like this (Once again, we've pared the identifiers down to make the code fit more neatly on the printed page, shortening `invoiceForm` to `f`, `table` to `tbl`, and `modifyInvoice` to `mod`):

```
<a  id="f:tbl:0:mod"
    href="#" title="Modify thisinvoice"
    onclick="document.forms['f']['f:tbl:0:mod].value='f:tbl:0:mod;
             document.forms['f'].submit(); return false;"
    class="Link">
        <span id="f:tbl:0:num">1001</span>
</a>
```

The zero that appears in several places in the HTML represents the row index, with the value zero indicating that this is the first row in the rendered table. For comparison, the second row's anchor tag would look like this:

```
<a  id="f:tbl:1:mod"
    href="#" title="Modify this invoice"
    onclick="document.forms['f']['f:tbl:1:mod].value='f:tbl:1:mod;
             document.forms['f'].submit(); return false;"
    class="Link">
        <span id="f:tbl:1:num">1002</span>
</a>
```

When the user clicks one of these links, the application's default `ActionListener` will invoke the `ViewInvoicePage` bean's `modifyInvoice()` method, which passes the selected invoice to the `ModifyInvoicePage` bean and then returns the string `modifyInvoice` as its navigation outcome. We will of course need to add a navigation rule to the application configuration file to handle the new outcome:

```
<navigation-rule>
  <from-tree-id>/ViewInvoicesList.jsp</from-tree-id>
  <navigation-case>
    <from-outcome>modifyInvoice</from-outcome>
      <to-tree-id>/ModifyInvoice.jsp</to-tree-id>
  </navigation-case>
</navigation-rule>
```

Rendering the Current Component Tree

Note that we didn't have to provide a navigation case for the sort links used in the column headings. That's because we don't need the framework to switch to a different view—we only need it to regenerate the current view so that the table will be rendered with the new sort order. The framework will do precisely that if the value returned by an `Action` doesn't match any navigation rule. It is left to our discretion whether we want to explicitly return `null`, or a string that won't be matched by an existing navigation rule, though returning `null` is probably clearer and less likely to result in bugs later on if the navigation rules are changed.

Initializing the Next Page

The primary responsibility of the `ViewInvoicesPage` class's `modifyInvoice()` method (Listing 7.9) is to return the outcome needed to navigate to the Modify Invoice page, which will be rendered by `ModifyInvoice.jsp` as shown in Listing 7.8.

```
<html>
<head>
    <meta http-equiv="Content-Type"
          content="text/html; charset=iso-8859-1">
    <title>Chaper 7, Example 1</title>
    <link rel="stylesheet" href="/ch7ex1/styles.css" type="text/css">
    <%@ taglib uri="http://java.sun.com/jsf/html" prefix="h" %>
    <%@ taglib uri="http://java.sun.com/jsf/core" prefix="f" %>
</head>
<body>
<f:view>
    <f:subview id="header"/>
        <jsp:include page="Header.jsp" flush="true">
            <jsp:param name="pageName" value="Modify Invoice"/>
            <jsp:param name="linkUrl" value="ViewInvoices.jsp"/>
            <jsp:param name="linkText" value="Back to List"/>
        </jsp:include>
    </f:subview>
    <p>
    <h:messages styleClass="ErrorMessage"/>
    <h:form id="invoiceForm">
        <h:panelGrid id="invoicePanel"
                     columns="2"
                     columnClasses="FieldLabel,TextInput"
                     footerClass="TableCellRight">
            <h:outputText
                id="invoiceNumberLabel"
                value="Invoice Number"/>
            <h:inputText
                id="invoiceNumber"
                styleClass="TextInput"
                required="true"
                value="#{modifyInvoicePage.invoice.invoiceNumber}">
                <f:validateLongRange minimum="1000"/>
            </h:inputText>
```

Listing 7.8 ModifyInvoice.jsp.

```
            <h:outputText
                id="invoiceDateLabel"
                value="Invoice Date"/>
            <h:inputText
                id="invoiceDate"
                styleClass="TextInput"
                required="true"
                value="#{modifyInvoicePage.invoice.invoiceDate}">
                <f:convertDateTime pattern="M/d/yyyy"/>
            </h:inputText>
            <h:outputText
                id="discountLabel"
                value="Discount"/>
            <h:inputText
                id="discount"
                styleClass="TextInput"
                value="#{modifyInvoicePage.invoice.discount}">
                <f:convertNumber type="percent"/>
            </h:inputText>
            <h:outputText
                id="amountLabel"
                value="Amount"/>
            <h:inputText
                id="amount"
                styleClass="TextInput"
                required="true"
                value="#{modifyInvoicePage.invoice.amount}">
                <f:convertNumber pattern="$#,###.00"/>
            </h:inputText>
            <f:facet name="footer">
                <h:panelGroup>
                    <h:commandButton
                        id="saveButton"
                        title="Save changes"
                        styleClass="Button"
                        value="Save"
                        action="#{modifyInvoicePage.save}"/>
                    <h:commandButton
                        id="cancelButton"
                        title="Cancel changes"
                        styleClass="Button"
                        value=" Cancel "
                        immediate="true"
                        action="viewInvoices">
<%-- Use this insteadif you need to do cleanup before navigating . . .
                        action="#{modifyInvoicePage.cancel}">--%>
                    </h:commandButton>
```

Listing 7.8 *(continued)*

```
                </h:panelGroup>
            </f:facet>
        </h:panelGrid>
    </h:form>
</f:view>
</body>
</html>
```

Listing 7.8 *(continued)*

The input tags in `ModifyInvoice.jsp` are bound to properties of an `InvoiceBean` nested in a `ModifyInvoicePage` bean. For example, the value reference expression for the Invoice Number field looks like this:

```
...
value="#{modifyInvoicePage.invoice.invoiceNumber}"
...
```

In order for these bindings to be evaluated correctly, the `modifyInvoice()` method must ensure that the `ModifyInvoicePage` bean contains an instance of `InvoiceBean` that corresponds to the invoice number the user clicked. There are a couple of different ways to do this. One would be to place the selected instance directly in the request or session, as in the following example:

```
public String modifyInvoice() {

    FacesContext facesContext = FacesContext.getCurrentInstance();
    UIViewRoot root = facesContext.getViewRoot();
    UIData table = (UIData)
        root.findComponent("invoiceForm").findComponent("table");

    HttpServletRequest request = (HttpServletRequest)
        facesContext.getExternalContext().getRequest();
    request.setAttribute(Constants.CURRENT_INVOICE_BEAN,
                         (InvoiceBean) table.getRowData());

    return "modifyInvoice";
}
```

The `ModifyInvoicePage` could then return the instance from its `get-Invoice()` method:

```
public InvoiceBean getInvoice() {
    FacesContext facesContext = FacesContext.getCurrentInstance();
    Map requestMap =
        facesContext.getExternalContext().getRequestMap();
    return (InvoiceBean)
        requestMap.get(Constants.CURRENT_INVOICE_BEAN);
}
```

When using this approach, make sure that the key used to store the object in the request or the session is globally unique for your application. Using a package path as a prefix is a common strategy:

```
public final static String CURRENT_INVOICE_BEAN =
    "com.wiley.masteringjsf.CURRENT_INVOICE_BEAN";
```

An alternate approach (and the one used in the example in Listing 7.9) is to make the `InvoiceBean` a property of `ModifyInvoicePage`, and set it directly by calling its mutator from within the `modifyInvoice()` method, as in the following example:

```
public String modifyInvoice() {

    FacesContext facesContext = FacesContext.getCurrentInstance();
    UIViewRoot root = facesContext.getViewRoot();
    UIData table = (UIData)
        root.findComponent("invoiceForm").findComponent("table");

    ValueBinding binding =
        Util.getValueBinding("#{modifyInvoicePage}");
    ModifyInvoicePage detailPage = (ModifyInvoicePage)
        binding.getValue(facesContext);

    detailPage.setInvoice((InvoiceBean) table.getRowData());

    return "modifyInvoice";
}
```

While the first approach may be a bit more flexible, the second approach has advantages in maintainability, especially in larger more complex applications.

One other detail is that it may be preferable for the `ModifyInvoicePage` to use a clone of the bean displayed on the `ViewInvoicesPage` rather than sharing the same instance. This is so because if the user makes some changes to the invoice but then cancels the transaction, we don't want the canceled changes to show up when the user navigates back to the View Invoices page. The version of `ViewInvoicesPage.java` shown in Listing 7.9 includes code to perform the clone operation.

```
package com.wiley.masteringjsf.ch7ex1;

import java.io.Serializable;
import java.util.*;

import javax.faces.component.UIData;
import javax.faces.component.UIViewRoot;
import javax.faces.context.FacesContext;
import javax.faces.el.ValueBinding;
import javax.faces.event.ActionEvent;

import com.sun.faces.util.Util;

/**
 * Presents a list of invoices and provides methods for sorting and
 * totalling the the list, and for drilling down to individual invoices
 */
public class ViewInvoicesPage implements Serializable
{
    /** A delegate for business services **/
    private static transient BusinessDelegate delegate =
        BusinessDelegate.getDelegate();
    /** The list of invoices to display */
    private List invoices;
    /** The account number for the current list */
    private Integer accountNumber;
    /** The name of the company associated with the account */
    private String companyName;

    public ViewInvoicesPage() { }

    public void sort(ActionEvent event) {
        String key = event.getComponent().getId();
        Collections.sort(invoices, InvoiceBean.getComparator(key));
    }

    /**
     * Sets up the detail page by getting the bean backing the current
     * row in the UIData table, and passing it to the detail page.
     * An alternative implementation would be to stuff the invoice
     * bean into the request under a well-known key and let the
     * detail page find it.
     *
     * @return the navigation outcome.
     */
    public String modifyInvoice() {
        FacesContext facesContext = FacesContext.getCurrentInstance();
```

Listing 7.9 ViewInvoicesPage.java.

```
        UIViewRoot root = facesContext.getViewRoot();
        UIData table = (UIData)
            root.findComponent("invoiceForm").findComponent("table");
        InvoiceBean invoice = (InvoiceBean) table.getRowData();

        // Clone the InvoiceBean so that changes applied from
        // the Modify Invoice page won't directly affect the invoices
        // in the local cache.
        InvoiceBean clonedInvoice = null;
        try {
            clonedInvoice = (InvoiceBean) invoice.clone();
        }
        catch (CloneNotSupportedException e) {
            throw new InvoiceAppUIException(e);
        }

        ValueBinding binding =
            Util.getValueBinding("#{modifyInvoicePage}");
        ModifyInvoicePage detailPage = (ModifyInvoicePage)
            binding.getValue(facesContext);

        detailPage.setInvoice(clonedInvoice);

        return "modifyInvoice";
    }


    /**
     * Totals the invoices.
     */
    public double getTotal() {
        double total = 0.0;
        Iterator invoiceIter = invoices.iterator();
        while (invoiceIter.hasNext()) {
            InvoiceBean invoice = (InvoiceBean) invoiceIter.next();
            Double amount = invoice.getAmount();
            if (amount != null)
                total += amount.doubleValue();
        }
        return total;
    }

    /*--------  Accessor methods --------*/

    public List getInvoices() {
        return invoices;
    }
    public void setInvoices(List invoices) {
```

Listing 7.9 *(continued)*

```
        this.invoices = invoices;
    }

    public String getCompanyName() {
        return companyName;
    }
    public void setCompanyName(String companyName) {
        this.companyName = companyName;
    }

    public Integer getAccountNumber() {
        return accountNumber;
    }
    public void setAccountNumber(Integer accountNumber) {
        this.accountNumber = accountNumber;
    }
}
```

Listing 7.9 *(continued)*

The version of InvoiceBean presented in Listing 7.10 includes several inner classes that implement the Comparator interface. These comparators are used in the ViewInvoicesPage sort() method when sorting the list of invoices by column values. Note that this implementation doesn't provide for sorting in descending order.

```
package com.wiley.masteringjsf.ch7ex1;

import java.io.Serializable;
import java.util.*;

/**
 * A bean that models a simple invoice. The provided Comparator
 * classes are used for sorting lists of InvoiceBeans.
 */
public class InvoiceBean implements Serializable, Cloneable
{
    /*--------  Inner classes (Comparators) --------*/

    static class InvoiceNumberComparator implements Comparator {
        public int compare(Object obj1, Object obj2) {
            Integer num1 = ((InvoiceBean) obj1).getInvoiceNumber();
            Integer num2 = ((InvoiceBean) obj2).getInvoiceNumber();
            return num1.compareTo(num2);
        }
    }
```

Listing 7.10 InvoiceBean.java.

```
static class AmountComparator implements Comparator {
    public int compare(Object obj1, Object obj2) {
        Double num1 = ((InvoiceBean) obj1).getAmount();
        Double num2 = ((InvoiceBean) obj2).getAmount();
        return num1.compareTo(num2);
    }
}

static class DiscountComparator implements Comparator {
    public int compare(Object obj1, Object obj2) {
        Double num1 = ((InvoiceBean) obj1).getDiscount();
        Double num2 = ((InvoiceBean) obj2).getDiscount();
        return num1.compareTo(num2);
    }
}

static class InvoiceDateComparator implements Comparator {
    public int compare(Object obj1, Object obj2) {
        Date num1 = ((InvoiceBean) obj1).getInvoiceDate();
        Date num2 = ((InvoiceBean) obj2).getInvoiceDate();
        return num1.compareTo(num2);
    }
}

/*--------  InvoiceBean --------*/

public static final String INVOICE_NUMBER_ID = "invoiceNumberId";
public static final String AMOUNT_ID = "amountId";
public static final String DISCOUNT_ID = "discountId";
public static final String INVOICE_DATE_ID = "invoiceDateId";

private Integer invoiceNumber;
private Date invoiceDate;
private Double amount;
private AccountBean account;
private Double discount;
private boolean selected;

public InvoiceBean() { }

public InvoiceBean(Integer invoiceNumber,
                   Date invoiceDate,
                   Double amount,
                   Double discount,
                   AccountBean account) {

    setInvoiceNumber(invoiceNumber);
    setInvoiceDate(invoiceDate);
```

Listing 7.10 *(continued)*

```
        setDiscount(discount);
        setAmount(amount);
        setAccount(account);
    }

    public static Comparator getComparator(String key) {
        if (key.equals(INVOICE_NUMBER_ID))
            return new InvoiceNumberComparator();
        if (key.equals(INVOICE_DATE_ID))
            return new InvoiceDateComparator();
        if (key.equals(AMOUNT_ID))
            return new AmountComparator();
        if (key.equals(DISCOUNT_ID))
            return new DiscountComparator();

        throw new IllegalArgumentException("Invalid key " + key);
    }

    protected Object clone() throws CloneNotSupportedException {
        return super.clone();
    }

    /*--------  Accessor methods --------*/

    ...
}
```

Listing 7.10 *(continued)*

Complex Navigation

Let's extend the preceding example a bit further to illustrate some additional navigation scenarios. The Modify Invoice page shown in Listing 7.9 contains not only a Save button to save any changes to the current invoice, but a Cancel button as well (Figure 7.4).

The desired behavior is that clicking Cancel should return the user to the View Invoices page. Clicking Save should cause the application to navigate to the Confirm Invoice page, where the user can decide whether to commit the changes or return to the Modify Invoice page to make further modifications. The navigational flow for the three pages is illustrated in Figure 7.5

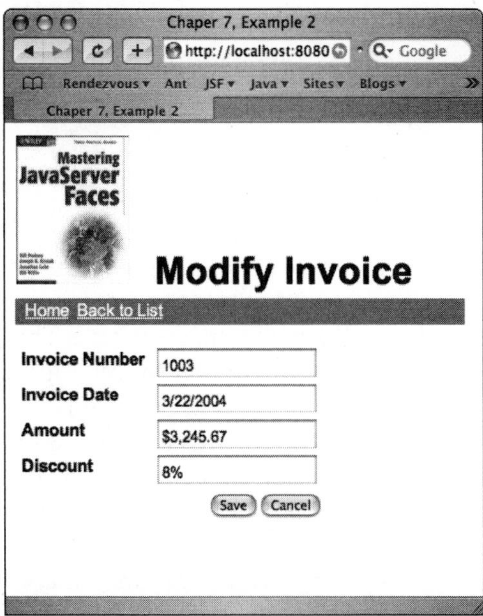

Figure 7.4 Modify Invoice page with Save and Cancel buttons.

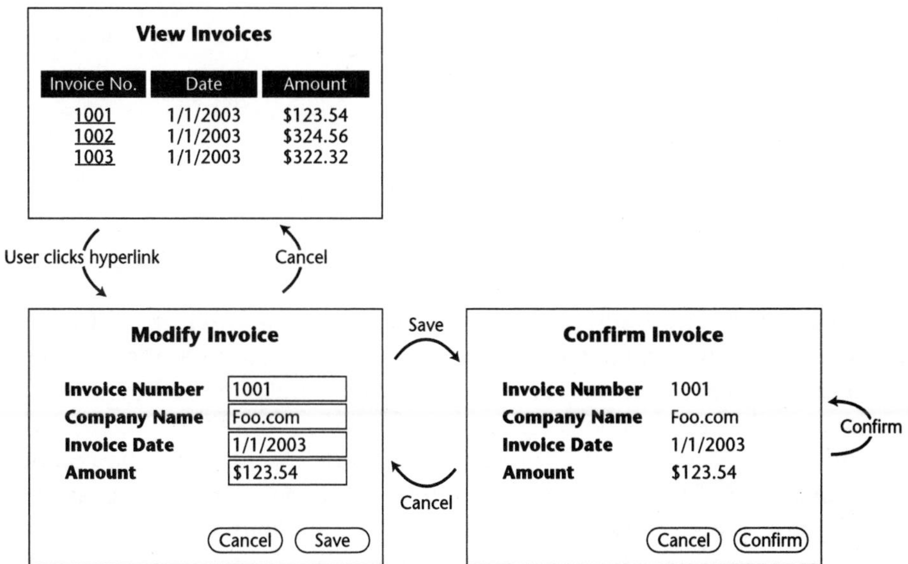

Figure 7.5 Navigational flow for View Invoices, Modify Invoice, and Confirm Invoice pages.

To implement the Modify Invoice page's cancellation behavior, the JSP in Listing 7.8 binds the Cancel button directly to a navigation outcome string:

```
<h:commandButton id="cancelButton"
                 ...
                 value="Cancel"
                 action="viewInvoices"/>
```

If we had set the `action` attribute's value to a method binding expression (as in `action="#{modifyInvoicePage.cancel}"`), then the framework would use the `action` method's return value as the navigation outcome. This would be useful if we needed to perform some cleanup or other processing as part of canceling the invoice transaction. However, in this case, all we really need to do is perform the navigation. Setting the component's action to a literal string will cause the framework to use the provided string directly as the navigation outcome. This saves us the nuisance of writing an extra method simply to return the outcome string.

We can now configure the navigation in the application configuration file, as follows:

```
<navigation-rule>
  <navigation-case>
    <from-outcome>viewInvoices</from-outcome>
    <to-view-id>/ViewInvoices.jsp</to-view-id>
  </navigation-case>
  <from-view-id>/ConfirmInvoice.jsp</from-view-id>
  <navigation-case>
    <from-outcome>modifyInvoice</from-outcome>
    <to-view-id>/ModifyInvoice.jsp</to-view-id>
    </navigation-case>
</navigation-rule>
```

This navigation rule defines two navigation cases. The first handles the outcome of the Cancel button by selecting the View Invoices page as the next view to render. The second navigation case handles the outcome returned by the `modifyInvoice()` method when the Save button is clicked.

There's one potential pitfall with Cancel buttons. The `UICommand` component provides an `immediate` attribute that we can set to `true` to cause the *Apply Request Values* phase to be skipped. This will avoid attempting to perform conversion and validation on the submitted form's input values, so if the user changed any of them before clicking Cancel, the modified values will be ignored. If we forget to set `immediate` to `true`, we will end up with an annoying bug.

If the user clicks Cancel after changing some of the values, and one of the changed values fails conversion or validation, instead of navigating to the

View Invoices page the application will rerender the Modify Invoice page, which will now display the error message. At this point the user is trapped, because repeated clicking of either the Save or the Cancel button will result in the same outcome.

Fortunately, the cure is simple: just set the Cancel button's `immediate` attribute to `true`:

```
<h:commandButton id="cancelButton"
                 ...
                 value="Cancel"
                 immediate="true"
                 action="viewInvoices"/>
```

The other potential path in the navigational flow occurs when a user clicks Save, and the submitted values are converted and validated successfully. In this case, the Save button's `action` will be evaluated. In the JSP shown in Listing 7.8, the Save button's `action` is a method reference expression:

```
<h:commandButton id="saveButton"
                 ...
                 value="Save"
                 action="#{modifyInvoicePage.save}"/>
```

The `save()` method shown in the listing for `ModifyInvoicePage.java` (Listing 7.11) uses a `ValueBinding` to get an instance of `ConfirmInvoicePage`, and then calls its `setInvoice()` method, passing the `InvoiceBean` as an argument. Finally, it returns confirmInvoice as its outcome.

```
package com.wiley.masteringjsf.ch7ex2;

import java.io.Serializable;

import javax.faces.context.FacesContext;
import javax.faces.el.ValueBinding;

import com.sun.faces.util.Util;

public class ModifyInvoicePage implements Serializable
{
    /** The invoice bean managed by this page */
    private InvoiceBean invoice;

    public ModifyInvoicePage() { }

    /**
```

Listing 7.11 ModifyInvoicePage.java. *(continued)*

```
         * Prepares the confirmation page by calling its
         * <code>saveInvoice()</code> method with the current invoice.
         * Doesn't actually perform the save. The save will be
         * performed by the confirmation page only if the user clicks
         * its Confirm button.
         */
        public String save() {
            FacesContext context = FacesContext.getCurrentInstance();

            ValueBinding binding =
                Util.getValueBinding("#{confirmInvoicePage}");
            ConfirmInvoicePage nextPage  = (ConfirmInvoicePage)
                binding.getValue(context);

            nextPage.setInvoice(invoice);

            return "confirmInvoice";
        }

        /*--------  Accessor methods --------*/

        public InvoiceBean getInvoice() {
            return invoice;
        }
        public void setInvoice(InvoiceBean invoice) {
            this.invoice = invoice;
        }
    }
```

Listing 7.11 *(continued)*

The Confirm Invoice page shown in Listing 7.12 is similar to the Modify Invoice page. It presents the same set of values to the user, though in a noneditable format, and provides Cancel and Confirm buttons. If the user clicks Cancel, we simply navigate to the previous page. If the user clicks Confirm, business tier code is executed to save the modified values. At this point, we want to redisplay the Confirmation page with a message informing the user of the status of the save request, rather than navigating to another page.

In order to do this, we return `null` from the `saveInvoice()` method. This tells the framework to rerender the current component tree, effectively leaving us where we are. Prior to returning from the `saveInvoice()` method, we place the message we wish to present to the user in the request. Here is the JSP code for the Confirm Invoice page:

```
<html>
<head>
   <meta http-equiv="Content-Type"
         content="text/html; charset=iso-8859-1">
   <title>Chaper 7, Example 2</title>
   <link rel="stylesheet" href="/ch7ex2/styles.css" type="text/css">
   <%@ taglib uri="http://java.sun.com/jsf/html" prefix="h" %>
   <%@ taglib uri="http://java.sun.com/jsf/core" prefix="f" %>
</head>
<body>
<f:view>
    <f:subview id="header"/>
        <jsp:include page="Header.jsp" flush="true">
            <jsp:param name="pageName" value="Confirm Invoice"/>
            <jsp:param name="linkUrl" value="ViewInvoices.jsp"/>
            <jsp:param name="linkText" value="Back to List"/>
        </jsp:include>
    </f:subview>
    <p>
    <h:messages styleClass="Message"/>
    <h:form id="invoiceForm">
        <h:panelGrid id="invoicePanel"
                     columns="2"
                     styleClass="SmallTable"
                     columnClasses="FieldLabel,FieldValue"
                     footerClass="TableCellRight">
            <h:outputText
                id="invoiceNumberLabel"
                value="Invoice Number"/>
            <h:outputText
                id="invoiceNumber"
                styleClass="FieldValue"
                value="#{confirmInvoicePage.invoice.invoiceNumber}"/>
            <h:outputText
                id="invoiceDateLabel"
                value="Invoice Date"/>
            <h:outputText
                id="invoiceDate"
                styleClass="FieldValue"
                value="#{confirmInvoicePage.invoice.invoiceDate}">
                <f:convertDateTime pattern="M/d/yyyy"/>
            </h:outputText>
            <h:outputText
                id="amountLabel"
                value="Amount"/>
```

Listing 7.12 ConfirmInvoice.jsp. *(continued)*

```
            <h:outputText
                id="amount"
                styleClass="FieldValue"
                value="#{confirmInvoicePage.invoice.amount}">
                <f:convertNumber pattern="$#,###.00"/>
            </h:outputText>
            <h:outputText
                id="discountLabel"
                value="Discount"/>
            <h:outputText
                id="discount"
                styleClass="FieldValue"
                value="#{confirmInvoicePage.invoice.discount}">
                <f:convertNumber type="percent"/>
            </h:outputText>

            <f:facet name="footer">
                <h:panelGroup>
                    <h:commandButton
                        id="confirmButton"
                        title="Confirm changes"
                        styleClass="Button"
                        value="Confirm"
                        action="#{confirmInvoicePage.save}"/>

                    <h:commandButton
                        id="cancelButton"
                        title="Cancel changes"
                        styleClass="Button"
                        value=" Cancel "
                        immediate="true"
                        action="modifyInvoice"/>
                </h:panelGroup>
            </f:facet>

        </h:panelGrid>
    </h:form>
</f:view>
</body>
</html>
```

Listing 7.12 *(continued)*

Figure 7.6 shows how the Confirm Invoice page looks when rendered by `ConfirmInvoice.jsp`.

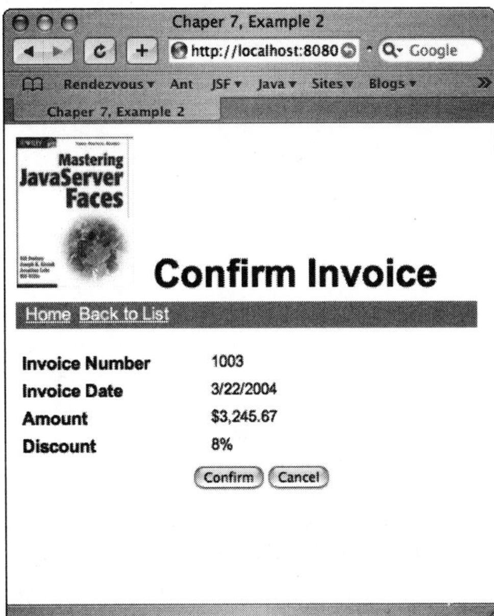

Figure 7.6 The Confirm Invoice page.

Listing 7.13 shows the `ConfirmInvoicePage` class. It implements a `save()` method that propagates the save to a business delegate, and then it adds a message to the `FacesContext` indicating whether the `Business Delegate's` save attempt succeeded or failed.

```
package com.wiley.masteringjsf.ch7ex2;

import java.io.Serializable;

import javax.faces.component.UIComponent;
import javax.faces.context.FacesContext;

import com.sun.faces.util.MessageFactory;

public class ConfirmInvoicePage implements Serializable
{
    /** The invoice bean displayed on this page */
    private InvoiceBean invoice;

    public ConfirmInvoicePage() { }

    /**
```

Listing 7.13 ConfirmInvoicePage.java. *(continued)*

```
     * Attempts to save the invoice in response to the user clicking
     * the Confirm button. A message is added to the FacesContext to
     * indicate whether the save attempt succeeded or failed.
     */
    public String save() {
        boolean saved = true;
        BusinessDelegate delegate = BusinessDelegate.getDelegate();

        try {
            delegate.saveInvoice(invoice);
        }
        catch (BusinessDelegate.DelegateException e) {
            saved = false;
        }

        FacesContext ctx = FacesContext.getCurrentInstance();
        String key = saved ? "invoiceSaved" : "invoiceSaveFailed";
        ctx.addMessage(null, MessageFactory.getMessage(ctx, key));
        return null;
    }

    /*--------  Accessor methods --------*/

    public InvoiceBean getInvoice() {
        return invoice;
    }
    public void setInvoice(InvoiceBean invoice) {
        this.invoice = invoice;
    }
}
```

Listing 7.13 *(continued)*

The navigation rule for the Confirm Invoice page need only concern itself with the Cancel outcome, because the `save()` method always returns `null`:

```
<navigation-rule>
  <from-view-id>/ConfirmInvoice.jsp</from-view-id>
  <navigation-case>
    <from-outcome>modifyInvoice</from-outcome>
    <to-view-id>/ModifyInvoice.jsp</to-view-id>
  </navigation-case>
</navigation-rule>
```

Until this point, we have focused on using action methods to respond to user actions. However, JSF also allows us to configure one or more listeners on instances of `UIComponent` that implement either the `EditableValueHolder` or the `ActionSource` interface, providing an additional mechanism to aid in handling user-generated events. Though you rarely need to implement listeners in JSF applications, the next section explores several situations where they will prove to be useful.

Events and Listeners

JSF provides two distinct event types, `ActionEvent` and `ValueChangeEvent`. Each of these event types has a corresponding listener type, `ActionListener`, and `ValueChangeListener`, respectively.

`ActionEvents` are queued by components that implement the `ActionSource` interface (such as `UICommand`) when activated by a user action—for example clicking a button or a hyperlink. `ValueChangeEvents` are queued by components that implement the `EditableValueSource` interface (such as `UIInput`) whenever their values change as a result of user input. Any events that have been queued are broadcast at the end of each life-cycle phase to any listeners that have registered an interest in receiving them.

The simplest way to implement a listener is to add a listener method to a backing bean. As with application action methods, listener method signatures must observe a convention in order to be called: They must return `void` and take a single argument of the event type for which they are registered. The method name can be any valid identifier. So an `ActionListener` method named *foo* would look like this:

```
void foo(ActionEvent event) { ... }
```

while a `ValueChangeListener` method named *bar* would look like this:

```
void bar(ValueChangeEvent event) { ... }
```

Tags backed by `UIInput` and `UICommand` components provide attributes to allow you to bind listener methods directly in JSP. Unsurprisingly, the `UIInput` attribute is `valueChangeListener` while the `UICommand` attribute is `actionListener`, as shown in the following code:

```
...
<h:inputText
    valueChangeListener="#{myBean.bar}"
    value="#{myBean.someProperty"/>
<h:commandButton
    value="Submit"
    actionListener="#{myBean.foo}"/>
...
```

It is also possible to manage a component's listeners programmatically by methods for manipulating a component's registered ActionListener instances:

```
public abstract void addActionListener(ActionListener listener);
public abstract ActionListener[] getActionListeners();
public abstract void removeActionListener(ActionListener listener);
```

Similarly, the EditableValueHolder interface provides the following API for managing a component's ValueChangeListener instances:

```
public abstract void addValueChangeListener(
    ValueChangeListener listener);
public abstract ValueChangeListener[] getValueChangeListeners();
public abstract void removeValueChangeListener(
    ValueChangeListener listener);
```

The other way to create a listener is to implement one of two provided interfaces, ActionListener or ValueChangeListener. Each interface defines a single method; taken together the two methods are analogs for the backing bean methods we just described. The method defined by ActionListener is as follows:

```
public abstract void processAction(ActionEvent event)
    throws AbortProcessingException;
```

The ValueChangeListener interface defines a similar method:

```
public abstract void processValueChange(ValueChangeEvent event)
    throws AbortProcessingException;
```

In spite of the impression given by the presence of the facilities we noted earlier in this section for registering listeners directly on tags, the role of listeners in JSF is primarily to support the development of components. For most usages, the combination of application action methods, Converters, and Validators should provide the most straightforward way to implement page-level functionality. Listeners should be used only in special cases where they provide a clear advantage over the ordinary processing techniques.

Implementing an ActionListener Method

Let's look at example of a situation where it might be preferable to implement an ActionListener method. The Confirm Invoice page in the previous section (Listing 7.12) renders a pair of buttons, one to confirm the transaction, and the other to cancel it. When the user clicks Confirm, the ConfirmInvoicePage bean's save() method attempts to save the changes, and places a message in the FacesContext to indicate whether it succeeded or not. In either case though, the method returns `null` to rerender the page, so that the user can view the message before navigating elsewhere (see Figure 7.7).

Note though, that the Confirm and Cancel buttons are now no longer relevant, because there is no transaction to confirm or cancel at this point. It would probably make sense to hide these buttons, perhaps replacing them with a hyperlink to the View Invoices page, or some other meaningful navigation target.

While we could simply add code to the `save()` method to make the necessary changes to the `UIComponents`, there are a couple of problems with this approach. One is that the `save()` method isn't passed any arguments, so there's no direct way to get a reference to the components. While it is possible to get the view root from the `FacesContext` and drill down from there to the components we're interested in, this approach requires more code, and it would couple the method's implementation to the structure of the JSP.

It would also reduce the cohesion of the `save()` method, making the code more complex. Using an `ActionListener` method to handle the changes to the `UIComponents` would allow the `save()` method to remain focused on functionality directly related to saving the invoice. The following is an example of an `ActionListener` method that would hide the buttons and replace them with a hyperlink.

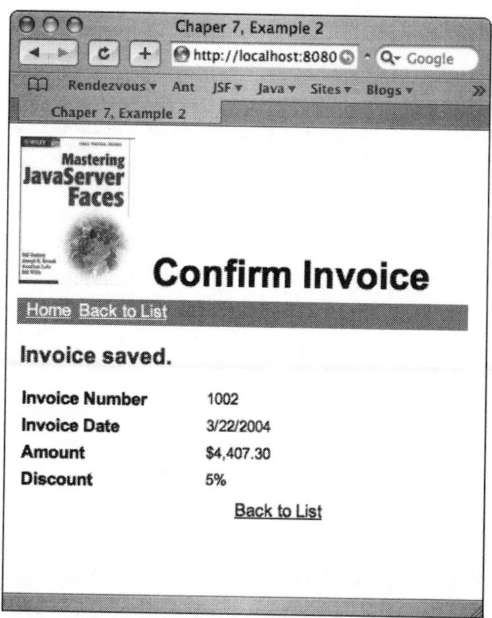

Figure 7.7 Confirm Invoice page with Confirm and Cancel buttons replaced by Back to List hyperlink.

```
/**
 * Once the Confirm button is clicked, it no longer makes sense
 * for the user to click Confirm or Cancel, so we hide the buttons.
 * In their place, we now show the 'Back to List' hyperlink.
 */
public void confirmed(ActionEvent event) {
    UIComponent confirmButton = event.getComponent();
    confirmButton.findComponent("confirmButton").setRendered(false);
    confirmButton.findComponent("cancelButton").setRendered(false);
    confirmButton.findComponent("viewListLink").setRendered(true);
}
```

Here's how the buttons and hyperlink would be configured:

```
<f:facet name="footer">
    <h:panelGroup>
        <h:commandButton
            id="confirmButton"
            title="Confirm changes"
            styleClass="Button"
            value="Confirm"
            actionListener="#{confirmInvoicePage.confirmed}"
            action="#{confirmInvoicePage.save}"/>

        <h:commandButton
            id="cancelButton"
            title="Cancel changes"
            styleClass="Button"
            value=" Cancel "
            immediate="true"
            action="modifyInvoice"/>

        <h:commandLink
            id="viewListLink"
            title="Return to View Invoices page"
            styleClass="Link"
            rendered="false"
            action="viewInvoices">
           <f:verbatim>Back to List</f:verbatim>
        </h:commandLink>
    </h:panelGroup>
</f:facet>
```

Now when the user clicks Confirm, the `confirmed()` `ActionListener` method will be invoked first, followed by the `save()` method. If the user interface requirements change later, we can modify the `confirmed()` method without being forced to tamper with the `save()` implementation.

Implementing the ActionListener Interface

ActionListener methods are more convenient for most purposes than are ActionListener classes. For one thing, ActionListener methods have the advantage of having direct access to the backing bean state. They also allow you to keep related functionality grouped together in the same class, which usually makes for better readability and easier maintenance.

However, there are occasions when it may make sense to create a class that implements the ActionListener interface. For example, suppose that we wanted to keep track of certain user actions in an application. We could add a managed bean to the session to provide a place to record the information. We could then create an ActionListener and register it on any UICommand components that we might be interested in tracking.

Here's the code for the UserActions managed bean we will use to record the user actions:

```
package com.wiley.masteringjsf.ch7ex3;

import java.io.Serializable;
import java.util.ArrayList;
import java.util.Date;
import java.util.Iterator;
import java.util.List;

public class UserActions implements Serializable {

    public static class LogItem {

        public LogItem(String name, String page, String component) {
            timestamp = new Date();
            this.command = name;
            this.page = page;
            this.component = component;
        }

        private Date timestamp;
        private String command;
        private String page;
        private String component;

        public Date getTimestamp() { return timestamp; }
        public void setTimestamp(Date timestamp) {
            this.timestamp = timestamp;
        }

        public String getCommand() { return command; }
        public void setCommand(String name) { this.command = name; }
```

```
        public String getPage() { return page; }
        public void setPage(String page) { this.page = page; }

        public String getComponent() { return component; }
        public void setComponent(String value) {
            this.component = value;
        }

        public String toString() {
            return timestamp + ": " +
                   "command=" + command +
                   ", page=" + page +
                   ", component=" + component;
        }
    }

    private List logItems = new ArrayList();

    public UserActions() { }

    public void addLogItem(String command,
                           String page,
                           String component) {
        logItems.add(new LogItem(command, page, component));
    }

    public List logItems() { return logItems; }

    public String toString() {
        StringBuffer buf = new StringBuffer();
        Iterator itemIter = logItems.iterator();
        while (itemIter.hasNext()) {
            buf.append(itemIter.next());
            buf.append("\n");
        }
        return buf.toString();
    }
}
```

We can configure the `UserActions` managed bean in the application configuration file as follows so it will be available in the session:

```
<managed-bean>
  <description>Used for logging user actions</description>
  <managed-bean-name>userActions</managed-bean-name>
  <managed-bean-class>
    com.wiley.masteringjsf.ch7ex3.UserActions
  </managed-bean-class>
  <managed-bean-scope>session</managed-bean-scope>
</managed-bean>
```

Now we can create an ActionListener implementation that records user actions in the UserActions bean:

```
package com.wiley.masteringjsf.ch7ex3;

import javax.faces.component.UICommand;
import javax.faces.context.FacesContext;
import javax.faces.el.ValueBinding;
import javax.faces.event.AbortProcessingException;
import javax.faces.event.ActionEvent;
import javax.faces.event.ActionListener;

import com.sun.faces.util.Util;

public class UserActionListener implements ActionListener {

    public void processAction(ActionEvent event)
        throws AbortProcessingException {

        FacesContext context = FacesContext.getCurrentInstance();
        ValueBinding binding = Util.getValueBinding("#{userActions}");
        UserActions actions = (UserActions) binding.getValue(context);
        UICommand component = (UICommand) event.getComponent();
        String commandName = (String) component.getValue();
        String pageName = context.getViewRoot().getViewId();
        String clientId = component.getClientId(context);

        actions.addLogItem(commandName, pageName, clientId);
    }
}
```

To register the UserActionListener on a component, we can use a nested actionListener tag. Note that the enclosing component must implement the ActionSource interface.

```
<h:commandButton
    id="saveButton"
    title="Save changes"
    styleClass="Button"
    value="Save"
    action="#{modifyInvoicePage.save}">
    <f:actionListener
        type="com.wiley.masteringjsf.ch7ex3.UserActionListener"/>
</h:commandButton>
```

The listener can also be registered programmatically, by calling `addActionListener()` on the target ActionSource:

```
...
FacesContext context = FacesContext.getCurrentInstance();
UIViewRoot view = context.getViewRoot();
ActionSource button = (ActionSource) view.findComponent("saveButton");

if (component != null)
    button.addActionListener(new UserActionListener());
...
```

We could then access the `UserActions` bean in the session whenever we wanted to display the tracked actions:

```
...
FacesContext context = FacesContext.getCurrentInstance();
ValueBinding binding = Util.getValueBinding("#{userActions}");
UserActions actions = (UserActions) binding.getValue(context);
System.out.println("User Actions = " + actions);
...
```

The resulting log entries would look something like the following:

```
...
Mon Mar 22 00:06:09 EST 2004: command=Save, page=/ModifyInvoice.jsp,
    component=invoiceForm:saveButton
Mon Mar 22 00:06:10 EST 2004: command=Confirm, page=/ConfirmInvoice.jsp,
    component=invoiceForm:confirmButton
Mon Mar 22 00:06:17 EST 2004: command=Save, page=/ModifyInvoice.jsp,
    component=invoiceForm:saveButton
Mon Mar 22 00:06:20 EST 2004: command=Confirm, page=/ConfirmInvoice.jsp,
    component=invoiceForm:confirmButton
...
```

Implementing a ValueChangeListener Method

Although `ValueChageListeners` are primarily intended to be used in implementing custom components (also true of `ActionListeners`, though perhaps to a lesser extent), they can also be used directly, either as methods on a backing bean or in the form of classes that implement the `ValueChange Listener` interface. Let's look at a concrete example of where it might make sense to use a `ValueChangeListener` method: adding support for an undo button on the Modify Invoice page from Listing 7.8.

First we will need to implement an undo manager. Here's a very simple one:

```
package com.wiley.masteringjsf.ch7ex3;

import java.io.Serializable;
import java.util.Stack;

import javax.faces.context.FacesContext;
import javax.faces.el.ValueBinding;

public class UndoManager implements Serializable {

    private class UndoItem {
        private ValueBinding binding;
        private Object previousValue;

        public UndoItem(ValueBinding binding, Object previousValue) {
            this.binding = binding;
            this.previousValue = previousValue;
        }

        public void undo() {
            FacesContext context = FacesContext.getCurrentInstance();
            binding.setValue(context, previousValue);
        }
    }

    private Stack undoStack;

    public UndoManager() {
        undoStack = new Stack();
    }

    public boolean undo() {
        if (undoStack.empty())
            return false;
        UndoItem item = (UndoItem) undoStack.pop();
        item.undo();
        return true;
    }

    public void add(ValueBinding binding, Object previousValue) {
        undoStack.push(new UndoItem(binding, previousValue));
    }
}
```

In order to get undo to work on the Modify Invoice page, we need our backing bean (`ModifyInvoicePage.java` from Listing 7.11) to be notified of every value change. We can get these notifications by implementing a

ValueChangeListener method and registering it on any UIComponents for which we wish to provide undo functionality. Here's the ValueChange-Listener method:

```
...
private UndoManager undoManager;
...
public ModifyInvoicePage() {
    ...
    undoManager = new UndoManager();
    ...
}
...
public void modified(ValueChangeEvent event) {
    UIInput component = (UIInput) event.getComponent();
    ValueBinding binding = component.getValueBinding("value");
    Object value = binding.getValue(FacesContext.getCurrentInstance());
    undoManager.add(binding, value);
}
...
```

We can now bind the input tags in the JSP to the new ValueChange Listener method. For example, here's the JSP for the Discount field with a valueChangeListener attribute setting added:

```
<h:inputText
    id="discount"
    styleClass="TextInput"
    valueChangeListener="#{modifyInvoicePage.modified}"
    value="#{modifyInvoicePage.invoice.discount}">
    <f:convertNumber type="percent"/>
</h:inputText>
```

We'll also need to add an undo() application action method to the Modify InvoicePage class:

```
...
public String undo() {
    boolean undone = undoManager.undo();
    if (!undone) {
        FacesContext ctx = FacesContext.getCurrentInstance();
        ctx.addMessage(null
            MessageFactory.getMessage("nothingToUndo", null));
    }
    return null;
}
...
```

Finally, we'll need to add a Submit button and an Undo button to the Modify Invoice page:

```
...
<h:commandButton
    id="submitButton"
    title="Submit changes"
    styleClass="Button"
    value="Submit"
    action=""/>
<h:commandButton
    id="undoButton"
    title="Undo"
    styleClass="Button"
    value="Undo"
    action="#{modifyInvoicePage.undo}"/>
...
```

Now when the user clicks Submit, any input components that are bound to the `modified()` `ValueChangeListener` method will queue `ValueChange Events` during the *Apply Request Values* phase. If no conversion or validation errors occur, the dispatch the events to the new method, giving it the opportunity to an `UndoItem` onto the undo stack for each of the changed values. If there are any items on the stack, clicking Undo will cause the most recent `UndoItem` to be popped off the stack and fired, thus reverting the associated property to its previous value.

Implementing the ValueChangeListener Interface

Although you should rarely need to create classes that implement the `Value ChangeListener` interface, they can occasionally provide a handy way to address troublesome issues such as synchronization between two or more related pages. Let's look at a specific example.

The `ViewInvoicesPage` class presented earlier in Listing 7.9 contains a list of `InvoiceBeans` that are rendered as rows in a table. The values in the Invoice Number column are rendered as hyperlinks that the user can click to navigate to the Modify Invoice page. The application action that handles the navigation also initializes the `ModifyInvoicePage` bean by passing it a clone of the `InvoiceBean` instance backing the table row. You'll recall that we cloned the bean to avoid the following scenario:

Imagine that the user clicks through to the Modify Invoice page, edits several of the fields, and then clicks Submit, but one of the fields fails validation. The user then decides to cancel the transaction and return to the View Invoices page. However, if the two pages share the same `InvoiceBean` instance, the user will see the changed values when the invoice list is redisplayed, even though the user canceled the transaction and the changes were never really saved (see Figure 7.8).

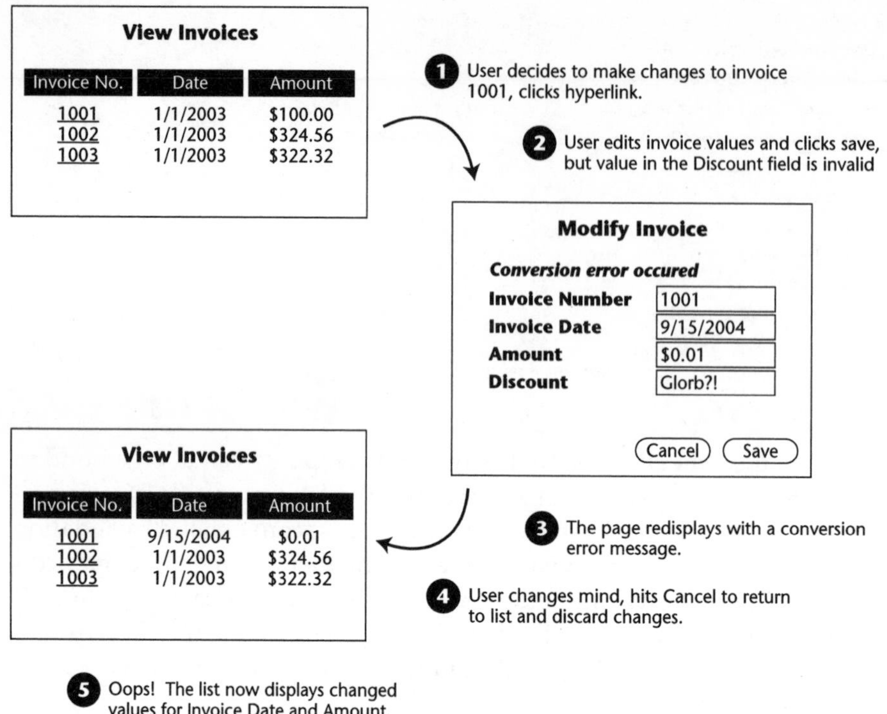

Figure 7.8 Invoice list synchronization glitch.

Unfortunately, if we clone the `InvoiceBean` we now face the opposite problem. If the user successfully submits changes on the Modify Invoice page and then navigates back to the View Invoices page, the invoice list will still display the old values. We could solve this by avoiding caching altogether, but allowing every page navigation to trigger a fetch probably wouldn't be terribly efficient.

Another potential solution would be to invalidate the `ViewInvoicePage` bean's cache when one or more `InvoiceBean` values change. We could register a `ValueChangeListener` to on the Modify Invoice page's input tags to listen for any changes. If one or more values were to change, the listener implementation could then invoke a method on the `ViewInvoicesPage` to cause it to invalidate its cache, forcing it to refetch the next time it is rendered.

Here's an example of a class that implements the `ValueChangeListener` interface to provide the needed functionality:

```
package com.wiley.masteringjsf.ch7ex3;

import javax.faces.context.FacesContext;
import javax.faces.el.ValueBinding;
import javax.faces.event.AbortProcessingException;
```

```
import javax.faces.event.ValueChangeEvent;
import javax.faces.event.ValueChangeListener;

import com.sun.faces.util.Util;

public class InvoiceListener implements ValueChangeListener {

    public void processValueChange(ValueChangeEvent event)
        throws AbortProcessingException {

        FacesContext context = FacesContext.getCurrentInstance();
        ValueBinding binding =
            Util.getValueBinding("#{viewInvoicesPage}");
        ViewInvoicesPage viewInvoicesPage = (ViewInvoicesPage)
            binding.getValue(context);
        viewInvoicesPage.invalidateCache();
    }
}
```

The `ViewInvoicesPage` class would need a few small code changes. Obviously, we would need to add an `invalidateCache()` method. In the following example we have also modified the existing `getInvoices()` method to automatically refresh the cache if it has been nullified. To make this possible, we have added an `accountNumber` property. The `accountNumber` value would be initialized by the search page before it passes control to the View Invoices page.

```
...
private Integer accountNumber = new Integer(101);
...
public Integer getAccountNumber() {
    return accountNumber;
}
public void setAccountNumber(Integer accountNumber) {
    this.accountNumber = accountNumber;
}
...
public void invalidateCache() {
    invoices = null;
}
...
public List getInvoices() {
    if (invoices == null && accountNumber != null) {
        setInvoices(delegate.findInvoices(accountNumber));
    }
    return invoices;
}
...
```

We can now use a valueChangeListener tag to bind the InvoiceListener to the Modify Invoice page's input tags; for example, here's the modified JSP for the Amount field:

```
...
<h:inputText
    id="amount"
    styleClass="TextInput"
    required="true"
    value="#{modifyInvoicePage.invoice.amount}">
    <f:valueChangeListener
        type="com.wiley.masteringjsf.ch7ex3.InvoiceListener"/>
    <f:convertNumber pattern="$#,###.00"/>
</h:inputText>
...
```

Using a ValueChangeListener class rather than a ValueChangeListener method in this situation helps us avoid coupling the ModifyInvoicePage to the ViewInvoicesPage.

Summary

In the examples in this chapter, you have seen how adding application action methods to a backing bean can lead to a very natural way of encapsulating a page's behavior along with its state, while the action attribute defined by UICommand makes it easy to bind the action methods to buttons and hyperlinks in JSP. You saw how this simple mechanism, coupled with declarative specification of navigation rules in XML, provides a straightforward way to implement application controller logic.

JavaServer Faces rounds out these capabilities with its Event/Listener model, which allows you to register ValueChangeListeners and ActionListeners on components, providing additional flexibility that can make it easier to craft solutions for some of the edge cases that arise when you are developing complex user interfaces.

But clearly the intent of the framework is that you should use application actions rather than ActionListeners wherever possible. Similarly, ValueChangeListeners are intended to be used sparingly, given that Validator classes and application actions provide more direct and natural mechanisms for most common situations.

CHAPTER

8

Validation and Conversion

JavaServer Faces provides extensible facilities for formatting, conversion and validation. The framework uses two distinct mechanisms to implement this functionality. This chapter covers both mechanisms in detail, including their extension points, and illustrates techniques for simplifying and automating formatting, conversion, and validation behavior in your applications.

The chapter is divided into two main parts, the first dealing with formatting and conversion, and the second with validation. With each topic, we begin by examining where and how these transformations take place within the JSF framework's processing model and then delve quickly into practical examples.

After working through examples that involve the standard classes and tags, we'll explore how to add custom behavior. Detailed code examples will help illustrate when and how to create your own custom Converters, Validators, and tags.

Overview

JavaServer Faces provides two separate facilities that can be used to assist in validating submitted HTML form values. One of these is the validation mechanism defined in the `javax.faces.validator` package, which includes the `Validator` interface and several concrete implementations. The other facility is provided by the built-in type conversion mechanism, as defined by the `javax.faces.convert.Converter` interface.

The Converter stereotype's primary role in the framework is to convert between the typed properties of JavaBeans that represent the application's model and the string representations of their values presented in the user interface. Converters are bidirectional; that is, they convert objects to strings and strings to objects. JSF applies Converters to inbound request values during the *Process Validations* phase, unless a component that implements the `EditableValueHolder` interface (such as `UIInput`) or the `ActionSource` interface (such as `UICommand`) has its `immediate` property set to true, in which case conversion takes place in the *Apply Request Values* phase. During outbound response processing, Converters are again invoked during evaluation of the JSP, as tags containing value reference expressions access bean properties that must be converted from Java types to their corresponding string representations.

During inbound processing, Converters throw a `ConversionException` if their component's string value cannot be coerced to the appropriate Java type. When this happens, the framework adds a conversion error message to the `FacesContext`, and marks the `UIComponent` as invalid (by setting its `valid` flag to `false`). A Converter can also optionally queue an event or directly call a method on the `FacesContext` to change the request processing flow. We'll discuss this in further detail in the "Conversion and Validation Processing" section later in this chapter.

Once all the Converters for a given view have been invoked, the framework processes validations. Validators typically implement logic that depends on the converted values of one or more components. Examples would be checking that a string value doesn't exceed a certain length, or that a numeric value falls within a given range. Thus, whereas a Converter can be used to guarantee that a given request parameter is valid as to its *type*, a Validator is used to guarantee that the parameter is valid as to its *value*.

Like the Converters, Validators typically post error messages whenever a rule fails. The Converter and Validator messages are coalesced into a list that can be presented to the user by inserting a `messages` tag or one or more `message` tags in the JSP.

The JavaServer Faces reference implementation supplies a set of default Converters and Validators to cover some of the more obvious cases, and to serve as examples to guide developers who may wish add their own custom implementations to the supplied set. The framework provides facilities to allow you to register your custom implementations at run time.

Converters and Validators can be bound to user interface components declaratively by using tags and attributes provided for that purpose in your JSPs. Alternatively, you can create custom tags that automatically apply predefined Converters or Validators.

Using Converters

The Converter interface defines a pair of methods—`getAsString()` and `getAsObject()`—to convert between the model's Java types and string representations suitable for presentation in the user interface (and for transmission via the character-based HTTP protocol). Often the presentation view of the data includes additional formatting that isn't stored in the model. For example, phone numbers might be internally represented as a string of 10 digits, but presented in the user interface with parentheses surrounding the area code and a dash to separate the three-digit exchange from the four-digit extension number. Obviously, this formatting information must be added to the value stored in the user interface during rendering, and removed during form submission.

During the *Process Validations* phase (or the *Apply Request Values* phase, if an `EditableValueHolder`'s or an `ActionSource`'s `immediate` attribute is set to `true`), the framework causes the `decode()` method of every `UIComponent` in the component tree to be invoked. `UIComponentBase`'s default implementation of `decode()` in turn delegates to the `decode()` method of the component's Renderer. If a `UIComponent` is a subtype of `UIInput`, its Renderer will find the Converter associated with the component and call its `getAsObject()` method to convert the string value to the required type, as depicted in Figure 8.1.

Similarly, during the *RenderResponse* phase, the framework invokes the `encodeXxx()` methods of each `UIComponent` in the component tree. The default implementation in `UIComponentBase` in turn delegates to the `encodeXxx()` methods of the component's Renderer. Renderers typically override `getFormattedValue()` to call the associated Converter's `getAs String()` method, which returns a formatted string representation of the underlying model attribute. Figure 8.2 illustrates this sequence.

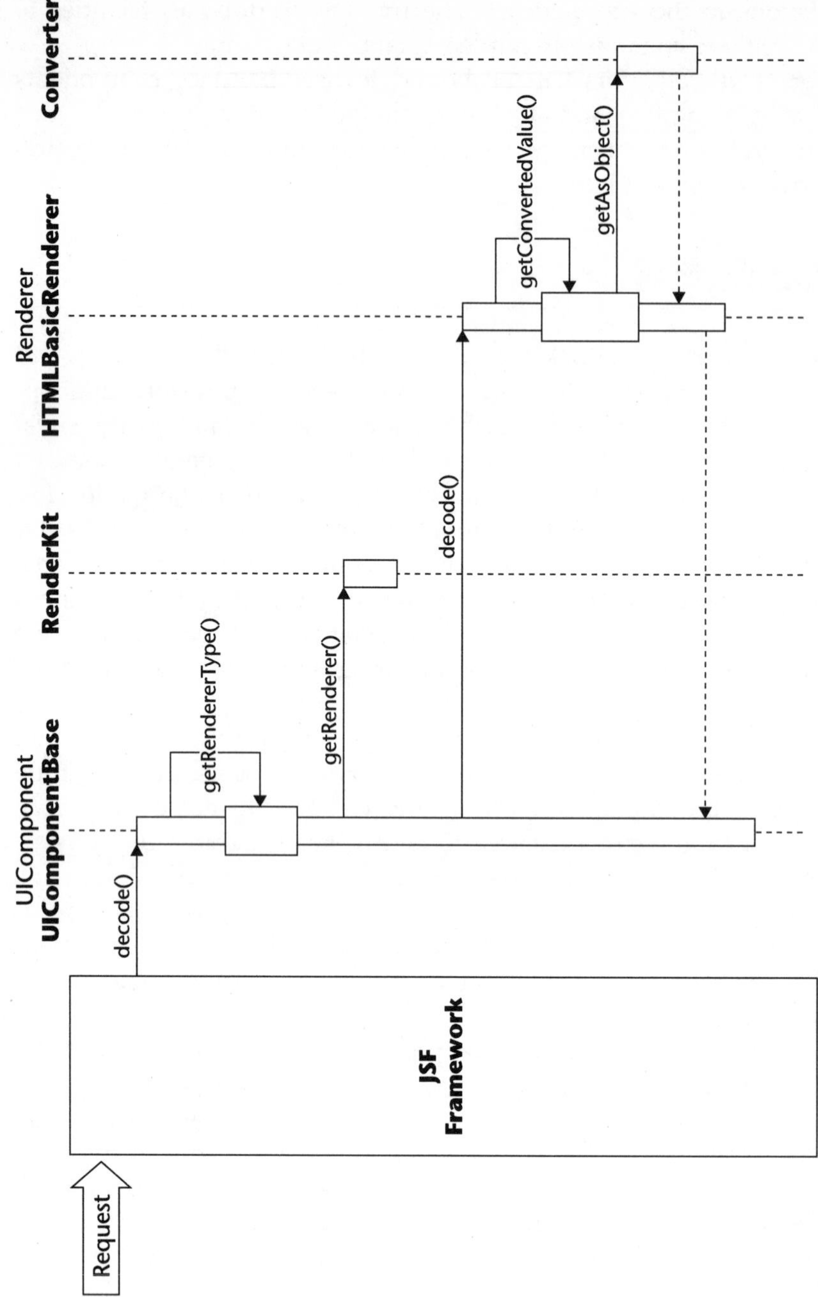

Figure 8.1 How the framework accesses Converters to convert inbound request values.

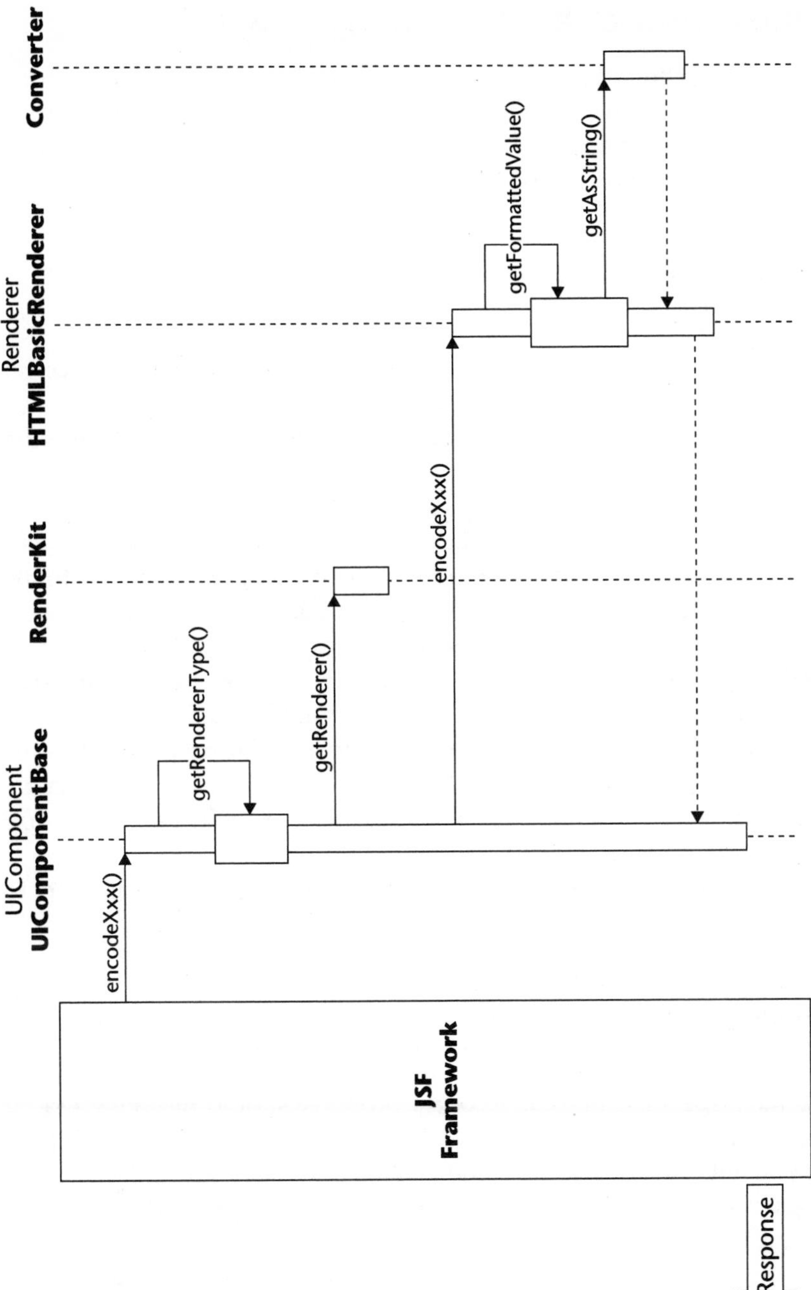

Figure 8.2 How the framework accesses Converters to format outbound response values.

Setting the converter Attribute in Input Tags

Several of the tags included in the JavaServer Faces reference implementation support a `converter` attribute that allows you to declaratively specify the Converter type to use. For example, here is an `inputText` tag that is bound to a `DoubleConverter`, one of the default Converters supplied with the framework:

```
<h:inputText  converter="Double"
              value="#{modifyInvoicePage.invoice.amount}"/>
```

This facility also permits developers to specify their own custom Converter classes using the same technique, as we shall see shortly. It is up to the developer, of course, to ensure that the specified Converter supports the underlying Java type.

The tags that support the `converter` attribute are `inputText`, `inputSecret`, `inputHidden`, and `outputText`. You can use any of the provided Converters, as well as any custom Converters you create and register with the system. The provided Converter classes are capable of performing conversions on a variety of standard Java types (see Table 8.4).

JSF supplies `NumberConverter` and `DateTimeConverter` classes that provide configuration attributes you can use to fine-tune their behavior. For example, suppose that you wanted to convert the amount property as a currency value. Setting the `converter` attribute of the `inputText` tag (as we did previously in several examples in Chapters 6 and 7) won't help us, because it won't allow us to configure the Converter's attributes.

Instead, we can use a nested `convertNumber` tag, which will allow us to specify configuration attributes for the `NumberConverter`:

```
<h:inputText value="#{modifyInvoicePage.invoice.amount}">
    <f:convertNumber type="currency"/>
</h:inputText>
```

Here, we have specified that the `amount` property should be converted by the `NumberConverter` as a currency value. Because Converters are bidirectional, this will not only format the value as a locale-specific currency amount, but it will also validate that values submitted by the user match the currency format for the locale and convert it to the appropriate object type. However, this bit of functionality depends on the `java.text.NumberFormat` class, which parses currency values in a fairly rigid fashion. In particular, it requires that currency values be prefixed with a currency symbol. That means submitting '4.99' instead of '$4.99' would result in a conversion error. We could set an attribute on the tag to eliminate the currency symbol, but then submitting the value *with* a currency symbol would cause a conversion error.

It would be nice if our UI could be flexible enough to allow either format. While the standard JSF Converters don't directly provide for this, you can easily create a custom Converter to provide the desired functionality. The section "Using Custom Converters for Validation" later in this chapter explores this in detail, and it even includes an example solution for the currency symbol problem.

Table 8.1 lists the attribute settings available for the `convertNumber` tag. Note that all of the attributes can work with value reference expressions, allowing you to bind the settings to a backing bean, if desired. Attribute settings for the `convertDateTime` tag are listed in Table 8.2.

Table 8.1 Attributes of the convertNumber Tag.

NAME	TYPE	VALUE
currencyCode	String	An ISO 4217 currency code to apply when formatting currency.
currencySymbol	String	The currency symbol to use when formatting currency.
groupingUsed	boolean	Indicates whether grouping separators should be used (for example, using comma as a thousands separator).
integerOnly	boolean	Indicates whether to use only the integer portion of the number.
locale	java.util.Locale	The locale to use; defaults to the value returned by `FacesContext.getViewRoot().getLocale()`.
maxFractionDigits	int	The maximum number of digits to use when formatting the fractional portion of the value.
maxIntegerDigits	int	The maximum number of digits to use when formatting the integer portion of the value.
minFractionDigits	int	The minimum number of digits to use when formatting the fractional portion of the value.
minIntegerDigits	int	The minimum number of digits to use when formatting the integer portion of the value.

(continued)

Table 8.1 *(continued)*

NAME	TYPE	VALUE
pattern	String	A custom formatting pattern that provides a precise specification of how the value is to be formatted and parsed; see the Javadoc for `java.text.NumberFormat` for more details.
type	String	One of a set of predefined parsing and formatting specifications. Possible values are `currency`, `percent`, and `number`. Default is `number`; see the Javadoc for `java.text.NumberFormat` for more details.

The `DateTimeConverter` can be used to convert the values of `java.util.Date` properties. Like the `NumberConverter`, it provides a variety of configuration attributes. Perhaps the most useful is the `pattern` attribute, which allows us to specify a format pattern as defined by the class `java.text.DateFormat`. For example, to convert and format a date value as '2/12/2004,' we could specify a format pattern of 'M/d/yyyy,' as in the following example:

```
<h:inputText id="invoiceDate"
             value="#{modifyInvoicePage.invoice.invoiceDate}">
    <f:convertDateTime pattern="M/d/yyyy"/>
</h:inputText>
```

Table 8.2 Attributes of the convertDateTime Tag.

NAME	TYPE	VALUE
dateStyle	String	One of the date styles defined by `java.text.DateFormat`. Must be one of `default`, `short`, `medium`, `long`, or `full`. Uses `default` if nothing is specified.
parseLocale	String or Locale	The locale to use. If nothing is specified, uses the Locale returned by `FacesContext.getLocale()`.
pattern	String	A format pattern used to determine how to convert the date/time string. If specified, `dateStyle`, `timeStyle`, and `type` attributes will be ignored.

Table 8.2 *(continued)*

NAME	TYPE	VALUE
timeStyle	String	One of the time styles specified by `java.text.DateFormat`. Must be one of `default`, `short`, `medium`, `long`, or `full`. Uses `default` if nothing is specified.
timeZone	String or TimeZone	The time zone to use.
type	String	A string that specifies whether the value is a date, a time, or both. Must be one of `date`, `time`, or `both`. Uses `date` if nothing is specified.

Standard Converters

JSF requires that all implementations provide a standard set of Converters that must be preregistered with the Application instance. The standard converters are listed in Table 8.3. Note that all of the standard Converters can be bound to model values of type `Number`. The `Date`, `DateFormat`, and `DateTime` Converters can also be bound to model values of type `Date`.

Table 8.3 Default Converter Classes.

CONVERTER CLASS	CONVERTER ID
BigDecimalConverter	BigDecimal
BigIntegerConverter	BigInteger
NumberConverter	Number
IntegerConverter	Integer
ShortConverter	Short
ByteConverter	Byte
CharacterConverter	Character
FloatConverter	Float
DoubleConverter	Double
BooleanConverter	Boolean
DateTimeConverter	DateTime

Some examples of Converter usage are given in Listing 8.1, which shows a version of the `ModifyInvoice.jsp` introduced in Chapter 6, "UI Components." The JSP has been updated by adding a number of different Converter settings.

```
<html>
<head>
    ...
</head>
<body>
...

<f:view>
    ...
    <h:messages styleClass="ErrorMessage"/>

    <h:form id="invoiceForm" action="#{modifyInvoicePage.save}">
        <h:panelGrid id="invoicePanel"
                     columns="2"
                     columnClasses="FieldLabel,TextInput"
                     footerClass="TableCellRight">

            <h:outputText
                id="invoiceNumberLabel"
                value="#{modifyInvoicePage.labels.invoiceNumber}"/>
            <h:inputText
                id="invoiceNumber"
                styleClass="TextInput"
                value="#{modifyInvoicePage.invoice.invoiceNumber}">
            </h:inputText>

            <h:outputText
                id="invoiceDateLabel"
                value="#{modifyInvoicePage.labels.invoiceDate}"/>
            <h:inputText
                id="invoiceDate"
                styleClass="TextInput"
                value="#{modifyInvoicePage.invoice.invoiceDate}">
                <f:convertDateTime pattern="M/d/yyyy"/>
            </h:inputText>

            <h:outputText
                id="amountLabel"
                value="#{modifyInvoicePage.labels.amount}"/>
            <h:inputText
                id="amount"
                styleClass="TextInput"
                converter="BigDecimal"
```

Listing 8.1 ModifyInvoice.jsp with several Converter settings added.

```
                value="#{modifyInvoicePage.invoice.amount}">
            </h:inputText>

            <h:outputText
                id="discountLabel"
                value="#{modifyInvoicePage.labels.discount}"/>
            <h:inputText
                id="discount"
                styleClass="TextInput"
                value="#{modifyInvoicePage.invoice.discount}">
                <f:convertNumber pattern="#.000%"/>
            </h:inputText>

            <f:facet name="footer">
                <h:panelGroup>
                    <h:commandButton
                        id="saveButton"
                        title="Save changes"
                        styleClass="Button"
                        value="Save"
                        action="#{modifyInvoicePage.save}">
                    </h:commandButton>
                </h:panelGroup>
            </f:facet>
        </h:panelGrid>
    </h:form>
</f:view>
</body>
</html>
```

Listing 8.1 *(continued)*

Using Custom Converters for Validation

The design of the JSF framework makes it easy for developers to use custom Converters in their applications. Let's consider a couple of scenarios where this type of customization might be useful.

First, suppose that one of the properties of a backing bean represents a product code. The product code is presented to the user as two letters followed by a dash and three digits, as in AZ-123, though it is stored without the dash in the database (see Figure 8.3). We want to ensure that values for this field entered in the user interface match the pattern. One way to do this would be to write a Validator. However, since we need to implement a Converter anyway in order to format the value for presentation (by inserting the dash) and to perform the inverse operation on submitted values, we'll be better off putting the validation logic in the Converter as well. This way we keep all the related logic together, while eliminating the need for an extra class and an additional setting in the JSP.

Our custom converter class, `ProductCodeConverter` (Listing 8.2), must implement the `javax.faces.convert.Converter` interface, which defines two methods with the following signatures:

```
public Object getAsObject(FacesContext, UIComponent, String)
    throws ConverterException

public Object getAsObject(FacesContext, UIComponent, Object)
    throws ConverterException
```

The `ProductCodeConverter's getAsString()` method first checks that the value in the backing bean is valid, and if not, throws a `Converter Exception`. Note that we have broken out the validation code into a separate method so that the implementation can be shared with the `getAsObject()` method, as we will see shortly. It then formats the bean value by simply inserting a dash between the second and third characters in the string.

The `ProductCodeConverter's getAsObject()` method will remove a dash (if there is one) in the third position and then validate that the resulting value is a string of five characters where the first two are letters and the rest are digits. It will throw a `ConverterException` if the value fails to meet this rule. Otherwise, it will return the resulting value with the letter portion uppercased.

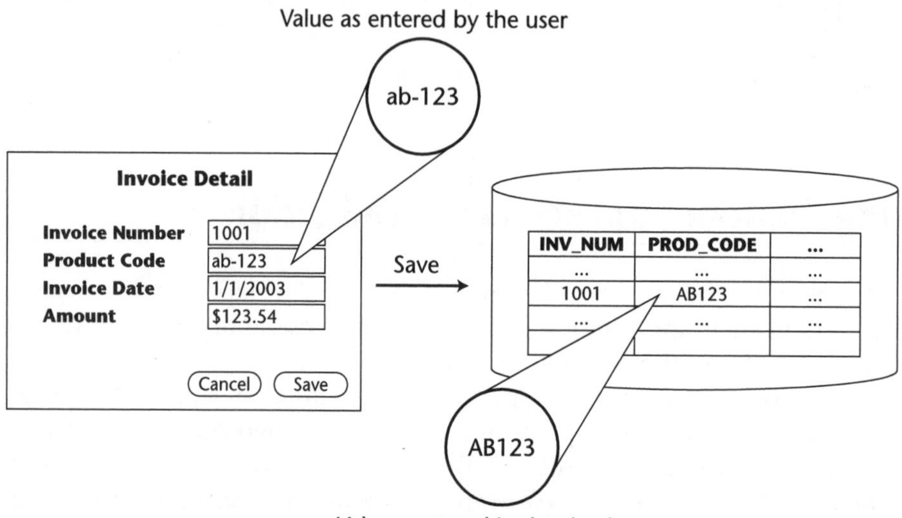

Figure 8.3 Product code value in the user interface and in the database.

Recall that the `UIInput` component will call its Converter's `getAsObject()` method during either the *Apply Request Values* phase or the *Process Validations* phase to convert the string submitted in the request to the type of the corresponding bean property. This call takes place even if, as in our case, the type of the corresponding property is typed as a `String`, as long as the framework can find a Converter registered for the component.

```
package com.wiley.masteringjsf.ch8ex1;

import javax.faces.component.UIComponent;
import javax.faces.context.FacesContext;
import javax.faces.convert.Converter;
import javax.faces.convert.ConverterException;

/**
 * A Converter for product codes
 */
public class ProductCodeConverter implements Converter {

    /**
     * Validates the target string as a product code, with the expected
     * format ZZ-999, or ZZ999. If validation is successful, returns
     * a string converted by trimming whitespace and removing the dash,
     * if one is present.
     *
     * @param context The FacesContext for this request
     * @param component The UIComponent that renders the value
     * @param target The string to be converted
     * @return a product code without a dash
     */
    public Object getAsObject(FacesContext context,
                              UIComponent component,
                              String target)
        throws ConverterException {

        if (target == null || target.trim().equals(""))
            return target;
        String stringValue = target.trim();
        String productCode = stringValue;

        // Remove dash, if present
        int dashPosition = stringValue.indexOf('-');
        if (dashPosition == 2)
            productCode = stringValue.substring(0, dashPosition) +
                          stringValue.substring(dashPosition + 1);

        // Validate the value.
```

Listing 8.2 ProductCodeCoverter.java. *(continued)*

```
        if (!isValidProductCode(productCode))
            throw new ConverterException());

        return productCode.toUpperCase();
    }

    /**
     * Formats the target string as a product code, with the format
     * ZZ-999. If target is not a valid product code, returns the
     * value entered by the user.
     *
     * @param context The FacesContext for this request
     * @param component The UIComponent that renders the value
     * @param target The object to be converted
     * @return a formatted product code
     */
    public String getAsString(FacesContext context,
                              UIComponent component,
                              Object target)
        throws ConverterException {
        String value = (String) target;
        if (value == null || value.trim().length() == 0)
            return value;

        // Throw if the value in the backing bean is invalid
        if (!isValidCompanyCode(value.trim()))
            throw new ConverterException();

        return value.substring(0, 2) + "-" + value.substring(2);
    }

    /**
     * Returns <code>true</code> if the provided product code is valid;
     * <code>false otherwise</code>. Valid product codes can be blank
     * strings, or strings formatted as either ZZ-999 or ZZ999. Case
     * of alphabetic characters is ignored.
     *
     * @param productCode a product code
     * @return true if the provided code is valid
     */
    protected static boolean isValidCompanyCode(String productCode) {
        if (!(productCode.length() == 5))
            return false;
        char[] chars = productCode.toCharArray();
        for (int i = 0; i < chars.length; i++) {
            if ((i < 2 && !Character.isLetter(chars[i])) ||
                (i > 1 && !Character.isDigit(chars[i])))
                return false;
```

Listing 8.2 *(continued)*

```
        }
        return true;
    }
}
```

Listing 8.2 *(continued)*

In Listing 8.2, the `getAsObject()` method removes a dash in the third position, if present, and then calls the local method `isValidProductCode()` to determine whether the resulting product code is valid. If not, a `ConverterException` is thrown to allow the caller to post an error message and invalidate the component. Otherwise, the product code is uppercased and the resulting string returned. In `getAsString()`, we simply insert a dash at the third position and return the resulting string.

Displaying Error Messages

To display conversion error messages generated during processing of a form submission, you can simply add a `messages` tag or one or more `message` tags to the JSP. The `messages` tag presents the entire list of error messages. If you wish to present inline messages, you can instead (or in addition) use `message` tags, which allow you to specify the `clientId` of the `UIComponent` that generated the error message, as in the following:

```
<h:inputText id="productCode"
             value="#{modifyInvoicePage.invoice.productCode}"/>
<h:message for="productCode"/>
```

You can apply a CSS style class as follows:

```
<h:message for="productCode" styleClass="ErrorStyle"/>
```

Registering the Converter

To use the ProductCodeConverter we created in the previous section (see Listing 8.2), we would need to register it with the application to allow it to be found at run time. Here's what the necessary setting would look like in the application configuration file:

```
...
<faces-config>
  ...
  <converter>
    <description>A Converter for product codes</description>
```

```
    <converter-id>ProductCode</converter-id>
    <converter-class>invoice.ProductCodeConverter</converter-class>
  </converter>
...
</faces-config>
```

The Faces tag library provides a generic converter tag that we could then nest inside other tags.

```
<h:inputText id="productCode"
             value="#{modifyInvoicePage.invoice.productCode}">
        <f:converter converterId="ProductCode"/>
</h:inputText>
```

In the previous example, the nested converter tag binds the ProductCodeConverter to the UIInput component backing the inputText tag for the Product Code field. Note that the converterId setting matches the converter-id value we specified in the application configuration file.

Using Converters to Validate Custom Value Types

The standard Converters provided with JSF can handle many routine conversions, but the framework makes it easy for you to add your own custom Converter to provide added functionality. For example, you might want to create custom Converters to handle some custom value types. Let's look at a simple example. In the section "Using Converters" earlier in this chapter, we mentioned that the NumberConverter can be a bit inflexible in dealing with certain number formats. For example, we can specify that currency values should be formatted either with or without a currency symbol, but then the user must input the values in precisely the same way. So, if we were to use the NumberConverter to format an input field as a currency value with a leading currency symbol, submitting a currency amount without a currency symbol would lead to a conversion error.

A more flexible approach would be to convert the value regardless of whether the user entered a currency symbol or not. Listing 8.3 presents a simple—you might even say naïve (because, among other things it doesn't provide for localization)—CurrencyConverter class that provides the needed functionality. We'll use BigDecimal as the target type in our example for simplicity's sake, and for its superior handling of decimal precision.

Writing a custom Converter will allow us to fine-tune the validation and formatting rules to meet our needs. Using the CurrencyConverter will also help ensure that currency values are validated and formatted consistently. From a maintenance perspective, it allows us to make a global change in formatting and conversion behavior by modifying a single file.

```
package com.wiley.masteringjsf.ch8ex2;

import java.math.BigDecimal;
import java.text.DecimalFormat;
import java.text.NumberFormat;
import java.text.ParsePosition;

import javax.faces.component.UIComponent;
import javax.faces.context.FacesContext;
import javax.faces.convert.Converter;
import javax.faces.convert.ConverterException;

/**
 *  A Converter for dollar-based currency values. Not locale-aware.
 */
public class CurrencyConverter implements Converter
{
    /** The default scale for money values */
    public final static int CURRENCY_SCALE = 2;
    /**  The default format for money values */
    public final static String CURRENCY_FORMAT = "#,##0.00";

    /**
     * Unformats its argument and returns a BigDecimal instance
     * initialized with the resulting string value
     */
    public Object getAsObject(FacesContext context,
                              UIComponent component,
                              String target)
        throws ConverterException {

        if (target == null || target.trim().length() < 1)
            return null;

        String stringValue = target.trim();
        if (stringValue.startsWith("$"))
            stringValue = stringValue.substring(1);
        ParsePosition parsePosition = new ParsePosition(0);
        DecimalFormat formatter = new DecimalFormat(CURRENCY_FORMAT);
        Number number = null;

        try {
            number = formatter.parse(stringValue, parsePosition);
        }
        catch (NumberFormatException e) {
            throw new ConverterException();
        }
```

Listing 8.3 CurrencyConverter.java. *(continued)*

```
        if (number == null ||
            parsePosition.getIndex() != stringValue.length())
                throw new ConverterException();

        return new Currency(number.doubleValue());
    }

    /**
     * Returns a string representation of its argument, formatted as a
     * currency value
     */
    public String getAsString(FacesContext context,
                              UIComponent component,
                              Object value)
        throws ConverterException {

        if (value == null)
            return null;

        // If the user entered a value that couldn't be converted
        // to BigDecimal, the value parameter contains the unconverted
        // string value, so just return it.
        if (!(value instanceof BigDecimal))
            return value.toString();

        BigDecimal bigDecValue = (BigDecimal)value;
        bigDecValue = bigDecValue.setScale(CURRENCY_SCALE,
                BigDecimal.ROUND_HALF_UP);

        // We're not using DecimalFormat.getCurrencyInstance() here
        // because it requires a leading currency symbol; we want
        // the currency symbol to be optional.
        NumberFormat formatter = DecimalFormat.getInstance();
        formatter.setMinimumFractionDigits(CURRENCY_SCALE);

        return formatter.format(bigDecValue.doubleValue());
    }
}
```

Listing 8.3 *(continued)*

The `getAsObject()` implementation in Listing 8.3 removes the leading dollar sign (if present) and then uses `java.text.DecimalFormat` to attempt to coerce the provided string to `BigDecimal`. If the type coercion fails, we throw a `ConverterException` to alert the caller.

In `getAsString()`, we apply default currency scale and rounding behavior, again using `java.util.DecimalFormat`, this time to convert from `BigDecimal` to `String`. If the method can't convert the supplied string, it simply returns it.

To start using the new CurrencyConverter, we have to register it in the application configuration file:

```
<converter>
  <description>Dollar-based currency converter</description>
  <converter-id>Currency</converter-id>
  <converter-class>
    com.wiley.masteringjsf.ch8ex2.CurrencyConverter
  </converter-class>
</converter>
```

Now, we need to modify the JSP from Listing 8.1 to use a CurrencyConverter instead of a NumberConverter to convert the value associated with the model property invoiceBean.amount. Here's the snippet of code we are going to change:

```
<h:inputText
    id="amount"
    styleClass="TextInput"
    value="#{modifyInvoicePage.invoice.amount}">
    <f:convertNumber type="currency"/>
</h:inputText>
```

We can simply replace the convertNumber tag with a converter tag and set the tag's converterId attribute to 'Currency', which is the converter-id we specified for the CurrencyConverter class in the application configuration file.

```
<h:inputText
    id="amount"
    styleClass="TextInput"
    value="#{modifyInvoicePage.invoice.amount}">
    <f:converter converterId="Currency"/>
</h:inputText>
```

The inputText tag's Renderer will now use our custom CurrencyConverter to convert and format its values, and we will no longer get conversion errors when entering currency values without the leading dollar sign.

Converter Registration by Type

JSF implementations register a set of default converters for basic Java types at startup time. This allows inputText and outputText tags to work with properties of types other than String, without requiring that you specify any converters at all in the JSP markup. Table 8.4 shows the standard converters that JSF registers by type at startup time.

Table 8.4 Standard Converter Class Registration.

CONVERTER CLASS	CONVERTER ID	NATIVE TYPE	JAVA CLASS
BigDecimalConverter	BigDecimal		java.math.BigDecimal
BigIntegerConverter	BigInteger		java.math.BigInteger
NumberConverter	Number		java.lang.Number
IntegerConverter	Integer	int	java.lang.Integer
ShortConverter	Short	short	java.lang.Short
ByteConverter	Byte		java.lang.Byte
CharacterConverter	Character	char	java.lang.Character
FloatConverter	Float	float	java.lang.Float
DoubleConverter	Double	double	java.lang.Double
BooleanConverter	Boolean	boolean	java.lang.Boolean

At run time, if a given component doesn't have an explicit converter setting, the framework will use introspection to determine the type of the underlying property and then check to see if there is a Converter registered for that type. If so, it will use that Converter to convert the component's value.

JSF also provides a way for your application to register custom Converters by type, so that you can take advantage of the same mechanism. You can register a custom Converter by adding a setting in the application configuration file. For example, earlier we created a `CurrencyConverter` that works with `BigDecimal` values. We could make this Converter the default for all `BigDecimal` values in our application by adding the following setting:

```
<converter>
  <description>Converter for BigDecimal type</description>
  <converter-for-class>
    java.math.BigDecimal
  </converter-for-class>
  <converter-class>
    com.wiley.masteringjsf.ch8ex3.CurrencyConverter
  </converter-class>
</converter>
```

This would set the default Converter for all backing bean properties of type `BigDecimal` in your application to the `CurrencyConverter` class. Setting a `converter` attribute or using a `converter` tag in JSP would allow you to override this setting for a given field if, for example, it contained a percentage rather than a currency value. If most of the `BigDecimal` fields in your application were currency values, this strategy could reduce the amount of specification needed in your JSPs. Note that this would work even if you had already registered the `CurrencyConverter` by ID:

```
<converter>
  <description>Currency converter registered by ID</description>
  <converter-id>Currency</converter-id>
  <converter-class>
    com.wiley.masteringjsf.ch8ex3.CurrencyConverter
  </converter-class>
</converter>
```

You could potentially further reduce the amount of Converter specification required in an application's JSPs through the use of custom value types. For example, suppose that your application used wrapper classes or custom subclasses for currency and percentage values. For example, instead of making the `CurrencyConverter` the default Converter for all `BigDecimal` properties, you might want to create a custom subclass of `BigDecimal` to explicitly represent currency values in your application. Registering the `Currency Converter` for this new class wouldn't affect the other `BigDecimal` properties in your application. If the custom subclass was named `'Currency'`, the setting would look like this:

```
<converter>
  <description>Converter for the custom Currency type</description>
  <converter-for-class>
    com.wiley.masteringjsf.ch8ex3.Currency
  </converter-for-class>
  <converter-class>
    com.wiley.masteringjsf.ch8ex3.CurrencyConverter
  </converter-class>
</converter>
```

You might then want to do the same thing for percentage values, so you could create another subclass of `BigDecimal` to use as the value class for percentages and create a custom Converter for it. You could then register the new Converter:

```
<converter>
  <description>Converter for custom Percentage type</description>
  <converter-for-class>
    com.wiley.masteringjsf.ch8ex3.Percentage
  </converter-for-class>
  <converter-class>
    com.wiley.masteringjsf.ch8ex3.PercentageConverter
  </converter-class>
</converter>
```

This would allow you to provide application-wide default formatting and conversion behavior by simply implementing your own `CurrencyConverter` and `PercentageConverter` classes. You can even register Converters by type dynamically, by calling the `addConverter()` method on the application instance, as in the following example:

```
...
Application app = FacesContext.getCurrentInstance().getApplication();
app.addConverter(Currency.class,
                 "com.wiley.masteringjsf.ch8ex2.CurrencyConverter");
app.addConverter(Percentage.class,
                 "com.wiley.masteringjsf.ch8ex2.PercentageConverter");
...
```

This code would have the same effect as the two previous settings. Note that it would also override any previous settings. While it might occasionally be handy to do something like this dynamically, applying the settings in the application configuration file would generally be clearer and more maintainable.

Using Validators

In the preceding section, we saw how Converters could be used to supply part of the functionality needed for validation by checking that the submitted values can be successfully converted to the underlying Java types to which they are bound.

In addition, JSF provides Validators to carry out more general types of validation during the *Process Validations* phase (or during the *Apply Request Values* phase if an `EditableValueHolder's` or an `ActionSource's` `immediate` attribute is set to `true`). Validators extend the `javax.faces.validator.Validator` interface, which defines a single method, `validate()`. In addition to the interface, the framework provides several standard Validators, as described in Table 8.5.

Table 8.5 Validator Classes.

VALIDATOR CLASS	JSF TAG	FUNCTION	ATTRIBUTES
DoubleRange Validator	validateDouble Range	Validates that the submitted value lies in the specified floating-point range; a minimum value, maximum value, or both may be specified.	minimum, maximum

Table 8.5 *(continued)*

VALIDATOR CLASS	JSF TAG	FUNCTION	ATTRIBUTES
Length Validator	validateLength	Validates that the length of the submitted string value; a minimum length, maximum length, or both may be specified.	minimum, maximum
LongRange Validator	validateLong Range	Validates that the submitted value lies in the specified integer range; a minimum value, maximum value, or both may be specified.	minimum, maximum

When the framework creates a component tree to service a given request, each component may register zero or more Validators. During the *Process Validations* phase, the framework calls `processValidators()` on the root component of the component tree. This message is then propagated recursively to all the components in the tree.

Adding Validator Bindings in JSP

You can specify one or more Validators within the context of any `UIInput` tag. For example, to validate that a product name doesn't exceed 24 characters, we can use a `validateLength` tag as follows:

```
<h:inputText id="productName"
             value="#{modifyInvoicePage.invoice.productName}">
        <f:validateLength maximum="24"/>
</h:inputText>
```

If the user submits a product name value that contains more than 24 characters, the framework will automatically add an error message and invalidate the `UIComponent`. If one or more error messages are set in the `FacesContext`, the current phase will pass control to the *Render Response* phase when all the validations have been completed, skipping the *Update Model Values* and *Invoke Application* phases. This way, if one or more values fail validation, the backing bean values remain unchanged.

Validator Tags

Table 8.6 contains a list of the tags that correspond to the Validator classes described in Table 8.5

Table 8.6 Validator Tags.

VALIDATOR CLASS	JSF TAG	FUNCTION	ATTRIBUTES
DoubleRange Validator	validateDouble Range	Any types that are convertible to floating-point	minimum, maximum
Length Validator	validateLength	java.lang.String	minimum, maximum
LongRange Validator	validateLong Range	Any numeric type or string that can be converted to a long	minimum, maximum

Multiple `Validator` tags can be associated with a single input tag. The following example adds a `validateLongRange` tag to an Invoice Number field. The new tag validates that the invoice number is greater than 1,000:

```
<h:inputText id="invoiceNumber"
             value="#{modifyInvoicePage.invoice.invoiceNumber}">
  <f:validateLongRange minimum="1001"/>
</h:inputText>
```

We can add a check for an upper bound by suppyling a `maximum` attribute, as in the following:

```
<f:validateLongRange  minumum="1001" maximum="99999"/>
```

We have now specified that the value should be constrained to lie between 1,001 and 99,999, inclusive. Note that you can also add one or more Validators to a `UIComponent` programmatically by invoking the component's `addValidator()` method at run time.

Required Fields Validation

One of the most common types of validation is to specify that a given field is required, that is, that the submitted value may not be blank. The `UIInput` component supports this directly by providing a built-in `required` property that can be set from any of the input tags. You need simply add a `required` attribute to any input tag to have it validated as a required field, as in the following example:

```
<h:inputText id="invoiceNumber"
             required="true"
             value="#{modifyInvoicePage.invoice.invoiceNumber}"/>
```

Validator Methods

There are a couple of reasons you might want to add custom validation functionality to a JSF application. One reason would be to provide a shared implementation of some generic field-level validation that could be used throughout the application—for example, validating a telephone number. The Validator interface makes it possible for us to write custom Validators for this purpose and then plug them in to the framework's validation mechanism. We'll explore an example of this approach in the section "Creating Custom Validators."

Another reason to add custom validation functionality is if the validation logic will require access to other page-related states—for example, cross-field validation. In these situations, you can simply add validation methods directly to your backing beans. Validation methods must have the following signature:

```
public void methodName(FacesContext context ,
                       UIComponent component,
                       Object value)
    throws ValidatorException
```

`UIInput` tags supply a `validator` attribute so that they can be bound directly to a validation method with a method reference expression, as in the following example:

```
 <h:inputText
    id="amount"
    validator="#{modifyInvoicePage.validateAmount}"
    value="#{modifyInvoicePage.invoice.amount}"/>
```

At run time, the framework will invoke the specified validation method. For example, the following method makes sure that an invoice item's amount is never greater than its unit price:

```
public void validateAmount(FacesContext context,
                           UIComponent component,
                           Object value)
    throws ValidatorException {

    UIInput comp = (UIInput) component.findComponent("unitPrice");
    Object unitPrice = comp.getValue();

    if (value == null || unitPrice == null
        || value instanceof String
        || unitPrice instanceof String)
        return;

    if (((BigDecimal)value).compareTo(unitPrice) > 0) {
```

```
            throw new ValidatorException(MessageFactory.
                getMessage(context, "invalidInvoiceAmount"));
        }
    }
```

If the amount is greater than the unit price, the previous method throws a ValidatorException containing an error message to be added to the `FacesContext`. The framework will automatically add the message and invalidate the `UIComponent` for us.

Displaying Error Messages

Validation error messages can be displayed by adding a `messages` or `message` tag to your JSP. See the previous description in the section on Converters earlier in this chapter.

Creating Custom Validators

Just as with Converters, you may wish to add your own custom Validator classes to those supplied by the framework. Custom Validators must implement the `javax.faces.validator.Validator` interface, which defines the `validate()` method:

```
public abstract void validate(FacesContext context,
                              UIComponent component
                              Object value)
    throws ValidatorException;
```

You can then either reference your custom Validator directly from JSP by using the `Validator` tag, or else write a custom `Validator` tag. We'll explore these two options in more detail shortly. First though, let's create a simple custom Validator.

Let's suppose that our application needs to validate that certain fields that are typed as `String` in the model contain only alphabetic characters. Listing 8.4 contains a simple `AlphaValidator` class that embodies this rule.

```
package com.wiley.masteringjsf.ch8ex3;

import javax.faces.component.UIComponent;
import javax.faces.context.FacesContext;
import javax.faces.validator.Validator;
import javax.faces.validator.ValidatorException;

import com.sun.faces.util.MessageFactory;
```

Listing 8.4 AlphaValidator.java.

```
public class AlphaValidator implements Validator
{
    /** The key used to look up the error message */
    public static final String MESSAGE_KEY = "invalidAlphaString";

    public AlphaValidator() { }

    /**
      * Validates that the component's value contains only
      * alpha characters
      *
      * @param context The FacesContext for this request.
      * @param component The component to be validated.
      * @param value The value to be validated.
      */
    public void validate(FacesContext context,
                         UIComponent component,
                         Object value)
        throws ValidatorException {

         if ((context == null) || (component == null)) {
             throw new IllegalArgumentException(
                context == null ? "Context" : "Component"
                + " cannot be null");
         }

         String val = (String) value;

         // Null input is considered valid.
         if (val == null || val.trim().length() == 0)
             return;

         if (!isAlphabeticString(val.trim())) {
             throw new ValidatorException(MessageFactory.
                getMessage(context, MESSAGE_KEY, new Object[] {val}));
         }
     }

     protected boolean isAlphabeticString(String string) {
         char[] chars = string.toCharArray();

         for ( int i = 0; i < chars.length; ++i ) {
             if (!Character.isLetter(chars[i])) {
                  return false;
             }
         }
         return true;
     }
}
```

Listing 8.4 *(continued)*

The AlphaValidator simply checks that the supplied string (if it is not blank) contains only alphabetic characters. If any character in the string fails this check, it posts an error message by calling addMessage() on the FacesContext.

In order to make the new Validator available to our JSP, we need to register it in the application configuration file, as follows:

```
<validator>
  <description>Alphabetic string validator</description>
  <validator-id>Alpha</validator-id>
  <validator-class>
    com.wiley.masteringjsf.ch8ex3.AlphaValidator
  </validator-class>
</validator>
```

Now, we can use the new Validator in a JSP by nesting a validator tag inside an inputText tag. We will need to set the validator tag's validatorId attribute to match the validator-id specified for the AlphaValidator in the application configuration file, as shown here:

```
<h:inputText id="productName"
             value="#{modifyInvoicePage.invoice.productName}">
    <f:validator validatorId="Alpha"/>
</h:inputText>
```

Adding Attributes to Custom Validators

Earlier in this section we saw an example of a Validator tag (validateLongRange) that had a pair of configuration attributes (minimum and maximum). Similarly, we can add configuration attributes to a custom validator. For example, we could make a more flexible version of the AlphaValidator by taking the existing code and parameterizing its behavior, so that in addition to checking for alphabetic characters it could also check for digits. We could then provide configuration attributes that would allow the developer to select validation for alphabetics, digits, or both.

The first step would be to create a copy of AlphaValidator—let's call it AlphanumValidator—and add several properties to contain the configuration parameters. Next, we'll modify the logic in its validate() implementation to make it responsive to the new settings. Listing 8.5 displays a suitably modified version.

```
package com.wiley.masteringjsf.ch8ex3;

import javax.faces.component.UIComponent;
```

Listing 8.5 AlphanumValidator.java.

```
import javax.faces.context.FacesContext;
import javax.faces.validator.Validator;
import javax.faces.validator.ValidatorException;

import com.sun.faces.util.MessageFactory;

public class AlphanumValidator implements Validator
{
    /** The key used to look up the error message */
    public static final String MESSAGE_KEY = "invalidAlphaString";
    private boolean letters;
    private boolean digits;
    private boolean whitespace;
    private String characters;

    public AlphanumValidator() { }

    /**
      * Validates that the component's value contains only
      * alphanumeric characters
      *
      * @param context The FacesContext for this request.
      * @param component The component to be validated.
      * @param value The value to be validated.
      */
     public void validate(FacesContext context,
                          UIComponent component,
                          Object value)
        throws ValidatorException {

        if ((context == null) || (component == null)) {
            throw new IllegalArgumentException(
               context == null ? "Context" : "Component" + " is null");
        }

        if (characters == null && letters == false &&
            digits == false && whitespace == false)
               throw new IllegalStateException(
                    "At least one configuration parameter must be set");

        String val = (String) value;

        // Null input is considered valid.
        if (val == null || val.trim().length() == 0)
            return;
        if (!isValidString(val.trim())) {
            throw new ValidatorException(MessageFactory.
               getMessage(context, MESSAGE_KEY, new Object[] {val}));
        }
```

Listing 8.5 *(continued)*

```
    }

    protected boolean isValidString(String string) {
        char[] chars = string.toCharArray();
        for ( int i = 0; i < chars.length; ++i ) {
            if (!isValidChar(chars[i]))
                return false;
        }
        return true;
    }

    protected boolean isValidChar(char c) {

        return (characters != null && characters.indexOf(c) > -1)
            || (letters && Character.isLetter(c))
            || (digits && Character.isDigit(c))
            || (whitespace && Character.isWhitespace(c));
    }

    /*--------  Accessor methods --------*/

    public String getCharacters() {
        return characters;
    }
    public void setCharacters(String characters) {
        this.characters = characters;
    }

    public boolean isWhitespace() {
        return whitespace;
    }
    public void setWhitespace(boolean whitespace) {
        this.whitespace = whitespace;
    }

    public boolean isDigits() {
        return digits;
    }
    public void setDigits(boolean digits) {
        this.digits = digits;
    }

    public boolean isLetters() {
        return letters;
    }
    public void setLetters(boolean letters) {
        this.letters = letters;
    }
}
```

Listing 8.5 *(continued)*

You'll notice that we added properties to contain the values of the configuration settings as well as a bit of extra logic to test the character values based on the settings. We will now need to register the new Validator class in the application configuration file, as follows:

```
<validator>
  <description>Alphanumeric string validator</description>
  <validator-id>Alphanum</validator-id>
  <validator-class>
    com.wiley.masteringjsf.ch8ex3.AlphanumValidator
  </validator-class>
</validator>
```

However, to allow the `AlphanumValidator` to be configured in a JSP, we will need to create a custom tag to support the new configuration attributes.

Creating a Custom Validator Tag

We can create a tag to support configuring custom Validator attributes in JSP by extending the `ValidatorTag` class. Listing 8.6 shows an example tag handler for the `AlphanumValidator` from Listing 8.5.

```
package com.wiley.masteringjsf.ch8ex3;

import javax.faces.validator.Validator;
import javax.faces.webapp.ValidatorTag;
import javax.servlet.jsp.JspException;

/**
 * A handler tag for validating the contents of alphanumeric strings
 */
public class AlphanumValidatorTag extends ValidatorTag
{
    private String letters;
    private String digits;
    private String whitespace;
    private String characters;
    public AlphanumValidatorTag() {
        super();
        super.setValidatorId("Alphanum");
    }

    protected Validator createValidator() throws JspException {
        AlphanumValidator validator =
            (AlphanumValidator) super.createValidator();
```

Listing 8.6 AlphanumValidatorTag.java. *(continued)*

```
        if (validator == null)
            throw new NullPointerException();

        validator.setDigits(
            Boolean.valueOf(digits).booleanValue());
        validator.setLetters(
            Boolean.valueOf(letters).booleanValue());
        validator.setWhitespace(
            Boolean.valueOf(whitespace).booleanValue());
        validator.setCharacters(characters);

        return validator;
    }

    /*--------  Accessor methods --------*/

    public String getLetters() { return letters; }
    public void setLetters(String letters) {
        this.letters = letters;
    }

    public String getDigits() { return digits; }
    public void setDigits(String digits) {
        this.digits = digits;
    }

    public String getWhitespace() { return whitespace; }
    public void setWhitespace(String whitespace) {
        this.whitespace = whitespace;
    }

    public String getCharacters() { return characters; }
    public void setCharacters(String characters) {
        this.characters = characters;
    }
}
```

Listing 8.6 *(continued)*

The `AlphanumValidatorTag` calls `super.setValidatorId()` from its constructor to allow the framework to find the `AlphanumValidator` class at run time, and it provides properties to capture attribute settings from the JSP. The key method in the tag handler is the overridden implementation of `createValidator()`, which constructs and initializes the validator.

Now, all that remains to be done is to add a tag library descriptor file (`.tld`) entry for the new tag, as shown in Listing 8.7. If you don't already have a `.tld` file, you can simply create one under your application's WEB-INF directory.

```
<?xml version="1.0" encoding="ISO-8859-1" ?>

<!DOCTYPE taglib
  PUBLIC "-//Sun Microsystems, Inc.//DTD JSP Tag Library 1.2//EN"
  "http://java.sun.com/dtd/web-jsptaglibrary_1_2.dtd">


<taglib>
  <tlib-version>0.01</tlib-version>
  <jsp-version>1.2</jsp-version>
  <short-name>Invoice Tag Library</short-name>
  <uri>/WEB-INF/invoice.tld</uri>
  <description>
    Tag library definitions for the Invoice application
  </description>

  ...

    <tag>
      <name>alphanumValidator</name>
      <description>Validates alphanumeric strings</description>
      <tag-class>
        com.wiley.masteringjsf.ch8ex2.AlphanumValidatorTag
      </tag-class>
      <attribute>
        <name>letters</name>
        <required>false</required>
        <rtexprvalue>false</rtexprvalue>
        <description>Are letters allowed?</description>
      </attribute>
      <attribute>
        <name>digits</name>
        <required>false</required>
        <rtexprvalue>false</rtexprvalue>
        <description>Are digits allowed?</description>
      </attribute>
      <attribute>
        <name>whitespace</name>
        <required>false</required>
        <rtexprvalue>false</rtexprvalue>
        <description>Is whitespace allowed?</description>
      </attribute>
      <attribute>
        <name>characters</name>
        <required>false</required>
        <rtexprvalue>false</rtexprvalue>
        <description>Additional allowable characters</description>
```

Listing 8.7 Tab library definition for the alphanumValidator tag. *(continued)*

```
        </attribute>
      </tag>

  ...

</taglib>
```

Listing 8.7 *(continued)*

To use the new tag, we will need to add an import statement for its tag library in the JSP.

```
<head>
    ...
    <%@ taglib uri="/WEB-INF/invoice.tld" prefix="invoice" %>
    ...
</head>
```

Now the custom tag can be nested inside input tags in a JSP.

```
<h:inputText
    id="description"
    value="#{modifyInvoicePage.invoice.description}">
        <invoice:alphanumValidator letters="true" digits="true"
            whitespace="true" characters="-_"/>
</h:inputText>
```

The settings on the `alphanumValidator` tag shown here specify that the `inputText` tag's value may only contain letters, digits, whitespace, and the hyphen and underscore characters.

Conversion and Validation Processing

JSF gives developers a great deal of flexibility in determining how their applications should respond to conversion and validation errors. We'll discuss the ways in which the framework allows us to modify its behavior shortly, but first let's examine the default processing flow.

The framework ordinarily invokes any converters registered for components in the current view during the *Process Validations* phase, though this behavior can be shifted to the *Apply Request Values* phase by setting the `immediate` attribute of a component that implements the `EditableValueHolder` or `ActionSource` interface to `true`. If there are no conversion or validation errors, the framework then passes control to the next sequential phase. However, if conversion or validation errors occur causing one or more error messages to be added to the `FacesContext`, the framework instead passes control directly to the *Render Response* phase. In other words, if there are any type conversion or validation errors the model will not be updated, and the application's processing code will not be invoked, as shown in Figure 8.4.

Figure 8.5 shows how setting the `immediate` attribute changes the default flow.

Standard Lifecycle Phases: Default Flow

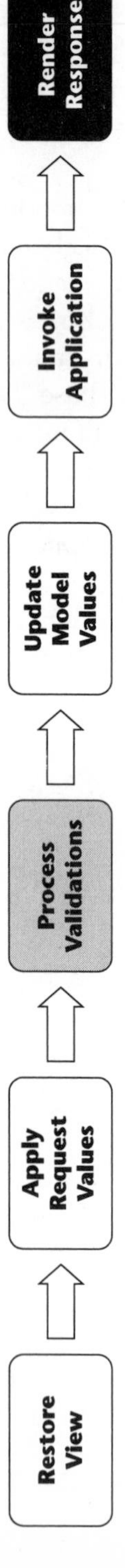

This is the default processing flow when no conversion or validation errors occur. Conversions and validations take place in the *Process Validations* phase.

Conversion and Validation Error Processing: Default Flow

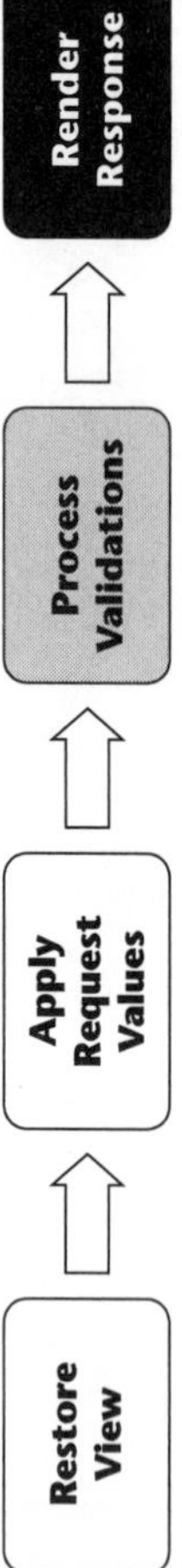

At the end of the *Process Validations* phase, control transfers directly to the *Render Response* phase if any error messages were added to the FacesContext.

Figure 8.4 How conversion and validation errors change the life-cycle flow.

Standard Lifecycle Phases: immediate Mode

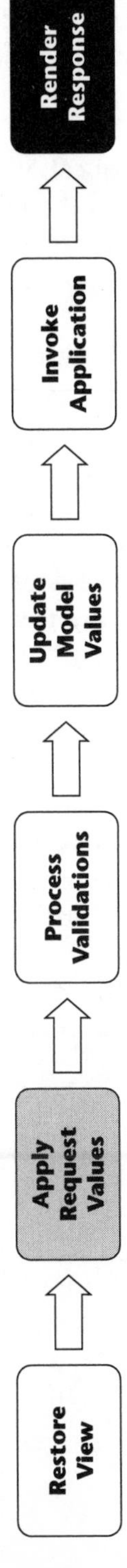

If a component that implements the ActionSource or EditableValueHolder interface has its immediate attribute set to true, conversion and validation take place in the *Apply Request Values* phase.

Conversion and Validation Error Processing: Default Flow

At the end of the *Apply Request Values* phase, control transfers directly to the *Render Response* phase if any error messages were added to the FacesContext.

Figure 8.5 How the `immediate` setting changes life-cycle flows.

For most situations, the default behavior ought to be sufficient. However, should your application need to do something different, there are a couple of ways to alter the standard processing flow. One way is to write a custom Converter that queues an event to be handled by an event listener. Listeners can then be coded to handle conversion error events by calling `renderResponse()` on the `FacesContext` instance for the current request, which would cause control to flow to the *Render Response* phase instead of the *Invoke Application* phase, (or the *Process Validations* phase, if the component is an `ActionSource` or an `EditableValueHolder` with its `immediate` attribute set to `true`).

Another way to change the default processing flow would be to write custom Renderers or UI components that catch the `ConversionException` thrown by a Converter. They could then call `renderResponse()` directly themselves. Note that it would also be possible in either case to call `responseComplete()` instead of `renderResponse()`. This would have the effect of aborting the request without rendering any new content for the user interface. As you might imagine, this would ordinarily be less useful, because it affords no means of providing feedback to the user about the error that aborted the request.

Summary

As you have seen in this chapter, JSF provides comprehensive, extensible facilities for converting and validating inbound request values, and for formatting outbound values for presentation in the user interface. The framework's standard `Converter` and `Validator` classes address many common situations, while the consistent use of interfaces where appropriate along with a dynamic registration system for custom implementations makes it easy to add custom conversion and validation behavior to JSF applications.

Applying JSF

CHAPTER

9

Building JSF Applications

To this point, we have covered all the aspects of JSF. In this chapter, we will put all these pieces together to show you how to build a whole application from start to finish. In this chapter, an architectural scheme will be presented to organize and build your JSF-based applications. First, you will see how to apply the MVC Pattern to the design of your JSF applications. Then, an application called iBank will be presented. This application will be discussed in light of the architectural vision that is laid out in the beginning of this chapter. Sample code from the application will also be presented and discussed in detail as well as design and implementation trade-offs.

Overview

Recall the discussion of the MVC Pattern in Chapter 1, "JSF Patterns and Architecture." This Pattern, or actually the problems this Pattern solves, is one of the driving forces behind the development of JSF in the first place. This Pattern is covered in detail in Chapter 1 as it relates to the architecture of JSF. In this brief section, it is important to go over various aspects of the Pattern again in light of all you have learned to this point, in order to understand the architecture of JSF applications. MVC provides two major benefits to applications that adopt it. The first benefit is the division of concerns between the model and the view. The view is focused strictly on displaying the information, and the model is focused strictly on implementing the business logic that makes up the application. The model and view are loosely coupled through the controller code. This division of concerns leads to better applications that are easier to maintain and modify.

The second major benefit of MVC is the ability to put a different user interface over the same business logic and still have the same application underneath the user interface. JSF's RenderKit is the most straightforward example of a realization of this benefit. Simply providing a new RenderKit can make the user interface of the application completely different (that is, replace the standard HTML RenderKit with a WML RenderKit). This is only a surface change though (that is, the same component trees exist; they are just rendered as WLM), if your application is architected properly, you can even change to a completely different user interface. For example, you could have a user interface that is crafted for the more expressive world of eXtensible User-Interface Language (XUL), one user interface for HTML and one for WML. All three user interfaces would drive the same back-end application but with very different user experiences.

As you build your JSF application, keep this division of responsibilities in mind. If you do not, chances are good that you will end up with an application that is much harder to maintain and extend than it would otherwise be.

Architectural Overview

Consider an application that displays a list of items and pages through the items 20 at a time as a quick example to illustrate the flexibility that comes from building applications with the MVC Pattern. Without using MVC as an organizing principal for the design of an application, inexperienced developers are likely to put the code for managing the list directly in a custom JSP tag or JSF component. While that approach would work, simple changes to the UI (like adding an additional column) forces the code that manages the list to be changed. When you use the MVC Pattern, however, the UI is free to change independently of the code that manages the list. Figure 9.1 shows the application built without MVC.

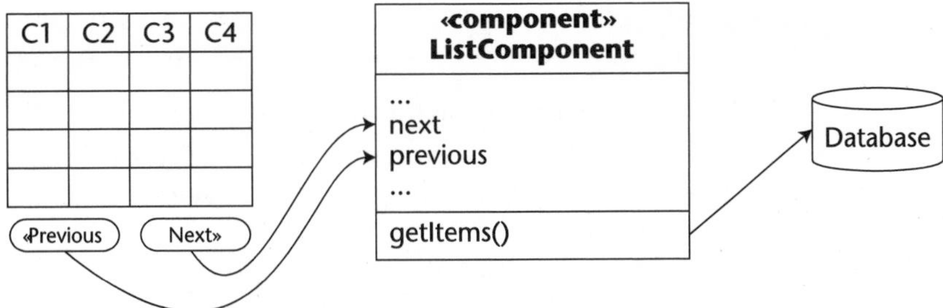

Figure 9.1 List Viewer without MVC.

This implementation too closely ties the presentation of the information to the application logic that delivers the information. In other words, changes in one area will require changes in the other area; for example, if anything changes in the schema (even very simple things like a column name), then the user interface component will have to be updated. This coupling makes changes hard to manage since small changes in one part of the system lead to a ripple effect throughout the application.

If, on the other hand, the application were to be implemented with MVC in mind changes would be more localized and thus easier to manage. Figure 9.2 shows what the List Viewer would look like implemented with MVC in mind.

This implementation hides the details of the handling of the list behind a controller object that manages getting the next and previous set of components. With this design, the underlying application can change without requiring the user interface to change, and vice versa.

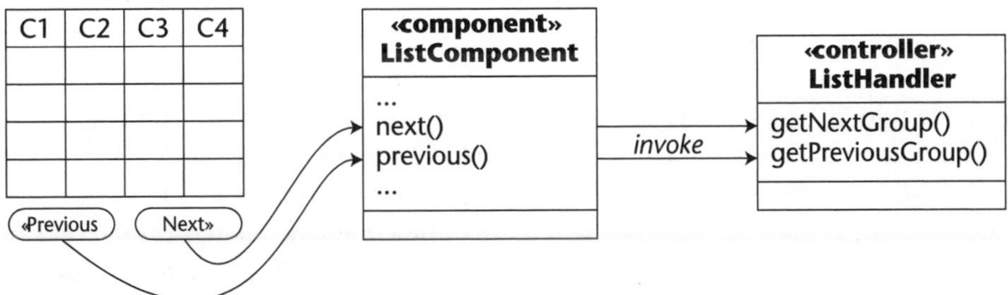

Figure 9.2 List Viewer with MVC.

JSF in the Architecture

The roles in the MVC Pattern are filled by many different pieces of the JSF framework. The UIComponents and their Renderers fulfill the View role and will most commonly be programmed via the JSP integration covered in detail in Chapter 5, "JSP Integration in JSF."

The Controller role is filled by a combination of JSF-supplied classes and custom code, provided by you, that is plugged into the JSF application. The supplied classes include the NavigationHandler, which manages the page flow of the application, and the Application class, which manages, among other things, Converters and Validators. There are many other abstract classes in JSF involved in the controller role that must be fleshed out by the developer. For example, developers provide action methods to tell the Navigation Handler which page (or which tree identifier) to choose next. The developer is also responsible for configuring the NavigationHandler via the `faces-config.xml` file. As you can see the controller role is quite broad and encompasses many different classes in JSF. The important thing to keep in mind here is that the controller is responsible for gluing the user interface to the application (for example, invoking business logic based on user actions) as well as managing the flow of the application. So, as you are writing your JSF application, focus on making sure that you keep controller code and not business logic in your controller classes.

Finally, the role of the Model is not really addressed by JSF. Either JavaBeans or EJB Session beans will typically fill the role of Model. Many inexperienced developers, however, end up ascribing the Model role to the JavaBeans that provide the data for the UIComponents and thus end up with model code in their controller or view classes.

BUSINESS LOGIC **The code that belongs in your model classes is often refered to as Business Logic. This code should be focused on the stuff the application needs to do, regardless of the type of user interface that is being used. A way to think through where a piece of functionality belongs is to decide if the functionality would be required in a Swing user interface, and if so would the implementation be exactlly the same? If you answer yes to both questions, then the functionality probably belongs in one of your model objects. If you answer no to either question, then the code probably belongs in a controller object. The list manager that was disussed earlier is a prime example of some functionality that these two questions could be applied to. Is the functionality needed in both types of user interfaces? Yes, it is needed because a very large list should never be brought into memory all at once; instead you should always page through it. Will the implementation be exactlly the same for both? Again the answer would be yes (with the possible exception of not needing the Session Facade). So this functionality belongs as part of the model code.**

The application of the MVC design Pattern is an undercurrent throughout the rest of this chapter. Without an understanding of this foundational Pattern many of the decisions made in the way JSF applications are built will leave you guessing why things are done the way they are. Hopefully, this brief review of the Pattern and its benefits has left you with a new perspective on the Pattern. If you are still scratching your head, then please read on; much of what is outlined here will be made clearer as you go through the chapter.

Connecting View, Controller, and Model Objects

In order for the MVC Pattern to work properly, the classes playing the different roles have to be able to communicate with each other. Figure 9.3 shows the usual connections that are established between the MVC roles in a typical JSF application.

The view is typically connected to the controller loosely through a string. The string is an identifier that is used to look up the controller object via the ValueBinding mechanism outlined in Chapter 6, "UI Components." Notice that the View is not typically connected directly to the model but instead gets its data from the controller. The controller is responsible for managing the in-memory life cycle of the model objects; in other words, the controller creates and/or fetches the model objects into memory as needed. The view invokes controller logic indirectly by posting events. The events make it to their respective targets because of the `action` strings evaluating to action methods. The controller is configured via the `faces-config.xml` file as well as may of the JSF core tags that can be used in JSP's. In JSF applications, unlike Swing applications, the model is typically passive from the controller and view's perspective; in other words, the model does not post events nor does it typically invoke any methods on the controller or view classes.

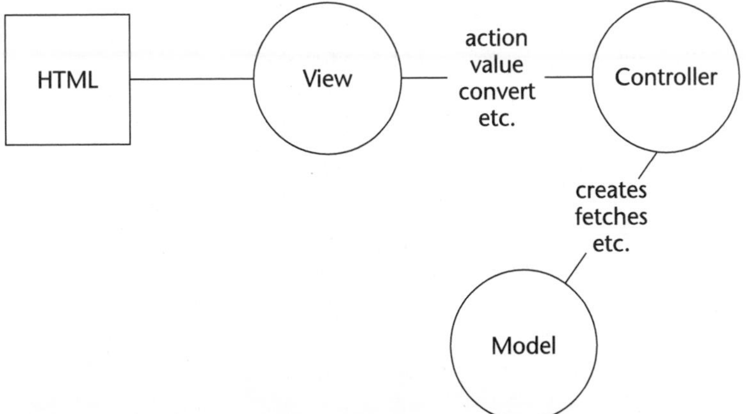

Figure 9.3 MVC Connections in a typical JSF application.

Again, most of this has been covered in one way or another in previous chapters; it is stated here again to give you a focused perspective from the point of view of implementing your applications in light of the MVC design Pattern. Next, we will start building the sample application.

iBank Bill Payment Application

The iBank application that we will architect and build (part of, anyway) allows users to log in and schedule payments. The payments are made to designated payees. This service is similar other bill payment services available on the Net. The use case model is shown in Figure 9.4.

The functions are organized into two groups, payment management and payee management. The payment management group has all the use cases to allow the user to add various kinds of payments as well as review the payments that will be made and have been made. The payee management group has the use cases that allow the user to specify who should get the payments. The Web site has the code for this application. Through the rest of this chapter the shaded use cases (that is, Login, Add New Payment, and Review Historical Payments) will be implemented. The use cases are also available on the Web site for your review.

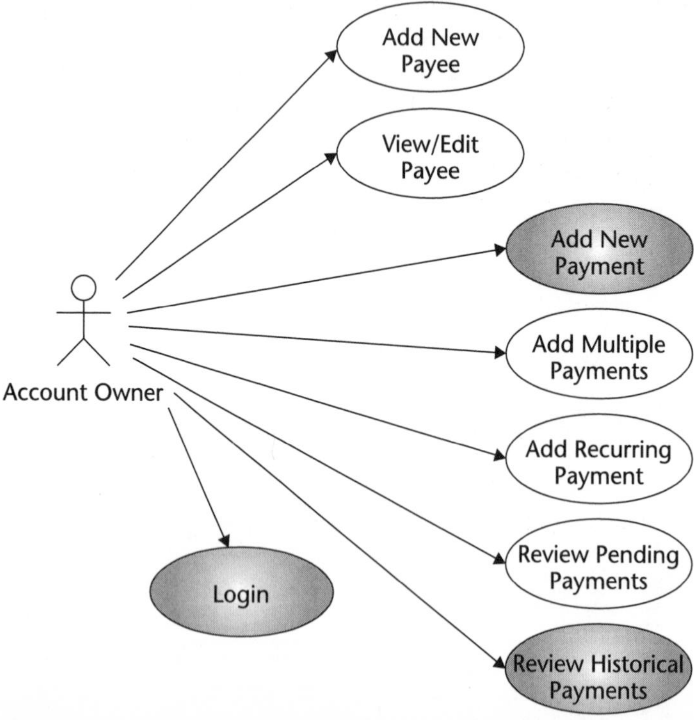

Figure 9.4 iBank use case model.

The screen flow shown in Figure 9.5 displays the way the application moves the user through the various functions.

A screen flow diagram will be very useful later as we develop the navigation rules that will go into the `faces-config.xml` file. After logging in, the user is taken to the summary screen where he or she is presented with a list of choices to go to any one of the other functions (that is, add a payment, review existing payees, and so on). And then from each of these screens the user is taken back to the summary screen. Now that we have the basic flow of the application, we can go over the screens that we will develop in detail in this chapter (shown shaded in Figure 9.5).

Login Screen

First, let's go over the Login screen. This screen provides a place for the user to specify his or her login ID or username, and password. After entering the information, the user clicks a button to submit the information and log in. The screen spec is shown in Figure 9.6.

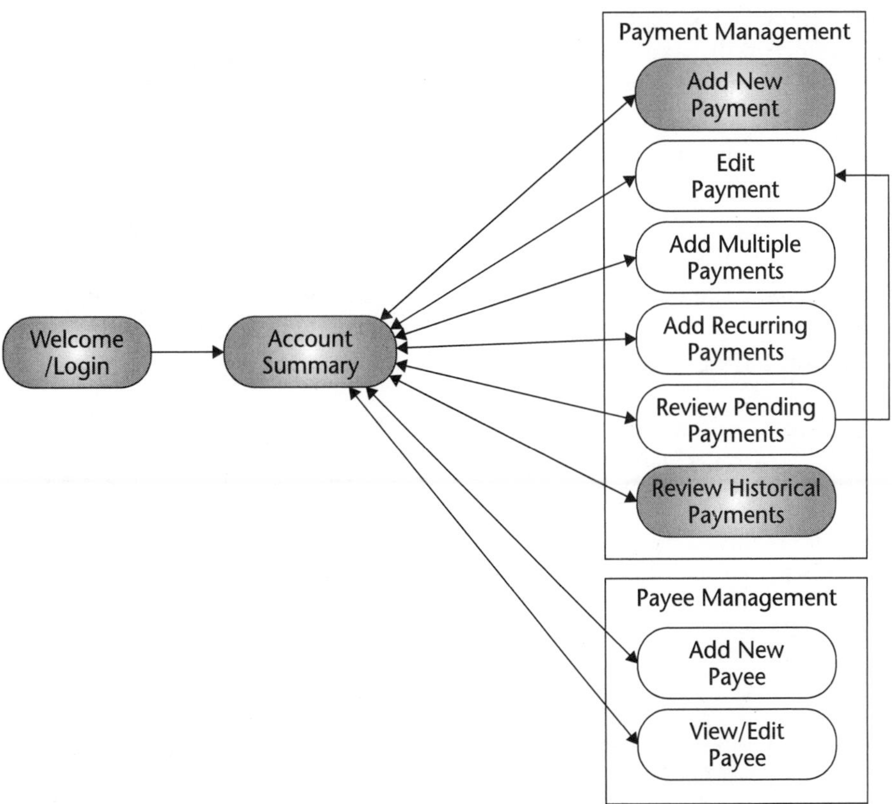

Figure 9.5 iBank screen flow diagram.

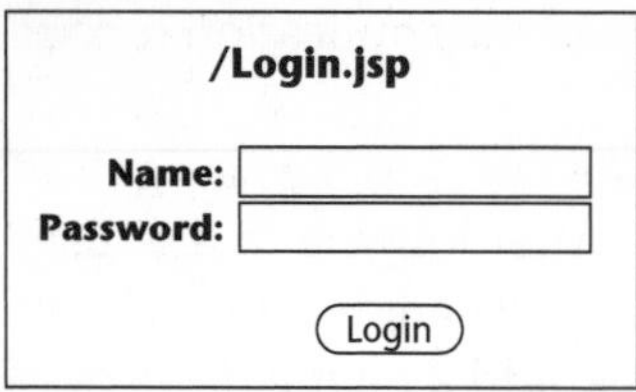

Figure 9.6 Login screen specification.

Notice that the screen is labeled `/Login.jsp`. It is a useful technique to label the screen specifications with their JSF tree identifiers. It makes writing the navigation rules easier when it comes time to build the `faces-config.xml` file. With a screen specification, you can also derive what components will be needed to make up the screen. For example, this screen will need two UIOutput components, two UIInput components, and one UICommand component.

Account Summary

The next screen specification is the Account Summary depicted in Figure 9.7.

This screen will have seven UICommand's rendered as links. These commands will be the actions that will bring the user to the various other named functions. In a real banking application, the right-hand side of this page would probably have some financial information as well as advertisements for products that the bank offers and so on.

The next screen we will build is the Add New Payment. This screen is shown in Figure 9.8.

Pushing the Save button will fire an action that will eventually result in a new Payment row being inserted into the database. The Cancel button will take the user back to the summary screen without anything being persisted.

/AccountSummary.jsp

Add New Payment
Add Multiple Payments
Add Recurring Payment
Review Pending Payments
Review Historical Payments
Add New Payee
View/Edit Payee

Total Balance: XXXX.XX

Figure 9.7 Account summary screen specification.

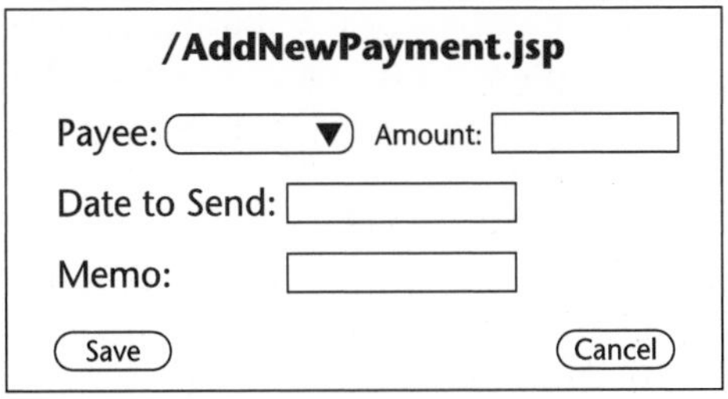

/AddNewPayment.jsp

Payee: [▼] Amount: [ ]

Date to Send: [ ]

Memo: [ ]

(Save) (Cancel)

Figure 9.8 Add New Payment screen specification.

Review Historical Payments

Finally, the review historical payments screen is shown. This screen allows the user to see a few historical payments at a time and then scroll through all the payments made in the last six months. Figure 9.9 shows the screen specification for this screen.

The iBank application is built as both a two-tier and three-tier application to illustrate the differences in the way that an application will be configured and built in the two different environments. The two-tier application is built with JavaBean model objects that the controllers interact with. In the three-tier model, the model is implemented as Session Façade's (Alur et al. 2003).

Hopefully, this brief overview of the iBank application and its use cases, screen flows, and screen specs has given you an understanding of what it takes to plan out and build a JSF application from scratch. Each of these pieces will be enormously helpful in fleshing out your application. The use cases, of course, help you to know what you are supposed to build, the screen flows help you to discover what `navigation-rule`'s should be in your `faces-config.xml` file, and the screen specifications give you a great staring point to know what goes into your JSP's.

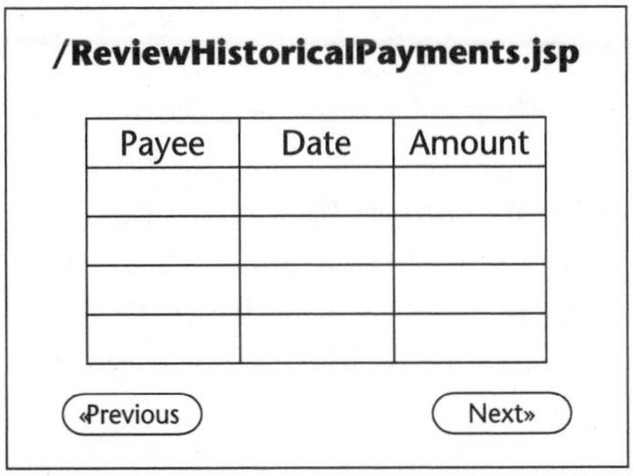

/ReviewHistoricalPayments.jsp

Payee	Date	Amount

(«Previous) (Next»)

Figure 9.9 Review Historical Payments screen specification.

Next, we will go into the detail of the implementation of the iBank application. You will see both two- and three-tier implementations as well as the trade-offs between the various implementation choices. Let's get started at the beginning, logging into the application.

Logging into iBank

Logging into the iBank application involves the user's supplying his or her username and password, and the application's validating that information with what is stored in the database. In order to be able to log in, the user must have established a login ID and password. We will assume that the username and password have been established for the sake of this application. The basic flow of the use case is that the user provides the information, the system validates the information, and if the information passes, the user is forwarded to the account summary screen. If the information is not validated, then an error message is displayed and the user is asked to repeat the login process.

Figure 9.6 has the screen specification for the view portion of the Login use case. When the user pushes the Login button, an action method will be invoked (through the `action` attribute, which we will see shortly) where the validation will take place. The controller for the login process is the `LoginPage` class. This class manages the process of validating the login and putting information into the session if the login is successful. The `LoginPage` also puts errors onto the queue if something goes wrong or the login is not valid. As discussed earlier, the model is implemented twice, once as plain old JavaBeans and ones as an EJB Session Façade. We will review both implementations in the discussion.

Figure 9.10 contains an overview of the layout of the Login process for the iBank application.

The login button is connected to the `login()` method through the `action` reference `loginPage.login`. After performing the validation the login method returns either valid or invalid. These Strings are used to decide which page to go to next based on navigation rules specified in the `faces-config.xml` file. If the login is successful, then the user is taken to the Account Summary page; if the login is not successful, the user is returned to the Login page. The two input fields are connected to the page object via `value` attributes. The string `loginPage.userName` evaluates to a `get/setUserName` method pair on the `LoginPage` class. You will see more of how all this is configured shortly, but first let's look at the code for the `LoginPage` class in Listing 9.1.

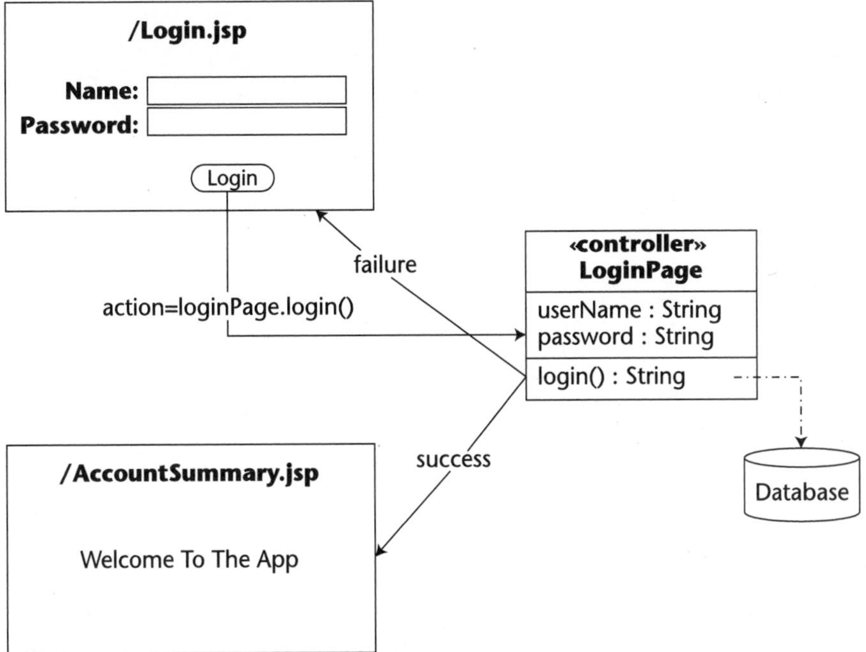

Figure 9.10 iBank architectural overview.

```
public class LoginPage extends Page implements Serializable {
  private static final Logger logger =
    Logger.getLogger("iBank.login.logger");
  // Constants used to signal success or failure
  public static final String INVALID_LOGIN_OUTCOME = "invalid login";
  public static final String VALID_LOGIN_OUTCOME = "valid login";
  // keys into the session
  public static final String CUSTOMER_KEY = "customer";
  private String userName = null;
  private String password = null;

  /**
   * @return
   */
  public String getPassword() {
    return password;
  }

  /**
   * @param password
   */
```

Listing 9.1 LoginPage.java. *(continued)*

```
public void setPassword(String password) {
  this.password = password;
}

/**
 * @return
 */
public String getUserName() {
  return userName;
}

/**
 * @param userName
 */
public void setUserName(String userName) {
  this.userName = userName;
}

public String login() {
  // defaults to valid
  String outcome = VALID_LOGIN_OUTCOME;
  FacesContext ctx = FacesContext.getCurrentInstance();
  try {
    LoginCommand delegate = LoginCommandLocal.getCommand();
    Customer customer =
      delegate.validateLogin(getUserName(), getPassword());
    if (customer != null) {
      Map sessionMap = ctx.getExternalContext().getSessionMap();
      sessionMap.put(CUSTOMER_KEY, customer);
       /*
      ValueBinding binding = Utils.getBinding(LoginPage.CUSTOMER_KEY);
      binding.setValue(ctx, customer);
      */
    } else {
      // The customer was null so the login must have failed.
      // Set the outcome to invalid and add an error message
      // to the faces context.
      outcome = INVALID_LOGIN_OUTCOME;
      addLoginNotFoundMessage(ctx);
    }
  } catch (HibernateException e) {
    // Something is wrong with the database.
    outcome = INVALID_LOGIN_OUTCOME;
    addInternalErrorMessage(ctx);
    // Log the exception so someone can fix it.
    logger.throwing(getClass().getName(), "login", e);
  } finally {
    // For security purposes set the password to null.
    setPassword(null);
```

Listing 9.1 *(continued)*

```
    }
    System.err.println("\n\nAbout to return " + outcome + "\n\n");
    return outcome;
  }

  private void addLoginNotFoundMessage(FacesContext ctx) {
      FacesMessage errMsg =
             new FacesMessage(
                     "Login Not Found",
                   "The login was not found. Please try again.");
             ctx.addMessage(null, errMsg);
      }
}
```

Listing 9.1 *(continued)*

As discussed in the introduction to this chapter, the login method is responsible for validating the input and then responding with a string saying whether or not the information was valid. Here is the code responsible for doing the validation:

```
LoginCommand delegate = LoginCommandLocal.getCommand();
Customer customer =
        delegate.validateLogin(getUserName(), getPassword());
```

The actual checking is delegated to another class that can be reused. The `validateLogin` method returns the `Customer` object if the login was valid and `null` if the username and password were invalid (that is, the username and password did not match anything in the database). The next thing the LoginPage has to do this is to check to see if `customer` is `null`. If the `customer` object was not `null` then it returns that the login was valid; if the `customer` object was `null` then it returns that the login was invalid and queues a message to let the user know what went wrong. The code to do that is listed here again for quick reference.

```
if (customer != null) {
    Map sessionMap = ctx.getExternalContext().getSessionMap();
    sessionMap.put(CUSTOMER_KEY, customer);
} else {
    // The customer was null so the login must have failed.
    // Set the outcome to invalid and add an error message
    // to the faces context.
    outcome = INVALID_LOGIN_OUTCOME;
    addLoginNotFoundMessage(ctx);
  }
```

Since the outcome defaults to valid, there is no reason to set it in the non-null case. Notice that the customer object is placed into the session under the CUSTOMER_KEY so that it can be used by the other parts of the application that need to know which customer is logged into the application.

The next piece of interesting code is the catch block:

```
} catch (HibernateException e) {
  // Something is wrong with the database.
  outcome = INVALID_LOGIN_OUTCOME;
  addInternalErrorMessage(ctx);
  // Log the exception so someone can fix it.
  logger.throwing(getClass().getName(), "login", e);


} finally {
  // For security purposes set the password to null.
  setPassword(null);
}
```

If the username/password validation throws an exception, then the outcome is set to invalid and an error message is added to the queue. Notice also that the exception is logged. It is very important that you always at least log any exceptions that happen. Silently ignored exceptions are the source of many bugs. And finally the password field is set to null just to make sure that there is no way for anyone to get at it.

When the login fails because the returned customer object is null, we have two options to get the user back to the Login page. If we specify the outcome (as we have done in this example), then the rules specified in the `faces-config.xml` file will be used. We could also just return null instead. This will cause faces to return to the last tree that was displayed. While this would work in this case, it is preferable to use a return value and configure the page to return to in the `faces-config.xml` file.

With this option, the application is more flexible; for example, instead of just displaying an error message the application might be changed to take the user to a registration page instead.

Configuration

Which brings us to the `faces-config.xml` file for the iBank application thus far, listed here in Listing 9.2.

```
<?xml version="1.0"?>

<!DOCTYPE faces-config PUBLIC
  "-//Sun Microsystems, Inc.//DTD JavaServer Faces Config 1.0//EN"
  "http://java.sun.com/dtd/web-facesconfig_1_0.dtd">

<faces-config>

  <navigation-rule>
    <from-view-id>/Login.jsp</from-view-id>
    <navigation-case>
      <from-outcome>invalid login</from-outcome>
      <to-view-id>/Login.jsp</to-view-id>
    </navigation-case>
    <navigation-case>
      <from-outcome>valid login</from-outcome>
      <to-view-id>/AccountSummary.jsp</to-view-id>
    </navigation-case>
  </navigation-rule>
  <!-- Page Objects -->
  <managed-bean>
    <description>
      This page manages the login process.
    </description>
    <managed-bean-name> loginPage </managed-bean-name>
    <managed-bean-class> ibank.page.LoginPage </managed-bean-class>
    <managed-bean-scope> session </managed-bean-scope>
  </managed-bean>
</faces-config>
```

Listing 9.2 faces-config.xml file for iBank's login processing.

The `LoginPage` is a `managed-bean` object. If you need a quick refresher on managed beans, you can go back to Chapter 4, "JSF Configuration," to get more info. The navigation-rule element specifies that if the string `invalid login` is returned from processing the form submission (from the login button being pressed) then the next tree identifier that should be shown to the user is `/Login.jsp`; if `valid login` is returned then show the user the `/AccountSummary.jsp` tree identifier. This string is referred to as the logical outcome of processing the action and is used to determine which navigation case should be used. The nice thing about the way that navigation works in JSF is that it all the information about navigation in JSF is externalized.

The components themselves and the application code do not have to know the names of any files or tree identifiers. All that information can be kept in the `faces-config.xml` file. This feature is really handy when you need to update the name of a JSP, instead of having to search through all your code to find references you can update the name in the configuration file once and be done with it. The navigation implementation in JSF can be thought of as an instance of the Front Controller Pattern defined in *Core J2EE Patterns* (Alur et al. 2003). The other interesting thing to note here is that application developers do not have to provide the whole controller implementation; instead, JSF delegates to action methods to return an identifier for what should happen next based on some business processing invoked from or contained in the method. In other words, all we have to worry about when building our applications is that the strings we return from the invoke method match one of the strings in one of the `from-outcome` elements defined in the `faces-config.xml` file.

The Two-Tiered Model for Login

As we discussed in the introduction to this chapter, there are two ways to approach the model in a JSF application. The model can be built to run inside the Web container alongside the JSF application classes or the model can be built to run in an EJB container. The two-tiered model has everything running in the Web container; the three-tiered model has the model in the EJB container.

Up till now we have been looking at the two-tiered implementation of logging into the iBank application. The `LoginPage` uses the two-tiered model for validating the username and password. The code from the `LoginPage` is repeated here for quick reference.

```
LoginCommand delegate = LoginCommandLocal.getCommand();
Customer customer =
        delegate.validateLogin(getUserName(), getPassword());
```

And Listing 9.3 is the code for the `LoginCommandLocal` class.

```
public class LoginCommandLocal
  extends CommandLocal
  implements LoginCommand {
  protected static LoginCommandLocal singleton = null;

  public static LoginCommandLocal getCommand() {
    return singleton;
  }

  static {
    singleton = new LoginCommandLocal();
  }

  public Customer validateLogin(String uname, String passwd)
    throws HibernateException {
```

Listing 9.3 LoginCommandLocal.java.

```
        Customer customer = null;
        Session session = getHibernateSession();
        StringBuffer query = new StringBuffer();
        query.append(
          "from ibank.domain.SiteUser user where user.uname = ?");
        query.append(" and user.passwd = ?");
        String args[] = { uname, passwd };
        Type types[] = { Hibernate.STRING, Hibernate.STRING };
        List users = session.find(query.toString(), args, types);
        if (users.size() != 0) {
          // Since its a one to one hibernate forces them
          // to have the same ID. Hibernate should be returning
          // the customer lazily, not sure why it does not.
          Long customerId = ((SiteUser) users.get(0)).getId();
          customer = (Customer) session.load(Customer.class, customerId);
          // This will cause the accounts to be pulled into memory--
          // not very efficient
          customer.getNetWorth();
          // This will cause the payees to be loaded too.
          customer.getPayees().iterator();
        }
        session.close();
        doneWithSession();
        return customer;
      }
    }
```

Listing 9.3 *(continued)*

Conceptually, this code is attaching to the database, looking for the username and password and returning the customer if the username and password are found. For many JSF applications, this two-tiered mode will work fine. In fact, it is often much simpler to build a two-tiered application than a three-tiered one. In a two-tiered world, you don't have to be concerned with the complexity that is inherent in a three-tiered application. You can sometimes get by with less hardware as well, since in a two-tiered configuration the server only needs to run Web containers.

As with most things in software, you have to give up something to get the simplicity and smaller resource footprint. A two-tiered application will not scale up as much as a three-tiered application will because you can't offload the Web serving to one box and the database access/business logic to another box. Everything must run in one address space.

For example, if the Login functionality were implemented behind a Session Façade, then it could be used remotely by many instances of the iBank Web interface at once. In a two-tiered environment, you also lose the ability to reuse the business functionality from another distributed client. In other words, if you wanted to put a different front end on the application (for example, make the application available via Web services), you would have significant work to do to expose the application functionality, whereas if you built the functionality in a three-tiered manner, the functionality would already be exposed.

Three-Tiered Model for Login

Here is the three-tiered implementation of the login functionality. Notice that from the perspective of the LoginPage class not much has changed.

```
LoginCommand delegate = LoginCommandEJB.getDelegate();
Customer customer = delegate.validateLogin(getUserName(),
                                           getPassword());
```

The implementation for the LoginCommandEJB is listed here in Listing 9.4.

```
public class LoginCommandEJB implements LoginCommand {
  private LoginManagementHome managerHome = null;
  private static LoginCommandEJB singleton = null;

  private LoginCommandEJB() {
    Hashtable env = new Hashtable();
    env.put(
      Context.INITIAL_CONTEXT_FACTORY,
      "org.jnp.interfaces.NamingContextFactory");
      env.put(Context.PROVIDER_URL, "jnp://localhost:1099");

      try {
        Context ctx = new InitialContext(env);
        managerHome =
          (LoginManagementHome) ctx.lookup("ibank/LoginManagement");
      } catch (NamingException e) {
        throw new InstantiationError(e.getMessage());
      }
  }

  public static LoginCommandEJB getCommand() {
    if(null == singleton) {
      singleton = new LoginCommandEJB();
    }
    return singleton;
  }

  public Customer validateLogin(String uname, String passwd)
    throws HibernateException {
    Customer customer = null;
    try {
```

Listing 9.4 LoginCommandEJB.java.

```
      LoginManagement manager = managerHome.create();
      customer = manager.validateLogin(uname, passwd);
      manager.remove();
    } catch (RemoveException e) {
      // TODO Auto-generated catch block
      e.printStackTrace();
    } catch (RemoteException e) {
      // TODO Auto-generated catch block
      e.printStackTrace();
    } catch (CreateException e) {
      // TODO Auto-generated catch block
      e.printStackTrace();
    }
    return customer;
  }
}
```

Listing 9.4 *(continued)*

Finally, the LoginCommandEJB interacts with the stateless LoginManagement session bean. The code for that class is show in Listing 9.5.

```
public class LoginManagementBean implements SessionBean {
  private SessionContext ctx;
  private SessionFactory sessionFactory = null;

  /**
   * @ejb.interface-method
   *     view-type="remote"
   */
  public Customer validateLogin(String uname, String passwd) {
    Customer customer = null;
    try {
      Session session = sessionFactory.openSession();
      StringBuffer query = new StringBuffer();
      query.append(
        "from ibank.domain.SiteUser user where user.uname = ?");
      query.append(" and user.passwd = ?");
      String args[] = {uname, passwd};
      Type types[] = {Hibernate.STRING, Hibernate.STRING};
      List users = session.find(query.toString(), args, types);
      if (users.size() != 0) {
        Long customerId = ((SiteUser) users.get(0)).getId();
        customer = (Customer) session.load(Customer.class, customerId);
        // This will cause the customer's accounts to be loaded
        // for display on the next screen.
        // TODO: look at a better way to do this lazily
```

Listing 9.5 LoginManagementBean.java. *(continued)*

```
            customer.getNetWorth();
          }
          session.close();
        } catch (HibernateException e) {
          throw new EJBException(e.getMessage());
        }
        return customer;
      }

      private SessionFactory getSessionFactory() throws HibernateException {
        return new Configuration().configure().buildSessionFactory();
      }

      public void ejbRemove() {
        sessionFactory = null;
      }

      public void ejbActivate() throws EJBException, RemoteException {
        try {
          if(null == sessionFactory) {
            sessionFactory = getSessionFactory();
          }
        } catch (HibernateException e) {
          throw new EJBException(e.getMessage());
        }
      }

      public void ejbPassivate() {
        try {
          sessionFactory.close();
          sessionFactory = null;
        } catch (HibernateException e) {
          e.printStackTrace();
        }
      }

      public void ejbCreate() {
        try {
          if(null == sessionFactory) {
            sessionFactory = getSessionFactory();
          }
        } catch (HibernateException e) {
          throw new EJBException(e.getMessage());
        }
      }

      public void setSessionContext(SessionContext c) {
        ctx = c;
```

Listing 9.5 *(continued)*

```
        ctx.getClass(); // Is just to use ctx so Eclipse does not complain
    }
}
```

Listing 9.5 *(continued)*

I know that this is a lot of code to have to digest in one sitting, so let us take you through a quick sequence of events to try to clarify what is happening with all this code. First, the user selects the login button, then JSF finds the `login` from the `loginPage` (that is, the loginPage is retrieved from the session, and then a call is made to the login method). JSF invokes the method once it is found. The login method then gets the `LoginCommand` object (in this case, the EJB version of the command) and calls `validateLogin` with the username and password as arguments. The command then invokes the `validateLogin` method on the `LoginManagement` Session Façade. The façade then looks up the username and password in the database and returns the Customer object if one is found.

As you can see this is a bit more complex (and we haven't even looked at deployment descriptors) than the two-tier model. So, you do pay a price in complexity for the ability to distribute the application across multiple servers. This arrangement will scale better though and is also easier for other user interfaces to reuse than the two-tiered architecture.

From a purely JSF perspective though, the difference is not that much. You must be aware of the remote nature of the Session Façade and not abuse the API with several calls but instead make single calls (which are probably already there in the API anyway). Now that we have covered the entire Login flow from screen to database for both two- and three-tier implementations, let's go on to the rest of the application. The next screen you will see is the Welcome to iBank screen, which contains an account summary. This screen is called Account Summary in the screen flow diagram in Figure 9.6.

Welcome to iBank

Recall from Listing 9.2 that upon successful login the user is taken to the `AccountSummary.jsp`, which displays a welcome message as well as a menu of options to navigate through the rest of the application. Here is a snippet of the `faces-config.xml` file from the listing.

```
<navigation-case>
  <from-outcome>valid login</from-outcome>
  <to-view-id>/AccountSummary.jsp</to-view-id>
</navigation-case>
```

Once the login method returns "valid login," the JSF runtime redirects the user to the `AccountSummary.jsp` file. Listing 9.6 has the code for the AccountSummary.jsp.

```
<%@ taglib prefix="h" uri="http://java.sun.com/jsf/html" %>
<%@ taglib prefix="f" uri="http://java.sun.com/jsf/core" %>
<HTML>
  <head>
    <meta HTTP-EQUIV="Content-Type"
        CONTENT="text/html;CHARSET=iso-8859-1">
    <title>Welcome To iBank</title>
  </head>
  <BODY>
      <f:view>
        <h:form>
        <h:panelGrid columns="2">
          <f:facet name="header">
            <%@ include file="header.jsp" %>
          </f:facet>
          <h:panelGroup id="one">
            <%@ include file="menu.jsp" %>
          </h:panelGroup>
          <h:panelGroup id="two">
            <%@ include file="summary.jsp" %>
          </h:panelGroup>
          <f:facet name="footer">
            <%@ include file="footer.jsp" %>
          </f:facet>
        </h:panelGrid>
        </h:form>
  </f:view>
  </BODY>
</HTML>
```

Listing 9.6 AccountSummary.jsp.

The interesting thing to note here is that the page is templatized. Each section is made up of imported JSP code.

Architecturally, there are no real surprises in the implementation of this page. All the data for the page was retrieved and placed into the session by the previous page, so we don't even have to hit the database. Next, we will go over how new objects are created and sent to the back end in a JSF application.

Making an iBank Payment

Making (or scheduling) a payment is the most important use case for the iBank application. After logging in, the user is presented with the menu and can choose to make a payment. Figure 9.8 shows the screen specification for the Make a Payment screen. From here, the user can enter all the pertinent information: payee, amount, date to send, and a memo. The new and interesting thing about this screen is that a new Payment object will be created and stored in the database. The JSP for this view is exactly what you would expect, so we will not include the code here; however, if you'd like to take a look at it please download it from the book's Web site.

The interesting part is the JavaBean that acts as the controller for this page. Here is the code in Listing 9.7:

```
public class PaymentPage extends Page implements Serializable {
  public static final String SAVE = "save";
  public static final String SAVE_ERROR = "save_error";
  public static final String CANCEL = "cancel";
  private SinglePayment payment;
  private Set payees;
  private Long payeeId;

  public PaymentPage() {
    super();
  }

  public String savePayment() {
    FacesContext ctx = FacesContext.getCurrentInstance();
    PaymentCommand command = PaymentCommandLocal.getCommand();
    try {
      ValueBinding binding = Utils.getBinding("#{customer.accounts}");
      Collection accts = (Collection) binding.getValue(ctx);
      Account acct = (Account) accts.iterator().next();
      getPayment().setAccount(acct);
      command.addPayment(getPayment());
    } catch (HibernateException e) {
      addInternalErrorMessage(ctx);
      e.printStackTrace();
      return SAVE_ERROR;
    }
    return SAVE;
  }

  public String cancelPayment() {
    return CANCEL;
```

Listing 9.7 PaymentPage.java. *(continued)*

```
  }

  public Long getPayeeId() {
    return payeeId;
  }

  public void setPayeeId(Long payeeId) {
    this.payeeId = payeeId;
    Iterator itr = getPayees().iterator();
    while (itr.hasNext()) {
      Payee payee = (Payee) itr.next();
      if (payee.getId().equals(payeeId)) {
        getPayment().setPayee(payee);
      }
    }
  }

  public Collection getPayeeIdItems() {
    Collection items = new ArrayList();
    Collection payees = getPayees();
    Iterator itr = payees.iterator();
    while (itr.hasNext()) {
      Payee payee = (Payee) itr.next();
      String value = payee.getId().toString();
      String label = payee.getName();
      items.add(new SelectItem(value, label));
    }
    return items;
  }

  public Set getPayees() {
    if (null == payees) {
      ValueBinding customerBinding =
        Utils.getBinding("#{customer.payees}");
      payees = new HashSet();
      Collection stuff =
        (Collection) customerBinding.getValue(
          FacesContext.getCurrentInstance());
      payees.addAll(stuff);
    }
    return payees;
  }

  public void setPayees(Set payees) {
    this.payees = payees;
  }

  public SinglePayment getPayment() {
```

Listing 9.7 *(continued)*

```
    if (null == payment) {
      payment = new SinglePayment();
      payment.setDateToSend(new Date());
      payment.setAmount(new Double(0.0));
    }
    return payment;
  }

  public void setPayment(SinglePayment payment) {
    this.payment = payment;
  }

}
```

Listing 9.7 *(continued)*

The ValueBinding mechanism is used to get at a value that was placed into the session by an earlier call. It is important to use the ValueBinding mechanism to be prepared for your JSF user interface to run in a portlet. If you use the HttpSession instead of the ValueBinding mechanism, your JSF user interface will not function properly in a portlet.

Another interesting method in the PaymentPage is `setPayeeId`. This method is responsible for setting the payee on the Payment. Here is the code again for quick reference:

```
public void setPayeeId(Long payeeId) {
    this.payeeId = payeeId;
    Iterator itr = getPayees().iterator();
    while (itr.hasNext()) {
      Payee payee = (Payee) itr.next();
      if (payee.getId().equals(payeeId)) {
        getPayment().setPayee(payee);
      }
    }
  }
```

Since the pull-down in the user interface is using IDs as keys, the JavaBean accepts these IDs. However, we are not really interested in the ID but the object that the ID represents. This method makes the connection for us.

Reviewing iBank Payments

The final part of the example covers the reviewing of historical payments that have been made through iBank. A user can schedule any number of payments, and then after they are made they can be reviewed. This is an important case because it is very likely that there will be way too many payments to show up on one page. This example will walk you through an implementation showing the way JSF should interact with a large list of objects.

In a three-tiered application, it is very important that a huge list of Entities not be fetched. Even if the entities are local, there is a certain amount of overhead associated with each entity. For example, consider the iBank historical payment page. Most of the time the user is only going to look at the first few payments (because the user comes often to check what has been paid) and will not usually go to the end of the list of payments. If we were to fetch and display all the payments for the last 6 months and the user only looked at 10 or 20, the application would have consumed a lot of memory and other resources for no reason. For more detail on this AntiPattern you can see *Dredge* in *J2EE AntiPatterns* (by Dudney et al.)

Even in three-tiered mode, however, the iBank application does not use entities, so it might seem unnecessary to be worried about fetching entities for this application. Even without entities it is not wise to have the Web tier fetch all 6 month's worth of Payment objects. The overhead is not as great as with entities but it could still be significant. Instead, the iBank application uses a slightly modified version of the Value List Handler Pattern (Alur, et al. 2003) to avoid the overhead of fetching too much. Since iBank does not use entities there is no reason to worry about DAOs; instead, we use the objects fetched by the Object Relational mapping tool. The interface for the command is included here.

```
public interface PaymentListCommand {
  public void openPaymentList(Customer customer)
    throws HibernateException;
  public void openPaymentList(Collection payees)
    throws HibernateException;
  public List getNextPayments() throws HibernateException;
  public boolean hasNextPayments();
  public List getPreviousPayments() throws HibernateException;
  public boolean hasPreviousPayments();
  public void closePaymentList();
}
```

I do not want to get bogged down in the intricacies of the Value List Handler and its implementation. Instead, I want to point out the interesting aspects of implementing the `PaymentListCommand` interface and show how iBank will interact with that interface as a JSF application.

In the `LoginCommand` that was discussed earlier (see Listing 9.3), the command object was stateless and could be reused from any thread at any time to perform the check, so it could be implemented as a Singleton (Gamma, et al. 1996). In the case of the `PaymentListCommand`, the command is stateful, so the local implementation of the command cannot be implemented as a Singleton. Instead, there must be one instance of the command per user session (that is, a session scoped variable). In this case, the `PaymentListPage` class manages the command. The code for the `PaymentListPage` is shown in Listing 9.8.

```
public class PaymentListPage extends Page {
  private PaymentListCommand command = null;
  private List currentPayments = null;
  private static final String DONE = "done";
  private static final String ERROR = "error";

  private PaymentListCommand getCommand() {
    if (null == command) {
      command = PaymentListCommandLocal.getCommand();
    }
    return command;
  }

  public void setCurrentPayments(List list) {
    currentPayments = list;
  }

  public List getCurrentPayments() {
    if (null == currentPayments) {
      try {
        ValueBinding binding = Utils.getBinding("#{customer.payees}");
        Collection payees =
          (Collection) binding.getValue(
            FacesContext.getCurrentInstance());
        System.err.println("payees = " + payees);
        getCommand().openPaymentList(payees);
        currentPayments = command.getNextPayments();
      } catch (PropertyNotFoundException e) {
        e.printStackTrace();
      } catch (HibernateException e) {
        e.printStackTrace();
      }
    }
    return currentPayments;
  }

  private void doneWithPage() {
    currentPayments = null;
    if (null != command) {
      command.closePaymentList();
    }
  }

  public String next() {
```

Listing 9.8 PaymentListPage.java. *(continued)*

```
    String outcome = null; // usually null so we come back
    FacesContext ctx = FacesContext.getCurrentInstance();
    try {
      if (getCommand().hasNextPayments()) {
        setCurrentPayments(getCommand().getNextPayments());
      }
    } catch (HibernateException e) {
      doneWithPage();
      this.addInternalErrorMessage(ctx);
      outcome = ERROR;
    }
    return outcome;
  }

  protected String done() {
    doneWithPage();
    return DONE;
  }

  public boolean getPreviousDisabled() {
    return true;
  }

  public String previous() {
    String outcome = null; // usually null so we come back
    FacesContext ctx = FacesContext.getCurrentInstance();
    try {
      if (getCommand().hasPreviousPayments()) {
        setCurrentPayments(getCommand().getPreviousPayments());
      }
    } catch (HibernateException e) {
      doneWithPage();
      this.addInternalErrorMessage(ctx);
      outcome = ERROR;
    }
    return outcome;
  }
}
```

Listing 9.8 *(continued)*

VALUE LIST HANDLER

The value list handler pattern documents several strategies to scroll through a large set of objects a few at a time with EJBs. If you need more information, go to java.sun.com and do a search for "value list handler." The pattern is documented in the J2EE blueprints section of the Web site.

Since the PaymentListPage manages the PaymentListCommand (through the getCommand method in Listing 9.8), and the page instance is configured through the `faces-config.xml` file and scoped at the session, the Payment ListCommand instance will be scoped at session level as well. And thus the state will be kept at session level.

Another interesting aspect to this implementation is the way that the payment list is maintained. There is no life-cycle-oriented API for managed beans (that is, a set of methods to inform the managed bean that was created or is about to be destroyed, and so on); the management of state must bemanaged in another way. In this case, the rendering of the page causes the state to be initialized and the state is discarded when the user navigates away from the page. Here is the code that manages that processing.

```
public List getCurrentPayments() {
    if (null == currentPayments) {
      try {
        ValueBinding binding = Utils.getBinding("#{customer.payees}");
        Collection payees =
          (Collection) binding.getValue(
            FacesContext.getCurrentInstance());
        System.err.println("payees = " + payees);
        getCommand().openPaymentList(payees);
        currentPayments = command.getNextPayments();
      } catch (PropertyNotFoundException e) {
        e.printStackTrace();
      } catch (HibernateException e) {
        e.printStackTrace();
      }
    }
    return currentPayments;
 }

 private void doneWithPage() {
    currentPayments = null;
    if (null != command) {
      command.closePaymentList();
    }
 }
```

A part of the code for the JSP is listed here.

```
<h:dataTable value="#{paymentListPage.currentPayments}"
             var="payment">
  <h:outputText value="#{payment.payee.name}"/>
  <h:outputText value="#{payment.dateToSend}"/>
  <h:outputText value="#{payment.amount}"/>
</h:dataTable>
```

When the page is rendered the `value` reference `paymentListPage.currentPayments` in the JSP invokes the `getCurrentPayments` method. That, in turn, initializes the state (via the call to `openPaymentList` on the command). Then, whenever the user navigates away from the list page (by pressing the Done button), the `doneWithPage` method is called by the action method associated with the Done button, which releases the state.

Summary

The iBank application presented is far from complete, but through the snapshots of the application that have been discussed in detail hopefully you have a good picture of what it will take to finish it up. The important thing to remember is that just because JSF is a new technology does not mean that all the old best practices from dealing with two- and three-tiered applications have to be rethought. Most of them still apply.

CHAPTER

10

Custom JSF Components

One of the most important ways that JSF is different from the user interface technologies for the Web that have come before is that it can be extended with new user interface elements. With the advent of JSF, you can write reusable user interface components that are not only capable of rendering in HTML, but also provide events, validations, and conversion. And all of it can be reused, just like any other standard JSF `UIComponent` that was covered in Chapter 6, "UI Components." In this chapter, you will see how to build your own JSF components, including all the supporting classes that go along with the component (that is, Renderers and JSP tags) that you can reuse. Let's get started by explaining what a custom component is in the first place.

Overview

In this chapter, we will go over what a custom JSF component is and how to build one. Like the other component UI frameworks that came before JSF (see Chapter 1, "JSF Patterns and Architecture") you can extend it by building your own components. A component consists of three parts, the subclass of UIComponent, the Renderer, and the custom JSP Tag. Not all custom components will require you to write all three pieces, but all components use these three pieces. The components you build can range in complexity from a simple new HTML element like `code` to a complex calendar component that renders dates in various locales.

In some cases, it is not necessary to build a whole new component, but instead you can sometimes customize the way an existing component is rendered to get the output that you want. We will also go over how you can customize the rendering of built-in components that come with JSF to get the final HTML that you want.

What Is a Custom Component?

A new component should customize (or extend) one or more of the general component responsibilities. A component is responsible for performing properly in the phases of the request-response life cycle (details can be found in Chapter 3, "JSF Request-Processing Life Cycle"). In other words, a component must be able to decode itself (or delegate to a Renderer), validate the user's inputs (or delegate this to a Validator), convert the input to local model values (or delegate this to a Converter), and finally render itself again (or delegate this to the Renderer again). Components are also responsible for processing any events that are queued up during any of these phases. An example of a component with extended functionality is a subclass of the `UIPanel` component that provides a column that could be filled with pull-downs. If one of the pull-downs is activated, a FacesEvent is posted. We will go into detail on how to build this kind of component later in this chapter. There are three kinds of custom components. The next three sections cover these types.

Aggregate Component

The first type of component is an aggregation of several existing components into one component. Typically, an aggregate component is built to help ensure consistency and to provide reuse. An aggregate component provides consistency because the way the aggregated components are presented is coded once in the aggregate instead of being duplicated each time the set of components is needed. The custom component provides easier reuse when compared to the JSP fragments (the JSP 2.0 specification allows for the creation of tags from JSP fragments, which will make JSP reuse more straightforward; however, JSP 2.0 is not required for JSF).

Another aspect of building an aggregate component is the ease of configuration. A single point of configuration is often simpler for a developer rather than having to configure all the components separately. Another aspect of the aggregate component is that the application developer can view that component as a single event source instead of multiple event sources. Having a single event source further simplifies application development. A confirm panel is a good example of an aggregate component. Most applications have the need to prompt the user for confirmation on significant actions such as deleting data. Figure 10.1 shows an example of what the panel could look like in a very simple form.

The simple confirmation panel component (shown in Figure 10.1) aggregates four components, a `UIOutput` rendered as simple text, two `UICommands` rendered as buttons, and finally a `UIPanel` rendered as a grid to hold it all together and present it nicely. Figure 10.2 is a diagram showing the parent child relationship of the components.

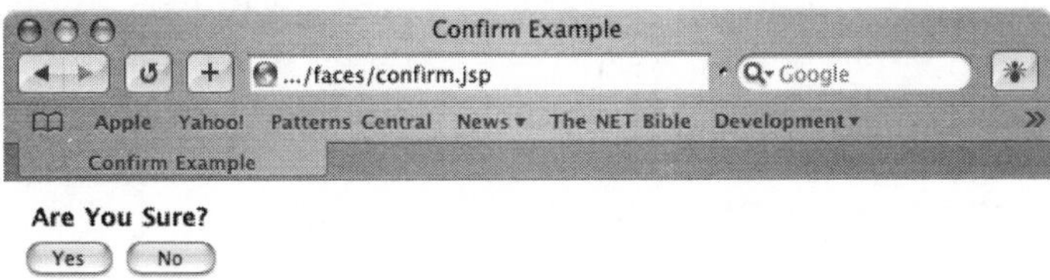

Figure 10.1 Simple confirmation panel.

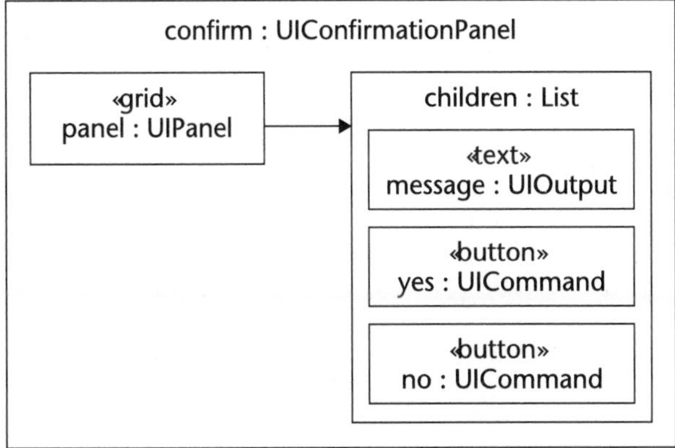

Figure 10.2 Simple confirmation panel aggregation.

New HTML Generator

The second type of component is a cover for some aspect of HTML that is not already provided by the JSF implementation you are using. You might also need to combine HTML in custom ways that are not easily representable via the existing components and Renderers. Most JSF implementations provide good coverage of the commonly used HTML features, but without complete coverage there is always the chance that you will need something that is not provided. If your JSF implementation does not provide the HTML element that you need, or if you want customized HTML and your JSF implementation does not provide the means to do the customization, you can easily write a new component.

For example, one of the sample components that was built for the *JSF Reference Implementation* is a component to manage client-side maps. The reference implementation (RI) does not provide a UIComponent to handle client-side image maps but the examples that ship with the RI does provide such a component. The `UIMap` component inherits the ability to respond to user input with an action event from UICommand. The `UIArea` component is intended solely to be the named areas for the image map and a child of a `UIMap` component. The `UIArea` component is a subclass of `UIComponentBase`. Figure 10.3 is a UML diagram for these components.

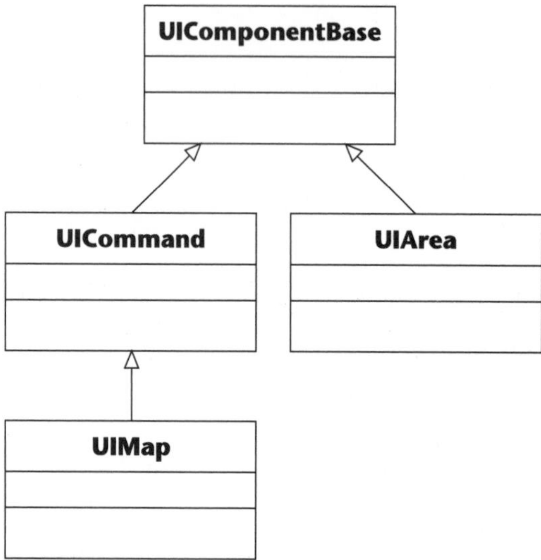

Figure 10.3 UIMap hierarchy.

New Client Type

The third component type is one that provides user interface for a client other than an HTML browser. This component type is the most extensive because it could entail writing a whole component suite as well as RenderKit.

Just as there are many different kinds of components there are many different reasons to build one; the next section documents these reasons.

Motivation for Building a Custom Component

The standard set of components included with any JSF implementation is enough to build rich HTML user interfaces. However, the standard components do not cover every aspect of HTML, and you probably have in mind new and interesting combinations of HTML that were not envisioned by the JSF specification.

You have a couple of choices to generate interesting combinations of HTML where components and Renderers do exist for the pieces. You can put together the standard components and their Renderers to accomplish your goal or you can build a custom component. Using the standard components and their Renderers to build your complex UI has the advantage that your UI is built from off-the-shelf components, which often leads to less maintenance costs. Using the standard components though can lead to increased complexity in the code used to set up the user interface. You can also have additional complexity in a custom component. With a custom component, you can hide some of the complexity from the developer using your component so that he or she does not have to worry about some of the details.

Let's look at a simple example. In many applications, the user needs the ability to either confirm or cancel a particular action. In this example, let's assume that we will implement this requirement as a pair of buttons titled `Submit` and `Cancel`. Here is the JSP code needed to build these two buttons using the standard JSF tags and components:

```
<h:commandButton id="submit"  action="#{calendar.submit}"
                  value="Submit"/>
<h:commandButton id="cancel" action="#{calendar.cancel}"
                  value="Cancel"/>
```

There are a couple of options to reuse this pair of buttons. We can put it into a JSP fragment and include that with the standard `jsp:include` tag, or we could simply copy and paste the JSP code from page to page. Of course, the copy-and-paste method is the absolute worst way to achieve reuse, so use the `jsp:include` instead.

If, on the other hand, you built a custom component to manage this part of your user interface, the JSP code could look something like this.

```
<custom:submitcancelButtonpair id="submitCancel"
              submit="#{calendar.submit}"
              cancel="#{calendar.cancel}"/>
```

In the background, without the JSP developer having to think about it, the `SubmitCancel` component is building the part of the component tree needed to end up with exactly the same HTML. The advantage of having this custom component is the ease of use for the JSP developer. After the *Render Response* phase is complete for either approach, the HTML sent back to the browser looks exactly the same; the difference is in what code the developer has to write.

The other reason you will want to build your own component is to cover a particular HTML element that is not currently covered by the standard JSF components. For example, there is no component that makes the client-side image map available. If you needed an image map, you could create a custom component instead of hard-coding the HTML. The great thing about the component-based approach (as opposed to hand-coding the HTML) is that you get the best of both worlds, quick feedback on the client side and server-side round trips when they are needed to refresh the view.

Keep in mind that you might be able to achieve your goal without resorting to creating a component. You might be able to get by with just creating a new Renderer for an existing component. For example, a standard JSF Renderer does not currently cover the `code` element. Even though you can achieve the same look with a class attribute and a CSS style using the UIOutput component, you might want the `code` element for some reason apart from the displaying of the HTML (that is, you might have a HTML reader that expects to find `code` elements). In this case, you could create a new Renderer for the UIOutput component and have it write `<code>` elements to the HTML output stream.

Just as important as knowing when you need a new component is to know when you do not. Remember that JSF has many built-in extension points that let you do a lot of customizations. Some things that might look like they need a custom component do not. For example, you do not need a new component simply to render a different element type in your HTML. In the case of the `code` element earlier, you could simply implement a new Renderer along with a new tag and use the existing `UIOutput` tag. The other extension points in JSF can also be used to customize the way existing components behave (that is, Validators, Converters, and so on). Before you build a new component, investigate the existing extension mechanisms to see if any can be exploited to fit your purposes.

Now that you have seen some of the motivations behind writing a custom component, let's take a look at some of the details that make up a custom component.

Aspects of Custom Components

The typical component requires a stack of objects to work properly. In many cases, you will not have to implement the entire stack to make your new component work. In this section, we will cover the various parts of the stack and how they work together to produce the user interface. Figure 10.4 is a graphical representation of the life cycle.

The life cycle was documented in detail back in Chapter 3. In this section, we will document the various aspects of the JSF component model and how they interact with the life cycle. Figure 10.5 is UML for the UIComponent and all its constituent parts that are required to fulfill its responsibility to perform the life cycle.

For each phase in the life cycle, we will see which classes are used and how, so that you will fully understand the responsibilities of your custom component implementation and which pieces of the stack you must implement to get your required functionality.

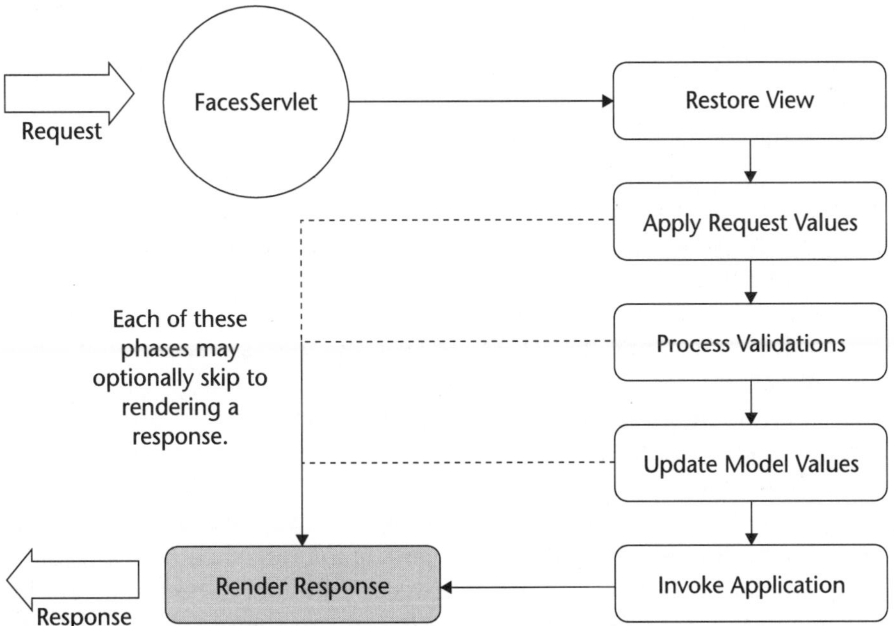

Figure 10.4 JSF Request Response life cycle.

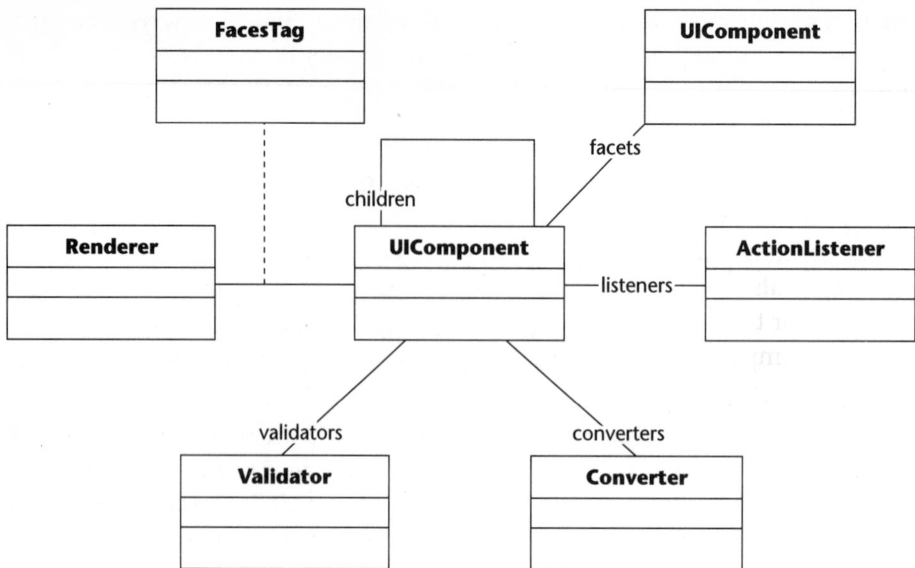

Figure 10.5 UIComponent and constituents.

Restore View

Recall from Chapter 3 that this phase is about getting the component tree back into memory. JSF provides two ways to store the view while the user is manipulating the rendered version of the view. The first is to store the state in a hidden parameter in the page as serialized objects. The second approach is to store the state on the server. There are advantages to both methods. When the state is stored in the page, the application server is free to load-balance in any way that is necessary instead of forcing the user to reconnect to the same session each time. On the other hand, the page-based approach can lead to potentially large pages that take too long to download. The server-side approach of keeping the tree in the session has the advantage of smaller download for the user. Either way, the important thing for you to keep in mind is to make your components implement `javax.faces.component.StateHolder`. Whichever way the application is deployed the component can be saved and restored with this interface. Your implementation of `saveState` and `restoreState` should be bidirectional. In other words they should do exactly the opposite things. If `saveState` returns an Array of `Serializable` objects then `restoreState` should expect the Object passed in is an `Array`.

All the Validators, Converters, action listeners, children, and facets will be back in memory and be ready to process the rest of the life cycle after this phase is complete. The Renderers that you write do not have their state stored. Only the identifier for the RenderKit is stored with the state of the objects and not the individual Renderers.

Apply Request Values

This phase is about getting the values that the user specified in the browser into the components that were just brought back into memory. In order to perform this phase, the component will be involved as well as a Renderer if the component delegates the decoding task. If the component has the `immediate` property set to true, then the validation that would normally happen in the Process Validations phase happens in this phase right after decoding. A Converter could also be involved to convert the value from the request into a suitable value for the component.

The most important decision you need to make for your custom component and its responsibility in this phase is how it will handle decoding the user request. Your component can fully implement its decoding, fully delegate its decoding to a `Renderer` subclass, or do a combination of both. The best approach is to do both—delegate where possible and have the component decode itself when necessary. Figure 10.6 is a UML sequence diagram showing how to implement delegation when possible and decoding locally when it's not possible to delegate.

Decoding is initiated by a call to the `processDecodes` method on the root component in the tree. Your custom component is told to decode by the JSF runtime (with `processesDecodes` sent to the root component of the tree) during the *Apply Request Values* phase. This method traverses the component graph in a depth first manner calling the `decode` method for each component from the bottom of the graph up. The `decode` method is responsible for taking any input from the request and decoding it into data suitable for the component (which could be a simple copy of the string value or involve a conversion through a Converter).

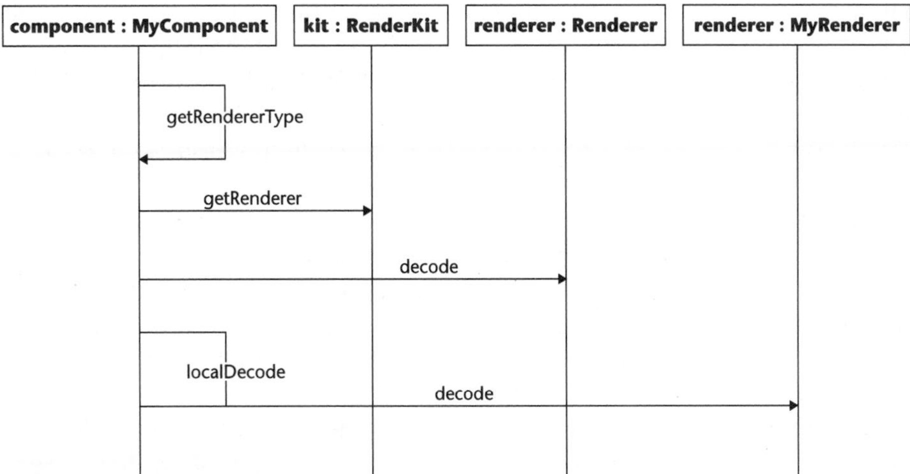

Figure 10.6 Rendering a custom component.

In most cases, your custom component need only implement the `decode` method since the `processDecodes` method is inherited from the `UI ComponentBase` class. The `decode` method (as shown in Figure 10.6) should first check for a render type, if one is found delegate to the Renderer from the RenderKit. If the render type is not set, then the component is responsible for its own rendering.

When you are building your custom component, it is important to put all the rendering code into one place (namely the Renderer) and always delegate to that class if the render type is not set. The interesting thing about this approach is that in most cases the RenderKit would find the same Renderer as it would if the render type were not set. In other words, the Renderer found by the RenderKit above in Figure 10.6 will usually be an instance of `MyRenderer`. This is by design; instead of putting rendering code into your component, you should put it into a Renderer and package the default Renderer with the component. Using this approach, you will provide rich default behavior as well as giving users of your component the ability to customize with their own Renderers in the future.

Aggregate components will typically not have to be concerned with this functionality since the constituent components will be rendered in the typical manner. Components that cover new HTML elements will need to handle decoding values from the request and thus will have to implement the `decode` method. In some cases, components that add new functionality will also need to have their own implementation of decode, especially if there is some special means of converting the request parameters into data the component can understand.

Process Validations

The next step in the life cycle is to validate the request parameters that were applied to the components in the last phase. Recall that if the immediate property is set on a component, then the validation has already occurred. If that is the case, then this phase does nothing. However, if the immediate property is not set, then this phase proceeds. In order to validate the inputs, the component will be involved as well as any Validators that are attached to the component. If your custom component has particular validation needs, you can implement that validation in either the component or a Renderer.

The `UIComponentBase` class provides a default implementation of the `processValidators` method that traverses the components in a depth first manner, so if your component subclasses from `UIComponentBase`, you only have to implement the `validate` method.

It is recommended that you only implement validation specific to the custom component in the `validate` method. You should never implement correctness checks in this method that are available through one of the standard Validators (that is, the `RequiredValidator` should be used instead of checking for `null` in the component's `validate` method). Instead, all validation done locally in the component should be related only to the component. For example, let's consider a date range chooser component. This component is an aggregation of six `UISelectOne` components (two each for the month, day, and year) for the start date and end date, along with two `UIOutput` components as labels (Start Date and End Date). Figure 10.7 is a containment diagram showing the various components and how they are contained.

A UML class diagram for the `UIDateRangeChooser` component is shown in Figure 10.8. This diagram shows the various components that the range chooser aggregates.

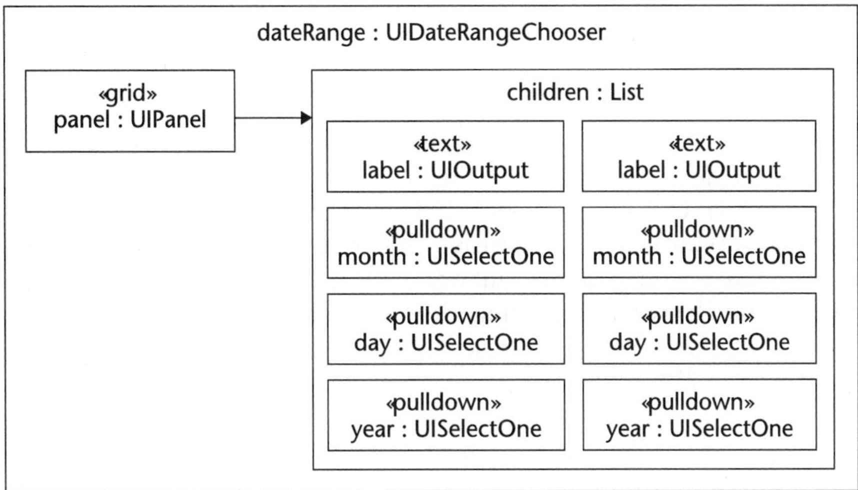

Figure 10.7 UIDateRangeChooser containment diagram.

UIDateRangeChooser
startDate : Date startLabel : UIOutput startMonth : UISelectOne startDay : UISelectOne startYear : UISelectOne stopDate : Date stopLabel : UIOutput stopMonth : UISelectOne stopDay : UISelectOne stopYear : UISelectOne maxDaysInRange : Integer

Figure 10.8 UIDateRangeChooser class diagram.

In addition to the child components, the `UIDateRangeChooser` component has an attribute that specifies the maximum number of days in the date range. The correctness check for the days in the range should be implemented in the component itself instead of as an external Validator, since the definition of validity is in the component itself. Of course, the validation could be implemented as a custom Validator that has its own configuration, but the probability of being able to reuse the validation functionality is slim, and the cost of having an additional class to maintain is higher than the gain.

No matter what kind of custom component you are building, it will have responsibility in this phase. The component with new behavior will have to manage the validation of the data related to the new behavior. Aggregating components will have to manage the validation of the aggregated data and finally components that manage additional HTML elements will have to validate any input the user made on the controls.

Update Model Values

This phase involves moving the validated data from the component to the model objects. Again the processing happens depth first. Each `UIInput` component in the tree is told to update its model with the `updateModel` method. Your custom component will then be responsible for applying its current value to the underlying model object. Remember not push the value down to the model object if any part of conversion or validation failed. The particular attribute to be updated is referred to by the `value` attribute.

In most cases, the default implementation of this method inherited from `UIComponentBase` will suffice, so you will not have to do anything specific for your components. The one caveat is the aggregated component.

Often the aggregated component has several different values that need to be applied to the underlying model. You have several options in the way you apply these updates. You can combine your aggregated data into a single JavaBean that is created during the conversion process in the *Apply Request Values* phase. This approach has the advantage of being most like the rest of the JSF components (that is, a component typically has one `value` attribute).

Alternately, you could provide more than one `value` for your aggregated component. For example, the date range chooser component we discussed earlier could have been implemented with a single value reference whose type was a JavaBean representing a date range, or the component could have had six `value` expressions representing the six choices the user had to make (they would of course have to have different names).

Both approaches are valid, but you should consider the simplicity of the interface and the implementation before you build your component. If you choose to have multiple `value` expressions for your component, you will expose a more difficult interface to the user of your component (that is, the developer using the range chooser would have to specify six value reference expressions). On the positive side, you will have a simpler implementation in your component because there is very little conversion to do. If you provide a single value reference interface to your component, the developer using it will have a simpler interface but you will have more to do in the implementation. We typically tend to lean towards a simpler interface for the developer because the developer using the component is probably building the code that will have to be changed and maintained more often. In other words, the simpler code needs to be in the class(es) that is more likely to change. The trade-off between these two options is not always obvious however, so keep them in mind while building your component and consciously make the choice.

Invoke Application

Most component types are not directly involved in this phase of the request response-processing life cycle. However subclasses of UICommand will be involved, although you typically can rely on the default implementation you inherit from UICommand. The UICommand subclass queues ActionEvents during the *Apply Request Values* phase. These events are then activated during this phase. As a subclass of UICommand, your component will inherit the ability to distribute the events. You will only have to override that functionality if you need to customize the way events are distributed to the listeners.

Render Response

This phase is responsible for building the response for the request that initiated this life cycle. The typical response is HTML sent back to a browser, but JSF is able to render many different types of responses. For your custom component, you will need to be concerned with rendering (the set of encode methods, `encodeBegin`, `encodeChildren`, and `encodeEnd`) your component either through a Renderer or by implementing the encoding locally. As we discussed in the *Apply Request Values* phase, it is always best to implement the encoding in a Renderer and then delegate to it directly if the RenderKit is unable to provide a render. In this way, you will allow others the ability to customize your component with their own rendering in the future.

The other interesting aspect of this phase is the involvement of the JSP tags. The most common way that a developer builds a component tree is through the use of JSF tags in a JSP. There is a lot of detail on this approach in Chapter 5, "JSP Integration in JSF." Figure 10.9 is a sequence diagram of the high-level processing that is involved in rendering a response from a JSP.

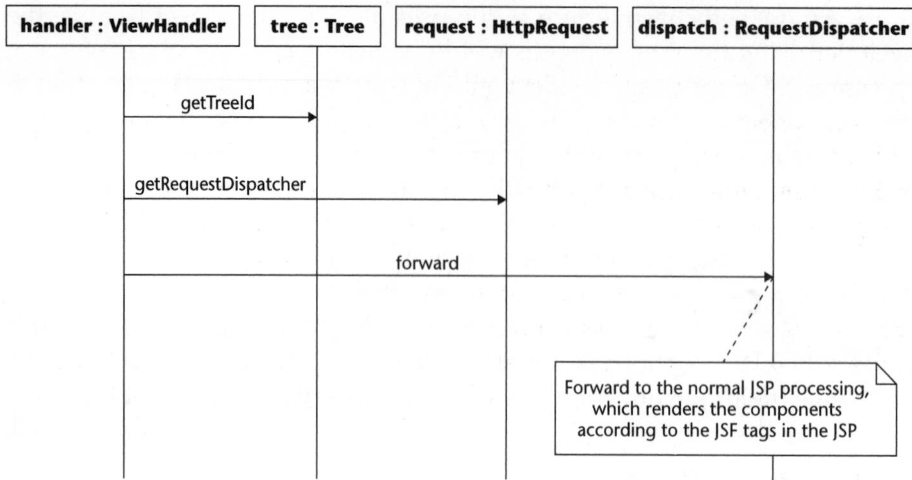

Figure 10.9 Rendering a response with JSP tags and the ViewHandler.

The JSP-based view handler (the default one in many JSF implementations) is responsible for forwarding data to the Web container, which will do the normal JSP processing, (see Chapter 5) to render the response. The next step in the rendering process is to invoke the JSP tags. The tags, in turn, attach Renderers (via the `setRenderType` method) to the components and then control the rest of the rendering of the component through translation of the JSP tag life-cycle methods into JSF rendering methods. Specifically the JSP tag life-cycle methods (`doStartTag`, `doAfterBody`, and `doEndTag`) are translated into calls on the JSF rendering methods (`encodeBegin`, `encodeChildren`, `encodeEnd`).

The users of your custom component will most likely interact with it first through the JSP tag that represents it. It is therefore very important that you build the tag so that it is easy to use and provides full control over the component.

Now that we have gone through the request response life cycle—specifically discussing how to make your custom component capable of performing properly—we will dive into a detailed discussion of a component.

Custom Component Example

To finish out this chapter, a sample component will be developed. The component represents a scroller that allows the user to move thru a list of choices one at a time by clicking on buttons. Figure 10.10 shows the scroller rendered in a Web browser.

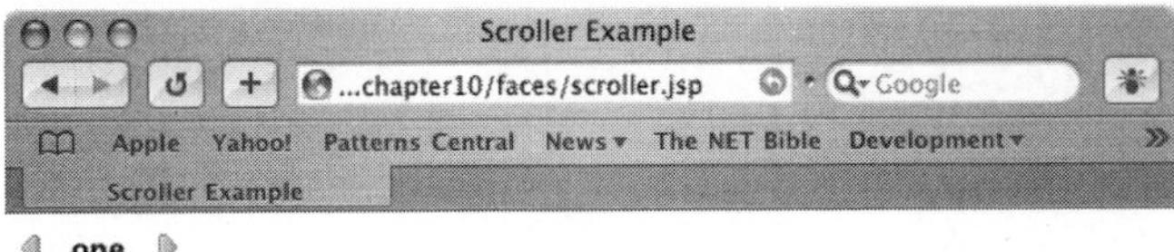

one

Figure 10.10 UIScroller component.

UIScroller Component Code

The `UIScroller` component has a list of string objects that represent the various choices the user can make. As the buttons on the right or left are clicked the selected (that is, displayed) option is changed (right is one higher or back to zero, left is one lower or to the end).

The scroller is made from three different classes: the component, the Renderer, and the JSP tag. The component is responsible for keeping track of the state of the component (that is, the list of choices and the currently selected choice) and handling the events that are produced from the button clicks. Each button click causes the selected choice to change as well as queuing an event to let any listeners know that the choice has changed.

The Renderer is responsible for turning the state of the component into HTML. The Renderer produces two `img` tags that represent the right and left buttons, and the selected options are rendered as simple bold text. The two images have JavaScript attached to their `onMouseDown` attributes that indicates which button was clicked then submits the form that contains the scroller.

The final class needed to implement the scroller component is the JSP tag. The tag allows a JSP author to specify the various aspects of the component. One item of note is the list of options. A comma-delimited string or a value reference can specify the options. If a value reference is used it should resolve to a `Collection` of String objects.

Listing 10.1 has the source code for the `UIScroller` component. We will go through each of the interesting pieces of the implementation in detail.

```
public class UIScroller extends UICommand {
  private static Logger logger =
               Logger.getLogger(Constants.LOGGER_NAME);
  // The type used by the render kit to find the
  // correct renderer for the component
  public static final String TYPE = "Scroller";

  private String rightScrollImg;
  private String leftScrollImg;
```

Listing 10.1 UIScroller Component. *(continued)*

```
private MethodBinding rightAction;
private MethodBinding leftAction;
private List options;
private String selectedOption;

public static final String DEFAULT_RIGHT_IMG = "right_small.gif";
public static final String DEFAULT_LEFT_IMG = "left_small.gif";

public UIScroller() {
  super();
  logger.entering(getClass().getName(), "noargs constructor");
  options = new ArrayList();
}

public void performRightAction(FacesContext context) {
  int index = options.indexOf(getSelectedOption());
  int size = options.size();
  if (0 != size) {
    index++;
    if (index == size)
      index = 0;
    setSelectedOption((String) options.get(index));
  }
  queueEvent(new ActionEvent(this));
}

public void performLeftAction(FacesContext context) {
  int index = options.indexOf(getSelectedOption());
  int size = options.size();
  if (0 != size) {
    if (index >= 0)
      index--;
    if (index == -1)
      index = size - 1;
    setSelectedOption((String) options.get(index));
  }
  queueEvent(new ActionEvent(this));
}

private Renderer getSharedRenderer(FacesContext context) {
  RenderKitFactory rkFactory =
    (RenderKitFactory) FactoryFinder.getFactory(
      RenderKitFactory.HTML_BASIC_RENDER_KIT);
  RenderKit renderKit =
    rkFactory.getRenderKit(context, context.
                           getViewRoot().getRenderKitId());
  return renderKit.getRenderer(UIScroller.FAMILY,
                               ScrollerRenderer.TYPE);
}
```

Listing 10.1 *(continued)*

```
public void decode(FacesContext context) {
  logger.entering(this.getClass().getName(), "decode");
  if (context == null) {
    NullPointerException npe = new NullPointerException(
      "FacesContext is null while trying "
        + "to decode "
        + getId());
    logger.throwing(this.getClass().getName(), "decode", npe);
    throw npe;
  }
  if (getRendererType() == null) {
    // local render
    Renderer renderer = getSharedRenderer(context);
    renderer.decode(context, this);
  } else {
    // render kit render
    super.decode(context);
  }
}

public void encodeBegin(FacesContext context) throws IOException {
  logger.entering(getClass().getName(), "encodeBegin");
  if (context == null) {
    NullPointerException npe = new NullPointerException(
      "FacesContext is null while trying "
        + "to encode "
        + getId());
    logger.throwing(this.getClass().getName(), "encode", npe);
    throw npe;
  }
  if (getRendererType() == null) {
    Renderer renderer = getSharedRenderer(context);
    renderer.encodeBegin(context, this);
  } else {
    // render kit render
    super.encodeBegin(context);
  }
}

public void encodeChildren(FacesContext context) throws IOException {
  logger.entering(getClass().getName(), "encodeChildren");
  if (context == null) {
    NullPointerException npe = new NullPointerException(
      "FacesContext is null while trying "
        + "to encodeChildren "
        + getId());
    logger.throwing(this.getClass().getName(), "encodeChildren", npe);
    throw npe;
  }
```

Listing 10.1 *(continued)*

```
    if (getRendererType() == null) {
      Renderer renderer = getSharedRenderer(context);
      renderer.encodeChildren(context, this);
    } else {
      // render kit render
      super.encodeChildren(context);
    }
  }

  public void encodeEnd(FacesContext context) throws IOException {
    logger.entering(getClass().getName(), "encodeEnd");
    if (context == null) {
      NullPointerException npe = new NullPointerException(
        "FacesContext is null while trying "
          + "to encodeEnd "
          + getId());
      logger.throwing(this.getClass().getName(), "encodeEnd", npe);
      throw npe;
    }
    if (getRendererType() == null) {
      Renderer renderer = getSharedRenderer(context);
      renderer.encodeEnd(context, this);
    } else {
      // render kit render
      super.encodeEnd(context);
    }
  }

  public String getLeftScrollImg() {
    return leftScrollImg;
  }

  public String getRightScrollImg() {
    return rightScrollImg;
  }

  public void setLeftScrollImg(String string) {
    leftScrollImg = string;
  }

  public void setRightScrollImg(String string) {
    rightScrollImg = string;
  }

  public List getOptions() {
    return options;
  }
```

Listing 10.1 *(continued)*

```
    public void setOptions(List options) {
      this.options = options;
    }

    public String getOption(int index) {
      return (String)options.get(index);
    }

    public void addOption(String option) {
      options.add(option);
    }

    public void removeOption(String option) {
      options.remove(option);
    }

    public String getSelectedOption() {
      return selectedOption;
    }

    public void setSelectedOption(String value) {
      selectedOption = value;
    }

    public void setLeftAction(MethodBinding binding) {
      leftAction = binding;
    }

    public MethodBinding getLeftAction() {
      return leftAction;
    }

    public void setRightAction(MethodBinding binding) {
      rightAction = binding;
    }

    public MethodBinding getRightAction() {
      return rightAction;
    }

}
```

Listing 10.1 *(continued)*

Events

The first method pair is used to manage the events that are generated when the buttons are pushed. Remember that as each button is pushed the selected option is changed as if the options were in a circularly linked list (that is, clicking past the end takes you back to the first option). In addition to changing the selected option, the component also needs to post an event to let all the listeners know that the option changed. Here is the code for quick reference:

```
public void performRightAction(FacesContext context) {
    int index = options.indexOf(getSelectedOption());
    int size = options.size();
    if (0 != size) {
      index++;
      if (index == size)
        index = 0;
      setSelectedOption((String) options.get(index));
    }
    queueEvent(new ActionEvent(this));
  }

  public void performLeftAction(FacesContext context) {
    int index = options.indexOf(getSelectedOption());
    int size = options.size();
    if (0 != size) {
      if (index >= 0)
        index--;
      if (index == -1)
        index = size - 1;
      setSelectedOption((String) options.get(index));
    }
    queueEvent(new ActionEvent(this));
  }
```

The first part of each method chooses the next option, which is basically making the list of options look like a circularly linked list. The final part of the method actually queues up a new `ActionEvent` for processing at the end of the *Invoke Application* phase. This is the only phase that the scroller component posts events in but your component might need to post events during the other phases. Reasons for doing so will vary but typically an action event posted later in the request response cycle requires some part of the functionality only performed later in the cycle to be complete before it can be properly posted and processed.

Rendering

The next method, `getSharedRenderer`, is key to only implementing the encoding and decoding once. The code is repeated here for quick reference.

```
private Renderer getSharedRenderer(FacesContext context) {
  RenderKitFactory rkFactory =
    (RenderKitFactory) FactoryFinder.getFactory(
```

```
        RenderKitFactory.DEFAULT_RENDER_KIT);
    RenderKit renderKit =
      rkFactory.getRenderKit(context.getViewRoot().getRenderKitId());
    return renderKit.getRenderer(UIScroller.TYPE);
  }
```

Decoding

As you recall from earlier discussion at the beginning of this chapter, it is very important that the code to render your new component be written only once. In many cases, the component will be simple enough that there is no need to build a separate Renderer. In these cases, it is very straightforward—implement the component to do its own rendering. In other words, put the decode and encode functionality directly into the `decode`, `encodeBegin`, `encode Children`, and `encodeEnd` methods on your component. In many cases, however, you will need to build a Renderer to manage the encoding and decoding of your component. Following is the `decode` method from the scroller that makes use of the `getSharedRenderer` method:

```
public void decode(FacesContext context) {
    logger.entering(this.getClass().getName(), "decode");
    if (context == null) {
      NullPointerException npe = new NullPointerException(
        "FacesContext is null while trying "
          + "to decode "
          + getId());
      logger.throwing(this.getClass().getName(), "decode", npe);
      throw npe;
    }
    if (getRendererType() == null) {
      // local render
      Renderer renderer = getSharedRenderer(context);
      renderer.decode(context, this);
    } else {
      // render kit render
      super.decode(context);
    }
}
```

Notice that the first test is to look for the Renderer type for the scroller. If it has not been set then the component Renderers itself; if it has been set, then the UIComponentBase implementation takes care of rendering. The inherited implementation looks up the Renderer from the RenderKit and delegates the decoding to the Renderer, which in essence is exactly like what is done here in the decode method. That seems odd to reimplement the superclasses functionality exactly. The difference is that the superclass is always looking for the

Renderer identified by whatever the component's `rendererType` method returns. The implementation of `getSharedRenderer` always looks up the Renderer for UIScroller.TYPE. This strategy provides great flexibility to your component in the hands of other developers. If another developer chooses to use the scroller component but wants to render it with a different Renderer, they are free to do that but they can always revert to the packaged Renderer by simply setting the `rendererType` attribute to `null`.

One final point about local rendering on components that is important to remember: The implementation of `decode` could have been done with a copy of the code from the Renderer (what we have been trying to avoid). In that case, the Renderer and the component would tend to have divergent implementations (that is, over time bugs would be fixed in one place but not the other, and so on), which could lead to a lot of confusion and trouble in using the scroller. Remember to implement the rendering functionality only once in a default Renderer, then delegate processing to that implementation.

Encoding

The next group of methods handles encoding the component into HTML. The encodeBegin method is shown again for quick reference:

```
public void encodeBegin(FacesContext context) throws IOException {
    logger.entering(getClass().getName(), "encodeBegin");
    if (context == null) {
      NullPointerException npe = new NullPointerException(
        "FacesContext is null while trying "
          + "to encode "
          + getId());
      logger.throwing(this.getClass().getName(), "encode", npe);
      throw npe;
    }
    if (getRendererType() == null) {
      Renderer renderer = getSharedRenderer(context);
      renderer.encodeBegin(context, this);
    } else {
      // render kit render
      super.encodeBegin(context);
    }
}
```

As you can see, much of the same functionality is present in this method as in the `decode` method we just looked at. In the same way that we want to avoid copying and pasting the decode functionality, we want to avoid copying and pasting the encode functionality. All three encode methods have the same basic structure—they just delegate processing to the appropriate method on the Renderer. Next, we will cover the Renderer for the `UIScroller` component.

UIScroller Renderer Code

Listing 10.2 is the code for the scroller Renderer. In the following paragraphs, we will cover each of the interesting aspects of the implementation in detail. Keep in mind that one of the key factors in the implementation of the Renderer is to enable reuse for both local and delegated rendering. The particulars of the implementation that were written a certain way to facilitate this reuse will be called out below in the discussion. Also, recall that the Renderer has two major functions: first it must encode and decode the response and request, respectively. Second the render needs to work properly with development tools. The particulars of the implementation pertaining to these two basic responsibilities will also be discussed later in this section.

```
public class ScrollerRenderer extends Renderer {
  private static Logger logger =
    Logger.getLogger(Constants.LOGGER_NAME);

  public static final String SELECTED_VALUE_CLASS_ATTR =
    "selectedClass";

  public static final String TYPE = "ScrollerRenderer";

  public ScrollerRenderer() {
    super();
  }

  public void decode(FacesContext context, UIComponent component) {

    checkState(context, component);

    UIScroller scroller = (UIScroller) component;
    decodeCommandName(context, scroller);
    UIForm parentForm = ComponentTreeUtils.getParentForm(scroller);
    if (null == parentForm) {
      queueMissingFormErrorMessage(context, scroller);
    }
  }

  private void decodeCommandName(
    FacesContext context,
    UIScroller scroller) {

    String clientId = scroller.getClientId(context);
    String rightClientId = getRightClientId(clientId);
    String leftClientId = getLeftClientId(clientId);
    Map requestParameterMap =
      context.getExternalContext().getRequestParameterMap();
```

Listing 10.2 ScrollerRenderer. *(continued)*

```
    String value = (String) requestParameterMap.get(clientId);

    String rightValue =
      (String) requestParameterMap.get(rightClientId);
    String leftValue =
      (String) requestParameterMap.get(leftClientId);

    String commandName = null;
    logger.fine("rightValue = " + rightValue);
    logger.fine("leftValue = " + leftValue);

    if (null != rightValue && clientId.equals(rightValue)) {
      scroller.performRightAction(context);
      commandName = rightValue;
    } else if (null != leftValue && clientId.equals(leftValue)) {
      scroller.performLeftAction(context);
      commandName = leftValue;
    } else {
      throw new IllegalStateException("no valid value returned to
decode:" +
          " rightValue = " + rightValue +" leftValue = " + leftValue +
          " clientId = " + clientId);
    }
  }

  private String getLeftClientId(String clientId) {
    String leftClientId = clientId + "L";
    return leftClientId;
  }

  private String getRightClientId(String clientId) {
    String rightClientId = clientId + "R";
    return rightClientId;
  }

  public void encodeBegin(FacesContext context, UIComponent component)
    throws IOException {
    checkState(context, component);
    if (!component.isRendered()) {
      return;
    }
    UIScroller scroller = (UIScroller) component;
    UIForm form = ComponentTreeUtils.getParentForm(scroller);
    if (null != form) {
      String formName = getFormName(form);
      String clientId = scroller.getClientId(context);
      String rightClientId = getRightClientId(clientId);
      String leftClientId = getLeftClientId(clientId);
      List elements = new ArrayList();
```

Listing 10.2 *(continued)*

```
      // Set up the left image.
      elements.add(
        imgElement(
          scroller.getLeftScrollImg(),
          leftClientId,
          clientId,
          formName));
      elements.add(selectedElement(scroller));
      // Set up the right image.
      elements.add(
        imgElement(
          scroller.getRightScrollImg(),
          rightClientId,
          clientId,
          formName));
      elements.add(hiddenElement(rightClientId));
      elements.add(hiddenElement(leftClientId));
      output(elements, context);
    } else {
      queueMissingFormErrorMessage(context, scroller);
    }
  }

  private void checkState(
    FacesContext context,
    UIComponent component) {
    if (null == context) {
      NullPointerException npe =
        new NullPointerException("Null Faces Context");
      logger.throwing(this.getClass().getName(), "encodeBegin", npe);
      throw npe;
    }
    if (null == component) {
      NullPointerException npe =
        new NullPointerException("Null Component");
      logger.throwing(this.getClass().getName(), "encodeBegin", npe);
      throw npe;
    }
  }

  public void encodeChildren(
    FacesContext context,
    UIComponent component)
    throws IOException {
    logger.entering(this.getClass().getName(), "encodeChildren");
    checkState(context, component);
    return;
  }
```

Listing 10.2 *(continued)*

```
public void encodeEnd(FacesContext context, UIComponent component)
  throws IOException {
  logger.entering(this.getClass().getName(), "encodeEnd");
  checkState(context, component);
  return;
}

private String getFormName(UIForm form) {
  String formName = null;
  Integer formNumber =
    (Integer) form.getAttributes().get("com.sun.faces.FormNumber");
  if (null != formNumber) {
    formName = "[" + formNumber.toString() + "]";
  } else {
    formName = "[0]";
  }
  return formName;
}

private Element selectedElement(UIScroller scroller) {
  // Set up the selected element.
  String selected = scroller.getSelectedOption();
  String selectedClass =
    (String) scroller.getAttributes().get(
      ScrollerRenderer.SELECTED_VALUE_CLASS_ATTR);
  Element option = null;
  if (null == selectedClass) {
    option = new Element("b");
  } else {
    option = new Element("span");
    option.setAttribute("class", selectedClass);
  }
  option.addContent(selected);
  return option;
}

private void queueMissingFormErrorMessage(
  FacesContext context,
  UIScroller scroller) {
  FacesMessage errMsg =
    new FacesMessage(
      "The UIScroller "
        + scroller.getClientId(context)
        + " is not in a Form",
      "Put the UIScroller "
        + scroller.getClientId(context)
        + " in a form");
  context.addMessage((scroller.getClientId(context)), errMsg);
}
```

Listing 10.2 *(continued)*

```
private void output(List elements, FacesContext context)
  throws IOException {
  XMLOutputter output = new XMLOutputter("  ", true);
  ResponseWriter responseWriter = context.getResponseWriter();
  CharArrayWriter writer = new CharArrayWriter(256);
  Iterator itr = elements.iterator();
  while (itr.hasNext()) {
    output.output((Element) itr.next(), writer);
  }
  writer.flush();
  String html = writer.toString();
  responseWriter.write(html);
}

private Element hiddenElement(String clientId) {
  Element hidden = new Element("input");
  hidden.setAttribute("type", "hidden");
  hidden.setAttribute("name", clientId);
  return hidden;
}

private Element imgElement(
  String uri,
  String commandName,
  String clientId,
  String formName) {
  Element imgElement = new Element("img");
  imgElement.setAttribute("border", "0");
  imgElement.setAttribute("src", uri);
  imgElement.setAttribute(
    "onClick",
    mouseDownString(clientId, commandName, formName));
  return imgElement;
}

private String mouseDownString(
  String clientId,
  String commandName,
  String formName) {
  StringBuffer buffer = new StringBuffer("document.forms");
  buffer.append(formName);
  buffer.append("['");
  buffer.append(commandName);
  buffer.append("'].value='");
  buffer.append(clientId);
  buffer.append("' ; document.forms");
  buffer.append(formName);
  buffer.append(".submit()");
```

Listing 10.2 *(continued)*

```
        return buffer.toString();
    }
}
```

Listing 10.2 *(continued)*

Decode

The first section of code in the listing is the decode method. The code is repeated here for quick reference.

```
public void decode(FacesContext context, UIComponent component) {
    checkState(context, component);

    UIScroller scroller = (UIScroller) component;
    decodeCommandName(context, scroller);
    UIForm parentForm = ComponentTreeUtils.getParentForm(scroller);
    if (null == parentForm) {
      queueMissingFormErrorMessage(context, scroller);
    }
}
```

The decode method is called during the request processing and is responsible for looking at what has come in on the request and understanding it. If the user clicked on either the right or left button, then the decode method will post an event. Renderers look at the attributes that are present in the request in order to find out what the user did. As you recall, the scroller is implemented with JavaScript attached to the onMouseDown event for the right and left img tags. The JavaScript places information into the request as an attribute of the request and then submits the form. The decode method then looks for the attributes on the request. If they are found, then an event is posted. Looking at the request is accomplished according to the following code from Listing 10.2:

```
private void decodeCommandName(
    FacesContext context,
    UIScroller scroller) {

    String clientId = scroller.getClientId(context);
    String rightClientId = getRightClientId(clientId);
    String leftClientId = getLeftClientId(clientId);
    Map requestParameterMap =
      context.getExternalContext().getRequestParameterMap();
    String value = (String) requestParameterMap.get(clientId);

    String rightValue =
      (String) requestParameterMap.get(rightClientId);
```

```
    String leftValue =
      (String) requestParameterMap.get(leftClientId);

    String commandName = null;
    logger.fine("rightValue = " + rightValue);
    logger.fine("leftValue = " + leftValue);

    if (null != rightValue && clientId.equals(rightValue)) {
      scroller.performRightAction(context);
      commandName = rightValue;
    } else if (null != leftValue && clientId.equals(leftValue)) {
      scroller.performLeftAction(context);
      commandName = leftValue;
    } else {
      throw new IllegalStateException("no valid value returned to
decode:" +
          " rightValue = " + rightValue +" leftValue = " + leftValue +
          " clientId = " + clientId);
    }
  }
```

Another interesting thing to note about the implementation of this method is that the processing of the internal state change for the component is accomplished via a method call to the component. This is done instead of performing the component's functionality here in the Renderer. Many custom component writers have the tendency to place all the event handling code in the Renderer. While this approach provides some level of encapsulation, it is at the wrong level. In order for this Renderer to be able to change the currently selected item, the whole process of making the list of options a circularly linked list would have to be public. That would expose too much of the internal workings of the `UIScroller`.

The important thing for you to keep in mind when building your Renderer is to make sure to keep the functionality of your component encapsulated so that details of its inner workings are not exposed to the Renderer just to meet a nonexistent requirement to keep all the event processing in one place.

Encode

The next section of code is related to encoding the component in HTML. The code for the `encodeBegin` method is included here for quick reference.

```
public void encodeBegin(FacesContext context, UIComponent component)
    throws IOException {
    checkState(context, component);
    if (!component.isRendered()) {
      return;
    }
```

```
    UIScroller scroller = (UIScroller) component;
    UIForm form = ComponentTreeUtils.getParentForm(scroller);
    if (null != form) {
      String formName = getFormName(form);
      String clientId = scroller.getClientId(context);
      String rightClientId = getRightClientId(clientId);
      String leftClientId = getLeftClientId(clientId);
      List elements = new ArrayList();
      // Set up the left image.
      elements.add(
        imgElement(
          scroller.getLeftScrollImg(),
          leftClientId,
          clientId,
          formName));
      elements.add(selectedElement(scroller));
      // Set up the right image.
      elements.add(
        imgElement(
          scroller.getRightScrollImg(),
          rightClientId,
          clientId,
          formName));
      elements.add(hiddenElement(rightClientId));
      elements.add(hiddenElement(leftClientId));
      output(elements, context);
    } else {
      queueMissingFormErrorMessage(context, scroller);
    }
  }
```

The code simply builds a bunch of elements and streams them out to the response. The use of JDom might seem a bit of overkill for such a simple component but I find that using JDom reduces the number of silly errors made in building the HTML so much that it is definitely worth the additional .jar file. The other aspect of this implementation is checking for and reporting failure to place the tag inside a form. Many Renderer developers provide poor error reporting when a fundamental assumption of the implementation is violated. Instead of relying on the user of your component to read all the documentation, provide decent error reporting so that it's obvious what is going wrong. We will cover some of the methods called from `encodeBegin` in more detail later in this section. The encodeChildren and encodeEnd methods are left blank for this Renderer. If your component has children, then you will have to implement both of these methods.

The last method we will look at for this Renderer is the method that builds the selected element output text. Recall that there is a Renderer-dependent attribute available to control how this text is rendered. If the attribute is specified (for example with the `f:attribute` tag in a JSP) then the value is rendered in a `span` element with its CSS class specified, otherwise the value is rendered as a `B` (that is, bold) element. Here is the code again for easy reference:

```
private Element selectedElement(UIScroller scroller) {
    // Set up the selected element.
    String selected = scroller.getSelectedOption();
    String selectedClass =
      (String) scroller.getAttributes().get(
        ScrollerRenderer.SELECTED_VALUE_CLASS_ATTR);
    Element option = null;
    if (null == selectedClass) {
      option = new Element("b");
    } else {
      option = new Element("span");
      option.setAttribute("class", selectedClass);
    }
    option.addContent(selected);
    return option;
  }
```

Notice that the generic attribute API on the component is used to look for the Renderer-dependent value. The generic attribute API is intended to support just this kind of flexible usage. Next, we will see how the JSP tag works that is used to integrate this component with JSP.

UIScroller JSP Tag Code

The next and final class needed to implement the scroller component is the JSP tag. As you recall, integration with JSP is a major goal of the JSF specification, and it is expected that JSP will be the way that most developers code their JSF user interfaces for some time to come. Listing 10.3 has the code for the scroller tag. We will cover each interesting aspect of the code in detail in this section.

```
/**
 * @jsp.tag name="simple" display-name="SimpleTag" body-content="JSP"
 * description="Simple JSP tag."
 */
public class ScrollerTag extends UIComponentTag {
  private static Logger logger =
    Logger.getLogger(Constants.LOGGER_NAME);
  private String selectedOption;
  private String options;
  private String rightImgURI;
  private String leftImgURI;
  private String rightAction;
```

Listing 10.3 ScrollerTag. *(continued)*

```
    private String leftAction;
    private String selectedClass;

    public ScrollerTag() {
      super();
      selectedOption = null;
      options = null;
      rightImgURI = null;
      leftImgURI = null;
      rightAction = null;
      leftAction = null;
    }

    public String getRendererType() {
      return ScrollerRenderer.TYPE;
    }

    public String getComponentType() {
      return UIScroller.TYPE;
    }

    private void setProperty(
      UIScroller scroller,
      String propertyName,
      String value) {
      if (value != null) {
        if (UIComponentTag.isValueReference(value)) {
          ValueBinding vb =
            FacesContext
              .getCurrentInstance()
              .getApplication()
              .createValueBinding(
              value);
          scroller.setValueBinding(propertyName, vb);
        } else {
          scroller.getAttributes().put(propertyName, value);
        }
      }
    }

    private void setLeftAction(UIScroller scroller, String value) {
      if (value != null)
        if (UIComponentTag.isValueReference(value)) {
          MethodBinding mb =
            FacesContext
              .getCurrentInstance()
              .getApplication()
              .createMethodBinding(
              value,
```

Listing 10.3 *(continued)*

```
            null);
        scroller.setLeftAction(mb);
      } else {
        throw new IllegalStateException(
          "the action property must be a method"
            + " binding expression on UIScroller:"
            + scroller.getId());
      }
  }

  private void setRightAction(UIScroller scroller, String value) {
    if (value != null)
      if (UIComponentTag.isValueReference(value)) {
        MethodBinding vb =
          FacesContext
            .getCurrentInstance()
            .getApplication()
            .createMethodBinding(
            value,
            null);
        scroller.setRightAction(vb);
      } else {
        throw new IllegalStateException(
          "the action property must be a method"
            + " binding expression on UIScroller:"
            + scroller.getId());
      }
  }

  protected void setProperties(UIComponent component) {
    super.setProperties(component);
    UIScroller scroller = (UIScroller) component;

    setOptions(scroller);
    setProperty(scroller, "selectedOption", selectedOption);
    setProperty(scroller, "selectedClass", selectedClass);
    if (null != rightImgURI) {
      setProperty(scroller, "rightScrollImg", rightImgURI);
    } else {
      setProperty(
        scroller,
        "rightScrollImg",
        UIScroller.DEFAULT_RIGHT_IMG);
    }
    if (null != leftImgURI) {
      setProperty(scroller, "leftScrollImg", leftImgURI);
    } else {
      setProperty(
        scroller,
```

Listing 10.3 *(continued)*

```
        "leftScrollImg",
        UIScroller.DEFAULT_LEFT_IMG);
    }
    setRightAction(scroller, rightAction);
    setLeftAction(scroller, leftAction);
  }

  private void setOptions(UIScroller scroller) {
    // If options is not null then we need to see if it's a value
    // reference or a simple value.
    // If it's a value binding, then get the binding and evaluate.
    // Other wise, tokenize the string.
    if (null != options) {
      if (UIComponentTag.isValueReference(options)) {
        ApplicationFactory factory =
          (ApplicationFactory) FactoryFinder.getFactory(
            FactoryFinder.APPLICATION_FACTORY);
        ValueBinding binding = Utils.getBinding(options);
        try {
          List valueOptions = (List) binding.
               getValue(FacesContext.getCurrentInstance());
          scroller.setOptions(valueOptions);
        } catch (PropertyNotFoundException e) {
          throw new PropertyNotFoundException(
            "Could not find the value specified as " + selectedOption);
        } catch (EvaluationException e) {
          throw new EvaluationException(
            "Could not evaluate the value specified as "
              + selectedOption);
        }
      } else {
        StringTokenizer tok = new StringTokenizer(options, ",");
        while (tok.hasMoreElements()) {
          scroller.addOption(tok.nextToken().trim());
        }
      }
    }
  }

  public int getDoAfterBodyValue() throws JspException {
    return BodyTag.EVAL_BODY_INCLUDE;
  }

  public int getDoStartValue() {
    return Tag.EVAL_BODY_INCLUDE;
  }

  public int getDoEndValue() {
    return Tag.EVAL_PAGE;
```

Listing 10.3 *(continued)*

```
  }


  /**
   * @jsp.attribute description="stuff" required="false"
   * rtexprvalue="false"
   */
  public String getLeftAction() {
    return leftAction;
  }

  public void setLeftAction(String string) {
    leftAction = string;
  }

  /**
   * @jsp.attribute description="stuff" required="false"
   * rtexprvalue="false"
   */
  public String getLeftImgURI() {
    return leftImgURI;
  }

  public void setLeftImgURI(String string) {
    leftImgURI = string;
  }

  /**
   * @jsp.attribute description="stuff" required="false"
   * rtexprvalue="false"
   */
  public String getRightAction() {
    return rightAction;
  }

  public void setRightAction(String string) {
    rightAction = string;
  }

  /**
   * @jsp.attribute description="stuff" required="false"
   * rtexprvalue="false"
   */
  public String getRightImgURI() {
    return rightImgURI;
  }

  public void setRightImgURI(String string) {
    rightImgURI = string;
```

Listing 10.3 *(continued)*

```
  }

  /**
   * @jsp.attribute description="stuff" required="false"
   * rtexprvalue="false"
   */
  public String getSelectedClass() {
    return selectedClass;
  }

  public void setSelectedClass(String selectedClass) {
    this.selectedClass = selectedClass;
  }

  /**
   * @jsp.attribute description="stuff" required="false"
   * rtexprvalue="false"
   */
  public String getSelectedOption() {
    System.err.println("getValue() -> " + selectedOption);
    return selectedOption;
  }

  public void setSelectedOption(String value) {
    this.selectedOption = value;
  }

  /**
   * @jsp.attribute description="stuff" required="false"
   * rtexprvalue="false"
   */
  public String getOptions() {
    return options;
  }

  public void setOptions(String options) {
    this.options = options;
  }

}
```

Listing 10.3 *(continued)*

Renderer Type

The first interesting method is `getRendererType`. The code is simple and is repeated here for quick reference:

```
public String getRendererType() {
    return ScrollerRenderer.TYPE;
}
```

This method is important because of the way that it is used. During the processing of the JSP, the value returned from `getRendererType` is set on the component that is created for this tag. Setting the Renderer type is how the tag achieves one of its primary purposes, tying together a particular Renderer with a particular component. Recall that any number of Renderers are capable of rendering a single component type The tag is responsible for specifying which one should be used. A straightforward example of this concept is the Renderers for `UICommand`. A `UICommand` can be rendered as a URL or a button. The tags specify which Renderer you want to use. For example, the tag `commandLink` tag ties the Link Renderer to the component created by the tag.

Creating the Component

The next method creates the component when necessary. Remember, the JSP tags are only active during the *Render Response* phase. While the response is being rendered, the JSP tag will either have to create the component that it represents or find the component in the component tree. During the first time the page is accessed, the components will have to be created. The code is simple and is included here for quick reference:

```
public UIComponent createComponent() {
  return new UIScroller();
}
```

Notice that the tag does no additional initialization other than creating a new instance. Any attributes that need to be set will be set when the tag is processing its attributes and setting the attributes of the component. You will see more about that next.

The next two methods translate the data specified in the JSP into attributes on the underlying component. The code for `setProperties` is repeated here for quick reference:

```
protected void setProperties(UIComponent component) {
    super.setProperties(component);
    UIScroller scroller = (UIScroller) component;

    setOptions(scroller);
    setProperty(scroller, "selectedOption", selectedOption);
    setProperty(scroller, "selectedClass", selectedClass);
    if (null != rightImgURI) {
      setProperty(scroller, "rightScrollImg", rightImgURI);
    } else {
      setProperty(
```

```
                scroller,
                "rightScrollImg",
                UIScroller.DEFAULT_RIGHT_IMG);
        }
        if (null != leftImgURI) {
            setProperty(scroller, "leftScrollImg", leftImgURI);
        } else {
            setProperty(
                scroller,
                "leftScrollImg",
                UIScroller.DEFAULT_LEFT_IMG);
        }
        setRightAction(scroller, rightAction);
        setLeftAction(scroller, leftAction);
    }
```

The important thing to keep in mind in your implementation of the `setProperties` method is that your tag will not replace any attribute that is already set on the component. This is so because the `setProperties` method won't be called unless the tag has to create a new component. Another interesting thing to consider is the default values to use for your component. If you don't want your users to have to specify all the attributes for the component every time they use it, you can provide default values. So your tag's `setProperties` method is the place to set default values.

Summary

You have now seen how to build your own component. You should be armed with the knowledge of how to build not only the component itself but all the surrounding classes as well. With what you have learned, you should be able to build a solid component that will integrate well with JSP's as well as with JSF development environments.

CHAPTER

11

Converting a Struts Application to JSF

Technologies build on previous technologies. Just as Struts was an improvement over its predecessor technologies of servlets and JSPs, so too is JSF an improvement over Struts. In fact, the original author of Struts, Craig McClanahan, has been directly involved with the design of JSF. As a result, many of the Struts concepts are reused in JSF.

Since the first release of Struts in June 2001, building Web applications with dynamic content using Struts has become popular. Struts provides a powerful framework enforcing the MVC pattern (actually Model 2), which separates design into the Model, view, and control architectural layers. This was a big improvement over the alternative patterns of mixing both presentation and business logic directly into a servlet or JSP.

So with the advent of JSF, many developers will be faced with the task of converting existing Struts applications to JSF in order to take advantage of the improvements that come with the newer JSF technology. What are the steps to conversion and how much change will be required?

The purpose of this chapter is to demonstrate the conversion to JSF of an example application built in Struts. We provide tangible steps and demonstrate an iterative process for conversion.

We begin the chapter by specifying a sample problem, SimpleBlogger, which we will use throughout the chapter to demonstrate our conversion. Next, we discuss the Struts design and implementation. Finally, we demonstrate the specific steps to convert the Struts example to JSF.

Overview

Conceptually, JSF has many similarities to Struts. For example, they both use the MVC paradigm, both depend heavily on configuration files, and both rely on JavaBeans. However, the details are different. For example, Struts Action and Form java classes and JSPs can be easily modified for JSF, but configuration files, while sharing similar concepts, are completely different.

The conversion process we present in this chapter can be summarized as reusing the domain objects from the Struts implementation, modifying configuration files, refactoring the JSP files, and morphing the Struts `Action` and `Form` classes. We recommend performing the conversion using an iterative approach—make a minimal set of changes, build, and retest. Trying to replace large amounts of code during a single iteration makes it difficult to debug and will only provide a frustrating conversion experience.

Defining the Example Problem: The SimpleBlogger

In this section, we define the sample project that we will use throughout the remainder of the chapter. In order to fully understand the sample problem, we will treat the problem definition as if it were part of a real project. More specifically, we will document *what* we are building with use cases, screen designs, a state diagram, and the domain model in order to clearly specify the problem. After all, the success of any conversion project depends on first understanding the problem space that is to be converted.

The Internet has brought us many new trendy concepts. One of the latest is a *blogger* (short for Web logger), in which Web users can create their own running log of information. Bloggers range from personal daily diaries to shared discussion groups—some open for all to see and some closed to all except a limited group.

Use Cases

One of the best ways to describe the requirements of an application is with use cases. The following set of use cases, as displayed in the SimpleBlogger use case diagram, shown in Figure 11.1, and given textually in the Logon use case, given in Listing 11.1; the Logout use case, given in Listing 11.2; the Add new message use case, given in Listing 11.3; the Edit existing message use case, given in Listing 11.4; and the Delete existing message use case, given in Listing 11.5, describes the behavior of the SimpleBlogger application.

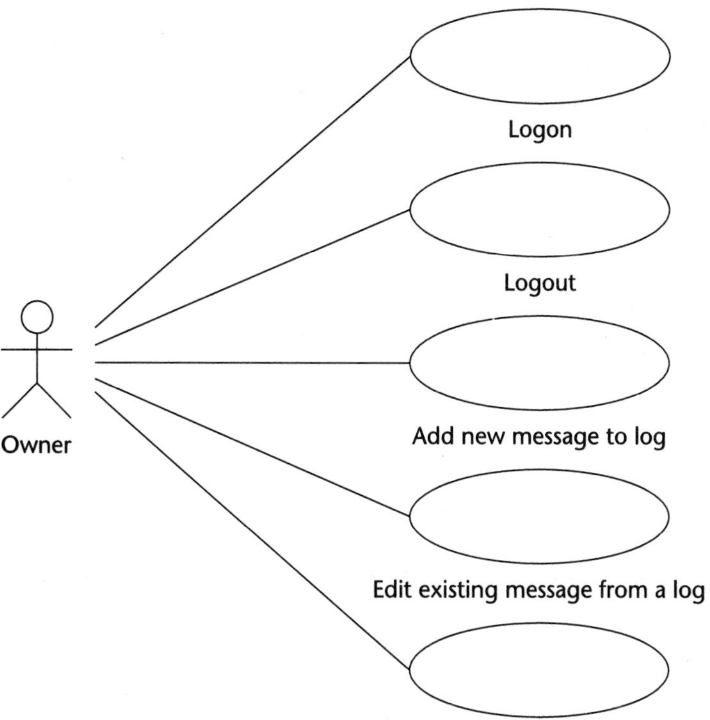

Figure 11.1 SimpleBlogger use case diagram.

```
Name: Logon
Description: Require the user to log onto the blogger.

Actors: Owner
Name: Basic Course
Steps:
1.  Enter the username.
2.  Enter the password.
3.  Submit the request.
    Exception Course: Logon Fails
    System Responsibilities:
    •  Validate the user.
    •  Persist a blog using the user's name.
Postconditions: Blog opens to the main page of log.

Exception Course:
Name: Logon Fails
Preconditions: Display message that logon fails.
```

Listing 11.1 Logon use case. *(continued)*

```
Steps:
1.  Retry logon.
Postconditions: When user resubmits the logon, the error message is
removed.
```

Listing 11.1 *(continued)*

```
Name: Logout
Description: Describes the process to logout

Actors: Owner
Name: Basic Course
Preconditions: The user is logged in.
Steps:
1.  Select Logout.
PostConditions: Blogger returns to the logon page.
```

Listing 11.2 Logout use case.

```
Name: Add new message to log
Description: Describes the steps to add new messages to a Web log

Actors: Owner
Name: Basic Course
Preconditions: Logged into the Web log
Steps:
1.  Enter message into the new message area.
2.  Submit the change.
Postconditions:
•  The message is added to the top of the log.
•  The message is time stamped.
```

Listing 11.3 Add new message use case.

```
Name: Edit existing message from a log
Description: Describes the steps to edit an existing message in the Web
log

Actors: Owner
Name: Basic Course
Preconditions: Web log exists with messages
Steps:
1.  Select a message to edit.
    Post Conditions: The text of the message is displayed in the message
editing area.
2.  Edit the message.
3.  Submit the changes.

Postconditions:
•  The message is redisplayed in the same location of the log as when it
   was first added.
•  The new text is displayed.
```

Listing 11.4 Edit existing message use case.

```
Name: Delete existing message from a log
Description: Describes the steps to remove an existing message from the
Web log

Actors: Owner
Name: Basic Course
Preconditions: Web log exists with messages.
Steps:
1.  Select a message to delete.
PostConditions: The message is removed from the list.
```

Listing 11.5 Delete existing message use case.

Screen Design

There are only two screens in our simple application, the Logon and Edit screens, shown in Figures 11.2 and 11.3, respectively. JSP files will be created for each screen.

Simple Blogger

Enter your username and password to log into your blog.

Username:

Password:

Figure 11.2 The Logon page design for SimpleBlogger.

Fred's Blog

The new message is ...Blah blah...
Blah, blah...

Save Clear Log Out

Oct. 16, 2003 12:30:02 — The new message is ... Now is the time for all people to do something... Blah blah... Blah, blah...

Edit Delete

Oct. 16, 2003 12:30:02 — The day started off great... Blah blah... Blah, blah...

Edit Delete

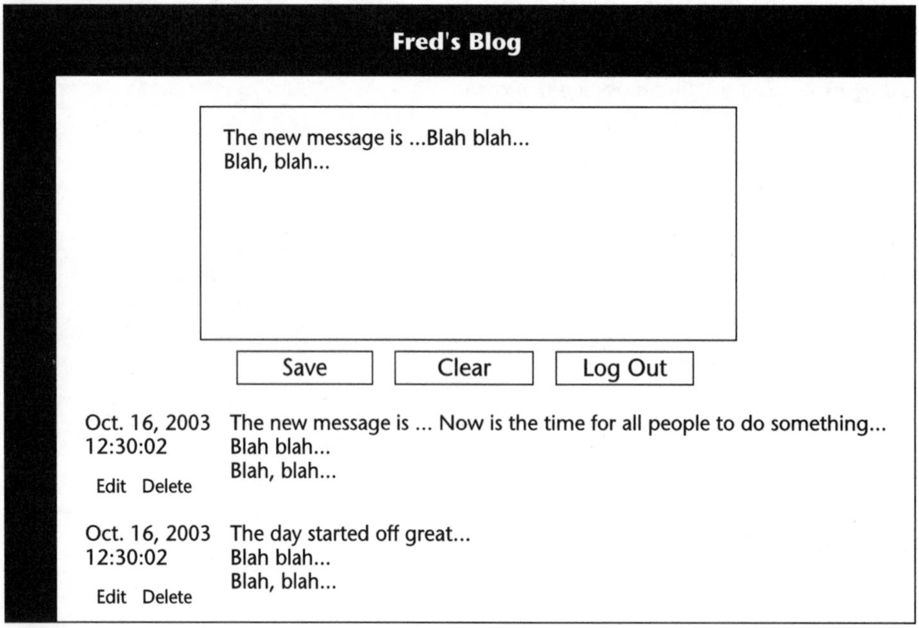

Figure 11.3 The Edit page design for SimpleBlogger.

State Diagram

The state diagram for the SimpleBlogger, shown in Figure 11.4, describes all the actions that are possible as derived from the use cases and screen designs. In general, the user first logs into the SimpleBlogger. The user begins a new blog by adding a message and saving it. Newly created messages are time-stamped and displayed in a log at the bottom of the screen. Users can edit or delete old messages. In our SimpleBlogger, each user creates his or her own blog.

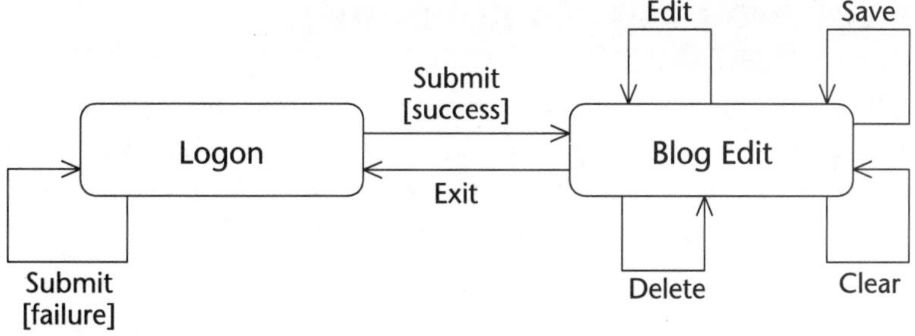

Figure 11.4 SimpleBlogger State Diagram.

Domain Classes

The domain classes in the SimpleBlogger, shown in Figure 11.5, deal with the creation, modification, and persisting of blogs. The `SecurityManager` class authenticates the user. The `BlogManager` is a factory that creates blogs or retrieves existing blogs for a particular user.

The persistence design for our SimpleBlogger is to store blogs as xml files, one for each user. The `BlogWriter` and `BlogSAXHandler` are used to manage the persistent XML store.

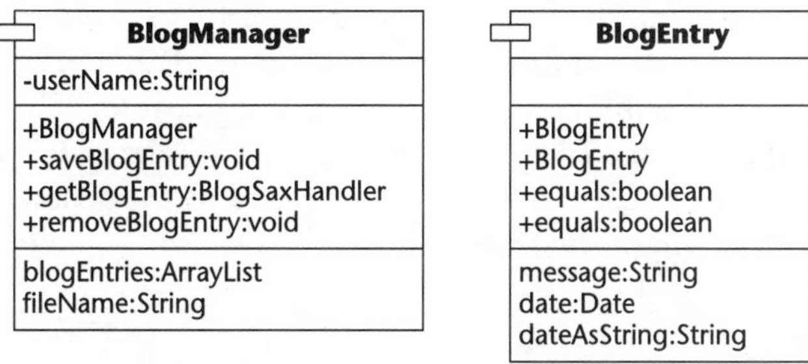

Figure 11.5 Domain classes for SimpleBlogger.

The Struts Version of the SimpleBlogger

Now that we have clearly defined the sample problem, this section defines the Struts implementation of SimpleBlogger. Because this is not a book on building Struts applications, we will focus our attention on those parts of a Struts application that will require change during a conversion to JSF.

Domain Classes

The domain classes, Figure 11.5, represent the business domain of our SimpleBlogger. By design, our Struts implementation isolates the domain layer from any Struts-specific dependencies. Keeping the domain independent of the presentation layer is a common practice in most Struts applications. As a result, both the Struts and JSF implementations of our SimpleBlogger use the exact same source code for their domain classes.

Because we will share the same domain class implementation, our conversion will only need to focus on the remaining Web tier. In order to save space, we have not included the source code for the domain classes in this chapter. However, a copy of the source code is available at the Web site.

Struts Configuration Files

Like JSF, Struts uses an external file, `struts-config.xml`, to configure the application. The `form-bean` declarations, given in Listing 11.6, declare the beans that will be used by the JSP pages of our Struts application. They are similar in concept to the managed beans of JSF. The `name` attribute of the `form-beans`, such as `logonForm` in our example, is used by the action mappings defined later in the configuration file.

```
<!--struts-config.xml -->
...
<!-- ======================================== Form Bean Definitions -->
  <form-beans>
    <form-bean name="logonForm"
               type="form.LogonForm"/>
    <form-bean name="blogEditForm"
               type="form.BlogEditForm"/>
  </form-beans>
...

<!-- ================================= Global Forward Definitions -->
  <global-forwards>
    <forward name="logon" path="/Logon.do"/>
```

Listing 11.6 The struts-config.xml file for our SimpleBlogger.

```
    <forward name="editBlog" path="/NavigateToBlog.do?action=navigate" />
    <forward name="saveBlog" path="/NavigateToBlog.do?action=save" />
    <forward name="deleteBlog" path="/DeleteBlog.do?action=delete" />
  </global-forwards>

<!-- ================================= Action Mapping Definitions -->
  <action-mappings>
    <action path="/Logon"
            type="org.apache.struts.actions.ForwardAction"
            parameter="/pages/Logon.jsp"
            name="logonForm"
            scope="request"/>
    <action path="/SubmitLogon"
            type="action.LogonAction"
            name="logonForm"
            scope="request"
            validate="true"
            input="/pages/Logon.jsp">
        <forward name="success"
                 path="/NavigateToBlog.do?action=navigate"/>
        <forward name="failure" path="/pages/Logon.jsp"/>
    </action>

    <action path="/NavigateToBlog"
            type="action.BlogAction"
            scope="request"
            name="blogEditForm"
            parameter="action">
        <forward name="success"
                 path="/pages/WebLogEdit.jsp"/>
    </action>

    <action path="/DeleteBlog"
            type="action.BlogAction"
            scope="request"
            name="blogEditForm"
            parameter="action">
        <forward name="success"
                 path="/pages/WebLogEdit.jsp"/>
    </action>

  </action-mappings>
...

<!-- =============================== Message Resources Definitions -->
  <message-resources parameter="resources.application"/>
<!-- ====================================== Plug Ins Configuration -->
...
```

Listing 11.6 *(continued)*

The global-forwards section of the struts-config.xml, given in Listing 11.6, is used to define forward paths with parameters, in our case, action parameters. Names are given to the forwards so they can be called from the JSPs as we will see later. The forward paths defined in our example include an action parameter that a DispatchAction class will use to call our action method. For example, the action=save parameter will inform the Struts framework to invoke the save() method of our LogonAction class defined later in this chapter.

The next section of the struts-config.xml file, Listing 11.6, is the action-mapping section. The action mappings are where the Web-tier of the application is wired together. Action mappings direct the flow of the application.

There is a lot going on in the Struts action mappings. For example, in our SubmitLogon action mapping in Listing 11.6, we declare the path, the action class that Struts will use, the ActionForm class it will instantiate, an alias name, the scope it will be placed in, whether to invoke validation, the path (input) to return validation failures, and action forwards (success). Most of these concepts are in JSF, but they are broken into different declarations. In general, JSF configuration is clean as compared to Struts.

And finally in our struts-config.xml file, Listing 11.6, we specify the resource file to use for messages. The resources.application is the path to the application.properties file. This is where Struts provides one of its most powerful features—support for internationalization. Different property files can be created for each language supported. In our simple example, we simply have names for buttons, titles, error messages, and more.

JSP Pages

The Web tier in Struts uses JSPs with special Struts tags. In our SimpleBlogger, we have two JSP pages, Logon.jsp and WebLogEdit.jsp. Our process for building Web applications includes screen designs mocked up in HTML. This first phase of development allows us to lay out the graphical design and colors and address usability issues with potential users prior to implementation. In order to simulate a real project, as compared to a trivial textbook example, we have left the HTML layout code that surrounds the Struts tags.

After the HTML mockups are approved, we replace HTML controls with their Struts replacement tags. Listing 11.7 is the Logon.jsp after replacement. We have bolded the Struts specific tags. All Struts-specific tags will eventually be replaced during our conversion to JSF.

```
<!-- Logon.jsp -->
<%@ taglib uri="/tags/struts-bean" prefix="bean" %>
<%@ taglib uri="/tags/struts-html" prefix="html" %>
```

Listing 11.7 The Logon.jsp file for our Struts SimpleBlogger.

```
<%@ taglib uri="/tags/struts-logic" prefix="logic" %>

<html:html locale="true">
<head>
<title> <bean:message key="logon.title"/> </title>
<html:base/>
</head>
<body bgcolor="white">
<html:form action="/SubmitLogon" >
  <table width="100%" border="0" cellspacing="0" cellpadding="0">
    <tr>
      <td width="75" bgcolor="#000066"></td>
      <td width="769" bgcolor="#000066"><div align="center">
        <font color="#FFFFFF" size="7">
          <bean:message key="logon.header"/>
        </font></div>
      </td>
    </tr>
    <tr>
      <td bgcolor="#000066"></td>
      <td><table width="100%" border="0" cellspacing="0"
           cellpadding="0">
        <tr>
          <td width="14%"> </td>
          <td width="62%"> </td>
          <td width="24%"> </td>
        </tr>
        <tr>
          <td> </td>
          <td><div align="center">
            <bean:message key="logon.instructions"/>
          </div></td>
          <td> </td>
        </tr>
        <tr>
          <td> </td>
          <td> </td>
          <td> </td>
        </tr>
        <tr>
          <td height="38"> </td>
          <td><table width="100%" border="0" cellspacing="0"
                cellpadding="0">
              <tr>
                <td width="45%"><div align="right">
                  <bean:message key="logon.username"/>
                </div></td>
                <td width="5%"></td>
               <td width="45%"> <div align="left">
```

Listing 11.7 *(continued)*

```
                    <html:text property="userName" size="10"
                     maxlength="10" />
                  </div></td>
                </tr>
                <tr>
                  <td><div align="right">
                    <bean:message key="logon.password"/>
                  </div></td>
                  <td></td>
                  <td> <div align="left">
                      <html:password property="password" size="10"
                       maxlength="10" />
                    </div></td>
                </tr>
              </table></td>
            <td> </td>
          </tr>
          <tr>
            <td> </td>
            <td> </td>
            <td> </td>
          </tr>
          <tr>
            <td> </td>
            <td><div align="center">
              <html:submit><bean:message key="logon.submit"/>
              </html:submit>
              </div></td>
            <td> </td>
          </tr>
        </table></td>
      </tr>
    </table>
</html:form>
<html:errors />
</body>
</html:html>
```

Listing 11.7 *(continued)*

The `WebLogEdit.jsp` is similar to the `Logon.jsp`, except for the special `logic:iterate` tag used to iterate over the collection of `blogEntries` in a blog. Listing 11.8 shows the Struts iteration section that we will have to replace with the new JSF tags for collections. The Struts tags are in bold. A complete version of the `WebLogEdit.jsp` is available from the Web site.

```
<!-- WebLogEdit.jsp -->
...
  </tr>
    <logic:iterate id="blogEntry" name="blogEditForm"
       property="blogEntries" type="domain.BlogEntry">
  <tr>
    <td>
    <table width="100%" border="0" cellspacing="0" cellpadding="0">
      <tr>
        <td><div align="center"><font size="-1">
          <bean:write name="blogEntry" property="dateAsString"/>
          </font></div>
        </td>
      </tr>
      <tr>
        <td><div align="center"><font size="-1">
          <html:link forward="editBlog" paramId="selection"
            paramName="blogEntry" paramProperty="dateAsString" > Edit
          </html:link>
           
          <html:link forward="deleteBlog" paramId="selection"
            paramName="blogEntry" paramProperty="dateAsString" > Delete
          </html:link>
          </font></div>
        </td>
      </tr>
    </table>
    </td>
    <td valign="top">
      <bean:write name="blogEntry" property="message"/>
    </td>
  </tr>
    </logic:iterate>
  <tr>
...
```

Listing 11.8 The WebLogEdit.jsp iterate section for our Struts SimpleBlogger.

Form Classes

The primary responsibility of the Struts `ActionForm` subclasses is to hold values for the presentation layer. They act as a temporary storage for user input values very similar to the JSF view beans. The properties in an `ActionForm` class must return String values for the JSPs.

In addition to storage, the Struts ActionForm classes are responsible for user input validation. The validate() method is called automatically by Struts if the validate attribute in the struts-config.xml file is set to true. If validation fails, the validate method is responsible for creating and returning error messages. The Struts error tag will automatically display error messages in the JSP. Our LogonForm implementation, given in Listing 11.9, is a typical example of a Struts ActionForm class that supports validation.

```
// LogonForm.java
...

public class LogonForm extends ActionForm {
  private String userName;
  private String password;

  /* Accessor methods */
  public String getPassword() {
    return password;
  }

  public void setPassword(String string) {
    password = string;
  }

  public String getUserName() {
    return userName;
  }

  public void setUserName(String string) {
    userName = string;
  }

  /**
   * The validate method checks for legal input.
   * @return errors if they occur
   * @return null if no errors
   */
  public ActionErrors validate(ActionMapping mapping,
                               HttpServletRequest request) {
    ActionErrors errors = new ActionErrors();

    if (userName != null) {
      int nameLength = userName.length();
      if (nameLength < 6 || nameLength > 10)
        errors.add(userName, new ActionError("logon.error.userName"));
    }

    if (password != null) {
```

Listing 11.9 The LogonForm for our Struts SimpleBlogger.

```
      int passwordLength = password.length();
      if (passwordLength < 6 || passwordLength > 10)
        errors.add(userName, new ActionError("logon.error.password"));
    }

    if (errors.size() > 0)
      return errors;

    return null;
  }
}
```

Listing 11.9 *(continued)*

In our Struts SimpleBlogger example, the BlogEditForm, shown in Listing 11.10, has properties with accessor methods just like the `LogonForm` class. In addition, it has a helper method required to support the Struts `logic:iterate` tag.

```
public Object getBlogEntry(int index);
// BlogEditForm.java
...

public class BlogEditForm extends ActionForm {
  private String currentMessage;
  private String currentTimestamp;
  private ArrayList blogEntries;

  /**
   * This method supports the html:iterate tag.
   * @param index
   * @return
   */
  public Object getBlogEntry(int index) {
    return blogEntries.get(index);
  }

  /* Accessor methods */
  public String getCurrentMessage() {
    return currentMessage;
  }

  public void setCurrentMessage(String string) {
    currentMessage = string;
  }

  public Collection getBlogEntries() {
```

Listing 11.10 The BlogEditForm for the Struts SimpleBlogger. *(continued)*

```
    if (blogEntries == null)
      blogEntries = new ArrayList();
    return (Collection)blogEntries;
  }

  public void setBlogEntries(ArrayList list) {
    blogEntries = list;
  }

  public String getCurrentTimestamp() {
    return currentTimestamp;
  }

  public void setCurrentTimestamp(String string) {
    currentTimestamp = string;
  }
}
```

Listing 11.10 *(continued)*

This helper method is used by the following `iterate` tag, from Listing 11.8, to return an item in the blogEntries list.

```
<logic:iterate id="blogEntry" name="blogEditForm"
       property="blogEntries" type="domain.BlogEntry">
```

Action Classes

The primary responsibility of the `Action` subclass in a Struts application is to handle action events from the user. For example, in our SimpleBlogger application, when the user presses the Submit button on the Logon page, our `LogonAction` class, Listing 11.11, is called. The Struts framework invokes the `execute()` method for the configured `Action` class as specified in the `struts-config.xml` file, Listing 11.6.

```
// LogonAction.java
...

public class LogonAction extends Action {

  public ActionForward execute(ActionMapping mapping,
                               ActionForm form,
                               HttpServletRequest request,
                               HttpServletResponse response)
                               throws Exception {
```

Listing 11.11 The LogonAction for the Struts SimpleBlogger.

```
      LogonForm logonForm = (LogonForm)form;
      SecurityManager user = new SecurityManager();
      ActionErrors errors = new ActionErrors();

      // Test for valid user
      boolean valid = user.isValidUser(logonForm.getUserName(),
                                       logonForm.getPassword());
      if (valid) {
        request.getSession().setAttribute("username",
                                          logonForm.getUserName());
        return mapping.findForward("success");
      }

      // Case invalid user
      errors.add(ActionErrors.GLOBAL_ERROR,
                 new ActionError("logon.error.unsuccessful"));
      saveErrors(request, errors);
      return mapping.findForward("failure");
    }
  }
```

Listing 11.11 *(continued)*

In Struts, a single instance of the `Action` class is instantiated for an application. Therefore, it is required to support multithreading. While this might be a good design for minimizing space and performance requirements, it imposes constraints on methods within the class. Saving state in an instance or class variable is unsafe because there may be more than one thread passing through the code at a single time. It is recommended that Struts `Action` methods be passed all the state they need as input parameters. By passing state through parameters, the call stack ensures thread safety within the scope of a method.

Our `BlogAction` class, Listing 11.12, is more interesting. It subclasses the Struts `DispatchAction` class, which uses the `action` parameter to invoke individual `action` methods by their name. The `ActionForwards` we declared in our `struts-config.xml` file, Listing 11.6, pass the action parameter (save, delete, or navigate) with the name of the action method to be invoked. The `action` methods act as the control in the MVC Struts Pattern.

```
// BlogAction.java
...

public class BlogAction extends DispatchAction {

  public ActionForward navigate(ActionMapping mapping,
                                ActionForm form,
```

Listing 11.12 The BlogAction for our Struts SimpleBlogger. *(continued)*

```
                                      HttpServletRequest request,
                                      HttpServletResponse response)
                                      throws IOException, ServletException {
    ActionErrors errors = new ActionErrors();
    BlogEditForm blogForm = (BlogEditForm)form;
    String userName = (String)request.getSession().
                      getAttribute("username");
    String blogPath = getResources(request).
                      getMessage("global.blogPath");
    BlogManager blogManager = new BlogManager(userName, blogPath);

    // Check for edit case
    String selection = request.getParameter("selection");
    if (selection != null) {
      BlogEntry blog = blogManager.getBlogEntry(selection);
      blogForm.setCurrentMessage(blog.getMessage());
      blogForm.setCurrentTimestamp(blog.getDateAsString());
    }

    ArrayList blogs = null;
    try {
      blogs = blogManager.getBlogEntries();
    } catch (IOException ex) {
      System.out.println(ex.getMessage());
      errors.add(
        ActionErrors.GLOBAL_ERROR,
        new ActionError("errors.fileCreateError"));
      saveErrors(request, errors);
    }
    blogForm.setBlogEntries(blogs);

    return mapping.findForward("success");
  }

  public ActionForward save(ActionMapping mapping,
                            ActionForm form,
                            HttpServletRequest request,
                            HttpServletResponse response)
                            throws IOException, ServletException {
    BlogEditForm blogForm = (BlogEditForm)form;
    String userName = (String)request.getSession().
                      getAttribute("username");
    String blogPath = getResources(request).
                      getMessage("global.blogPath");
    BlogManager blogManager = new BlogManager(userName, blogPath);
    blogManager.saveBlogEntry(
      blogForm.getCurrentTimestamp(),
      blogForm.getCurrentMessage());
    ArrayList blogs = null;
```

Listing 11.12 *(continued)*

```
    blogs = blogManager.getBlogEntries();
    blogForm.setBlogEntries(blogs);
    blogForm.setCurrentMessage(null);
    blogForm.setCurrentTimestamp(null);

    return mapping.findForward("success");
  }

  public ActionForward delete(ActionMapping mapping,
                              ActionForm form,
                              HttpServletRequest request,
                              HttpServletResponse response)
                              throws IOException, ServletException {
    BlogEditForm blogForm = (BlogEditForm)form;
    String userName = (String)request.getSession().
                      getAttribute("username");
    String blogPath = getResources(request).
                      getMessage("global.blogPath");
    BlogManager blogManager = new BlogManager(userName, blogPath);

    // Get the selection.
    String selection = request.getParameter("selection");
    if (selection != null) {
      blogManager.removeBlogEntry(selection);
    }

    ArrayList blogs = null;
    blogs = blogManager.getBlogEntries();
    blogForm.setBlogEntries(blogs);

    return mapping.findForward("success");
  }
}
```

Listing 11.12 *(continued)*

The JSF Version of the SimpleBlogger

Now that we have reviewed our Struts design and implementation, we are finally ready to address the topic of this chapter—conversion to JSF.

Our approach to conversion is to keep it as iterative as possible—modify a minimal set of artifacts, rebuild, rerun, and retest. This will minimize the possibility of spending a lot of time trying to figure out what went wrong after making too many simultaneous changes.

In general, we use the following steps for conversion from Struts to JSF.

1. Set up the Environment. Build and test the basic stubbed-out project.
2. Copy the Business Model objects. Build and test for compilation errors.
3. Convert the Struts `ActionForm` Classes to managed beans. Work on a single bean at a time.
4. Convert the JSPs.
5. Build the navigation model.
6. Add the action handlers.

We begin by simply setting up the environment as a place to begin copying reusable Struts components. Our general approach to conversion is to keep as much as possible from our Struts implementation.

Set Up the Environment

The first step to converting a Struts application to a JSF application is to create the environment for the JSF project. This can be done manually or by copying an existing JSF application. The following steps describe the manual process.

1. Begin by creating a JSF Web application directory and naming it with the project name.
2. Create a directory structure as shown in Figure 11.6.
3. Copy the.jar, .tld, and .dtd files from the `..\jwsdp-1.3\jsf\lib` directory to the `WEB-INF` directory of the new Web application.
4. Create a `faces-config.xml` file in the `WEB-INF` directory (or copy it from an existing JSF application).
5. Create a `Web.xml` file in the `WEB-INF` directory (or copy it from an existing JSF application).

As a convenience, the source code at our Web site includes the `blank-jsf` template for creating new JSF applications. Use the following steps to start a new JSF application from the template.

1. Copy the `blank-jsf` project to a work area, for example, `c:\workarea`.
2. Rename the directory to the new application name, for example, `SimpleBloggerJSF`.
3. If it is not already present, make a copy of the `..\jwsdp-1.3\jsf\samples\build.properties.sample` file and place it in the new `workarea` (the parent directory of `SimpleBloggerJSF`).

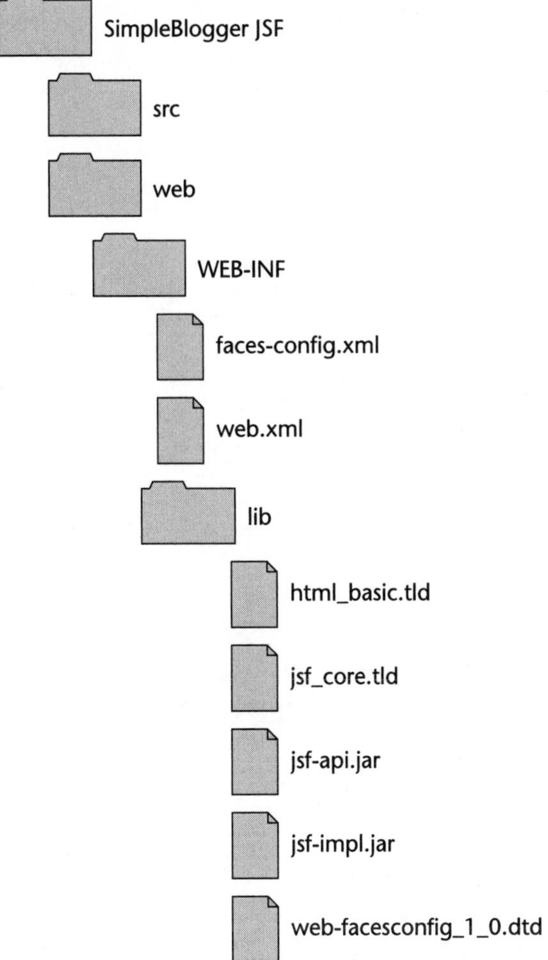

Figure 11.6 Directory structure for a typical JSF application.

4. Modify the `build.xml` file inside of `blank-jsf` by replacing all occurrences of `blank-jsf` with the name of the new project, `Simple-BloggerJSF` (see Listing 11.13).
5. Modify the `build.xml` file propertyBundlePath to the location where the `*.properties` files will be located in the new project (see Listing 11.13).
6. Update the `jsf.home` (see Listing 11.13).

```
<!— build.xml —>
<project name="SimpleBloggerJSF" default="build" basedir=".">
  <target name="init" depends="verifyPreconditions">
      <tstamp/>
  </target>

  <!-- Configure the following specific for this application -->
  <property name="context.path" value="/SimpleBloggerJSF"/>
  <property name="webAppName" value="SimpleBloggerJSF" />
  <property name="propertyBundlePath" value="form/bundles" />
  <property name="build"   value="${basedir}/build" />

  <!-- LM added this to allow direct deployment to server -->
  <property name="jsf_home" value="c:\jwsdp-1.3" />
  <property name="webDeployDir" value="${jsf_home}/webapps" />
  ...

  ...
```

Listing 11.13 Modified build.xml from blank-jsf project.

7. Modify the `SimpleBloggerJSF\Web\WEB-INF\Web.xml\` file by changing the name and description of the new application (see Listing 11.14).

```
<!-- Web.xml -->
...
<Web-app>
    <description>
        SimpleBlogger written using JSF.
    </description>
    <display-name>SimpleBloggerJSF</display-name>
...
```

Listing 11.14 Modified Web.xml file.

8. Test the modified `build.xml` by running `ant` with no arguments in the same directory as the build file. If successful, a .war file will be created in the application root and copied to the `"${jsf_home}/webapps"` deployment directory.
9. Test the build by restarting the server or hot deploy the WAR using the Web Application Manager provided in the jwsdp-1.3 distribution from Sun Microsystems (that is, http://localhost:8080/manager/html). Open the newly created application, `http://localhost:8080/SimpleBloggerJSF` in a browser. The Welcome page should open in the browser.

Copy the Business Model Objects

Because Struts and JSF are based on the MVC pattern, the business model objects for conversion from Struts to a JSF application typically require little to no changes.

Examine the business object capabilities for returning attribute types as Strings. Some objects might require Converters to translate them from native objects to Strings. In these situations, many Struts implementations use Converters in their `ActionForm`. However, it is common but not required for business object classes to provide methods that return Strings for objects, that is, `getDate()` versus `getDateAsString()`.

Unlike Struts, Converters in JSF can be attached to `UIComponent` tags. JSF provides converters for basic types (int, double . . .) and some of the reference objects such as Date, String, Number, and more. In some conversions, custom Converters might be required.

For our application, SimpleBlogger, the business model objects require no changes. Simply copy the domain classes from the Struts version to the new work area, `..\workarea\SimpleBloggerJSF\src\domain\`. Test the building of the domain classes by running ant.

Convert the Struts ActionForm Classes to Managed Beans

In a Struts application, the `ActionForm` classes are used primarily as a staging area. Although they have other responsibilities, their main purpose is to hold String values submitted by the presentation layer. They act as a staging area between the actual business objects and the GUI (graphical user interface).

JSF components simply require beans (any bean) to interact with GUI components. In JSF applications these beans are usually specified in the application configuration file `faces-config.xml` as managed beans or created directly within the JSP using the standard JSP tag, `<jsp:useBean>`. (Note: managed beans can also be created dynamically using a value-binding API, which we will not cover in this chapter).

Struts `ActionForm` classes are easily converted to JSF managed beans as follows. Primarily the properties of the `ActionForm` classes are a good starting place for the managed beans. Use the following steps to convert the SimpleBlogger:

1. Copy the `ActionForm` classes to the new JSF `..\src\form` directory.
2. Remove `ActionForm` as the superclass.
3. Remove the `validate` method and any supporting helper methods for validation.

4. Remove any helper methods for Struts tags. For example, the `iterate` tag requires helper methods such as `getBlogEntry(int index)` to return indexed entries generated from the tag.

Our managed beans for SimpleBlogger, after the first pass, are shown in Listings 11.15 and 11.16.

```
// LogonForm.java
package form;

public class LogonForm extends Object {
  private String userName;
  private String password;

  /* Accessor methods */
  public String getPassword() {
    return password;
  }

  public void setPassword(String string) {
    password = string;
  }

  public String getUserName() {
    return userName;
  }

  public void setUserName(String string) {
    userName = string;
  }
}
```

Listing 11.15 LogonForm.java after first pass of conversion.

```
// BlogEditForm.java
package form;

import java.util.ArrayList;

public class BlogEditForm {
  private String currentMessage;
  private String currentTimestamp;
  private ArrayList blogEntries;
  private BlogManager blogManager;
```

Listing 11.16 BlogEditForm.java after first pass of conversion.

```
  public String getCurrentMessage() {

    return currentMessage;
  }

  public void setCurrentMessage(String string) {
    currentMessage = string;
  }

  public Collection getBlogEntries() {
    if (blogEntries == null)
      blogEntries = new ArrayList();
    return (Collection)blogEntries;
  }

  public void setBlogEntries(ArrayList list) {
    blogEntries = list;
  }

  public String getCurrentTimestamp() {
    return currentTimestamp;
  }

  public void setCurrentTimestamp(String string) {
    currentTimestamp = string;
  }
}
```

Listing 11.16 *(continued)*

Now we are ready to add the new JSF beans as managed beans to the `faces-config.xml` file, as shown in Listing 11.17.

```
<!--faces-config.xml -->

...
<!-- Managed Beans -->
  <managed-bean>
    <description> Form bean that supports the logon page. </description>
    <managed-bean-name> logonForm </managed-bean-name>
    <managed-bean-class> form.LogonForm </managed-bean-class>
    <managed-bean-scope> request </managed-bean-scope>
  </managed-bean>
  <managed-bean>
    <description> Form bean that supports the Web Log Edit page.
    </description>
```

Listing 11.17 faces-config.xml managed beans declaration. *(continued)*

```
        <managed-bean-name> blogEditForm </managed-bean-name>
        <managed-bean-class> form.BlogEditForm </managed-bean-class>
        <managed-bean-scope> session </managed-bean-scope>

    </managed-bean>
  ...
```

Listing 11.17 *(continued)*

The JSF framework will create managed objects according to the scope specified in the `faces-config.xml`. In our SimpleBlogger application, we create two managed beans. Each bean is responsible for the behaviors defined in the state diagram for the SimpleBlogger (see Figure 11.4).

The `logonForm` bean is only used to validate the user and allow access to the user's blog. The submit action either fails and returns the user to the logon page or succeeds and allows the user to edit his or her blog. The existence of the `logonForm` bean only requires request scope and is specified in the `faces-config.xml` file (see Listing 11.17). The JSF framework will create a new instance of `logonForm` for each user request to logon. However, as we will see later, only the name of the user is placed in session scope and will be used to store the actual blog using the user's name.

The `blogEditForm` bean does the actual work of the user's blog editing session. The allowable actions while editing the user's blog are save, edit, delete, clear, and exit, as shown in the SimpleBlogger state diagram, Figure 11.4. In our JSF implementation of the SimpleBlogger, we set the scope for the `blogEditForm` to `session` in the `faces-config.xml` file (see Listing 11.17). The JSF framework will create a single instance of the `blogEditForm` for each user who logs into the application.

At this point in our conversion, we have not dealt with the application actions when pages are loaded or modified as the result of user or system Actions. We will address converting Actions later in this chapter.

Convert the JSP Pages

Now that we have converted our forms and configured them as managed beans, we are ready to convert the presentation layer (in our case the JSPs). Conversion of JSPs written in Struts to JSF is not a difficult process and is primarily centered on keeping the same format while replacing the Struts tags with JSF tags.

Begin by copying the Struts JSPs to the new work area `..\SimpleBlogger JSF\Web\`. Use the following steps to morph a Struts JSP to a JSF JSP. Listing 11.18 is the `Logon.jsp` converted to JSF. The following JSP conversion steps are included in the listing in bold:

1. Replace the Struts TagLibs with JSF equivalents.
2. Add support for resource bundles.
3. Surround the JSF tags with the `f:view` tags.
4. Remove unnecessary JavaScript.
5. Replace the simple tags first.
6. Add the `validation` attribute or core validation tags.
7. Replace navigation tags.

```
<!-- Logon.jsp -->

<!-- 1. Replace the Struts taglibs with JSF equivalents. -->
<%@ taglib uri="http://java.sun.com/jsf/html" prefix="h" %>
<%@ taglib uri="http://java.sun.com/jsf/core" prefix="f" %>

<!-- 2. Add support for resource bundles. -->
<f:loadBundle basename="form.bundles.logon" var="bloggerBundle"/>

<!-- 3. Surround JSF tags with the view tag. -->
<f:view>

<!-- 4. Remove unnecessary javascript. -->
<head>
  <title>
    <!-- 5. Replace tags. -->
    <h:outputText value="#{bloggerBundle.title}" />
  </title>
</head>
<body bgcolor="white">

<!-- 5. Replace tags. -->
<h:form>
<table width="100%" border="0" cellspacing="0" cellpadding="0">
  <tr>
    <td width="75" bgcolor="#000066"></td>
    <td width="769" bgcolor="#000066"> <div align="center">
      <font color="#FFFFFF" size="7">
      <!-- 5. Replace tags. -->
      <h:outputText value="#{bloggerBundle.header}" />
      </font></div>
    </td>
  </tr>
  <tr>
    <td bgcolor="#000066"></td>
    <td>
```

Listing 11.18 Logon.jsp after conversion to JSF. *(continued)*

```
<table width="100%" border="0" cellspacing="0" cellpadding="0">
  <tr>
    <td width="14%"> </td>
    <td width="62%"> </td>
    <td width="24%"> </td>
  </tr>
  <tr>
    <td> </td>
    <td><div align="center">
      <!-- 5. Replace tags. -->
      <h:outputText value="#{bloggerBundle.instructions}" />
    </div></td>
    <td> </td>
  </tr>
  <tr>
    <td> </td>
    <td> </td>
    <td> </td>
  </tr>
  <tr>
    <td height="38"> </td>
    <td><table width="100%" border="0" cellspacing="0"
      cellpadding="0">
      <tr>
        <td width="45%"><div align="right">
          <!-- 5. Replace tags. -->
          <h:outputText value="#{bloggerBundle.username}" />
        </div></td>
        <td width="5%"></td>
        <td width="45%"> <div align="left">
          <!-- 5. Replace tags. -->
          <!-- 6. Add validator attribute -->
          <h:inputText id="username"
                  value="#{logonForm.username}"
                  size="10" maxlength="10"
                  validator="#{logonForm.validateUsername}"/>
        </div></td>
      </tr>
      <tr>
        <td><div align="right">
          <!-- 5. Replace tags. -->
          <h:outputText
                value="#{bloggerBundle.password}" />
        </div></td>
        <td></td>
        <td> <div align="left">
          <!-- 5. Replace tags. -->
          <!-- 6. Add validator attribute -->
          <h:inputSecret id="password"
```

Listing 11.18 *(continued)*

```
                        value="#{logonForm.password}"
                        size="10" maxlength="10"
                        validator="#{logonForm.validatePassword}"/>
                </div></td>
              </tr>
              </table></td>
            <td> </td>
          </tr>
          <tr>
            <td> </td>
            <td> </td>
            <td> </td>
          </tr>
          <tr>
            <td> </td>
            <td><div align="center">
                <!-- 7. Replace navigation tags. -->
                <h:commandButton value="#{bloggerBundle.submit}"
                    action="#{logonForm.logon}" /> </div></td>
            <td> </td>
          </tr>
        </table></td>
    </tr>
</table>
<!-- 5. Replace tags. -->
</h:form>
<!-- 5. Replace tags. -->
<h:messages showSummary="true" showDetail="false"
    layout="table"/><br>
<!-- 4. Surround JSF tags with the f:view tags.  -->
</f:view>
</body>
```

Listing 11.18 *(continued)*

Replace the Struts TagLibs with JSF Equivalents

Begin by replacing the Struts taglibs with JSF equivalents, given in Listing 11.18, Step 1. The format for declaring JSP tags is identical for Struts and JSF. The only difference is the name of the tag libraries. JSF includes the HTML and core tag libraries. Table 11.1 lists the JSF HTML tags in JWSDP and their counterpart(s) in Struts.

Not all Struts tags have JSF equivalent tags. Struts logic, bean, and nested tag libraries do not have specific JSF tag equivalents. Converting Struts applications that depend on these libraries will require either redesign or an implementation using a combination of Struts and JSF.

Table 11.1 html_basic.tld Tags Cross-Referenced to Struts Tag Libraries.

JSF:HTML TAGS	STRUTS-HTML TAGS
column	
commandButton	button; reset; submit; cancel
commandLink	link
dataTable	
form	form
graphicImage	image; img
inputHidden	hidden
inputSecret	password
inputText	text
inputTextarea	textarea
message	errors; messages
messages	errors; messages
outputLabel	text
outputLink	link
outputMessage	errors; messages
outputText	text
panelGrid	
panelGroup	
selectBooleanCheckbox	checkbox
selectManyCheckbox	multibox
selectManyListbox	select; options; optionsCollection
selectManyMenu	select; options; optionsCollection
selectOneListbox	select; option
selectOneMenu	select; option
selectOneRadio	radio

Table 11.2 lists the JSF core tags shipped with JWSDP from Sun Microsystems and their counterpart(s) in Struts.

Table 11.2 jsf_core.tld Tags Cross-Referenced to Struts Tag Libraries.

JSF:CORE TAGS	STRUTS-HTML TAGS	STRUTS-BEAN TAGS
actionListener		
attribute	parameter	
convertDateTime		
convertNumber		
converter		
facet		
loadBundle		
parameter	parameter	
selectItem	option	
selectItems	options; optionsCollection	
subview		
validateDoubleRange		
validateLength		
validateLongRange		
validator		
valueChangeListener		
verbatim		
view		

Add Support for Resource Bundles

Next, we add support for resource bundles (`.properties` files), as shown in Listing 11.18, Step 2. Bundles enable the application designer to define strings for labels, messages, and errors in external files.

The JSF framework promotes using multiple resource bundles, whereas Struts applications typically use only one resource bundle (the `struts-config.xml` file) for the entire application. For medium to large applications, a Struts resource bundle becomes large and difficult to maintain.

JSF applications are not as restricted as Struts applications in loading resource bundles. Developers can create `*.properties` files as needed. For example, resource bundles could be organized into packages to more closely reflect the application's package structure. Or, as we have done in the SimpleBloggerStruts design, resource bundles can reflect the application's form structure—one bundle per form.

Refactor the SimpleBloggerStruts `application.properties` file (see Listing 11.19) into the `application.properties` (see Listing 11.20), `logon.properties` (see Listing 11.21), and the `blogEditForm.properties` (see Listing 11.22). Make sure the "`propertyBundlePath`" in the `build.xml` file (see Listing 11.13) is modified as shown in the following code to include the path to the resource bundle files.

```
<property name="propertyBundlePath" value="form/bundles" />
# Struts application.properties

# -- special properties --
global.blogPath=c:\\temp\\

# -- standard errors --
errors.header=<UL>
errors.prefix=<LI>
errors.suffix=</LI>
errors.footer=</UL>

# -- validator --
errors.invalid={0} is invalid.
errors.maxlength={0} cannot be greater than {1}
characters.errors.minlength={0} cannot be less than {1}
characters.errors.range={0} is not in the range {1} through {2}.
errors.required={0} is required.
errors.byte={0} must be an byte.
errors.date={0} is not a date.
errors.double={0} must be an double.
errors.float={0} must be an float.
errors.integer={0} must be an integer.
errors.long={0} must be an long.
errors.short={0} must be an short.
errors.creditcard={0} is not a valid credit card number.
errors.email={0} is an invalid email address.

# -- other --errors.cancel=Operation
cancelled.errors.detail={0}errors.general=The process did not complete.
Details should follow.errors.token=Request could not be completed.
Operation is not in sequence.
errors.fileCreateError=Can't create new blog file.

# -- logon --
```

Listing 11.19 Struts application.properties before conversion to JSF.

```
logon.title=Simple Blogger
logon.username=Username:
logon.password=Password:
logon.submit=Submit
logon.header=Welcome to Simple Blogger.
logon.instructions=Enter your username and password to <br> log into
your blog.
logon.error.userName=Valid username is 6 to 10 characters. (try
"blogger")
logon.error.password=Valid password is 6 to 10 characters. (try
"blogger")
logon.error.unsuccessful=Unauthorized user, please try again.

# -- webLogEdit --
webLogEdit.title=Blogger
webLogEdit.save=Save
webLogEdit.clear=Clear
webLogEdit.logout=Exit
```

Listing 11.19 *(continued)*

```
# JSF application.properties

# -- special properties --
global.blogPath=c:\\temp\\
```

Listing 11.20 JSF application.properties after conversion to JSF.

```
# -- logon.properties

title=Simple Blogger
username=Username:
password=Password:
submit=Submit
header=Welcome to Simple Blogger.
instructions=Enter your username and password to log into your blog.

# error messages for the logon page
usernameError=Valid username is 6 to 10 characters. (try "blogger")
passwordError=Valid password is 6 to 10 characters. (try "blogger")
unsuccessfulError=Unauthorized user, please try again.
usernameRequired=Username Required
passwordRequired=Password Required
```

Listing 11.21 JSF logon.properties after conversion to JSF.

```
# -- blogEditForm.properties

title=Blogger
save=Save
clear=Clear
logout=Exit
edit=edit
delete=delete
```

Listing 11.22 JSF blogEditForm.properties after conversion to JSF.

Modify the `Logon.jsp` file (see Listing 11.18) as shown in the following code to load the `logon.properties` resource bundle and specify a local page variable.

```
<f:loadBundle basename="form.bundles.logon" var="bloggerBundle"/>
```

Modify the `WebLogEdit.jsp` file as shown in the following code to load the `blogEditForm.properties` resource bundle and specify a local page variable.

```
<f:loadBundle basename="form.bundles.logon" var="bloggerBundle"/>
```

Remove Unnecessary JavaScript

A consistent goal of JSF design is to keep programming out of the JSP pages. If the Struts application being converted contains JavaScript functions, evaluate them to see if they are still needed after the conversion to JSF. Remove them if possible.

Surround JSF Tags with the View Tag

In order to use JSF tags in a JSP, surround the JSP code that will use JSF tags with `<f:view>` and `</f:view>`. Modify `Logon.jsp` and `WebLogEdit.jsp` as shown in Listing 11.18, Step 3.

Replace the Simple Tags

In the SimpleBlogger example, replacing the Struts tags is fairly straightforward. For simple tags, Struts to JSF conversion is easy. However, for more complex tags, the replacement might not be a 1 to 1 replacement. For example, the logic and nesting tags of Struts are not present in JSF. Replacing logic and nesting tags would require rethinking the design of the JSP.

Instead of replacing all the tags in a single step, we recommend using an iterative approach. Do the easy ones first. For example, set up the form, replace the labels, text, and text areas. Save the navigation, validation, and error-handling areas until later. At the end of each iteration, test the basic structure.

As shown in Listing 11.18, Step 5, begin replacing tags in the `Logon.jsp` and `WebLogEdit.jsp` files. Replace `<html:form>` with `<h:form>` and `</html:form>` with `</h:form>` tags.

Continue replacing the struts tags with JSF tags. For example, replace `<bean:message key="WebLogEdit.title"/>` with `<h:outputTextvalue="#{bloggerBundle.title}"/>`.

Add Validation Attributes or Tags

One of the biggest differences between the design of Struts and JSF is the validation of user input. In Struts, the `ActionForm` subclasses are responsible for implementing a `validate` method that is automatically called by the Struts framework (if specified in the `struts-config actionForward` declaration). Errors are collected and then displayed back to the user if the set of errors is not empty.

In JSF, input validation is managed by either `validation` tags that are included in the presentation layer or by using a `validate` attribute associated with input tags. It should be noted that other layers in the application are still responsible for validating their own inputs. But the goal of user input validation is to try and catch errors before they descend the layers of the architecture. See Table 11.2 for a complete list of validations shipped in JSF from Sun Microsystems.

In the `Logon.jsp` file, we could have added the standard `validateLength` tag (as shown in the following code) to the `username` and password fields. However, the error messages generated from the core validation tags are standard and not customizable for a particular input tag.

```
<h:inputText id="username"
             required="true"
             size="10" maxlength="10"
             value="#{logonForm.username}">
    <f:validateLength maximum="10" minimum="6"/>
</h:inputText>
```

In our SimpleBlogger conversion, we wanted to mimic the Struts implementation where the error messages were customized. Instead of using the core standard validation tags and their generic error messages, we use the `validator` attribute for the `inputText` tag as shown in the following code.

```
<h:inputText id="username"
             value="#{logonForm.username}"
             size="10" maxlength="10"
             validator="#{logonForm.validateUsername}"/>
```

Next we add validation methods to the `LogonForm` class to support the `validator` attribute (Listing 11.23). Validation methods must meet two requirements to work correctly in the JSF framework. First, the validation methods must take a `FacesContext`, a `UIComponent`, and an `Object` as parameters. Second, the validation methods should throw a `Validator Exception` if there is a validation error. In our LogonForm implementation we create all messages from the logon.properties resource bundle when an instance of `LogonForm` is created.

```
// LogonForm.java
...

public class LogonForm extends Object {
  private String username;
  private String password;
  private ResourceBundle bundle;
  private FacesMessage loginErrorMessage;
  private FacesMessage usernameErrorMessage;
  private FacesMessage passwordErrorMessage;
  private FacesMessage usernameRequiredMessage;
  private FacesMessage passwordRequiredMessage;

  public LogonForm() {
    initializeMessages();
  }

  private void initializeMessages() {
    bundle = ResourceBundle.getBundle("form.bundles.logon");
    String message = bundle.getString("unsuccessfulError");
    loginErrorMessage = new FacesMessage(FacesMessage.SEVERITY_INFO,
        message, null);
    message = bundle.getString("usernameError");
    usernameErrorMessage = new FacesMessage(FacesMessage.SEVERITY_INFO,
        message, null);
    message = bundle.getString("passwordError");
    passwordErrorMessage = new FacesMessage(FacesMessage.SEVERITY_INFO,
        message, null);
    message = bundle.getString("usernameRequired");
    usernameRequiredMessage = new FacesMessage(
        FacesMessage.SEVERITY_INFO, message, null);
    message = bundle.getString("passwordRequired");
    passwordRequiredMessage = new FacesMessage(
```

Listing 11.23 LogonForm.java validation methods.

```
        FacesMessage.SEVERITY_INFO, message, null);
  }

  ...

  /* Validation Methods */
  public void validateUsername(FacesContext context,
              UIComponent toValidate,
              Object value) throws ValidatorException {
    int max = 10;
    int min = 6;
    String name = (String) value;
    int length = name.length();
    if(length < min || length > max) {
      throw new ValidatorException(usernameErrorMessage);
    }
    return; // validation passed
  }

  public void validatePassword(FacesContext context,
              UIComponent toValidate,
              Object value) throws ValidatorException {
    int max = 10;
    int min = 6;
    String name = (String) value;
    int length = name.length();
    if(length < min || length > max) {
      throw new ValidatorException(passwordErrorMessage);
    }
    return; // validation passed
  }
  ...
```

Listing 11.23 *(continued)*

To finish the validation changes for the SimpleBlogger, we need to replace the Struts `html:errors` tag in `Logon.jsp` (see Listing 11.18) with the JSF `h:messages` tag as shown in the following code. The `layout="table"` attribute automatically formats multiple errors as rows in a table.

```
<h:messages showSummary="true" showDetail="false" layout="table"/>
```

Replace Navigation Tags

Replace navigation tags, like buttons and hypertext links, iteratively while building the navigation model and action classes, as described later in this chapter. The basic process is to define the navigation model, add support for actions, replace the navigation tag, and test. Using an iterative approach is best.

Build the Navigation Model

Both Struts and JSF externalize navigation into configuration files—`struts-config.xml` and `faces-config.xml`, respectively. The logic behind this design is to simplify page flow modifications for an application.

For the SimpleBlogger application, we start with the UML state diagram from the analysis phase of our project, shown in Figure 11.4, to help us define our navigation requirements. We can simplify this diagram if we focus on event outcomes with respect to navigation, as shown in Figure 11.7. In this diagram, the literal events are generalized into success or failure. The net result of this effort is to minimize the number of navigation rules required. We could have defined a separate rule for every literal event, but many of the rules would only differ by name.

To define navigation in JSF, use the `navigation-case` with `from-outcome` and `to-view-id` tags, as shown in Listing 11.24 below.

```
<!-- faces-config.xml -->
...
<!-- Navigation rules -->
  <navigation-rule>
    <from-view-id>/Logon.jsp</from-view-id>
    <navigation-case>
      <from-outcome>success</from-outcome>
      <to-view-id>/WebLogEdit.jsp</to-view-id>
    </navigation-case>
    <navigation-case>
      <from-outcome>failure</from-outcome>
      <to-view-id>/Logon.jsp</to-view-id>
    </navigation-case>
  </navigation-rule>

  <navigation-rule>
    <from-view-id>/WebLogEdit.jsp</from-view-id>
    <navigation-case>
      <from-outcome>success</from-outcome>
      <to-view-id>/WebLogEdit.jsp</to-view-id>
    </navigation-case>
    <navigation-case>
      <from-outcome>failure</from-outcome>
      <to-view-id>/WebLogEdit.jsp</to-view-id>
    </navigation-case>
    <navigation-case>
      <from-outcome>logout</from-outcome>
      <to-view-id>/Logon.jsp</to-view-id>
    </navigation-case>
  </navigation-rule>
...
```

Listing 11.24 faces-config.xml navigation rules.

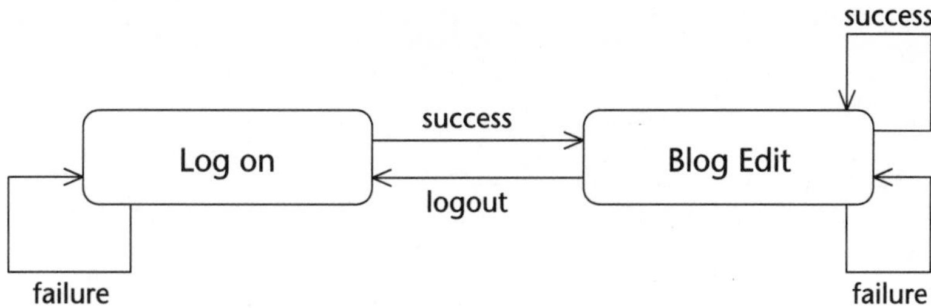

Figure 11.7 SimpleBlogger generalized navigation state diagram.

Add the Action Handlers

Now it is time to wire the application together using our navigation rules and define methods to handle the application actions.

In JSF, application actions are generated from `UICommand` components such as `HtmlCommandButton` or `HtmlCommandLink`, which implement the `javax.faces.component.ActionSource` interface. The application designer can use either the `action` or `actionListener` attributes of the associated `UICommand` component tags to specify how actions will be handled.

Two examples of using the `action` attribute are demonstrated below. In the first case, the actual `from-outcome` name is specified, for example, `action="success"`. Navigation is transferred to the `to-view-id` as specified in the `faces-config.xml` navigation rule (see Listing 11.24). In the second case, the `action` attribute delegates control to the bean and method, `logonform.logon`, that will process, make decisions, and route the final navigation. This logon bean method is responsible for handling any specific application action processing and returning the name of a `from-outcome` as specified in the `faces-config.xml` (see the logon method in Listing 11.25).

```
// case 1:
<h:commandButton value="#{bloggerBundle.submit}"
                 action="success" />

// case 2:
<h:commandButton value="#{bloggerBundle.submit}"
                 action="#{logonform.logon}" />
```

We use the second case in our implementation of the JSF SimpleBlogger. The basic logic from the Struts `LogonAction.execute()` method is replicated in our JSF version. The `logon()` method validates the user with the `SecurityManager`. If it is a valid user, then it stores the key/value pair for `username` in the `Session` scope and returns "success." If the result is invalid, then it returns "failure."

```
// LogonForm.java

import javax.faces.context.FacesContext;
import javax.faces.component.UIInput;
import javax.faces.application.FacesMessage;
import java.util.ResourceBundle;
import java.util.Map;

import domain.SecurityManager;

public class LogonForm extends Object {

...

  public String logon() {
    SecurityManager security = new SecurityManager();
    FacesContext facesContext = FacesContext.getCurrentInstance();
    boolean hasErrorMessages = false;

    validateRequiredFields();
    hasErrorMessages = facesContext.getMessages().hasNext();
    // test for valid user
    boolean valid = security.isValidUser(getUsername(), getPassword());
    if (!hasErrorMessages && valid) {
      Map sessionMap = facesContext.getExternalContext().
                       getSessionMap();
      sessionMap.put("username", getUsername());
      return "success";
    }
    else if(hasErrorMessages==false)
      facesContext.addMessage(null, loginErrorMessage);

    return "failure";
  }

...


  protected boolean validateRequiredFields() {
    boolean missingField = false;
    FacesContext facesContext = FacesContext.getCurrentInstance();
    if(username!=null && username.length()<=0) {
      facesContext.addMessage(null, usernameRequiredMessage);
      missingField = true;
    }
    if(password!=null && password.length()<=0) {
      facesContext.addMessage(null, passwordRequiredMessage);
      missingField = true;
    }
```

Listing 11.25 LogonForm.java with added methods for logon Actions.

```
    if(missingField) {
      return false;
    }
    return true;
  }
...
```

Listing 11.25 *(continued)*

In the Logon.jsp, replace the Struts submit Action:

```
<html:submit><bean:message key="logon.submit"/></html:submit>
```

```
with the JSF actionCommand:<h:commandButton
value="#{bloggerBundle.submit}"
                    action="#{logonForm.logon}" />
```

Build and test the navigation and logon Action implementation. At this point in the conversion, the user should be able to launch the application, enter a valid username and password, and navigate to the BlogEdit page.

Converting the Blog Edit Actions involves the same basic steps as the logon Action. Add support for edit, save, and delete Actions. In addition, we need to load an existing blog when the `BlogEditForm` is first loaded (see Listing 11.26).

```
// BlogEditForm.java

package form;

import java.io.IOException;
import java.util.ArrayList;
import java.util.Collection;
import java.util.ResourceBundle;
import java.util.Map;
import javax.faces.context.FacesContext;
import javax.faces.event.ActionEvent;
import javax.faces.component.UIData;
import domain.BlogEntry;
import domain.BlogManager;

public class BlogEditForm extends Object {
  private String currentMessage;
  private String currentTimestamp;
  private ArrayList blogEntries;
  private BlogManager blogManager;
```

Listing 11.26 BlogEditForm.java action methods for save, edit, and delete. *(continued)*

```
public BlogEditForm() {
    initialize();
    refreshForm();
  }

  protected void initialize() {
    FacesContext context = FacesContext.getCurrentInstance();
    Map sessionMap = FacesContext.getCurrentInstance().
                   getExternalContext().getSessionMap();
    String username = (String)sessionMap.get("username");
    ResourceBundle bundle = ResourceBundle.getBundle(
                          "form.bundles.application");
    String blogPath = bundle.getString("global.blogPath");
    blogManager = new BlogManager(username, blogPath);
  }

  protected void refreshForm() {
    try {
      setBlogEntries(blogManager.getBlogEntries());
    } catch (IOException e) {
      System.out.println("Refresh Error: Blog File Not Found");
      e.printStackTrace();
    }
    setCurrentMessage("");
    setCurrentTimestamp("");
  }

  public String save() {
    try {
      blogManager.saveBlogEntry(getCurrentTimestamp(),
                              getCurrentMessage());
    } catch (IOException e) {
      System.out.println("Save failed");
      e.printStackTrace();
      return "failure";
    }
    refreshForm();

    return "success";
  }

  public void edit(ActionEvent event) {
    // 1st parent is a Column, 2nd is the table
    UIData table = (UIData)event.getComponent().getParent().getParent();
    BlogEntry selection = (BlogEntry)table.getRowData();
    if (selection != null) {
      setCurrentMessage(selection.getMessage());
      setCurrentTimestamp(selection.getDateAsString());
```

Listing 11.26 *(continued)*

```
    }
  }

  public void delete(ActionEvent event) {
    // 1st parent is a Column, 2nd is the table
    UIData table = (UIData)event.getComponent().getParent().getParent();
    BlogEntry selection = (BlogEntry)table.getRowData();
    if (selection != null) {
      blogManager.removeBlogEntry(selection);
      refreshForm();
    }
// Force a refresh to the UITable - bug in current JSF 1.0 beta release
    table.setValue(null);
  }

  public String logout() {
    Map sessionMap = FacesContext.getCurrentInstance().
                     getExternalContext().getSessionMap();
    sessionMap.remove("blogEditForm");
    return "logout";
  }

  public String getCurrentMessage() {
    return currentMessage;
  }

  public void setCurrentMessage(String string) {
    currentMessage = string;
  }

  public Collection getBlogEntries() {
    if (blogEntries == null)
      blogEntries = new ArrayList();
    return (Collection)blogEntries;
  }

  public void setBlogEntries(ArrayList list) {
    blogEntries = list;
  }

  public String getCurrentTimestamp() {
    return currentTimestamp;
  }

  public void setCurrentTimestamp(String string) {
    currentTimestamp = string;
  }

}
```

Listing 11.26 *(continued)*

In order to create the BlogEditForm the first time it is called, we add a constructor. The constructor calls the initialize() method, which gets the username from the session scope. Next, it retrieves from the application resource bundle the path to the location where the blogs are stored. Finally, it creates a BlogManager and stores it in an instance variable to be reused for future requests. When we declared the BlogEditForm as a managed bean, we set the scope to session (see Listing 11.17). The JSF framework will create an instance of BlogEditForm for each user session in the application. Had we set the scope to request, the constructor would have been called for each request, creating a new instance of BlogManager—an expensive operation we choose to limit.

In JSF, the ability to store state between actions is a more powerful and flexible design than that provided by Struts. This stateful versus stateless design is a major difference between Struts and JSF. Struts Action class instances are multithreaded singletons, which are shared between users in the same application. Their primary purpose is to dispatch events. Therefore, by design, they should not keep state in instance (or class) variables. Class properties cannot be shared between method invocations within the same Action class.

In Struts Action class implementations, all shared values must be passed as parameters between method invocations. As a result, Action class design ends up being a collection of functions with no shared state. This can be annoying to say the least, and typically results in writing long complex functions with redundant code. In the real world, the cyclomatic complexity of Struts Action class methods is often high. Functional decomposition is the only means available to developers to break up complexity.

JSF action design does not impose such restrictions. It is left to the designer to choose which Pattern is most effective in dealing with Action events.

For each of the edit, save, and delete Actions, we follow the same basic logic used in our Struts Action class implementation. The edit() method retrieves the selection parameter from the request and sets the current Message to the selection. The save() method invokes the blogManager to save the current message text as a new entry in the blog. The delete() method retrieves the selection from the request parameter and invokes the blogManager to delete the selected message.

Replace the Struts action tags with their JSF counterparts in the WebLogEdit.jsp. Begin by replacing the buttons, as shown in Listing 11.27.

```
<!-- WebLogEdit.jsp -->
...
  <tr>
    <td> </td>
    <td><div align="center">
        <table width="60%" border="0" cellspacing="0" cellpadding="0">
```

Listing 11.27 WebLogEdit.jsp commandButton tags.

```
            <tr>
              <td><div align="center">
                <h:commandButton value="#{bloggerBundle.save}"
                                 action="#{blogEditForm.save}" />
              </div></td>
              <td><div align="center">
                <h:commandButton value="#{bloggerBundle.clear}"
                                 type="reset" />
              </div></td>
              <td><div align="center">
                <h:commandButton value="#{bloggerBundle.logout}"
                                 action="#{blogEditForm.logout}" />
              </div></td>
            </tr>
          </table>
        </div></td>
    </tr>

...
```

Listing 11.27 *(continued)*

Note that the Save and Logout buttons are examples of invoking a bean `action` method directly. The Clear button is an example of using HTML only.

Finally, we address one of the more difficult tag conversions from Struts to JSF—replacing the dynamic list of messages. In Struts, we used the `logic:iterate` tag to iterate over a collection (list) of blog messages. In Listing 11.28, we replace the `logic:iterate` tag with the `h:dataTable` and `h:column` tags.

The main problem in our conversion is that the basic semantics are different in JSF and Struts. They both iterate over a collection and retrieve entities. However, the JSF tag implementation assumes that it has the responsibility for rendering the table. The Struts version leaves table controls with the HTML tags. So, we begin by removing all the HTML table tag information replacing it with only the JSF tags.

The `dataTable` tag uses the bean method `getBlogEntries()` to return a collection of blog entries to iterate over. The `var="item"` attribute assigns a local variable that is the current item in the collection.

```
<!-- WebLogEdit.jsp -->
...

    </tr>
      <h:dataTable id="table" rowClasses="list-row"
                   value="#{blogEditForm.blogEntries}" var="item">
```

Listing 11.28 WebLogEdit.jsp panel_data and command_hyperlink tags. *(continued)*

```
        <h:column>
          <h:outputText styleClass="small" value="#{item.dateAsString}"/>
        </h:column>
        <h:column>
          <h:commandLink id="editLink"
                         actionListener="#{blogEditForm.edit}">
              <h:outputText value="#{bloggerBundle.edit}" />
          </h:commandLink>
        </h:column>
        <h:column>
          <h:commandLink id="deleteLink"
                         actionListener="#{blogEditForm.delete}">
              <h:outputText value="#{bloggerBundle.delete}" />
          </h:commandLink>
        </h:column>
        <h:column>
          <h:outputText value="#{item.message}" />
        </h:column>
      </h:dataTable >
    <tr>
...
```

Listing 11.28 *(continued)*

In the `WebLogEdit.jsp`, `h:command_link` tags are used for the edit and delete actions. The `actionListener` attribute identifies the bean and method that will handle the `ActionEvent`.

In our SimpleBlogger, the `actionListener` methods `delete` and `edit` use the `ActionEvent` to get the `UIComponent` that generated the `Action Event` and walk the view tree upwards by calling `getParent()` until they reach the table. Once the table has been retrieved, the `getRowData()` method is called to get the `blogEntry` (see Listing 11.26 for details).

At this point of the conversion, you should be able to run the JSF application in its entirety.

Summary

Because Struts and JSF applications are built using the MVC pattern, the conversion is conceptually easy. However, as we have seen on this simple application, there remains a lot of work to do in the details.

Learning a new set of tags and a new configuration file format is not difficult. If anything, the JSF implementation is cleaner and more consistent in these areas. After all, it is the next generation after Struts. Future releases of JSF will add new and improved tags.

Adding the event listener Patterns to the view is a powerful improvement over Struts. However, depending on the design of the Struts application, this might prove to be the most difficult to convert.

JSF is new, and when it matures we expect it will be the framework of choice. The best of Struts, JSTL, and JSF will ultimately emerge as the de facto standard for Java Web applications and hopefully for microdevices. Time will tell.

APPENDIX

What's on the Web Site

This appendix provides you with information on the contents of the download that accompanies this book. For the latest information, please refer to the ReadMe file located in the zip file for download. Here is what you will find:

- System requirements
  - JDK 1.3.1 or higher
  - JWSDP 1.2 or higher (`http://java.sun.com/webservices/download.html`)
  - Hibernate 2.*x* (`http://www.hibernate.org/`)
  - JUnit 3.8.1 or more (`http://www.junit.org`)
- What's in the download
- Source code for the examples in the book

System Requirements

Make sure that your computer meets the minimum system requirements listed in this section. If your computer doesn't match up to most of these requirements, you may have a problem using the software recommended by the author.

For Windows 9*x*, Windows 2000, Windows NT4 (with SP 4 or later), Windows Me, or Windows XP:

- PC with a Pentium processor running at 600 MHz or faster
- At least 128 MB of total RAM installed on your computer; for best performance, we recommend at least 256 MB
- Ethernet network interface card (NIC) or modem with a speed of at least 28,800 bps
  - A CD-ROM drive
  - JDK 1.3.1 or higher (tested with Sun's JDK)

For Linux:

- PC with a Pentium processor running at 600 MHz or faster
- At least 64 MB of total RAM installed on your computer; for best performance, we recommend at least 128 MB
- Ethernet network interface card (NIC) or modem with a speed of at least 28,800 bps
  - A CD-ROM drive
  - JDK 1.3.1 or higher

For Macintosh:

- Mac OS X computer with a G3 or faster processor running OS 10.1 or later
  - At least 64 MB of total RAM installed on your computer; for best performance, we recommend at least 128 MB
  - JDK 1.3.1 or higher

If you still have trouble with the CD-ROM, please call the Wiley Product Technical Support phone number: (800) 762-2974. Outside the United States, call 1 (317) 572-3994. You can also contact Wiley Product Technical Support at `www.wiley.com/techsupport`. Wiley Publishing will provide technical support only for installation and other general quality control items; for technical support on the applications themselves, consult the program's vendor or author.

To place additional orders or to request information about other Wiley products, please call (800) 225-5945.

References

Alur, Deepak, John Crupi, and Dan Malks. *Core J2EE Patterns: Best Practices and Design Strategies*. Second Edition, Upper Saddle River, NJ: Prentice Hall PTR, 2003.

Dudney, Bill, Stephen Asbury, Joseph Krozak, Kevin Wittkopf. *J2EE AntiPatterns*. Indianapolis, Indiana: Wiley Publishing, Inc. 2003.

Gamma, Erich, Richard Helm, Ralph Johnson, and John Vlissides. *Design Patterns: Elements of Reusable Object-Oriented Software*. Reading, MA: Addison-Wesley Pub. Co., 1995.

Goldberg, Adele, D. Robson. *Smalltalk-80: The Language and Its Implementation*. Addison-Wesley, 1983.

Husted, Ted, Ed Burns, and Craig R. McClanahan. *Struts User Guide*, `http://jakarta.apache.org/struts/userGuide/index.html`. Apache Software Foundation, 2003.

Liskov, Barbara. "Data Abstraction and Hierarchy," OOPSLA 1987 Addendum to the Proceedings, October 1987, pages 17–34.

Index

SYMBOLS AND NUMBERS

M

R

T

V